Singapore
a country study

Federal Research Division
Library of Congress
Edited by
Barbara Leitch LePoer
Research Completed
December 1989

On the cover: Singapore past and present

Second Edition, 1991; First Printing, 1991.

Library of Congress Cataloging-in-Publication Data

Singapore : a country study / Federal Research Division, Library of
   Congress ; edited by Barbara Leitch LePoer.—2d ed.
      p.   cm. — (Area handbook series) (DA pam ; 550-184)
   "Research completed October 1989."
   "Supersedes the 1977 edition of Area Handbook for Singapore
written by Nena Vreeland, et al."—T.p. verso.
   Includes bibliographical references (pp. 285-301) and index.
   1. Singapore   I. LePoer, Barbara Leitch, 1941-   II. Library of
Congress. Federal Research Division.   III. Area handbook for
Singapore. IV. Series. V. Series: DA pam ; 550-184.
DS609.S55   1991   90-25755
959.57—dc20   CIP

Headquarters, Department of the Army
DA Pam 550-184

Foreword

This volume is one in a continuing series of books now being prepared by the Federal Research Division of the Library of Congress under the Country Studies—Area Handbook Program. The last page of this book lists the other published studies.

Most books in the series deal with a particular foreign country, describing and analyzing its political, economic, social, and national security systems and institutions, and examining the interrelationships of those systems and the ways they are shaped by cultural factors. Each study is written by a multidisciplinary team of social scientists. The authors seek to provide a basic understanding of the observed society, striving for a dynamic rather than a static portrayal. Particular attention is devoted to the people who make up the society, their origins, dominant beliefs and values, their common interests and the issues on which they are divided, the nature and extent of their involvement with national institutions, and their attitudes toward each other and toward their social system and political order.

The books represent the analysis of the authors and should not be construed as an expression of an official United States government position, policy, or decision. The authors have sought to adhere to accepted standards of scholarly objectivity. Corrections, additions, and suggestions for changes from readers will be welcomed for use in future editions.

>Louis R. Mortimer
>Chief
>Federal Research Division
>Library of Congress
>Washington, D.C. 20540

Acknowledgments

The editor and authors are grateful to numerous individuals in the international community, in various agencies of the United States government, and in private organizations who gave of their time, research materials, and special knowledge to provide data and perspective for this study. Especially appreciated are the helpful suggestions and economic insights of Edward Chesky and Morris Crawford and the generous assistance of the staff of the Embassy of Singapore, Washington.

The editor and authors also wish to express their appreciation to staff members of the Federal Research Division, Library of Congress, whose high standards and dedication helped shape this volume. These include Martha E. Hopkins, who managed editing; Marilyn L. Majeska, who reviewed editing and managed book production; and Barbara Edgerton and Izella Watson, who did word processing. David P. Cabitto and Sandra K. Ferrell prepared the maps and other graphics for the book, Carolina E. Forrester reviewed the maps, and Arvies J. Staton contributed to the charts on military ranks and insignia. Special thanks go to Kimberly A. Lord, who designed the illustrations for the cover of the volume and the title pages of the chapters, and Donald R. DeGlopper, who assisted with many of the editorial duties.

The following individuals are gratefully acknowledged as well: Shari Villarosa of the Department of State for reviewing all the chapters; Mimi Cantwell for editing the chapters; Cissie Coy for the final prepublication editorial review; Joan Cook for preparing the index; and Linda Peterson of the Printing and Processing Section, Library of Congress, for phototypesetting, under the direction of Peggy Pixley. The inclusion of photographs in the book was made possible by the generosity of private individuals and public agencies, especially Ong Tien Kwan of Kuala Lumpur and Chiang Yin-Pheng and Joyce Tan of the Singapore Ministry of Communications and Information.

Finally, the editor and authors wish to thank Federal Research Division staff members Andrea M. Savada, Sandra W. Meditz, and Richard Nyrop for reviewing all or parts of the manuscript, and Robert L. Worden for assisting in the final stages of editing the completed manuscript.

Contents

	Page
Foreword	iii
Acknowledgments	v
Preface	xi
Country Profile	xiii
Introduction	xxi
Chapter 1. Historical Setting	1
Barbara Leitch LePoer	
PRECOLONIAL ERA	5
Temasek and Singapura	6
Johore Sultanate	7
FOUNDING AND EARLY YEARS, 1819–26	9
Anglo-Dutch Competition	9
Raffles' Dream	10
Early Administration and Growth	13
A FLOURISHING FREE PORT, 1826–67	16
Financial Success	17
A Cosmopolitan Community	21
CROWN COLONY, 1867–1918	24
BETWEEN THE WORLD WARS, 1919–41	32
WORLD WAR II, 1941–45	35
The Japanese Malaya Campaign	36
Shōnan: Light of the South	38
AFTERMATH OF WAR, 1945–55	41
Economic and Social Recovery	42
Political Awakening	43
ROAD TO INDEPENDENCE, 1955–65	47
People's Action Party	48
Singapore as Part of Malaysia	55
TWO DECADES OF INDEPENDENCE, 1965–85	57
Under Lee Kuan Yew	57
Toward New Leadership	62
Chapter 2. The Society and Its Environment	65
Donald R. DeGlopper	
PHYSICAL SETTING	68
POPULATION	70

  Population, Vital Statistics, and Migration 70
  Population Control Policies 73
  Population Distribution and Housing Policies 75
ETHNIC AND LINGUISTIC GROUPS 78
  Ethnic Categories 78
  The Chinese 79
  The Malays 82
  The Indians 87
  Singaporean Identity 88
  Language Planning 90
THE SOCIAL SYSTEM 92
  Ethnicity and Associations 92
  Social Stratification and Mobility 96
  Family, Marriage, and Divorce 100
RELIGION 103
  Temples and Festivals 103
  Religion and Ethnicity 106
  Religious Change 108
HEALTH AND WELFARE 110
  Medical Services and Public Health 110
  Mortality and Morbidity 111
  AIDS Policy 112
EDUCATION 112
  The School System 112
  Education and Singaporean Identity 116

Chapter 3. The Economy 119
             Margaret Sullivan

PATTERNS OF DEVELOPMENT 123
ECONOMIC ROLES OF THE GOVERNMENT 127
  Budgeting and Planning 127
  Economic Boards 128
  Land Management and Development 131
  Forced Savings and Capital Formation 133
  State-Owned Enterprises 135
  Public Utilities 136
  Policies for the Future 137
  Privatization 138
MANPOWER AND LABOR 140
  Industrial Relations and Labor Unions 140
  Wage Policies 143
  Foreign Labor 144
  Manpower Training 145

INDUSTRY 146
    Industrialization Policy 146
    Information Technology 149
    Petroleum 150
TRADE, TOURISM, AND TELECOMMUNICATIONS ... 151
    Foreign Trade 151
    Trading Partners 152
    Tourism 157
    Telecommunications 158
FINANCE 159
    Currency, Trade, and Investment Regulation 160
    Financial Center Development 161
    International Financial Organizations 165
TRANSPORTATION 165
    Sea 165
    Land 167
    Air 169
AGRICULTURE 171

Chapter 4. Government and Politics 175
Ronald J. Cima and Donald R. DeGlopper

GOVERNMENT STRUCTURE 177
    Form of Government 177
    Constitutional Framework 180
    Major Governmental Bodies 181
    The Public Service 185
    The Public Bureaucracy 186
    Statutory Boards 188
    Public Enterprises 190
    Parapolitical Institutions 191
POLITICAL PARTIES 192
POLITICAL DYNAMICS 195
    Power Structure 195
    Political Culture 197
KEY POLITICAL ISSUES 198
    Succession 198
    Relations Between State and Society 200
    Political Opposition 205
FOREIGN POLICY 207
    Governing Precepts and Goals 207
    Regional 209
    Superpowers 211
THE MEDIA 214

Chapter 5. National Security 217
Rodney P. Katz

   THE ARMED FORCES 220
      Historical Development 221
      Organization and Mission of the Armed Forces 230
      Military Establishment 237
      Strategic Perspective 248
   PUBLIC ORDER AND INTERNAL SECURITY 252
      Subversive Threats 256
      Crime and Law Enforcement 261
      Civil Defense 269

Appendix. Tables 273

Bibliography 285

Glossary 303

Index 307

List of Figures
1 Singapore, 1989 xx
2 The Johore Sultanate, ca. 1700 8
3 The Straits Settlements, 1826 14
4 Plan of the Town of Singapore by Lieutenant Phillip
   Jackson, 1828 18
5 Age-Sex Distribution, 1986 72
6 Sources of Government Revenue, Fiscal Year (FY) 1988 ... 126
7 Government Expenditures, Fiscal Year (FY) 1988 128
8 Gross Domestic Product (GDP), by Sector, Fiscal
   Year (FY) 1988 148
9 Expressway System, 1989 168
10 Mass Rapid Transit System, 1990 170
11 Governmental Structure, 1989 178
12 Association of Southeast Asian Nations (ASEAN), 1989 208
13 Japanese Campaign on Malay Peninsula, 1941–42 226
14 Organization of the Armed Forces, 1989 232
15 Military Rank Insignia, 1989 242
16 Organization of the Police Force, 1989 264
17 Organization of the Civil Defence Force, 1989 268

Preface

The first edition of the *Area Handbook for Singapore* was published in 1977. Prior to that edition, Singapore was included in the *Area Handbook for Malaysia and Singapore*, which was published in 1965 just before Singapore became a separate, independent nation. The current volume, a complete revision of the 1977 edition, covers a period of remarkable economic growth and political stability for a nation in existence for only a quarter century. During the 1977-89 period, Singapore moved assuredly into the category of newly industrializing economy, and its renowned port grew from being fourth in the world in terms of volume of shipping to being the world's busiest port.

Singapore: A Country Study is an attempt to present an objective and concise account of the dominant social, economic, political, and national security concerns of contemporary Singapore within an historical framework. The volume represents the combined efforts of a multidisciplinary team, which used as its sources a variety of scholarly monographs and journals, official reports of government and international organizations, and foreign and domestic newspapers and periodicals. Brief commentary on some of the more useful and readily accessible English-language sources appears at the end of each chapter. Full references to these and other sources appear in the Bibliography.

The authors have limited the use of foreign and technical terms, which are defined when they first appear in the study. Readers are also referred to the Glossary at the back of the book. Spellings of Singaporean personal names used in the study conform to standard Singaporean usage, and contemporary place names are generally those approved by the United States Board on Geographic Names. All measurements are given in the metric system (see table 1, Appendix).

Country Profile

Country

Formal Name: Republic of Singapore

Short Form: Singapore

Term for Citizens: Singaporeans

Capital: Singapore

Date of Independence: August 9, 1965 (from Malaysia)

Geography

Location and Size: Located at narrow point of Strait of Malacca off southern tip of Malay Peninsula; connected with Malaysia by causeway. Land area in 1988 about 636 square kilometers, consisting of one main island and 58 islets. Main island 42 kilometers long and 23 kilometers wide, with coastline of 138 kilometers.

Topography: Mainly low-lying, with hills reaching 165 meters in island's center. Extensive reclamation and landfill along coasts.

Climate: Tropical climate, with daily high temperatures moderated by sea breezes. Rainfall throughout the year but usually heaviest from November to January.

Society

Population: 2,674,362 in July 1989. Low birth and death rates; at some points in the 1980s, negative rate of population increase.

Languages and Ethnic Groups: Multiethnic population; 76.4 percent Chinese, 14.9 percent Malay, 6.4 percent Indian, 2.3 percent other. National language Malay but language of administration English. Four official languages—Malay, English, Chinese, and Tamil—but English predominates. Government policy for all citizens to be bilingual—competent in English and an Asian "mother tongue." Large resident alien population composed of unskilled laborers from neighboring countries and skilled managers and professionals from developed countries.

Religion: Religious diversity reflects ethnic diversity. Major religions in 1988: Buddhist, 28.3 percent; Christian, 18.7 percent: no religion, 17.6 percent; Islam, 16 percent; Daoist, 13.4 percent; Hindu, 4.9 percent; "other," 1.1 percent. Rapid growth of Christianity and decline of Chinese folk religion in 1980s.

Health: Conditions approach those of developed countries; adequate number of physicians and hospitals. Government enforces strict sanitation and public health regulations. Heart disease, cancer, stroke, and pneumonia major causes of death. In 1987 life expectancy 71.4 years for males and 76.3 years for females.

Education: British-inspired system with six-year primary and four-year secondary schools and two-year junior colleges for quarter of student population preparing for higher education. English primary language of instruction. Six institutions of higher education, government supported. Education system emphasizes English, science and technology, and vocational skills.

Economy

Salient Features: Export-oriented economy with large government role. Dependent on international trade, sale of services, export of manufactures. Consistently high rates of economic growth (11 percent in 1988), balance of payments surplus, large foreign investment, large foreign reserves (S$33 billion in 1988), minimal foreign debt.

Gross Domestic Product (GDP): S$47.9 billion in 1988, S$17,950 per capita. Manufacturing contributed 29 percent, financial and business services 27 percent, commerce 18 percent, transport and communications 14 percent, other services 12 percent.

Industry: Major industries: electronics, petroleum refining and petrochemicals, machinery, shipbuilding, and ship repair.

Foreign Trade: S$167.3 billion in 1988. Usual deficit in merchandise trade offset by surplus in services for positive balance of trade. Major exports: electronics, machinery, refined petroleum products. Major imports: machinery and electronic components, chemicals, fuels, and food. Major trading partners: United States, Japan, Malaysia, and European Community.

Exchange Rates: Singapore dollar allowed to float since 1973. In late 1989, US$1 = S$1.94.

Transportation and Communications

Ports: Port of Singapore, world's busiest port in 1988, serves more than 36,000 ships per year. Five port terminals, each specializing in different type of cargo; fifteen kilometers of wharf; extensive warehouse and oil storage facilities. Singapore has fifteenth largest merchant fleet in world.

Railroads: Malayan Railways provides service to Singapore. Main station in central business district. Major public transport 67-kilometer mass rapid transit system serving 800,000 passengers daily scheduled for completion in 1990.

Roads: 2,810 kilometers of roads in 1989, mostly paved; five expressways, totalling 95 kilometers, with total 141 kilometers by 1991.

Airports: Two major airports, Singapore Changi Airport for international flights and Seletar for charter and training flights, and three smaller fields.

Telecommunications: Excellent telecommunications facilities. Domestic telephone system with optical fiber network, 26 exchanges, and 48.5 telephones per 100 residents. Two satellite ground stations and submarine cable connections to neighboring countries.

Government and Politics

Government: Parliamentary system with written constitution. Unicameral parliament of eighty-one members (in 1989) elected by universal suffrage. President largely ceremonial head of state; government run by prime minister and cabinet representing majority of parliament. British-influenced judiciary; Supreme Court divided into High Court, Court of Appeal, and Court of Criminal Appeal. Subordinate courts include district courts and magistrate's courts.

Politics: Nineteen registered political parties in mid-1980s, but People's Action Party (PAP) won every general election from 1959 to 1988, usually holding every seat in parliament. Opposition parties divided and weak. Lee Kuan Yew prime minister from 1959 through 1989, providing unusual continuity in leadership and policy. PAP policies stressed economic development, government management of economy and society, firm government with little tolerance for dissent.

Administrative Divisions: Unitary state with no second-order administrative divisions. Some advisory bodies based on fifty-five parliamentary electoral districts.

Foreign Relations: Primary goals of maintaining sovereignty, stability in Southeast Asia, and free international trade. Member of Association of Southeast Asian Nations, Commonwealth of Nations, Nonaligned Movement, World Bank, Asian Development Bank, United Nations.

Media: Seven newspapers, five radio stations, and three television channels publishing and broadcasting in four official languages. Government operates radio and television and supervises newspapers.

National Security

Armed Forces: In 1989 regular armed forces of 55,500: army—45,000, air force—6,000, navy—4,500. Reserves totaled 182,000, and 30,000 in People's Defence Force, a national guard. All males eligible for conscription at age eighteen; most conscripts served twenty-four to thirty months active duty, with reserve obligation to age forty for enlisted personnel and fifty for officers.

Military Units and Equipment: Army composed of one active and one reserve armored brigade, three active and six reserve infantry brigades, two commando battalions, and seventeen artillery battalions. Equipment included light weapons, light tanks, armored personnel carriers, and 155mm howitzers. Navy had corvettes, missile craft squadrons, patrol squadrons, transport ships, and minesweepers. Major weapons were Gabriel and Harpoon ship-to-ship missiles. Air force had twenty F-16 fighter-bombers on order for early 1990s, and in 1989 had estimated 125 combat aircraft in 6 squadrons and 60 helicopters. Air defense provided by army and air force antiaircraft artillery and by Bloodhound 2, Rapier, and HAWK surface-to-air missiles.

Military Budget: In 1988 estimated at US$1.003 million, 6 percent of Gross National Product (GNP).

Foreign Military Relations: No formal military alliances or treaty relations, but participated in Five-Powers Defence Agreement with Britain, Malaysia, Australia, and New Zealand. Shared integrated air defense system with Malaysia. Singapore armed forces trained in or held joint exercises with Malaysia, Indonesia, Brunei, Taiwan, and Australia.

Police: In 1989 regular force of 7,000 supplemented by 3,000 conscripts assigned to police and 2,000 citizen volunteers. Additional forces provided by 300-member Port of Singapore police and Commercial and Industrial Security Corporation whose 2,000 armed guard and escort personnel had police powers. Prison security and security force reserve provided by 700-member Gurkha contingent.

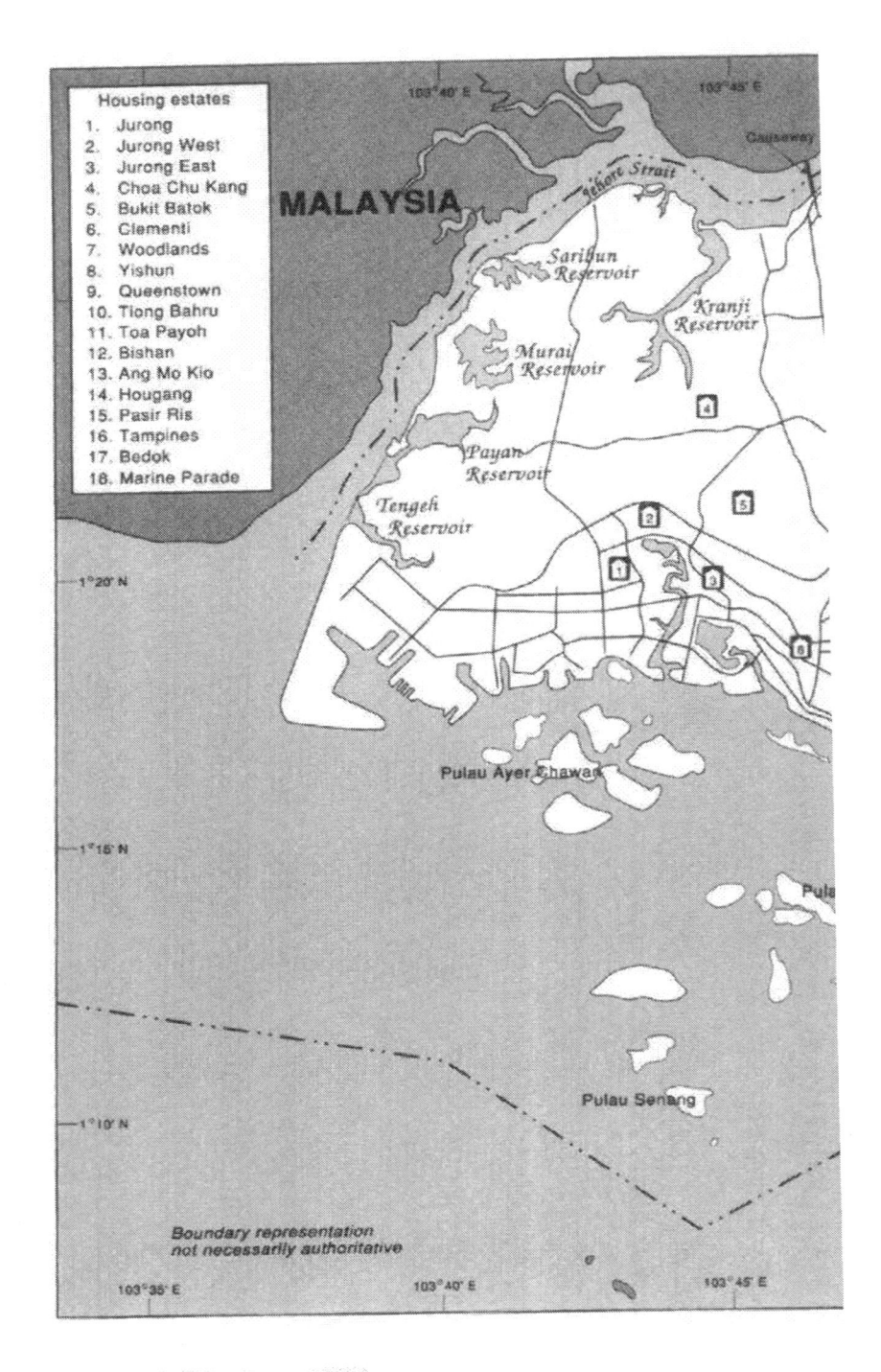

Figure 1. Singapore, 1989

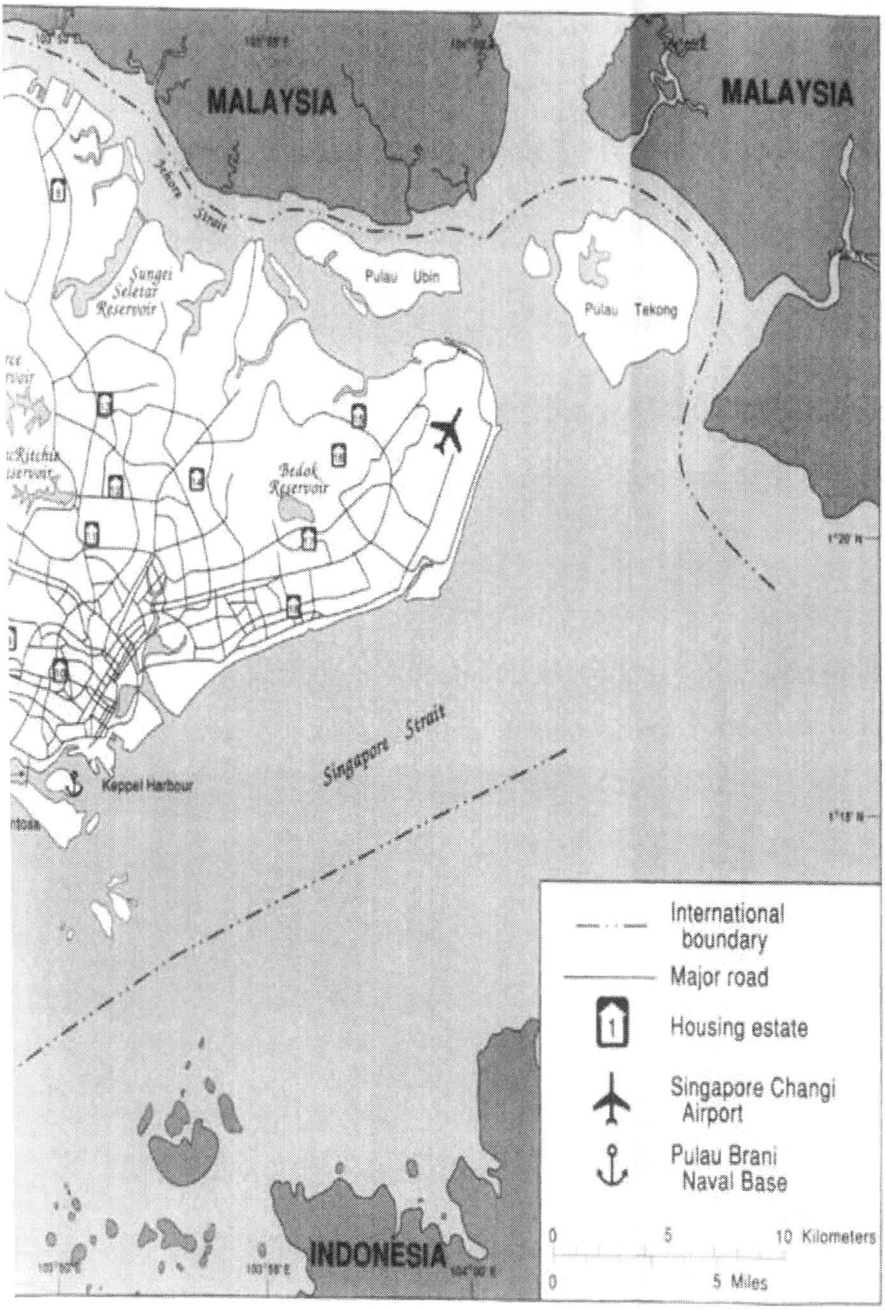
MALAYSIA
MALAYSIA
Johore Strait
Sungei Seletar Reservoir
Pulau Ubin
Pulau Tekong
Bedok Reservoir
Keppel Harbour
Singapore Strait
INDONESIA
International boundary
Major road
Housing estate
Singapore Changi Airport
Pulau Brani Naval Base
0
5
10 Kilometers
0
5 Miles

Introduction

The world's busiest port, the modern nation of the Republic of Singapore, was founded as a British trading post on the Strait of Malacca in 1819. Singapore's location on the major sea route between India and China, its excellent harbor, and the free trade status conferred on it by its visionary founder, Sir Thomas Stamford Raffles, made the port an overnight success. By 1990 the multiethnic population attracted to the island had grown from a few thousand to 2.6 million Singaporeans, frequently referred to by Prime Minister Lee Kuan Yew as his nation's greatest resource. If Raffles had set the tone for the island's early success, Lee had safeguarded the founder's vision through the first quarter-century of Singapore's existence as an independent nation, providing the leadership that turned it into a global city that offered trading and financial services to the region and to the world.

Modern Singapore would be scarcely recognizable to Raffles, who established his trading center on an island covered with tropical forests and ringed with mangrove swamps. Towering skyscrapers replace the colonial town he designed, and modern expressways cover the tracks of bullock carts that once led from the harbor to the commercial district and the countryside beyond. Hills have been leveled, swamps filled, and the island itself expanded in size through extensive land reclamation projects (see fig. 1). Offshore islands are used for recreation parks, oil refineries, and military training bases. Despite the scarcity of land for real estate, the government has worked to maintain and expand the island's parks, gardens, and other green spaces. By housing 88 percent of its population in mostly multistoried public housing, Singapore has kept a rein on suburban sprawl. In Raffles's town plan, separate areas were set aside for the various ethnic groups of the time: Malays, Chinese, Arabs, Bugis, and Europeans. Government resettlement programs begun in the 1960s broke up the former ethnic enclaves by requiring that the public housing projects—called housing estates—that replaced them reflect the ethnic composition of the country as a whole. As a result, modern Singapore's three main ethnic groups—Chinese, Malays, and Indians—live next door to each other and share the same housing development facilities, shops, and transportation.

Despite efforts to maintain an ethnic balance in housing, however, the stated goal of the nation's leaders is not that Singapore become a mini-melting pot, but, rather, a multiethnic society.

Of the country's 2.6 million inhabitants, about 76 percent are Chinese, 15 percent Malay, 6.5 percent Indian, and 2.5 percent other. There are, however, mixtures within this mixture. The designation Chinese lumps together speakers of more than five mutually unintelligible dialects; Singaporean Malays trace their forebears to all of the major islands of the Indonesian archipelago, as well as to the Malay Peninsula; and the ancestral homes of Indians include what are the modern states of India, Pakistan, Bangladesh, and Sri Lanka. Out of this diversity, the government leadership has attempted to establish what it calls "Singaporean identity," which would include certain unifying and modernizing elements but yet retain essential variations, based on Asian culture and values. One of the unifying factors is the English language, selected as the medium for educational instruction both because of its neutrality in the eyes of the three dominant ethnic groups and because of its position as the international language of business, science, and technology. In order not to lose touch with their Asian heritage, however, Singaporean school children are also required to study an appropriate "mother tongue," designated by the government as either Malay, Tamil, or Mandarin Chinese—a vast oversimplification of the polyglot of Singaporean native languages.

Singaporean identity, as envisioned by the country's leadership, calls for rugged individualism with an emphasis on excellence; the government constantly exhorts its citizens to be the best they can be. Education, home ownership, and upward mobility are all considered appropriate goals. Although Singaporeans are expected to be modern in their outlook, they also are encouraged to retain a core of traditional Asian values and culture. In a society in which all share a common education system, public housing, recreation facilities, and military training, the government considers it important to highlight the uniqueness of the three official ethnic groups—Chinese, Malays, and Indians—through the setting aside of national ethnic holidays and the sponsorship of ethnic festivals. Singaporean ethnic differences are usually maintained, however, not so much by these somewhat self-conscious displays of ethnicity but rather by membership in ethnically exclusive associations. Usually religious, charitable, or business in nature, many of these associations had their origins in colonial Singapore and represent finer distinctions of ethnicity than those supported by the government. Chinese trade associations, for example, are usually restricted to speakers of a particular dialect. Hindu temples are sometimes associated with worshipers who trace their heritage to a particular region of India.

Singapore is multireligious as well as multiethnic. Major religious preferences reported in 1988 were Buddhism (28 percent), Christian (19 percent), no religion (17 percent), Islam (16 percent), Daoist (13 percent), and Hindu (5 percent). Singapore's nineteenth-century immigrants valued the social as well as religious aspects of their congregations, and their descendants are more likely to concern themselves with social activities centered around their temples and mosques than with elaborate ritual or ceremony. The government, although secular, views religion as a positive force for instilling moral values in the society. At the same time, it keeps a watchful eye out for social or political activism within religious groups. Muslim fundamentalists and over-zealous Christian proselytizers alike are kept under careful scrutiny, lest they upset the religious and ethnic harmony of the country.

Singapore closely resembles developed countries in terms of its low birth rates, high life expectancy (73.8 years at birth), and major causes of death—heart disease, cancer, and stroke. Although in the early years of independence the government mounted campaigns to lower the country's high birth rate, it became concerned in the 1980s when the rate dropped below the replacement level. Campaigns and incentives were instituted to encourage those who could afford it to have more than two children. College-educated women were especially encouraged by exhortations and incentives to marry and have children.

In terms of public health, Singapore also closely resembles developed countries. Although some observers criticize the country's modern, sanitized environment and mourn the loss of the old port's charm, they probably either have forgotten or never knew the open sewers, tuberculosis sanatoriums, and opium dens of colonial Singapore. Whereas the manufacture and sale of opium continued to be a major source of revenue for the colonial government up until World War II, the government effectively combats drug use in modern Singapore through antidrug campaigns, rehabilitation centers, and a mandatory death penalty for trafficking. The government heavily subsidizes services in order to make them affordable to all and sets aside 6 percent of the monthly income of each worker into a personal Medisave account, which can be used to pay hospitalization costs for any family member. The Medisave account is part of the Central Provident Fund, which is Singapore's compulsory national social security savings plan. Contribution rates due to be phased in in the early 1990s mandate a contribution of 40 percent of the gross wages of employees under fifty-five, with employee and employer sharing the burden equally. Singaporeans can use these funds to invest in approved securities, to purchase homes in government housing projects, or to pay for hospitalization and retirement. By 1990 some 88 percent of Singaporeans lived in Housing and Development Board apartments, a vast public housing and urban redevelopment project initiated in the early postwar years. Under the program, which began in earnest after independence, Singapore's slums and ethnic neighborhoods gradually were replaced with modern housing estates, self-contained units providing shopping, restaurants, and recreation facilities as well as apartments of various sizes, scattered outward from the old central city. A network of superhighways and a state-of-the-art mass rapid transit system connect Singapore's housing estates with commercial and industrial areas.

Although Singapore's founder and other nineteenth-century residents would no longer recognize the island, they would at least be able to identify with certain aspects of its modern economy. The principle of free trade laid down by Raffles was still largely in effect in the late 1980s, with only a few revenue tariffs levied on such things as tobacco and liquor. Trade continued to be the island's lifeblood; in 1988 the value of Singapore's international trade was triple the total of its gross domestic product (GDP). Although some aspects of the trade have changed, others remained the same. The island's initial success resulted from its role as a conveniently located and duty-free entrepôt for the three-way trade among China, India, and various parts of the Malay Archipelago. This trade was an ancient commerce, and trading posts probably had flourished intermittently at that favored location for two millenia. In early colonial times, silks from China, manufactures from Europe, incense from India, and spices from the Moluccas all were shipped on the various seasonal trade winds to Singapore, where they were bought, sold, traded, or stored for a future customer. By the late nineteenth century, however, the British overlords of Singapore had extended their influence or control throughout the Malay Peninsula, and the port acquired a large hinterland rich in resources. Singapore became the outlet for Malaya's tin and rubber, as well as the gateway through which were funneled supplies and workers for the peninsula's mines and plantations. Tin smelting and rubber processing were added to the list of services that Singapore provided—a long list that already included wholesaling, ship repair and provisioning, warehousing, and a host of banking and financial services.

In 1990 the economy of modern Singapore was still based on the same services that were performed by the colonial port, although most of these services had been greatly expanded or modified and new ones added. The major sectors of the economy were the regional entrepôt trade, export-oriented manufacturing, petroleum refining and shipping, production of goods and services for the domestic economy, and a vastly expanded services industry.

When independence was suddenly thrust upon Singapore in 1965, its economic prospects looked bleak, if not precarious. In the aftermath of World War II, Singapore had faced staggering problems of high unemployment, slow economic growth, inadequate housing, decaying infrastructure, and labor and social unrest. Separation from Malaysia meant the loss of its economic hinterland, and Indonesia's policy of military Confrontation directed at Singapore and Malaysia had dried up the entrepôt trade from that direction. Moreover, with the announcement in 1968 of Britain's departure from the island's bases, Singapore faced the loss of 20 percent of its jobs. These problems led Singapore's leadership to take a strong role in guiding the nation's economy. The government aggressively promoted export-oriented, labor-intensive industrialization through a program of incentives designed to attract foreign investment. By 1972 one-quarter of Singapore's manufacturing firms were either foreign-owned or joint-venture companies, with the United States and Japan both major investors. The response of foreign investors to Singapore's favorable investment climate and the rapid expansion of the world economy at that time were factors in the annual double-digit growth of the country's GDP during most of the period from 1965 through 1973. By the late 1970s, however, government planners had adopted a policy of replacing Singapore's labor-intensive manufacturing with skill- and technology-intensive, high value-added industries. Information technology was particularly targeted for expansion, and by 1989 Singapore was the world's largest producer of disk drives and disk drive parts. In that year, earnings from manufacturing accounted for 30 percent of the country's GDP.

Although Singapore lost its former hinterland when it separated from Malaysia, its northern neighbor remained the leading source of primary imports and a major destination for Singapore's manufactured exports. Malaysia was Singapore's third largest overall trading partner in 1988, and Singaporean companies were major investors in Malaysia's southern state of Johor. The entrepôt trade with Indonesia had long since revived following the end of Confrontation in 1966. By the late 1980s, Singapore was the world's third largest petroleum-refining center as well as third largest oil-trading center, serving the needs of oil-rich Indonesia and Malaysia. By 1988 Singapore had nosed out Rotterdam as the world's busiest port in terms of tonnage. Some 700 shiplines used its modern facilities each year, including Singapore's own merchant fleet, which ranked fifteenth worldwide. Four major shipyards employed about 70,000 workers, about 40 percent of whom were from neighboring Asian countries.

One of the fastest growing sectors of the economy was Singapore's international banking and financial services sector, which accounted for nearly 25 percent of the country's GDP in the late 1980s. Historically, Singapore served as the financial services center for Southeast Asia, and in the late 1980s it ranked with Hong Kong as the two most important Asian financial centers after Tokyo. The government provided incentives for the continuing diversification and automation of financial services, and Singapore's political stability and top-notch infrastructure were important attractions for international bankers and investors. Trade, manufacturing, and international financial services were closely linked in Singapore, which in 1990 hosted more than 650 multinational companies and several thousand international financial institutions and trading firms. Singapore's reliance on the international economy, over which it had little control, provided incentive for the government to play a strong role in regulating domestic conditions. Soon after independence, the government brought under control the serious labor unrest of the 1950s and early 1960s in order to present a more favorable climate for foreign investment. Discipline imposed on the labor force was counterbalanced, however, by provisions for workers' welfare. While the booming economy of the late 1960s and 1970s brought new jobs to the private sector, government provision of subsidized housing, education, health services, and public transportation created jobs in the public sector. The Central Provident Fund, built up by compulsory contributions by both employer and employee, provided the necessary capital for government projects as well as for the country's comprehensive social security scheme.

Singapore, Inc., as some observers refer to the country, spent the first twenty-five years of its independence under the same management. Led by Lee Kuan Yew, the country's first and only prime minister, the People's Action Party (PAP—see Glossary) won all or nearly all of the seats in parliament in the six elections held between 1959 and 1988. Based on a British parliamentary system, with free and open elections, the Singapore government was recognized for its stability, honesty, and effectiveness. Critics complained, however, that the government's authoritarian leadership reserved for itself all power of decision making and blocked the rise of an effective opposition. A small nucleus of leaders centered around Lee had indeed closely guided the country from its turbulent preindependence days and crafted the policies that led to Singapore's economic development. During the 1980s, however, a second generation of leaders was carefully groomed to take over, and in early 1990, only Lee remained of the first generation leaders.

In late 1989, Lee announced that he would step down in late 1990 and that his successor, First Deputy Prime Minister Goh Chok Tong, had already largely taken over the day-to-day management of the government. However, based on the prime minister's own assertions that he was not yet ready to relinquish all control, observers speculated on just what powers Lee would continue to hold. Goh acknowledged in late 1989 the growing sophistication and rising expectations of younger Singaporeans, who want a greater participation in the country's political life, and noted that he expected the opposition to claim a larger share of seats in parliament in the 1990s. In contrasting his leadership style with that of Lee, Goh stated that Lee "believes in firm government from the center . . . whereas our style is a little more consultative, more consensus-building." Behind Goh in the Singapore leadership queue was believed to be Lee Kuan Yew's son, Brigadier General Lee Hsien Loong, who served in the cabinet as minister for trade and industry and second minister for defence. His meteoric rise in the late 1980s through the ranks of bureaucratic and political responsibility was regarded with interest by both foreign and domestic observers.

The transition to a new generation of leaders was a phenomenon not unique to Singapore. In neighboring Malaysia and Indonesia, the independence generation was also rapidly dwindling, and the 1990s will surely mark the passing from the scene of Prime Minister Mahathir Mohamad and President Soeharto as well as Lee Kuan Yew. The close relationship between Singapore and both its neighbors had been built to a large extent on personal ties between Lee and his counterparts in Malaysia and Indonesia. Nonetheless, the new leadership of these countries will very likely continue to build on the foundation laid by their predecessors.

In late 1989, Goh discussed the prospect of Johor State, the nearby Indonesian island of Batam (currently being developed), and Singapore forming a "triangle of growth" within the region in a cooperative rather than competitive effort. There were also signs of increased military cooperation among the three countries. Singapore, for example, conducted bilateral land exercises for the first time with both Malaysia and Indonesia in 1989. Bilateral air and naval exercises had been conducted with both countries during most of the 1980s. All three countries (along with Thailand, Brunei, and the Philippines) were members of the Association of Southeast Asian Nations (ASEAN—see Glossary), formed in 1967 to promote closer political and economic cooperation within the region. The invasion of Cambodia by Vietnam in 1978 brought increased unity to the organization throughout the 1980s, as it sought to find a peaceful solution to the Cambodian problem. Although there was considerable bilateral military cooperation among ASEAN states, the organization was not viewed by its members as a military alliance. However, Singapore and Malaysia, along with Britain, Australia, and New Zealand, were also members of the 1971 Five-Powers Defence Agreement, which provided for consultation and support by the latter three nations in the event of an attack on Singapore or Malaysia. Cooperation under the agreement diminished during the 1970s, but by the late 1980s extensive military exercises involving all five participants were again being held.

In August 1989, Lee Kuan Yew created a stir within the region by stating that Singapore was "prepared to host some United States facilities to make it easier for the Philippines to host the United States bases there." Malaysia reacted negatively to the announcement, and other ASEAN countries expressed some dismay. In October, however, the Singapore foreign ministry clarified the issue by stating that an increased use of Singapore's maintenance and repair facilities by United States ships had been agreed on by the two countries, as had short-term visits by United States aircraft to Singapore's Paya Lebar Air Base. The agreement followed a period of somewhat strained relations between the two nations, during which the United States had been critical of Singapore's use of its Internal Security Act to detain dissidents indefinitely, and Singapore had accused Washington of meddling in its internal affairs. The United States, however, was Singapore's largest trading partner and foreign investor, and the relationship was one that neither country was eager to upset.

By the last decade of the twentieth century, the former colonial port of Singapore had become a global financial, trading, and industrial center that continued to live by its wits in the world of international trade, just as it had done in the nineteenth century. Singapore's leadership and its people have always managed to adapt to the changing demands of the world economy, on which so much of their livelihood depended. In the coming decade, however, a new generation of leaders will take full control of the nation's government and economy. Before them lies the task of reconciling the need to steer a steady course in the nation's continuing development with the people's growing aspirations for an increased share in political and economic decision making.

March 17, 1990

As Singapore faced what its policy planners refer to as "the next lap," the future of the island nation appeared bright. The economic growth rate for 1990 topped 8 percent, led by a booming financial services sector and strong performances in industry and tourism. Not ones to rest on their accomplishments, Singapore's planners began unveiling strategies to internationalize the country's economy. Singaporean capital and management expertise increasingly was being invested abroad, not just in the growth triangle being formed among Singapore, Johor, and Indonesia's Riau Islands, but in Hong Kong, China (with which diplomatic relations were established in 1990), New Zealand, and other parts of the Asia-Pacific region.

In August 1990, Singapore celebrated twenty-five years of independence, and a few months later, on November 28, Goh Chok Tong was sworn in as the nation's second prime minister. As Lee Kuan Yew prepared to leave the office he had held for thirty-one years, former Foreign Minister Sinnathamby Rajaratnam remarked that there was no need to erect any monuments in honor of Lee because "Singapore is his monument." Lee, in any event, was expected to remain close at hand; he will continue to serve as a senior minister in the Singapore cabinet and as secretary general of the People's Action Party. Moreover, in January 1991, Parliament passed legislation converting the appointive ceremonial post of president to a directly elected office with wide executive powers that appeared to some observers to be designed specifically with Lee in mind. Prime Minister Goh, at his swearing in ceremony, summed up the task that lay before him: "My mission is clear: to ensure that Singapore thrives and grows after Lee Kuan Yew; to find a new group of men and women to help me carry on where he and his colleagues left off; and to build a nation of character and grace where people live lives of dignity, fulfillment and care for one another."

June 14, 1991   Barbara Leitch LePoer

Chapter 1. Historical Setting

Statue of Sir Thomas Stamford Raffles, founder of modern Singapore

FAVORABLY LOCATED AT the southern end of the Strait of Malacca, the shortest sea route between China and India, the island of Singapore was known to mariners as early as the third century A.D. By the seventh century, the Srivijaya Empire, the first in a succession of maritime states to arise in the region of the Malay Archipelago, linked numerous ports and cities along the coasts of Sumatra, Java, and the Malay Peninsula. Singapore probably was one of many outposts of Srivijaya, serving as an entrepôt and supply point for Chinese, Thai, Javanese, Malay, Indian, and Arab traders. An early chronicle refers to the island as Temasek and recounts the founding there, in 1299, of the city of Singapura ("lion city"). In the following three centuries, Singapura came under the sway of successive Southeast Asian powers, including the empires of Srivijaya, Majapahit, and Ayutthaya and the Malacca and Johore sultanates. In 1613 the Portuguese, the newest power in the region, burned down a trading post at the mouth of the Singapore River, and the curtain came down on the tiny island for two centuries.

In 1818 Singapore was settled by a Malay official of the Johore Sultanate and his followers, who shared the island with several hundred indigenous tribespeople and some Chinese planters. The following year, Sir Thomas Stamford Raffles, an official of the British East India Company, arrived in Singapore and secured permission from its Malay rulers to establish a trading post on the island. Named by Raffles for its ancient predecessor, Singapore quickly became a successful port open to free trade and free immigration. Before the trading post's founding, the Dutch had a monopoly on the lucrative three-way trade among China, India, and the East Indies. Now Indian, Arab, European, Chinese, Thai, Javanese, and Bugis traders alike stopped in their passage through the Strait of Malacca to anchor in the excellent harbor and exchange their wares. Malays, Chinese, Indians, Arabs, and Europeans flocked to the growing settlement to make their fortunes servicing the needs of the sea traders.

The next half century brought increased prosperity, along with the growing pains of a rapidly expanding seaport with a widely diverse population. During this period Singapore, Penang, and Malacca were ruled together as the Straits Settlements (see Glossary) from the British East India Company headquarters in India. In 1867, when Singapore was a bustling seaport of 85,000 people, the Straits Settlements was made a crown colony ruled directly

Singapore: A Country Study

from London. Singapore continued to grow and prosper as a crown colony. The opening of the Suez Canal in 1869, the advent of steamships, the expansion of colonialism in Southeast Asia, and the continuing spread of British influence in Malaya combined to establish Singapore's position as an important trade and manufacturing center in the late nineteenth century.

In the early twentieth century, financial institutions, transportation, communications, and government infrastructure expanded rapidly to support the booming trade and industry. Social and educational services lagged far behind, however, and a large gulf separated the upper classes from the lower classes, whose lives were characterized by poverty, overcrowding, malnutrition, disease, and opium addiction. Singapore was largely unaffected by World War I. Following the war, the colony experienced both boom and depression, but on the whole, expanded and prospered.

During the period between the world wars, Singapore's Chinese took increasing interest in events in China, and many supported either the Chinese Communist Party or the Guomindang (Kuomintang—Chinese Nationalist Party). The Malayan Communist Party (MCP—see Glossary) was organized in 1930 and competed with the local branch of the Guomindang. Beginning in the early 1930s, both groups strongly supported China against the rising tide of Japanese aggression. Japan's lightning attack on Malaya in December 1941 took the British by surprise, and by mid-February the Japanese were in control of both Malaya and Singapore. Renamed Shōnan ("Light of the South"), Singapore suffered greatly during the Japanese occupation.

Although Singaporeans tumultuously welcomed the return of the British in 1945, their view of the colonial relationship had changed forever. Strikes and student demonstrations organized by the MCP increased throughout the 1950s. The yearning for independence was beginning to be felt in Singapore and Malaya as it was all over the colonial world. In 1953 a British commission recommended partial internal self-government for Singapore, which had been governed as a separate crown colony following the formation of the Federation of Malaya in 1948. Political parties began to form. In 1954 a group of anticolonialists led by David Marshall formed the Labour Front, a political party that campaigned for immediate independence within a merged Singapore and Malaya. That same year saw the formation of the People's Action Party (PAP—see Glossary) under Lee Kuan Yew, which also campaigned for an end to colonialism and union with Malaya. The Labour Front formed a coalition government with David Marshall as chief minister following elections in 1955 for the newly established Legislative

Assembly. In 1956-58, Merdeka (freedom in Malay) talks were held in London to discuss the political future of Singapore. As a result of the discussions, Singapore was granted internal self-government, whereas defense and foreign affairs were left in the hands of the British.

In the May 1959 election, the PAP swept the polls, and Lee became prime minister. Singapore's foreign and local business communities were greatly alarmed by the turn of events, fearing that the communist wing of the PAP would soon seize control of the government. The PAP moderates under Lee, however, favored independence through merger with Malaya. Singaporean voters approved the PAP merger plan in September 1962, and on September 16, 1963, Singapore joined Malaya and the former British Borneo territories of Sabah and Sarawak to form an independent Malaysia. After two years of communal strife, pressure from neighboring Indonesia, and political wrangling between Singapore and Kuala Lumpur, however, Singapore was forced to separate from Malaysia and became an independent nation on August 9, 1965.

Singaporeans and their leaders immediately accepted the challenge of forging a viable nation on a tiny island with few resources other than the determination and talent of its people. The leaders sought to establish a unique "Singaporean identity" and to strengthen economic and political ties with Malaysia, Indonesia, and the other countries of the region. The government also began to reorient the economy toward more high-technology industries that would enhance the skills of the labor force and attract increased foreign investment. By the 1970s, Singapore was among the world leaders in shipping, air transport, and oil refining. By the mid-1980s, the first generation of leaders under Lee Kuan Yew had successfully guided the nation for more than two decades, and a new generation was beginning to take charge.

Precolonial Era

Located astride the sea routes between China and India, from ancient times the Malay Archipelago served as an entrepôt, supply point, and rendezvous for the sea traders of the kingdoms and empires of the Asian mainland and the Indian subcontinent. The trade winds of the South China Sea brought Chinese junks laden with silks, damasks, porcelain, pottery, and iron to seaports that flourished on the Malay Peninsula and the islands of Sumatra and Java. There they met with Indian and Arab ships, brought by the monsoons of the Indian Ocean, carrying cotton textiles, Venetian glass, incense, and metalware. Fleets of swift *prahu* (interisland craft) supplied fish, fruit, and rice from Java and pepper and spices from the Moluccas in the eastern part of the archipelago. All who came brought not only their trade goods but also their cultures, languages, religions, and technologies for exchange in the bazaars of this great crossroads.

In time, the ports of the peninsula and archipelago formed the nucleus of a succession of seabased kingdoms, empires, and sultanates. By the late seventh century, the great maritime Srivijaya Empire, with its capital at Palembang in eastern Sumatra, had extended its rule over much of the peninsula and archipelago. Historians believe that the island of Singapore was probably the site of a minor port of Srivijaya.

Temasek and Singapura

Although legendary accounts shroud Singapore's earliest history, chroniclers as far back as the second century alluded to towns or cities that may have been situated at that favored location. Some of the earliest records of this region are the reports of Chinese officials who served as envoys to the seaports and empires of the Nanyang (southern ocean—see Glossary), the Chinese term for Southeast Asia. The earliest first-hand account of Singapore appears in a geographical handbook written by the Chinese traveler Wang Dayuan in 1349. Wang noted that Singapore Island, which he called Tan-ma-hsi (Danmaxi), was a haven for several hundred boatloads of pirates who preyed on passing ships. He also described a settlement of Malay and Chinese living on a terraced hill known in Malay legend as Bukit Larangan (Forbidden Hill), the reported burial place of ancient kings. The fourteenth-century Javanese chronicle, the *Nagarakertagama*, also noted a settlement on Singapore Island, calling it Temasek.

A Malay seventeenth-century chronicle, the *Sejarah Melayu* (Malay Annals), recounts the founding of a great trading city on the island in 1299 by a ruler from Palembang, Sri Tri Buana, who named the city Singapura ("lion city") after sighting a strange beast that he took to be a lion. The prosperous Singapura, according to the *Sejarah Melayu*, in the mid-fourteenth century suffered raids by the expanding Javanese Majapahit Empire to the south and the emerging Thai kingdom of Ayutthaya to the north, both at various times claiming the island as a vassal state.

The *Sejarah Melayu*, as well as contemporaneous Portuguese accounts, note the arrival around 1388 of King Paramesvara from Palembang, who was fleeing Majapahit control. Although granted asylum by the ruler of Singapura, the king murdered his host and seized power. Within a few years, however, Majapahit or Thai forces again drove out Paramesvara, who fled northward to found eventually the great seaport and kingdom of Malacca. In 1414 Paramesvara converted to Islam and established the Malacca Sultanate, which in time controlled most of the Malay Peninsula, eastern Sumatra, and the islands between, including Singapura. Fighting ships for the sultanate were supplied by a senior Malaccan official based at Singapura. The city of Malacca served not only as the major seaport of the region in the fifteenth century, but also as the focal point for the dissemination of Islam throughout insular Southeast Asia.

Johore Sultanate

When the Portuguese captured Malacca in 1511, the reigning Malaccan sultan fled to Johore in the southern part of the Malay Peninsula, where he established a new sultanate (see fig. 2). Singapura became part of the new Johore Sultanate and was the base for one of its senior officials in the latter sixteenth century. In 1613, however, the Portuguese reported burning down a trading outpost at the mouth of the Temasek (Singapore) River, and Singapura passed into history.

In the following two centuries, the island of Temasek was largely abandoned and forgotten as the fortunes of the Johore Sultanate rose and fell. By 1722 a vigorous seafaring people from the island of Celebes (modern Sulawesi, Indonesia) had become the power behind the throne of the Johore Sultanate. Under Bugis influence, the sultanate built up a lucrative entrepôt trade, centered at Riau, south of Singapore, in present-day Sumatra. Riau also was the site of major plantations of pepper and gambier, a medicinal plant used in tanning. The Bugis used waste material from the gambier refining process to fertilize pepper plants, a valuable crop, but one that quickly depletes soil nutrients. By 1784 an estimated 10,000 Chinese laborers had been brought from southern China to work the gambier plantations on Bintan Island in the Riau Archipelago (now part of Indonesia). In the early nineteenth century, gambier was in great demand in Java, Siam, and elsewhere, and cultivation of the crop had spread from Riau to the island of Singapore.

The territory controlled by the Johore Sultanate in the late eighteenth century was somewhat reduced from that under its precursor, the Malacca Sultanate, but still included the southern part of the Malay Peninsula, the adjacent area of Sumatra, and the islands between, including Singapore. The sultanate had become increasingly weakened by division into a Malay faction, which controlled the peninsula and Singapore, and a Bugis faction, which controlled the Riau Archipelago and Sumatra. When the ruling sultan died without a royal heir, the Bugis had proclaimed as

Singapore: A Country Study

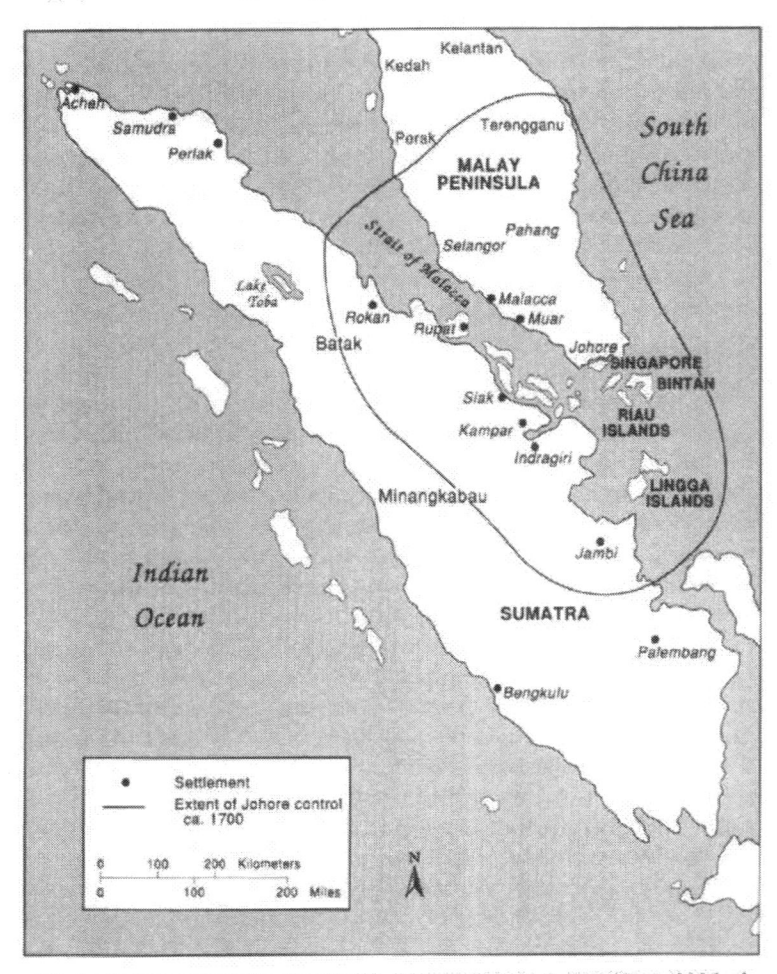

Source: Based on information from Constance M. Turnbull, *A Short History of Malaysia, Singapore, and Brunei,* Stanmore, N.S.W., 1980, 61; and Tan Ding Eing, *Portrait of Malaysia and Singapore,* Singapore, 1975, 22.

Figure 2. *The Johore Sultanate, ca. 1700*

sultan the younger of his two sons by a commoner wife. The sultan's elder son, Hussein (or Tengku Long) resigned himself to living in obscurity in Riau.

Although the sultan was the nominal ruler of his domain, senior officials actually governed the sultanate. In control of Singapore and the neighboring islands was Temenggong Abdu'r Rahman, Hussein's father-in-law. In 1818 the *temenggong* (a high Malay official) and some of his followers left Riau for Singapore shortly after the Dutch signed a treaty with the Bugis-controlled sultan, allowing them to station a garrison at Riau. The *temenggong's* settlement on the Singapore River included several hundred *orang laut* (sea gypsies in Malay) under Malay overlords who owed allegiance to the *temenggong*. For their livelihood the inhabitants depended on fishing, fruit growing, trading, and occasional piracy. Large pirate fleets also used the strait between Singapore and the Riau Archipelago as a favorite rendezvous. Also living on the island in settlements along the rivers and creeks were several hundred indigenous tribespeople, who lived by fishing and gathering jungle produce. Some thirty Chinese, probably brought from Riau by the *temenggong*, had begun gambier and pepper production on the island. In all, perhaps a thousand people inhabited the island of Singapore at the dawn of the colonial era.

Founding and Early Years, 1819-26

By the early seventeenth century, both the Dutch and the English were sending regular expeditions to the East Indies. The English soon gave up the trade, however, and concentrated their efforts on India. In 1641 the Dutch captured Malacca and soon after replaced the Portuguese as the preeminent European power in the Malay Archipelago. From their capital at Batavia on Java, they sought to monopolize the spice trade. Their short-sighted policies and harsh treatment of offenders, however, impoverished their suppliers and encouraged smuggling and piracy by the Bugis and other peoples. By 1795, the Dutch enterprise in Asia was losing money, and in Europe the Netherlands was at war with France. The Dutch king fled to Britain where, in desperation, he issued the Kew Letters, by which all Dutch overseas territories were temporarily placed under British authority in order to keep them from falling to the French.

Anglo-Dutch Competition

In the late eighteenth century, the British began to expand their commerce with China from their bases in India through both private traders and the British East India Company. The company had occupied a small settlement at Bencoolen (Bengkulu) on the western coast of Sumatra since 1684; from there it had engaged in the pepper trade after being forced out of Java by the Dutch. Acutely aware of the need for a base somewhere midway between Calcutta and Guangzhou (Canton), the company leased the island of Penang, on the western coast of the Malay Peninsula, from the sultan of Kedah in 1791. From these posts at Penang and Bencoolen, the British began in 1795 to occupy the Dutch possessions placed temporarily in their care by the Kew Letters, including Malacca and Java. After war in Europe ended in 1814, however, the British agreed to return Java and Malacca to the Dutch. By 1818 the Dutch had returned to the East Indies and had reimposed their restrictive trade policies. In that same year, the Dutch negotiated a treaty with the Bugis-controlled sultan of Johore granting them permission to station a garrison at Riau, thereby giving them control over the main passage through the Strait of Malacca. British trading ships were heavily taxed at Dutch ports and suffered harassment by the Dutch navy. Meanwhile, the British government and the British East India Company officials in London, who were concerned with maintaining peace with the Dutch, consolidating British control in India, and reducing their commitments in the East Indies, considered relinquishing Bencoolen and perhaps Penang to the Dutch in exchange for Dutch territories in India.

Raffles' Dream

Sir Thomas Stamford Raffles, the lieutenant governor of Bencoolen in 1818, vigorously opposed his government's plan to abandon control of the China trade to the Dutch. Raffles, who had started his career as a clerk for the British East India Company in London, was promoted at the age of twenty-three to assistant secretary of the newly formed government in Penang in 1805. A serious student of the history and culture of the region and fluent in Malay, Raffles served as governor general of Java (1811-16). In 1818 Raffles sailed from Bencoolen to India, where he convinced Governor General Lord Hastings of the need for a British post on the southern end of the Strait of Malacca. Lord Hastings authorized Raffles to secure such a post for the British East India Company, provided that it did not antagonize the Dutch. Arriving in Penang, Raffles found Governor General James Bannerman unwilling to cooperate. When he learned that the Dutch had occupied Riau and were claiming that all territories of the sultan of Johore were within their sphere of influence, Raffles dispatched Colonel William Farquhar, an old friend and Malayan expert, to survey the Carimon Islands (modern Karimun Islands near Riau). Disregarding Bannerman's orders to him to await further instructions from Calcutta, Raffles slipped out of Penang the following night aboard a private trading ship and caught up with Farquhar. Raffles knew of Singapore Island from his study of Malay texts and determined to go there.

On January 28, 1819, Raffles and Farquhar anchored near the mouth of the Singapore River. The following day the two men went ashore to meet Temenggong Abdu'r Rahman, who granted

Singapore Malay fishing village, nineteenth century
Courtesy Library of Congress
Rattan harvesting in nineteenth-century Singapore
Courtesy Library of Congress

provisional permission for the British East India Company to establish a trading post on the island, subject to the approval of Hussein. Raffles, noting the protected harbor, the abundance of drinking water, and the absence of the Dutch, began immediately to unload troops, clear the land on the northeast side of the river, set up tents, and hoist the British flag. Meanwhile, the *temenggong* sent to Riau for Hussein, who arrived within a few days. Acknowledging Hussein as the rightful sultan of Johore, on February 6 Raffles signed a treaty with him and the *temenggong* confirming the right of the British East India Company to establish a trading post in return for an annual payment (in Spanish dollars, the common currency of the region at the time) of Sp$5,000 to Hussein and Sp$3,000 to the *temenggong*. Raffles then departed for Bencoolen, leaving Farquhar in charge, with instructions to clear the land, construct a simple fortification, and inform all passing ships that there were no duties on trade at the new settlement.

The immediate reaction to Raffles' new venture was mixed. Officials of the British East India Company in London feared that their negotiations with the Dutch would be upset by Raffles' action. The Dutch were furious because they considered Singapore within their sphere of influence. Although they could easily have overcome Farquhar's tiny force, the Dutch did not attack the small settlement because the angry Bannerman assured them that the British officials in Calcutta would disavow the whole scheme. In Calcutta, meanwhile, both the commercial community and the *Calcutta Journal* welcomed the news and urged full government support for the undertaking. Lord Hastings ordered the unhappy Bannerman to provide Farquhar with troops and money. Britain's foreign minister Lord Castlereagh, reluctant to relinquish to the Dutch "all the military and naval keys of the Strait of Malacca," had the question of Singapore added to the list of topics to be negotiated with the Dutch, thus buying time for the new settlement.

The opportunity to sell supplies at high prices to the new settlement quickly attracted many Malacca traders to the island. Word of Singapore's free trade policy also spread southeastward through the archipelago, and within six weeks more than 100 Indonesian interisland craft were anchored in the harbor, as well as one Siamese and two European ships. Raffles returned in late May to find that the population of the settlement had grown to nearly 5,000, including Malays, Chinese, Bugis, Arabs, Indians, and Europeans. During his four-week stay, he drew up a plan for the town and signed another agreement with Hussein and the *temenggong* establishing the boundaries of the settlement. He wrote to a friend that Singapore "is by far the most important station in the East; and,

Historical Setting

as far as naval superiority and commercial interests are concerned, of much higher value than whole continents of territory."

Early Administration and Growth

Although the India-China trade was partly responsible for the overnight success of Singapore, even more important was the well-established entrepôt trade of the East Indies that the new port captured from Riau and other trade centers. The news of the free port brought not only traders and merchants but also permanent settlers. Malays came from Penang, Malacca, Riau, and Sumatra. Several hundred boatloads of Hussein's followers came from Riau, and the new sultan had built for himself an *istana* (palace in Malay), thus making Singapore his headquarters. The growing power of the Dutch in Riau also spurred several hundred Bugis traders and their families to migrate to the new settlement. Singapore was also a magnet for the Nanyang Chinese who had lived in the region for generations as merchants, miners, or gambier farmers. They came from Penang, Malacca, Riau, Manila, Bangkok, and Batavia to escape the tariffs and restrictions of those places and to seek their fortunes. Many intermarried with Malay women, giving rise to the group known as the Baba Chinese (see Glossary). The small Indian population included both soldiers and merchants. A few Armenian merchants from Brunei and Manila were also attracted to the settlement, as were some leading Arab families from Sumatra. Most Europeans in the early days of Singapore were officials of the British East India Company or retired merchant sea captains.

Not wanting the British East India Company to view Singapore as an economic liability, Raffles left Farquhar a shoestring budget with which to administer the new settlement. Prevented from either imposing trade tariffs or selling land titles to raise revenue, Farquhar legalized gambling and the sale of opium and *arak*, an alcoholic drink. The government auctioned off monopoly rights to sell opium and spirits and to run gambling dens under a system known as tax farming, and the revenue thus raised was used for public works projects. Maintenance of law and order in the wide-open seaport was among the most serious problems Farquhar faced. There was constant friction among the various immigrant groups, particularly between the more settled Malays and Chinese from Malacca and the rough and ready followers of the *temenggong* and the sultan. The settlement's merchants eventually funded night watchmen to augment the tiny police force.

When Raffles returned to Singapore from Bencoolen in October 1822, he immediately began drawing up plans for a new town (see fig. 3). An area along the coast about five kilometers long and one

Singapore: A Country Study

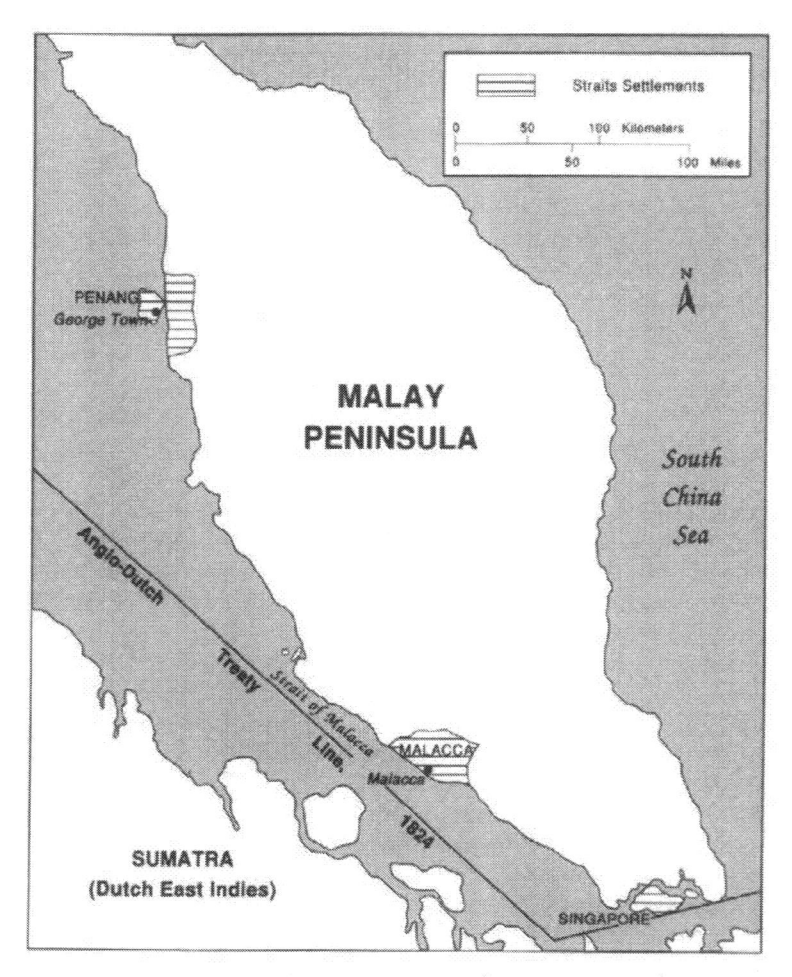

Source: Based on information from Gerald Percy Dartford, *A Short History of Malaya*, London, 1957, 102; and Constance M. Turnbull, *The Straits Settlements, 1826-67*, London, 1972.

Figure 3. The Straits Settlements, 1826

kilometer deep was designated the government and commercial quarter. A hill was leveled and the dirt used to fill a nearby swamp in order to provide a place for the heart of the commercial area, now Raffles Place. An orderly and scientifically laid out town was the goal of Raffles, who believed that Singapore would one day be "a place of considerable magnitude and importance." Under Raffles' plan, commercial buildings were to be constructed of brick

Historical Setting

with tiled roofs, each with a two-meter covered walkway to provide shelter from sun and rain. Spaces were set aside for shipyards, markets, churches, theaters, police stations, and a botanical garden. Raffles had a wooden bungalow built for himself on Government Hill.

Each immigrant group was assigned an area of the settlement under the new plan. The Chinese, who were the fastest growing group, were given the whole area west of the Singapore River adjoining the commercial district; Chinatown was further divided among the various dialect groups. The *temenggong* and his followers were moved several kilometers west of the commercial district, mainly in an effort to curtail their influence in that area. The headmen or *kapitans* of the various groups were allotted larger plots, and affluent Asians and Europeans were encouraged to live together in a residential area adjacent to the government quarter.

In the absence of any legal code, Raffles in early 1823 promulgated a series of administrative regulations. The first required that land be conveyed on permanent lease at a public auction and that it must be registered. The second reiterated Singapore's status as a free port, a popular point with the merchants. In his farewell remarks, Raffles assured them that "Singapore will long and always remain a free port and no taxes on trade or industry will be established to check its future rise and prosperity." The third regulation made English common law the standard, although Muslim law was to be used in matters of religion, marriage, and inheritance involving Malays.

Raffles was an enlightened administrator for his time. He believed in the prevention of crime and the reform, rather than the mere punishment, of criminals. Payment of compensation to the injured by the offender was to be considered as important as punishment. Only murder was to be considered a capital offense, and various work and training programs were used to turn prisoners into useful settlers. Raffles shut down all gambling dens and heavily taxed the sale of liquor and opium. He abolished outright slavery in 1823, but was unable to eradicate debt bondage, by which immigrants often were forced to work years at hard labor to pay for their passage.

Raffles felt that under Farquhar the *temenggong* and the sultan had wielded too much power, receiving one-third of the proceeds from the opium, liquor, and gambling revenues, and demanding presents from the captains of the Asian ships that dropped anchor there. Hussein and the *temenggong*, however, viewed Singapore as a thriving entrepôt in the mold of the great port cities of the Malay maritime empires of Srivijaya, Malacca, and Johore. As rulers

15

Singapore: A Country Study

of the island, they considered themselves entitled to a share of the power and proceeds of the settlement. In June 1823, Raffles managed to persuade Hussein and the *temenggong* to give up their rights to port duties and their share in the other tax revenues in exchange for a pension of Sp$1,500 and Sp$800 per month, respectively. Because the Dutch still contested the British presence in Singapore, Raffles did not dare push the issue further. On March 17, 1824, however, the Anglo-Dutch Treaty of London was signed, dividing the East Indies into two spheres of influence. The British would have hegemony north of a line drawn through the Strait of Malacca, and the Dutch would control the area south of the line. As a result, the Dutch recognized the British claim to Singapore and relinquished power over Malacca in exchange for the British post at Bencoolen. On August 3, with their claim to Singapore secure, the British negotiated a new treaty with the sultan and the *temenggong*, by which the Malay rulers were forced to cede Singapore and the neighboring islands to the British East India Company for cash payments and increased pensions. Under the treaty, the Malay chiefs also agreed to help suppress piracy, but the problem was not to be solved for several more decades.

In October 1823, Raffles left Singapore for Britain, never to return. Before leaving, he replaced Farquhar with the Scotsman John Crawfurd, an efficient and frugal administrator who guided the settlement through three years of vigorous growth. Crawfurd continued Raffles' struggles against slavery and piracy, but he permitted the gambling houses to reopen, taxed them, and used the revenue for street widening, bridge building, and other civic projects. He failed to support, however, Raffles' dream of higher education for the settlement. As his last public act, Raffles had contributed Sp$2,000 toward the establishment of a Singapore Institution, which he had envisioned as a training ground for Asian teachers and civil servants and a place where European officials could gain an appreciation of the rich cultural heritage of the region as Raffles himself had. He had hoped that the institution would attract the sons of rulers and chiefs of all the region. Crawfurd, however, advised the company officials in Calcutta that it would be preferable to support primary education. In fact, education at all levels was neglected until much later.

A Flourishing Free Port, 1826-67

In the first half-century after its founding, Singapore grew from a precarious trading post of the British East India Company populated by a few thousand to a bustling, cosmopolitan seaport of 85,000 (see fig. 4). Although the general trend of Singapore's economic status was upward during this period, the settlement endured economic recessions as well as prosperity, fires and floods as well as building booms, and bureaucratic incompetence as well as able administration. In 1826 the British East India Company combined Singapore with Penang and Malacca to form the Presidency of the Straits Settlements, with its capital at Penang. The new bureaucratic apparatus proved to be expensive and cumbersome, however, and in 1830 the Straits Settlements were reduced to a residency, or subdivision, of the Presidency of Bengal. Although Singapore soon overshadowed the other settlements, Penang remained the capital until 1832 and the judicial headquarters until 1856. The overworked civil service that administered Singapore remained about the same size between 1830 and 1867, although the population quadrupled during that period. Saddled with the endless narrative and statistical reports required by Bengal, few civil servants had time to learn the languages or customs of the people they governed.

Although the European and Asian commercial community was reasonably satisfied with the administration of the settlement under Bengal, an economic depression in the 1840s caused some to consider the merits of Singapore being administered directly as a crown colony. The advent of the steamship had made Singapore less dependent on Calcutta and more closely tied to the London commercial and political scene. By mid-century, the parent firms of most of Singapore's British-owned merchant houses were located in London rather than Calcutta. In 1851, following a visit to Singapore, Lord Dalhousie, the governor general of India, separated the Straits Settlements from Bengal and placed them directly under his own charge. In the following sixteen years, a number of issues arose that caused increased agitation to remove the Straits Settlements completely from India's administration and place it directly under the British Colonial Office. Among these issues were the need for protection against piracy and Calcutta's continuing attempts to levy port duties on Singapore. Mostly as a result of the need for a place other than fever-ridden Hong Kong to station British troops in Asia, London designated the Straits Settlements a crown colony on April 1, 1867.

Financial Success

Trade at Singapore had eclipsed that of Penang by 1824, when it reached a total of Sp$11 million annually. By 1869 annual trade at Singapore had risen to Sp$89 million. The cornerstone of the settlement's commercial success was the entrepôt trade, which was carried on with no taxation and a minimum of restriction. The

Singapore: A Country Study

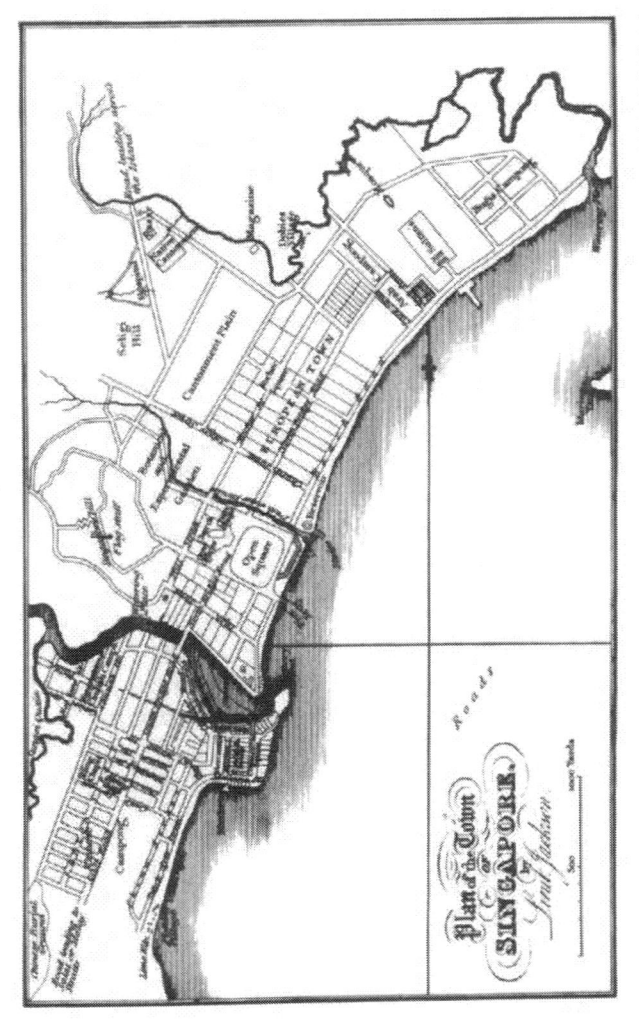

Source: Based on information from J. Crawfurd, *Journal of an Embassy from the Governor-General of India to the Courts of Siam and Cochin China*, London, 1828, 2, 383.

Figure 4. Plan of the Town of Singapore by Lieutenant Phillip Jackson, 1828.

main trading season began each year with the arrival of ships from China, Siam, and Cochinchina (as the southern part of Vietnam was then known). Driven by the northeast monsoon winds and arriving in January, February, and March, the ships brought immigrant laborers and cargoes of dried and salted foods, medicines, silk, tea, porcelain, and pottery. They left beginning in May with the onset of the southwest monsoons, laden with produce, spices, tin, and gold from the Malay Archipelago, opium from India, and English cotton goods and arms. The second major trading season began in September or October with the arrival of the Bugis traders in their small, swift *prahu*, bringing rice, pepper, spices, edible bird nests and shark fins, mother-of-pearl, gold dust, rattan, and camphor from the archipelago. They departed carrying British manufactures, cotton goods, iron, arms, opium, salt, silk, and porcelain. By mid-century, there were more than twenty British merchant houses in Singapore, as well as German, Swiss, Dutch, Portuguese, and French firms. The merchants would receive cargoes of European or Indian goods on consignment and sell them on commission.

Most of the trade between the European and Asian merchants was handled by Chinese middlemen, who spoke the necessary languages and knew the needs of their customers. Many of the middlemen had trained as clerks in the European trading firms of Malacca. With their experience, contacts, business acumen, and willingness to take risks, the middlemen were indispensable to the merchants. For the Chinese middlemen, the opportunities for substantial profit were great; but so were the risks. Lacking capital, the middlemen bought large quantities of European goods on credit with the hope of reselling them to the Chinese or Bugis ship captains or themselves arranging to ship them to the markets of Siam or the eastern Malay Peninsula. If, however, buyers could not be found or ships were lost at sea, the middlemen faced bankruptcy or prison. Although the merchants also stood to lose under such circumstances, the advantages of the system and the profits to be made kept it flourishing.

The main site for mercantile activity in mid-century Singapore was Commercial Square, renamed Raffles Place in 1858. Besides the European merchant houses located on the square, there were in 1846 six Jewish merchant houses, five Chinese, five Arab, two Armenian, one American, and one Indian. Each merchant house had its own pier for loading and unloading cargo; and ship chandlers, banks, auction houses, and other businesses serving the shipping trade also were located on the square. In the early years, merchants lived above their offices; but by mid-century most had established themselves in beautiful houses and compounds in a fashionable section on the east bank of the Singapore River.

Construction of government buildings lagged far behind commercial buildings in the early years because of the lack of tax-generated revenue. The merchants resisted any attempts by Calcutta to levy duties on trade, and the British East India Company had little interest in increasing the colony's budget. After 1833, however, many public works projects were constructed by the extensive use of Indian convict labor. Irish architect George Drumgold Coleman, who was appointed superintendent of public works in that year, used convicts to drain marshes, reclaim seafront, lay out roads, and build government buildings, churches, and homes in a graceful colonial style.

Probably the most serious problem facing Singapore at midcentury was piracy, which was being engaged in by a number of groups who found easy pickings in the waters around the thriving port. Some of the followers of the *temenggong's* son and heir, Ibrahim, were still engaging in their "patrolling" activities in the late 1830s. Most dangerous of the various pirate groups, however, were the Illanun (Lanun) of Mindanao in the Philippines and northern Borneo. These fierce sea raiders sent out annual fleets of 50 to 100 well-armed *prahu*, which raided settlements, attacked ships, and carried off prisoners who were pressed into service as oarsmen. The Illanun attacked not only small craft from the archipelago but also Chinese and European sailing ships. Bugis trading captains threatened to quit trading at Singapore unless the piracy was stopped. In the 1850s, Chinese pirates, who boldly used Singapore as a place to buy arms and sell their booty, brought the trade between Singapore and Cochinchina to a standstill. The few patrol boats assigned by the British East India Company to protect the Straits Settlements were totally inadequate, and the Singapore merchants continually petitioned Calcutta and London for aid in stamping out the menace.

By the late 1860s, a number of factors had finally led to the demise of piracy. In 1841, the governor of the Straits Settlements, George Bonham, recognized Ibrahim as *temenggong* of Johore, with the understanding that he would help suppress piracy. By 1850 the Royal Navy was patrolling the area with steam-powered ships, which could navigate upwind and outmaneuver the pirate sailing ships. The expansion of European power in Asia also brought increased patrolling of the region by the Dutch in Sumatra, the Spanish in the Philippines, and the British from their newly established protectorates on the Malay Peninsula. China also agreed to cooperate in suppressing piracy under the provisions of treaties signed with the Western powers in 1860.

Singapore's development and prosperity at mid-century were largely confined to the coast within a few kilometers of the port area. The interior remained a dense jungle ringed by a coastline of mangrove swamps. Attempts to turn the island to plantation agriculture between 1830 and 1840 had met with little success. Nutmeg, coffee, sugar, cotton, cinnamon, cloves, and indigo all fell victim to pests, plant diseases, or insufficient soil fertility. The only successful agricultural enterprises were the gambier and pepper plantations, numbering about 600 in the late 1840s and employing some 6,000 Chinese laborers. When the firewood needed to extract the gambier became depleted, the plantation would be moved to a new area. As a result, the forests of much of the interior of the island had been destroyed and replaced by coarse grasses by the 1860s, and the gambier planters had moved their operations north to Johore. This pressure on the land also affected the habitats of the wildlife, particularly tigers, which began increasingly to attack villagers and plantation workers. Tigers reportedly claimed an average of one victim per day in the late 1840s. When the government offered rewards for killing the animals, tiger hunting became a serious business and a favorite sport. The last year a person was reported killed by a tiger was 1890, and the last wild tiger was shot in 1904.

A Cosmopolitan Community

As Singapore prospered and grew, the size and diversity of its population kept pace. By 1827, the Chinese had become the most numerous of Singapore's various ethnic groups. Many of the Chinese came from Malacca, Penang, Riau, and other parts of the Malay Archipelago to which their forebears had migrated decades or even generations before. More recent Chinese immigrants were mainly from the southeastern provinces of Guangdong and Fujian and spoke either the Hokkien, Teochiu, Cantonese, or Hakka dialects. In an extension of the common Chinese practice of sojourning, in which men temporarily left their home communities to seek work in nearby or distant cities, most migrants to Singapore saw themselves as temporary residents intending to return to home and family after making a fortune or at least amassing enough capital to buy land in their home district. Many did return; more did not. Even those who never returned usually sent remittances to families back home.

To help them face the dangers, hardships, and loneliness of the sojourner life, most men joined or were forced to join secret societies organized by earlier immigrants from their home districts. The secret societies had their origin in southern China, where, in the late seventeenth century, the Heaven, Earth, and Man (or Triad) Society was formed to oppose the Qing (1644-1911) dynasty. By the nineteenth century, secret societies in China acted as groups that organized urban unskilled labor and used coercion to win control of economic niches, such as unloading ships, transporting cotton, or gambling and prostitution. The same pattern extended all over Southeast Asia, where immigrants joined secret societies whose membership was restricted to those coming from the same area and speaking the same dialect. Membership gave the immigrants some security, in the form of guaranteed employment and assistance in case of illness, but required loyalty to the leaders and payment of a portion of an already meager wage. Although the societies performed many useful social functions, they were also a major source of crime and violence. By 1860 there were at least twelve secret societies in Singapore, representing the various dialect and subdialect groups. Invariably friction arose as each society sought to control a certain area or the right to a certain tax farm. Civil war in China in the 1850s brought a flood of new migrants from China, including many rebels and other violent elements. Serious fighting between the various secret societies broke out in 1854, but it remained a domestic dispute within the Chinese community. Although not directed at the government or the non-Chinese communities, such outbreaks disrupted commerce and created a tense atmosphere, which led to the banning of secret societies in 1889.

Just as the European merchant community used Chinese middlemen in conducting their business, the Straits government relied on prominent Chinese businessmen to act as go-betweens with the Chinese community. In the early years, the Baba Chinese, who usually spoke English, served in this capacity. By mid-century, however, immigrant Chinese from the various dialect groups had begun to act as intermediaries. Some, such as Seah Eu Chin, who was the go-between with the Teochiu community, were well educated and from respected families. Seah, who made his fortune in gambier and pepper plantations, was an early member of the Singapore Chamber of Commerce, established in 1837, and a justice of the peace. Probably the wealthiest and most prominent Chinese immigrant in the nineteenth century was Hoo Ah Kay, nicknamed "Whampoa" after his birthplace near Guangzhou, who served as a go-between with the Cantonese-speaking community. Hoo came as a penniless youth and made his fortune in provisioning ships, merchandising, and speculating in land. He later became the first Asian member of Singapore's Legislative Council and a member of the Executive Council. Despite their close connections to the European ruling class, Seah, Hoo, and other prominent Chinese carefully retained their Chinese culture and values, as did the less prominent immigrants.

Most Chinese immigrants fared far less well. If they survived the rigors of the voyage, they were forced to work at hard labor for a year or more to pay off their passage. Some were sent directly to the gambier plantations or even to the tin mines of the Malay Peninsula. Others were sent to toil on the docks or become construction workers. After paying off their passage, they began earning a meager wage, which, unless diverted for opium or gambling debts, was sent as a remittance to families back in China. Wives were in short supply, since very few Chinese women came to Singapore in the first few decades of the settlement. Even by the mid-1860s, the ratio of Chinese men to women was fifteen to one.

Until about 1860, Malays were the second largest group. The followers of the *temenggong* mostly moved to Johore, where many of them died of smallpox. The *orang laut* by mid-century merged with other groups of Malay, who were drawn from Riau, Sumatra, and Malacca. Generally peaceful and industrious, the Malays usually worked as fishermen, boatmen, woodcutters, or carpenters.

Most of the Bugis sea traders migrated to Macassar after the Dutch made it a free port in 1847, and by 1860 the Bugis population of Singapore had declined to less than 1,000. Small numbers of Arabs, Jews, and Armenians, many of them already well-to-do, were drawn to Singapore, where they amassed even greater wealth. Another small group numbered among Singapore's upper class were the Parsis, Indians of Iranian descent who were adherents of Zoroastrianism.

Indians had become Singapore's second largest community by 1860, numbering more than 11,000. Some of these people were laborers or traders, who, like the Chinese, came with the hope of making their fortune and returning to their homeland. Some were troops garrisoned at Singapore by the government in Calcutta. Another group were convicts who were first brought to Singapore from the detention center in Bencoolen in 1825, after Bencoolen was handed over to the Dutch. Singapore then became a major detention center for Indian prisoners. Rehabilitation rather than punishment was emphasized, and prisoners were trained in such skills as brick making, carpentry, rope making, printing, weaving, and tailoring, which later would enable them to find employment. Singapore's penal system was considered so enlightened that Dutch, Siamese, and Japanese prison administrators came to observe it. Convict labor was used to build roads, clear the jungle, hunt tigers, and construct public buildings, some of which were still in use in the late twentieth century. After completing their sentences, most convicts settled down to a useful life in Singapore. As with Chinese and Europeans, Indian men far outnumbered women because few Indian women came to Singapore before the 1860s. Some Indian Muslims married Malay women, however, and their descendants were known as Jawi-Peranakan (see Glossary).

The highly unbalanced sex ratio in Singapore contributed to a rather lawless, frontier atmosphere that the government seemed helpless to combat. Little revenue was available to expand the tiny police force, which struggled to keep order amid a continuous influx of immigrants, often from the fringes of Asian society. This tide of immigration was totally uncontrolled because Singapore's businessmen, desperate for unskilled laborers, opposed restriction on free immigration as vehemently as they resisted any restraint on free trade. Public health services were almost nonexistent, and cholera, malnutrition, smallpox, and opium use took a heavy toll in the severely overcrowded working-class areas.

Crown Colony, 1867-1918

After years of campaigning by a small minority of the British merchants, who had chafed under the rule of the Calcutta government, the Straits Settlements became a crown colony on April 1, 1867. Under the crown colony administration, the governor ruled with the assistance of executive and legislative councils. The Executive Council included the governor, the senior military official in the Straits Settlements, and six other senior officials. The Legislative Council included the members of the Executive Council, the chief justice, and four nonofficial members nominated by the governor. The numbers of nonofficial members and Asian council members gradually increased through the years. Singapore dominated the Legislative Council, to the annoyance of Malacca and Penang.

By the 1870s, Singapore businessmen had considerable interest in the rubber, tin, gambier, and other products and resources of the Malay Peninsula. Conditions in the peninsula were highly unstable, however, marked by fighting between immigrants and traditional Malay authorities and rivalry among various Chinese secret societies. Singapore served as an entrepôt for the resources of the Malay Peninsula and, at the same time, the port of debarkation for thousands of immigrant Chinese, Indians, Indonesians, and Malays bound for the tin mines and rubber plantations to the north. Some 250,000 Chinese alone disembarked in Singapore in 1912, most of them on their way to the Malay states or to the Dutch East Indies.

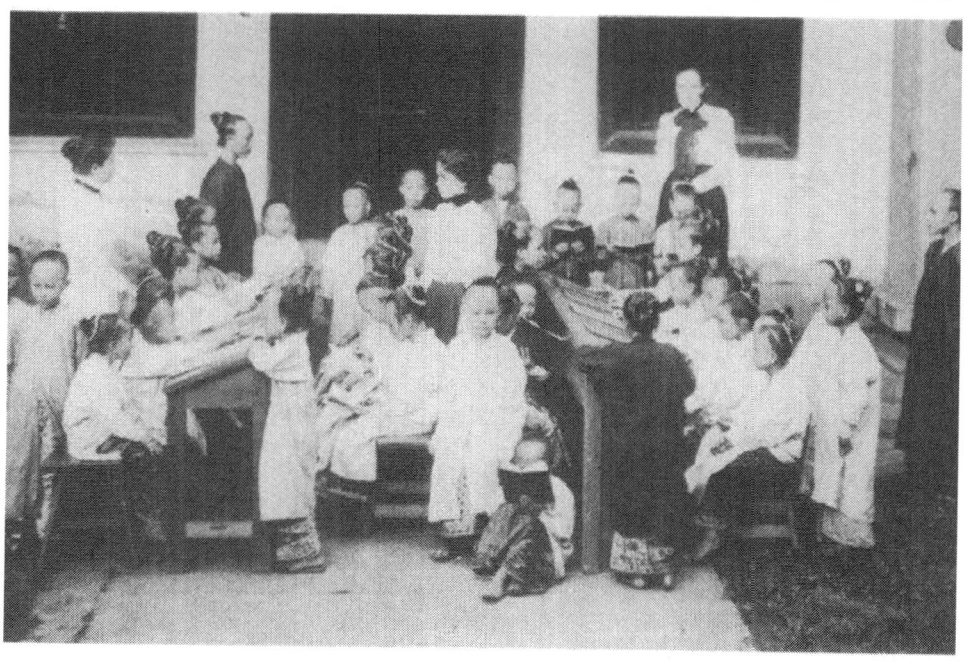

Singapore Malay family, nineteenth century
Courtesy Library of Congress
School for Singapore Chinese girls, nineteenth century
Courtesy Library of Congress

Although most Chinese immigrants merely passed through Singapore, the Chinese population of the island grew rapidly, from 34,000 in 1878 to 103,000 in 1888. The colonial government established the Chinese Protectorate in 1877 to deal with the serious abuses of the labor trade. William Pickering, the first appointed Protector of Chinese, was the first British official in Singapore who could speak and read Chinese. Pickering was given power to board incoming ships and did much to protect the newly arrived immigrants. In the early 1880s, he also extended his protection to Chinese women entering the colony by working to end forced prostitution. Because of his sympathetic approach and administrative ability, the protector soon spread his influence and protection over the whole Chinese community, providing arbitration of labor, financial, and domestic disagreements, thereby undermining some of the powers of the secret societies. Although no longer able to engage in illegal immigration practices, the societies continued to cause problems by running illegal gambling houses and supporting large-scale riots that often paralyzed the city. In 1889, Governor Sir Cecil Clementi-Smith sponsored a law to ban secret societies, which took effect the following year. The result was to drive the societies underground, where many of them degenerated into general lawlessness, engaging in extortion, gambling operations, gang fights, and robbery. The power of the secret societies, however, was broken.

The largest Chinese dialect group in the late nineteenth century were the Hokkien, who were traditionally involved in trade, shipping, banking, and industry. The next largest group, the Teochiu, engaged in agricultural production and processing, including gambier, pepper, and rubber production, rice and lumber milling, pineapple canning, and fish processing. Cantonese served as artisans and laborers and a few made their fortunes in tin. The two smallest groups, the Hakka and Hainanese, were mostly servants, sailors, or unskilled laborers. Because wealth was the key to leadership and social standing within the Chinese community at that time, the Hokkien dominated organizations such as the Singapore Chinese Chamber of Commerce and supplied most of the Chinese members of the Legislative Council and the Chinese Advisory Board. The latter, established in 1889 to provide a formal link between the British government of the colony and the Chinese community, served as a place to air grievances but had no power.

The affluent among Singapore's Chinese community increasingly saw their prosperity and fortunes tied to those of the crown colony and the British Empire. Western education, customs, and pastimes were adopted, and the sons of Chinese businessmen were

Historical Setting

often sent to Britain for university training. The Straits Chinese British Association was formed in 1900 by Baba Chinese leaders to promote loyalty to the British Empire as well as to advance the education and welfare of Singapore's Chinese. Visiting British royalty were warmly received and British causes and victories enthusiastically supported. The Straits Chinese (see Glossary) contributed generously to the British war effort in World War I (1914-18).

Although the Chinese upper class, particularly the Straits-born Chinese, grew increasingly Westernized, the homeland exerted a continuing pull on its loyalties that increased during this period. Visits to China by Singapore Chinese became more common with the advent of steamship travel. The relaxation by the 1870s of China's law forbidding emigration (repealed in 1893) and the protection afforded Singaporeans by British citizenship made it relatively safe for prosperous businessmen to visit their homeland and return again to Singapore. Upper-class Singapore Chinese frequently sent their sons to school in China and encouraged them to find brides there, although they themselves had often married local women.

In the latter part of the nineteenth century, China's ruling Qing dynasty began to take an interest in the Nanyang Chinese and sought to attract their loyalty and wealth to the service of the homeland. Chinese consulates were established in Singapore, Malaya, the Dutch East Indies, and other parts of the Nanyang. Hoo Ah Kay was appointed Singapore's first consul in 1877. He and his successors worked diligently to strengthen the cultural ties of the Singapore Chinese to China by establishing a cultural club, a debating society, Singapore's first Chinese-language newspaper (*Lat Pau*), and various Chinese-language schools, in which the medium of instruction was Chinese. One of the most important functions of the consul, however, was to raise money for flood and famine relief in China and for the general support of the Qing government. With the upheaval in China following the Hundred Days' Reform Movement in 1898, and its suppression by the Qing conservatives, the Singapore Chinese and their pocketbooks were wooed by reformists, royalists, and revolutionaries alike. Sun Yat-sen founded a Singapore branch of the Tongmeng Hui, the forerunner of the Guomindang (Kuomintang—Chinese Nationalist Party), in 1906. Not until the successful Wuchang Uprising of October 10, 1911, however, did Sun receive the enthusiastic support of Singapore Chinese.

Much smaller than the Chinese community and less organized in the late nineteenth century was the Singapore Indian community. By 1880 there were only 12,000 Indians, including Hindus,

Muslims, Sikhs, and Christians, each group with its own temple, mosque, or church. South Indians tended to be shopkeepers or laborers, particularly dockworkers, riverboatmen, and drivers of the ox carts that were the major transport for goods to and from the port area. North Indians were usually clerks, traders, and merchants. Both groups came to Singapore expecting to return to their homeland and were even more transient than the Chinese.

Malays continued to be drawn to Singapore from all over the archipelago, reaching a population of 36,000 by 1901. Malay traders and merchants lost out in the commercial competition with Chinese and Europeans, and most Malay immigrants became small shopkeepers, religious teachers, policemen, servants, or laborers. The leadership positions in the Malay-Muslim community went to the Jawi-Peranakan, because of their facility in English, and to wealthy Arabs. In 1876 the first Malay-language newspaper of the region, *Jawi Peranakan,* was published in Singapore. Several other Malay-language journals supporting religious reform were begun in the early twentieth century, and Singapore became a regional focal point for the Islamic revival movement that swept the Muslim world at that time.

A number of events beginning in the late nineteenth century strengthened Singapore's position as a major port and industrial center. When the Suez Canal opened, the Strait of Malacca became the preferred route to East Asia. Steamships began replacing sailing ships, necessitating a chain of coaling stations, including Singapore. Most of the major European steamship companies had established offices in Singapore by the 1880s. The expansion of colonialism in Southeast Asia and the opening of Siam (as Thailand was known at that time) to trade under King Chulalongkorn (Rama V) brought even more trade to Singapore. The spread of British influence in Malaya increased the flow of rubber, tin, copra, and sugar through the island port, and Singapore moved into processing and light manufacturing, some of which was located on its offshore islands. To serve the growing American canning industry a tin smelter was built in 1890 on Pulau Brani (*pulau* means island). Rubber processing expanded rapidly in response to the demands of the young automobile industry. Oil storage facilities established on Pulau Bukum made it the supply center for the region by 1902.

In the early twentieth century, Singapore had expanded its financial institutions, communications, and infrastructure in order to support its booming trade and industry. British banks predominated, although by 1905 there were Indian, Australian, American, Chinese, and French-owned banks as well. Telegraph service from India and Europe reached Singapore in 1870, and telephone service within Singapore was installed in 1879 and extended to Johore in 1882 (see Telecommunications, ch. 3). The more than sixty European-owned companies in the Straits Settlements crown colony in the 1870s were largely confined to Singapore and Penang. Far more prosperous were some of the Chinese firms in Singapore that were beginning to expand their business links throughout Asia.

Singapore's port facilities failed to keep up with its commercial development until the publicly owned Tanjong Pagar Dock Board (renamed Singapore Harbour Board in 1913) set about replacing old wharves and warehouses and installing modern machinery and a new graving dock (dry dock). Trucks gradually replaced ox carts for transporting goods from the harbor to the town, and by 1909 it was possible to travel from Singapore to Penang by train and railroad ferry. The Johore Causeway linked road and rail transportation between Singapore and the peninsula after 1923.

At the turn of the century, social advancement lagged far behind economic development in Singapore. While the wealthy enjoyed their social clubs, sports facilities, mansions, and suburban estates, the lower classes endured a grim existence marked by poverty, overcrowding, malnutrition, and disease. Malaria, cholera, and opium addiction were chiefly responsible for Singapore's mortality rate, which in 1896 was higher than that of Hong Kong, Ceylon, or India. A 1907 government commission to investigate the opium problem found that the majority of opium deaths were among the poor, who were reduced to smoking the dregs of used opium. Campaigns by missionaries and European-educated Chinese to ban opium use were successfully opposed by tax farmers and businessmen. By 1900 the opium tax provided one-half of the revenue of the colonial government, and both Asian and European businessmen resisted its replacement with an income tax. As an alternative, the government in 1910 took over all manufacture and sale of opium, setting up a factory at Pasir Panjang. Opium sales continued to constitute half of the government's revenue, but the most dangerous use of the drug had been curtailed.

Education was generally in a backward state. Most primary schools in which Malay, Chinese, or Tamil was the medium of instruction were of poor quality. English-language primary schools were mostly run by Christian missionaries, and the only secondary education was provided by Raffles Institution beginning in 1884. In 1902 the government formulated an Education Code, under which it took responsibility for providing English-language primary schools; the following year it took over Raffles Institution.

With the support of the Chinese community, the government opened a medical school in 1905 that had a first class of twenty-three students. Upgraded to the King Edward Medical College in 1920, the school formed the cornerstone of the future Singapore University. The affluent of Singapore sent their children to the English-language schools, which had steadily improved their standards. The brightest students vied for the Queen's Scholarships, founded in 1889, which provided for university education in Britain for Asian students. Many prosperous Asian families themselves sent their children to school in Britain. An English-language education at either the secondary or university level provided many Asians with the key to government, professional, or business employment. It also created a bond among the upper classes of all ethnic groups.

Under the leadership of reformist Chinese, Singapore's Chinese-language schools were also expanded and modernized at this time. A scientific curriculum was added to the traditional education in Chinese classics and Confucian morality. Students from Chinese-language schools often continued their education in China, where a school for Nanyang students had been opened in Nanjing in 1907 to prepare them for a role in Singapore's Chinese community. At the turn of the century, schools were even established in Singapore for Chinese women, who before that time had led severely sheltered lives under the domination of their husbands and mothers-in-law. By 1911 Chinese women were receiving instruction in Malay, English, Chinese, music, sewing, and cooking. Malay and Tamil-language primary schools continued to decline, and few students were able to progress from them to the English-language secondary level.

Responsibility for Singapore's defense had been a contentious issue between London and Singapore almost since its founding. The Singapore merchants resisted any attempts to levy taxes for fortifications and even objected to paying the cost of maintaining a small garrison on the island. In 1886 troubles with Russia over Afghanistan and worry over the Russian navy in the Pacific, prompted the British to begin fortifying the port area and building new barracks and other military facilities. The Singapore business community resisted strenuously London's proposal to double the colony's annual military contribution, insisting that the island was a critical link in the imperial chain. The colony, nonetheless, was required to pay a larger sum although slightly less than originally demanded. The British signed a defensive treaty with Japan in 1902. The Japanese defeat of the Russian navy in 1905 removed

Singapore Indian family, nineteenth century
Courtesy Library of Congress

that threat to Britain's seapower in Asia, thus enabling Britain to concentrate its navy in its home waters in response to a German naval buildup.

Singapore essentially sat out World War I. Fear that the island would be attacked by Germany's East Asiatic Squadron never materialized. Singapore's German business community, nonetheless, was rounded up and interned comfortably at their Teutonia Club. The only incident of the war period was the mutiny of Singapore's small garrison, the 800 troops of the Fifth Light Infantry Regiment. The regiment, composed entirely of Punjabi Muslims, was angered that Britain was at war with the Muslim Ottoman Empire. When the regiment was ordered to Hong Kong in February 1915, rumors spread through the unit that the troops were actually being sent to fight in France or Turkey. On the eve of its departure, the regiment mutinied, killed the officers, and terrorized the town. Within ten days the rebellion had been put down by a combined force of the Singapore Volunteer Artillery (a unit of 450 volunteers formed in 1914), police, Malay troops from Johore, the crews of British, French, Japanese, and Russian warships in port, and several hundred civilians. After the mutineers were rounded up, thirty-six were shot in public executions and the others were imprisoned or sent on active duty elsewhere.

Subsequently, hard feelings were created in Singapore's Indian community by a requirement that its members register with the government. A small British detachment was brought in to garrison the post for the rest of the war, with the aid of the Singapore Volunteer Artillery.

Between the World Wars, 1919-41

The Singapore economy experienced much the same rollercoaster effect that Western economies did in the period between the world wars. A postwar boom created by rising tin and rubber prices gave way to recession in late 1920 when prices for both dropped on the world market. By the mid-1920s, rubber and tin prices had soared again and fortunes were made overnight. Tan Kah Kee, who had migrated from Xiamen (Amoy) at age seventeen, reportedly made S$8 million (for value of the Singapore dollar—see Glossary) in 1925 in rubber, rice milling, and shipping; and Hakka businessman Aw Boon Haw earned the nickname "Tiger Balm King" for the multimillion-dollar fortune he made from the production and sale of patent medicines. Although they never amassed the great fortunes of Singapore's leading Asian businessmen, the prosperous European community increasingly lived in the style and comfort afforded by modern conveniences and an abundance of servants.

The Baba Chinese leaders focused their attention on improving educational opportunities, which meant lobbying for free English-language primary schools and more scholarships for English-language secondary schools. Although English-language schools expanded rapidly, most educated Straits-born Chinese studied at Chinese-language schools. Of the 72,000 children in Singapore schools in 1939, 38,000 were in Chinese schools, 27,000 in English schools, 6,000 in Malay schools, and 1,000 in Tamil schools (See Education, ch. 2).

The Straits-born Chinese increased their share of Singapore's Chinese population from 25 percent in 1921 to 36 percent in 1931. Chinese immigration was drastically cut by the Immigration Restriction Ordinance of 1930, which limited immigration of unskilled male laborers. Put in force to combat unemployment resulting from the Great Depression, the ordinance dropped the quota of Chinese immigrants from 242,000 in 1930 to 28,000 in 1933. Immigration was further restricted by the Aliens Ordinance of 1933, which set quotas and charged landing fees for aliens. Executive Council member Tan Cheng Lock and others bitterly opposed the policy in the Legislative Council as anti-Chinese.

The administration of the colony continued to be carried out by the governor and top-level officials of the Malayan Civil Service, posts that could be held only by "natural-born British subjects of pure European descent on both sides." The governor continued to consult with the Legislative Council, which included a handful of wealthy Asian business and professional leaders, who served as nonofficial members of the council. The mid-level and technical civil service positions were open to British subjects of all races. Very few Asians opposed the system, which gave the official members the majority on the legislative and executive councils. In the 1930s, Tan agitated unsuccessfully for direct popular representation and a nonofficial majority for the legislative council, but most Chinese were satisfied to devote their attention to commercial and professional affairs and the growing interest in nationalism in China.

The sympathies of even the Straits-born Chinese lay with their homeland in the period between the wars. A Singapore branch of the Guomindang was active for a few years beginning in 1912, and China-oriented businessmen led boycotts in 1915 against Japanese goods in response to Japan's Twenty-One Demands against China. These demands were a set of political and economic ultimatums, which if acceded to, would have made China a protectorate of Japan. Mass support for Chinese nationalism became more evident in 1919 when demonstrations, which turned violent, were staged in Singapore. In the early 1920s, Sun Yat-sen was successful in convincing Singapore's China-born businessmen to invest heavily in Chinese industry and to donate large sums of money for education in China. Tan Kah Kee contributed more than S$4 million for the founding of Amoy (Xiamen) University in 1924. The Guomindang also sent teachers and textbooks to Singapore and encouraged the use of Mandarin (or Guoyu) in Singapore's Chinese schools.

Although Mandarin was not the language of any of Singapore's major dialect groups, it was considered a unifying factor by the various Chinese leadership factions of both Singapore and China. Singapore's first Chinese secondary school, established by Tan in 1919, taught in Mandarin, as did a growing number of Chinese primary schools. In 1927 the Guomindang increased the number of promising students brought to China for university education and began a concerted effort to extend its control over Chinese schools in the Nanyang by supervising their curriculum and requiring the use of Mandarin. In the late 1920s, the colonial authorities had become increasingly aware of growing left-wing politics in the Chinese schools and sought to discourage the use of Mandarin as required by the Guomindang. By 1935, however, Mandarin had become the medium of instruction in all of Singapore's Chinese schools.

Following the breakup of the short-lived collaboration between the Guomindang and the Chinese Communist Party, the communists established a Nanyang Communist Party in 1928. Outlawed and harassed by the Singapore police, the party was reorganized in 1930 as the Malayan Communist Party (MCP—see Glossary), centered in Singapore. For the remainder of that year, it had some success in infiltrating teacher and student organizations and staging student strikes. In early 1931, however, the seizure by the police of an address book containing information on the newly organized party and its connections with the Far Eastern Bureau of the Communist International (Comintern—see Glossary) in Shanghai, led to arrests and the near destruction of the MCP by the following year. The Guomindang also had its problems during this period. The party's membership in Singapore had expanded rapidly until 1929, when the colonial administration banned the Singapore branch of the Guomindang and fund-raising for the party in China. Concerned about the increase of anticolonial propaganda, the Singapore government censored the vernacular press, severely restricted immigration, and cut off aid to Chinese and Tamil schools. During the 1930s, attempts by the communists and the Guomindang to organize labor and lead strikes were also suppressed by the colonial government.

Chinese nationalism and anti-Japanese sentiment in Singapore increased throughout the 1930s. The fortunes of both the Guomindang and the MCP rose with invasion of Manchuria by Japan in 1931 and the start of the Sino-Japanese War in 1937. The Chinese Communist Party and the Guomindang formed a united front in December 1936 to oppose Japanese aggression. The Guomindang called upon the Nanyang Chinese for volunteer and financial support for the Republic of China, which had promulgated a Nationality Law in 1929, by which it claimed all persons of Chinese descent on the paternal side as Chinese nationals. Tan Kah Kee headed both the Nanyang Chinese National Salvation Movement and the Singapore Chinese General Association for the Relief of Refugees, as well as the fund-raising efforts for the homeland among the Malayan Chinese. Chinese government agents used the Singapore Chinese Chamber of Commerce and other local organizations to organize highly effective boycotts against Japanese goods. Singapore's Chinese also boycotted Malay or Indian shops selling Japanese goods, and Chinese merchants who ignored the boycott were severely punished by extremist groups.

The British authorities struggled vainly to control the tide of anti-Japanese feeling by forbidding anti-Japanese demonstrations and by banning importation of anti-Japanese textbooks from China, which was at war with Japan, and the teaching of anti-Japanese slogans and songs in Chinese schools. They were alarmed at the communist infiltration of the Nanyang Chinese National Salvation Movement and other Chinese patriotic groups. The banned MCP claimed a membership of more than 50,000 by early 1940. Although nominally partners in a united front in opposition to the Japanese, the MCP and the Guomindang competed for control of such organizations as the Nanyang Chinese Relief General Association. Nonetheless, Singapore's Chinese contributed generously to the support of the Chinese government.

World War II, 1941-45

The British had begun building a naval base at Singapore in 1923, partly in response to Japan's increasing naval power. The project was costly and unpopular, and construction of the base proceeded slowly until the early 1930s when Japan began moving into Manchuria and northern China. A major component of the base was completed in March 1938, when the King George VI Graving Dock was opened; more than 300 meters in length, it was the largest dry dock in the world at the time. The base, completed in 1941 and defended by artillery, searchlights, and the newly built nearby Tengah Airfield, caused Singapore to be ballyhooed in the press as the "Gibralter of the East." The floating dock, 275 meters long, was the third largest in the world and could hold 60,000 workers. The base also contained dry docks, giant cranes, machine shops, and underground storage for water, fuel, and ammunition. A self-contained town on the base was built to house 12,000 Asian workers, with cinemas, hospitals, churches, and seventeen soccer fields. Above-ground tanks held enough fuel for the entire British navy for six months. The only thing the giant naval fortress lacked was ships.

The Singapore naval base was built and supplied to sustain a siege long enough to enable Britain's European-based fleet to reach the area. By 1940, however, it was clear that the British fleet and armed forces were fully committed in Europe and the Middle East and could not be spared to deal with a potential threat in Asia. In the first half of 1941, most Singaporeans were unaffected by the war on the other side of the world, as they had been in World War I. The main pressure on the Straits Settlements was the need to produce more rubber and tin for the Allied war effort. Both the colonial government and British military command were for the most part convinced of Singapore's impregnability.

Even by late autumn 1941, most Singaporeans and their leaders remained confident that their island fortress could withstand an attack, which they assumed would come from the south and from the sea. Heavy fifteen-inch guns defended the port and the city, and machine-gun bunkers lined the southern coast. The only local defense forces were the four battalions of Straits Settlements Volunteer Corps and a small civil defense organization with units trained as air raid wardens, fire fighters, medical personnel, and debris removers. Singapore's Asians were not, by and large, recruited into these organizations, mainly because the colonial government doubted their loyalty and capability. The government also went to great lengths to maintain public calm by making highly optimistic pronouncements and heavily censoring the Singapore newspapers for negative or alarming news. Journalists' reports to the outside world were also carefully censored, and, in late 1941, reports to the British cabinet from colonial officials were still unrealistically optimistic. If Singaporeans were uneasy, they were reassured by the arrival at the naval base of the battleship *Prince of Wales*, the battle cruiser *Repulse*, and four destroyers on December 2. The fast and modern *Prince of Wales* was the pride of the British navy, and the *Repulse* was a veteran cruiser. Their accompanying aircraft carrier had run aground en route, however, leaving the warships without benefit of air cover (See Historical Development, ch. 5).

The Japanese Malaya Campaign

On December 8, 1941, the Japanese troops of two large convoys, which had sailed from bases in Hainan and southern Indochina, landed at Singora (now Songkhla) and Patani in southern Thailand and Kota Baharu in northern Malaya. One of Japan's top generals and some of its best trained and most experienced troops were assigned to the Malaya campaign. By the evening of December 8, 27,000 Japanese troops under the command of General Yamashita Tomoyuki had established a foothold on the peninsula and taken the British air base at Kota Baharu. Meanwhile, Japanese airplanes had begun bombing Singapore. Hoping to intercept any further landings by the Japanese fleet, the *Prince of Wales* and the *Repulse* headed north, unaware that all British air bases in northern Malaya were now in Japanese hands. Without air support, the British ships were easy targets for the Japanese air force, which sunk them both on December 10.

The main Japanese force moved quickly to the western side of the peninsula and began sweeping down the single north-south road. The Japanese divisions were equipped with about 18,000 bicycles.

Historical Setting

Whenever the invaders encountered resistance, they detoured through the forests on bicycles or took to the sea in collapsible boats to outflank the British troops, encircle them, and cut their supply lines. Penang fell on December 18, Kuala Lumpur on January 11, 1942, and Malacca on January 15. The Japanese occupied Johore Baharu on January 31, and the last of the British troops crossed to Singapore, blowing a fifty-meter gap in the causeway behind them.

Singapore faced Japanese air raids almost daily in the latter half of January 1942. Fleeing refugees from the peninsula had doubled the 550,000 population of the beleaguered city. More British and Commonwealth of Nations (see Glossary) ships and armed forces were brought to Singapore during January, but most were poorly trained raw recruits from Australia and India and inexperienced British troops diverted from the war in the Middle East. Singapore's Chinese population, which had heard rumors of the treatment of the Malayan Chinese by the invading Japanese, flocked to volunteer to help repel the impending invasion. Brought together by the common enemy, Guomindang and communist groups banded together to volunteer their services to Governor Shenton Thomas. The governor authorized the formation of the Chung Kuo Council (China National Council), headed by Tan Kah Kee, under which thousands volunteered to construct defense works and to perform other essential services. The colonial government also reluctantly agreed to the formation of a Singapore Chinese Anti-Japanese Volunteer Battalion, known as Dalforce for its commander, Lieutenant Colonel John Dalley of the Federated Malay States police force. Dalley put his volunteers through a ten-day crash training course and armed them with basic weapons, including shotguns, knives, and grenades.

From February 1–8, 1942, the two armies faced each other across the Johore Strait. The Japanese stepped up their air raids, bombing the airfields, naval base, and harbor area. Bombs also fell in the commercial and residential sections of the city, causing great destruction and killing and wounding many civilians. With their mastery of the skies, the Japanese could choose the time and place for invasion and maintain an element of surprise. Yamashita, however, had only 30,000 troops and limited ammunition available to launch against a British force of about 70,000 armed personnel. Lieutenant General Arthur E. Percival, Commander of Commonwealth forces in Malaya, commanded the defense of Singapore under the direction of General Archibald Wavell, the newly appointed commander in chief Far East, who was headquartered in Java. Percival's orders from British prime minister Winston

Churchill through Wavell called for defending the city to the death, while executing a scorched-earth policy: "No surrender can be contemplated .... every inch of ground ... defended, every scrap of material or defences ... blown to pieces to prevent capture by the enemy ...." Accordingly, the troops set about the task of destroying the naval base, now useless without ships, and building defense works along the northern coast, which lay totally unprotected.

On the night of February 8, using collapsible boats, the Japanese landed under cover of darkness on the northwest coast of Singapore. By dawn, despite determined fighting by Australian troops, they had two divisions with their artillery established on the island. By the next day the Japanese had seized Tengah Airfield and gained control of the causeway, which they repaired in four days. The British forces were plagued by poor communication and coordination, and, despite strong resistance by Commonwealth troops aided by Dalforce and other Chinese irregulars, the Japanese took Bukit Timah—the highest point on the island—on February 11. The British forces fell back to a final perimeter around the city, stretching from Pasir Panjang to Kallang, as Yamashita issued an invitation to the British to surrender. On February 13, the Japanese broke through the final perimeter at Pasir Panjang, putting the whole city within range of their artillery.

As many as 2,000 civilians were killed daily as the Japanese continued to bomb the city by day and shell it at night. Governor Thomas cabled London that "there are now one million people within radius of three miles. Many dead lying in the streets and burial impossible. We are faced with total deprivation of water, which must result in pestilence . . . ." On February 13, Percival cabled Wavell for permission to surrender, hoping to avoid the destruction and carnage that would result from a house-to-house defense of the city. Churchill relented and on February 14 gave permission to surrender. On the evening of February 15, at the Japanese headquarters at the Ford factory in Bukit Timah, Yamashita accepted Percival's unconditional surrender.

Shōnan: Light of the South

The Japanese occupied Singapore from 1942 until 1945. They designated it the capital of Japan's southern region and renamed it Shōnan, meaning "Light of the South" in Japanese. All European and Australian prisoners were interned at Changi on the eastern end of the island—the 2,300 civilians at the prison and the more than 15,000 military personnel at nearby Selarang barracks. The 600 Malay and 45,000 Indian troops were assembled by the Japanese and urged to transfer their allegiance to the emperor of

*Admiral Lord Louis Mountbatten, the Supreme Allied Commander
in Southeast Asia, reading the order of the day following
the Japanese surrender in September 1945
Courtesy National Archives
Parade celebrating return of British to Singapore in 1945
Courtesy National Archives*

Japan. Many refused and were executed, tortured, imprisoned, or sent as forced laborers to Thailand, Sumatra, or New Guinea. Under pressure, about 20,000 Indian troops joined the Japanese-sponsored Indian National Army to fight for India's independence from the British.

The Asian civilian population watched with shock as their colonial rulers and supposed protectors were marched off to prison and the Japanese set about establishing their administration and authority. The Chinese were to bear the brunt of the occupation, in retribution for support given by Singapore Chinese to China in its struggle against Japan. All Chinese males from ages eighteen to fifty were required to report to registration camps for screening. The Japanese military police arrested those alleged to be anti-Japanese, meaning those who were singled out by informers or who were teachers, journalists, intellectuals, or even former servants of the British. Some were imprisoned, but most were executed, and estimates of their number range from 5,000 to 25,000. Many of the leaders of Singapore's anti-Japanese movement had already escaped, however, and the remnants of Dalforce and other Chinese irregular units had fled to the peninsula, where they formed the Malayan People's Anti-Japanese Army.

The harsh treatment by the Japanese in the early days of the occupation undermined any later efforts to enlist the support of Singaporeans for the Japanese vision of a Greater East Asia Co-Prosperity Sphere, which was to comprise Japan, Korea, China, Manchukuo, and Southeast Asia. Singapore's prominent Chinese leaders and businessmen were further disaffected when the Japanese military command bullied them into raising a S$10 million "gift" to the Japanese as a symbol of their cooperation and as reparation for their support for the government of China in its war against Japan. The Chinese and English schools were pressured to use Japanese as the medium of instruction. The Malay schools were allowed to use Malay, which was considered the indigenous language. The Japanese-controlled schools concentrated on physical training and teaching Japanese patriotic songs and propaganda. Most parents kept their children at home, and total enrollment for all the schools was never more than 7,000. Although free Japanese language classes were given at night and bonuses and promotions awarded to those who learned the language, efforts to replace English and Chinese with Japanese were generally unsuccessful.

Serious disruption of not only the economy but the whole fabric of society marked the occupation years in Singapore. Food and essential materials were in short supply since the entrepôt trade that Singapore depended on to provide most goods was severely curtailed by the war. Chinese businessmen collaborated with corrupt Japanese officials to establish a flourishing black market for most items, which were sold at outrageous prices. Inflation grew even more rampant as Japanese military scrip flooded the economy. Speculation, profiteering, bribery, and corruption were the order of the day, and lawlessness against the occupation government almost a point of honor.

As the war wound down and Japanese fortunes began to fade, life grew even more difficult in Shōnan. Military prisoners, who suffered increasing hardship from reduced rations and brutal treatment, were set to work constructing an airfield at Changi, which was completed in May 1945. Not only prisoners of war but also Singapore's unemployed civilians were impressed into work gangs for labor on the Burma-Siam railroad, from which many never returned. As conditions worsened and news of Japanese defeats filtered in, Singaporeans anxiously awaited what they feared would be a bloody and protracted fight to reoccupy the island. Although Japan formally surrendered to the Allies on August 15, 1945, it was not announced in the Singapore press until a week later. The Japanese military quietly retreated to an internment camp they had prepared at Jurong. On September 5, Commonwealth troops arrived aboard British warships, cheered by wildly enthusiastic Singaporeans, who lined the five-kilometer parade route. A week later, on the steps of the municipal building, the Japanese military command in Singapore surrendered to the supreme Allied commander in Southeast Asia, Admiral Lord Louis Mountbatten.

Aftermath of War, 1945-55

The abrupt end of the war took the British by surprise. Although the Colonial Office had decided on the formation of a Malayan Union, which would include all the Malay states, Penang, and Malacca, no detailed plans had been worked out for the administration of Singapore, which was to be kept separate and serve as the headquarters of the British governor general for Southeast Asia. Many former colonial officials and businessmen opposed the separation of Singapore from peninsular Malaya, arguing that the two were economically interdependent and to exclude Singapore would "cut the heart out of Malaya." The Colonial Office maintained that the separation did not preclude union at some future date, but that union should not be forced on "communities with such widely different interests." In September 1945, Singapore became the headquarters for the British Military Administration under Mountbatten. Although Singaporeans were relieved and happy at the arrival of the Commonwealth troops, their first-hand witnessing of the defeat of the British by an Asian power had changed forever the perspective from which they viewed their colonial overlords.

Economic and Social Recovery

The British returned to find their colonies in sad shape. Food and medical supplies were dangerously low, partly because shipping was in total disarray. Allied bombing had taken its toll on Singapore's harbor facilities, and numerous wrecks blocked the harbor. Electricity, gas, water, and telephone services were in serious disrepair. Severe overcrowding had resulted in thousands of squatters living in shanties, and the death rate was twice the prewar level. Gambling and prostitution, both legalized under the Japanese, flourished, and for many opium or alcohol served as an escape from a bleak existence. The military administration was far from a panacea for all Singapore's ills. The British Military Administration had its share of corrupt officials who helped the collaborators and profiteers of the Japanese occupation to continue to prosper. As a result of the inefficiency and mismanagement of the rice distribution, the military administration was cynically known as the "Black Market Administration." However, by April 1946, when military rule was ended, the British Military Administation had managed to restore gas, water, and electric services to above their prewar capacity. The port was returned to civilian control, and seven private industrial, transportation, and mining companies were given priority in importing badly needed supplies and materials. Japanese prisoners were used to repair docks and airfields. The schools were reopened, and by March 62,000 children were enrolled. By late 1946, Raffles College and the King Edward Medical College both had reopened.

Food shortages were the most persistent problem; the weekly per capita rice ration fell to an all-time low in May 1947, and other foods were in short supply and expensive. Malnutrition and disease spawned outbreaks of crime and violence. Communist-led strikes caused long work stoppages in public transport, public services, at the docks, and at many private firms. The strikers were largely successful in gaining the higher wages needed by the workers to meet rising food prices.

By late 1947, the economy had begun to recover as a result of a growing worldwide demand for tin and rubber. The following year, Singapore's rubber production reached an all-time high, and abundant harvests in neighboring rice-producing countries ended the most serious food shortages. By 1949 trade, productivity, and social services had been restored to their prewar levels. In that year a five-year social welfare plan was adopted, under which benefits were paid to the aged, unfit, blind, crippled, and to widows with dependent children. Also in 1949, a ten-year plan was launched to expand hospital facilities and other health services. By 1951 demand for tin and rubber for the Korean War (1950-53) had brought economic boom to Singapore.

By the early post-World War II years, Singapore's population had become less transitory and better balanced by age and sex. The percentage of Chinese who were Straits-born rose from 36 percent in 1931 to 60 percent by 1947, and, of those born in China, more than half reported in 1947 that they had never revisited and did not send remittances there. Singapore's Indian population increased rapidly in the postwar years as a result of increased migration from India, which was facing the upheavals of independence and partition, and from Malaya, where the violence and hardships of the anticommunist Emergency (see Glossary) caused many to leave. Although large numbers of Indian men continued to come to Singapore to work and then return to India, both Indians and Chinese increasingly saw Singapore as their permanent home.

In 1947 the colonial government inaugurated a ten-year program to provide all children with six years of primary education in the language of the parents' choice, including English, Malay, Chinese, and Tamil. Seeing an English education as offering their children the best opportunity for advancement, parents increasingly opted to send their children to English-language schools, which received increased government funding while support for the vernacular schools declined. In 1949 the University of Malaya was formed through a merger of Raffles College and the King Edward Medical College.

Political Awakening

The Colonial Office established an advisory council in November 1945 to work with the British Military Administration on the reconstruction of Singapore. Among the seventeen members appointed to the council was Wu Tian Wang, a former guerrilla leader and chairman of the communist Singapore City Committee. The MCP enjoyed great popularity in the early postwar days because of its association with the resistance and the Malayan People's Anti-Japanese Army, which also included many noncommunists. In January 1946, the anti-Japanese army was formally disbanded following a final parade at which Mountbatten presented medals to the guerrilla commander, Chin Peng, and the other resistance leaders. All arms and ammunition, which the guerrillas had received in airdrops from the British during the war or captured from the Japanese, were supposed to be surrendered at that

Singapore: A Country Study

time. The MCP, however, secretly retained large stocks of its weapons.

The British legally recognized the MCP in late 1945, largely because of its resistance efforts and its popularity. The party by that time commanded about 70,000 supporters. The MCP at first concentrated its efforts on organizing labor, establishing the General Labour Union, which covered more than sixty trade unions. It organized numerous strikes in 1945 and early 1946, including a two-day general strike in January in which 173,000 workers struck and transport was brought to a halt. In February, after the formation of a Pan-Malayan Federation of Trade Unions claiming 450,000 members in Singapore and the peninsula, the British Military Administration arrested twenty-seven leading communists, banishing ten of them without trial. Thereafter, the MCP adopted a lower profile of quietly backing radical groups that were working for constitutional changes and increasing its control over the labor movement.

In April 1946, the British Military Administation ended with the formation of the Malayan Union, at which time Singapore became a separate crown colony with a civil administration. The two entities continued to share a common currency, institutions of higher learning, and the administration of immigration, civil aviation, posts and telegraphs, and income tax. Opposition to the separation of Malaya and Singapore motivated the formation in December 1945 of Singapore's first indigenous political party, the Malayan Democratic Union. Although most leaders of the new party were not communist, there were several prominent communists among its founders, including Wu Tian Wang, who saw the Malayan Union as a threat to the vision of a communist, united Malayan republic. The Malayan Democratic Union proposed eventual inclusion of Singapore in an independent Malaya within the Commonwealth of Nations. Meanwhile, on the peninsula, conservative Malay leaders, who were concerned about provisions in the Malayan Union scheme that conferred equal political status on immigrant communities, formed the United Malays National Organization (UMNO) in March 1946. After various mass rallies, movements and countermovements, proposals and counterproposals, the British acceded to UMNO wishes. February 1948 marked the formation of the Federation of Malaya, which provided for the gradual assimilation of immigrants into a Malay state working toward independence under British guidance. Singapore remained a separate crown colony.

Elections in Singapore were scheduled for March 1948, at which time a new constitution would go into effect. That document called for an Executive Council of colonial officials and a Legislative Council comprising nine officials and thirteen nonofficials, four nominated by the governor, three chosen by the chambers of commerce, and six elected by adult British subjects who had been resident in Singapore for one year prior to the election. The appointed governor retained power over certain items and veto power over the proceedings of the Legislative Council. The Malayan Democratic Union, by then a communist front organization, boycotted the elections and organized mass rallies opposing the new constitution. The moderate Progressive Party was formed in August 1947 by British-educated business and professional men who advocated gradual constitutional reform aimed at eventual self-government. Of the six elected seats on the Legislative Council, three were won by independents and three by Progressives, the only party to contest the elections. In the first municipal election in 1949, the Progressive Party won thirteen of the eighteen seats on the twenty-seven member municipal commission. Voter interest was very low in both elections, however, with only about 10 percent of those eligible registering to vote.

Meanwhile, the MCP had abandoned the moderate stance advocated by its secretary general Lai Teck, who was replaced in March 1947 by Chin Peng. Soon after, it was discovered that Lai Teck not only had disappeared with the party's funds but also had been a double agent, serving both the Japanese and the British. Following the establishment of the Federation of Malaya in February 1948, Singapore's communist leaders moved to the peninsula, where they reactivated the Malayan People's Anti-Japanese Army and began fomenting acts of violence and terrorism. This led to the declaration of a state of emergency in Malaya on June 18 and in Singapore a week later. Although the twelve-year struggle was largely confined to the peninsula, restrictions were placed on meetings and strikes, and the detention of individuals without trial was permitted under the Emergency regulations. The MCP was proscribed by the colonial government in Singapore, and the Malayan Democratic Union, fearing the same fate, voluntarily dissolved itself. Left-wing political movements were thus stifled, and the only political party that arose to challenge the Progressives was the Singapore Labour Party formed in 1948. Like the Progressive Party, its positions were moderate and its leadership mostly British educated. Nevertheless, as a result of personal squabbles and factions, the Singapore Labour Party had largely disintegrated by 1952.

The number of elected seats in the Legislative Council was increased to nine in 1951, and the Progressive Party won six of the nine seats in the election that year. The membership of the party never numbered more than about 4,000, the majority of whom were upper or middle class and British educated. The interests of the members of the Legislative Council and the leadership of the Progressive Party were so closely aligned with those of the colonial government that they were out of touch with the masses. Participation in politics was restricted to Straits-born or naturalized British subjects who were literate in English. This exclusion of immigrants and those not educated in English meant that, in the late 1940s, about one-half of Singapore's adult population was disenfranchised.

Although the Chinese-educated took little interest in the affairs of the Legislative Council and the colonial government, they were stirred with pride by the success of the Chinese Communist Party in China. Fearful that support by Singapore's Chinese for the Chinese communists would translate to support for the MCP, the colonial government attempted to curtail contacts between the Singapore Chinese and their homeland. When Tan Kah Kee returned from a trip to China in 1950, the colonial government refused to readmit him, and he lived out his days in his native Fujian Province.

For graduates of Singapore's Chinese high schools, there were no opportunities for higher education in the colony. Many went to universities in China, despite the fact that immigration laws prohibited them from returning to Singapore. To alleviate this problem, wealthy rubber merchant and industrialist Tan Lark Sye proposed formation of a Chinese-language university for the Chinese-educated students of Singapore, Malaya, and other parts of Southeast Asia. Singaporean Chinese, rich and poor, donated funds to found Nanyang University, which was opened in Singapore in 1956.

By the early 1950s, large numbers of young men whose education had been postponed by the Japanese occupation were studying at Chinese-language high schools. These older students were particularly critical of the colonial government's restrictive policies toward Chinese and of its lack of support for Chinese-language schools. The teachers in these schools were poorly paid, the educational standards were low, and graduates of the schools found they could not get jobs in the civil service or gain entrance to Singapore's English-language universities. While critical of the colonial government, the students were becoming increasingly proud of the success of the communist revolution in China, reading with interest the publications and propaganda put out by the new regime.

As the Emergency on the peninsula began to go badly for the communists, the MCP took a renewed interest in Singapore and began organizing protest demonstrations among the disaffected students. Among the brightest and most capable of the older Chinese

Panoramic view of Singapore's waterfront in mid-1940s
Courtesy National Archives

high school students were Lim Chin Siong and Fong Swee Suan, who both became involved in organizing class boycotts that resulted in a police raid on the Chinese High School in 1952. The two left the school, took low-paying jobs at bus companies, and began working to build communist influence among workers and students. In May 1954, mass student protest demonstrations were organized to oppose a new National Service Ordinance requiring males between the ages of eighteen and twenty to register for part-time national service. Also in May, the Singapore Factory and Shop Workers' Union registered with the government, with Lim as its secretary general; Fong, who was by then general secretary of the Singapore Bus Workers' Union, and C.V. Devan Nair, of (at that time) the Singapore Teachers' Union, were members of the executive board. Dedicated and charismatic, Lim led several well-organized small strikes that were successful in gaining better conditions for the union's workers and in attracting thousands of recruits for the union. By late 1955, the Singapore Factory and Shop Workers' Union included thirty industrial unions and had a membership of about 30,000.

Road to Independence, 1955–65

In 1953 the colonial government appointed Sir George Rendel to head a commission to review the Singapore constitution and devise a "complete political and constitutional structure designed to enable Singapore to develop as a self-contained and autonomous unit in any larger organization with which it may ultimately become associated." The commission recommended partial internal self-government for Singapore, with Britain retaining control of internal security, law, finance, defense, and foreign affairs. It also proposed a single-chamber Legislative Assembly of thirty-two members, twenty-five of whom would be elected, and a nine-member council of ministers that would act as a cabinet. The governor retained his power to veto legislation. The British government accepted the commission's recommendations, and the Rendel constitution went into effect in February 1954, with elections scheduled for the Legislative Assembly for April 1955. Voters were to be automatically registered, which was predicted to greatly enlarge the size of the turnout over previous elections. Although the new constitution was a long way from offering Singapore full independence, election fever gripped the country as new political alliances and parties were formed.

Two former members of the Singapore Labour Party, Lim Yew Hock and Francis Thomas, and a prominent lawyer, David Marshall, formed a new political party, the Labour Front, in July 1954. Marshall, who was a member of Singapore's small Jewish community, had studied law in Britain, fought with the Singapore Volunteer Corps during the Japanese invasion, and worked in the coal mines of Hokkaidō as a prisoner of war. Under the leadership of Marshall, a staunch anticolonialist, the party campaigned for immediate independence within a merged Singapore and Malaya, abolishing the Emergency regulations, Malayanization of the civil service within four years (by which time local officials would take over from colonial officials), multilingualism, and Singapore citizenship for its 220,000 China-born inhabitants. Marshall, a powerful speaker, promised "dynamic socialism" to counter "the creeping paralysis of communism" as he denounced colonialism for its exploitation of the masses.

People's Action Party

In November 1954, the People's Action Party (PAP—see Glossary) was inaugurated at a gathering of 1,500 people in Victoria Memorial Hall. The party was formed by a group of British-educated, middle-class Chinese who had returned to Singapore in the early 1950s after studying in Britain. Led by twenty-five-year-old Lee Kuan Yew, as secretary general, Toh Chin Chye, Goh Keng Swee, and S. Rajaratnam, the party sought to attract a following among the mostly poor and non-English-speaking masses. Lee had served as a legal adviser to a number of trade unions and, by 1952, had earned a reputation for his successful defense of the rights of workers. He also helped defend Chinese students arrested during the 1954 student demonstrations protesting national service. Lee, a fourth-generation Singaporean, was educated at Raffles Institution and Cambridge University, where he took a double first (first-class honors in two subjects) in law. Through his work with the unions and student groups, Lee had made many contacts with anticolonialists, noncommunists and communists alike.

Present at the inauguration of the PAP were a number of noted communists and procommunists, including Fong Swee Suan and Devan Nair, who both joined the new party. Also present were Malayan political leaders Tunku Abdul Rahman, president of UMNO, and Sir Tan Cheng Lock, president of the Malayan Chinese Association (MCA). The PAP proposed to campaign for repeal of the Emergency regulations, union with Malaya, a common Malayan citizenship, Malayanization of the civil service, and free compulsory education. Ending colonialism, however, was the first priority of Lee and the PAP leadership, although they concluded this could be accomplished only with support from the Chinese-educated public and the communist-controlled trade unions. The PAP, calculating that a united front with the communists was necessary to end colonialism, declared itself noncommunist, neither pro- nor anticommunist, preferring to put off until after independence any showdown with the communists.

Meanwhile, two other political parties prepared to contest the upcoming election. The Progressive Party, whose leaders had earned a reputation as the "Queen's Chinese" for their procolonial positions and conservative economic policies, had little appeal for the masses of working-class Chinese who were newly enfranchised to vote in the 1955 election. Automatic registration of voters had increased the electorate from 76,000 in 1951 to more than 300,000. Shortly before the elections, wealthy and influential members of the Chinese Chamber of Commerce formed the new Democratic Party, which championed the causes of improved Chinese education, establishment of Chinese as an official language, and liberal citizenship terms for the China-born. Although these issues appealed to Singapore's China-born lower classes, this same group was disenchanted with the party's conservative economic platform, which closely resembled that of the Progressive Party.

Election fever gripped Singapore during the month-long campaign, and the results of the April 2 contest sent shock waves as far as Britain, where it had been expected that the Progressive Party would win handily. Surprising even itself, the Labour Front won ten of the twenty-five seats and formed a coalition government with the UMNO-MCA Alliance, which won three seats. Three ex-officio members and two nominated members joined with the coalition, forming a group of seventeen in the thirty-two-member assembly. The Progressives won only four seats and the Democratic Party just two, in a clear rejection of colonial rule and procolonial politics. The PAP won three of the four seats it had contested, including a seat in one of Singapore's poorest sections won by Lee Kuan Yew and one seat won by Lim Chin Siong. Lim had the backing of organized labor and led the procommunist wing of the party while Lee led the noncommunist wing.

The Labour Front government, with David Marshall as Singapore's first chief minister, faced serious problems from the start. The communists launched a campaign of strikes and student unrest in an attempt to destabilize the government. Only about one-third of the 275 strikes called in 1955 were for better wages and working conditions; the remainder were sympathy strikes or strikes to protest imprisonment of labor union officials. Riots broke out on May 12 when police attempted to break up an illegal picket line formed by striking bus workers and Chinese school students. Four people were killed and thirty-one injured in that single incident, which became known as "Black Thursday." Although the government arrested some students, Marshall eventually backed down and agreed to the registration of the Singapore Chinese Middle School Students' Union because he was in sympathy with the students' grievances against the colonial education system. In registering their union, the students agreed to the condition that the union keep out of politics; the communist leaders of the union, however, had no intention of keeping the agreement.

Along with problems with labor and students, Marshall faced constant conflict with the colonial government over his determination not to be a figurehead controlled by the governor. When the governor, Sir Robert Black, refused to allow Marshall to appoint four assistant ministers, Marshall threatened to resign unless Singapore was given immediate self-government under a new constitution. The Colonial Office agreed to hold constitutional talks, which came to be known as *Merdeka* (freedom in Malay) talks, in London in April 1956. Marshall led to the talks a thirteen-man delegation comprising members of all the legislative parties and including Lee and Lim Chin Siong. The British offered to grant Singapore full internal self-government but wanted to retain control over foreign affairs and internal security. They proposed a Defence and Internal Security Council, with three delegates each from Britain and Singapore, to be chaired by the British high commissioner in Singapore, who would have the casting ballot (the deciding vote in case of a tie). Marshall had promised he would resign if he failed to obtain internal self-government, and the talks broke down over the issue of the casting ballot. The delegation returned to Singapore, and Marshall resigned in June and was succeeded by the deputy chief minister, Lim Yew Hock.

By July the Singapore Chinese Middle Schools Students' Union had begun planning a campaign of agitation against the government. The Lim Yew Hock government moved first, however, dissolving seven communist-front organizations, including the student union, and closing two Chinese middle schools. This touched off a protest sit-in at Chinese high schools organized by Lim Chin Siong that ended in five days of rioting in which thirteen people were killed. British troops were brought in from Johore to end the disturbance, and more than 900 people were arrested, including Lim Chin Siong, Fong Swee Suan, and Devan Nair. The British approved of the Singapore government's tough action toward the agitators, and when Lim Yew Hock led a delegation to London for a second round of constitutional talks in March 1957, the Colonial Office proposed a compromise on the internal security issue. The Singapore delegation accepted a proposal whereby the Internal Security Council would comprise three Singaporeans, three Britons, and one delegate from what was soon to be the independent Federation of Malaya, who would hold the casting ballot. The Singapore delegation returned to a hero's welcome; the Legislative Assembly accepted the proposals, and a delegation was scheduled to go to London in 1958 for a third and final round of talks on the new constitution.

Although the moderates led by Lee Kuan Yew retained control of the PAP Central Executive Committee, by 1956 the procommunists held sway over the membership and many of the mass organizations and PAP branches. At the annual general meeting in August 1957, the procommunists won six of the twelve seats on the committee. Lee Kuan Yew and the other moderates refused to take office in order to avoid becoming front men for the leftists. On August 21, the Lim Yew Hock government reacted to the situation by arresting thirty-five communists, including five of the new members of the PAP Central Executive Committee, some PAP branch officials, and labor and student leaders. Lee and the moderates were able to regain control of the party and, the following November, amended the party's constitution to consolidate moderate control by limiting voting for the Central Executive Committee to the full cadres (full members), who were literate Singapore citizens over the age of twenty-one who had been approved as cadres by the Central Executive Committee.

Meanwhile, the Lim Yew Hock government continued to make further progress on issues related to Singapore's self-government. The Citizenship Ordinance passed in 1957 provided Singapore citizenship for all born in Singapore or the Federation of Malaya and for British citizens of two years' residence; naturalization was offered to those who had resided in Singapore for ten years and would swear loyalty to the government. The Legislative Assembly voted to complete Malayanization of the civil service within four years beginning in 1957. The Education Ordinance passed in 1957 gave parity to the four main languages, English, Chinese, Malay, and Tamil. By 1958 the Ministry of Education had opened nearly 100 new elementary schools, 11 new secondary schools, and a polytechnic school and set up training courses for Malay and Tamil teachers.

Lim Yew Hock led the Singapore delegation to the third round of constitutional talks in April 1958. The talks resulted in an agreement on a constitution for a State of Singapore with full powers of internal government. Britain retained control over foreign affairs and external defense, with internal security left in the hands of the Internal Security Council. Only in the case of dire emergency could Britain suspend the constitution and assume power. In August 1958, the British Parliament changed the status of Singapore from a colony to a state, and elections for the fifty-one-member Legislative Assembly were scheduled for May 1959. Voting was made compulsory for all adult Singapore citizens, but the British refused to allow persons with records of subversive activity to stand for election. Ten parties contested the election, but none was as well organized as the PAP, which under Lee Kuan Yew ran a vigorous campaign with huge weekly rallies. Campaigning on a platform of honest efficient government, social and economic reform, and union with the Federation of Malaya, the PAP scored a stunning victory by winning forty-three of the fifty-one seats. The badly divided and scandal-ridden Labour Front had reorganized as the Singapore People's Alliance, which won four seats, including one for Lim Yew Hock. The remaining seats were won by three UMNO–MCA Alliance candidates and one independent. Marshall's Workers' Party failed to win any seats.

Both foreign and local businesses feared that the PAP victory signaled Singapore's slide toward communism, and many moved their headquarters to Kuala Lumpur. Lee indeed refused to take office until the eight procommunist PAP detainees arrested in 1956 and 1957 were released, and he appointed several of them, including Lim Chin Siong, Fong Swee Suan, and Devan Nair, to government posts. Lee's closest advisors, however, were moderates Goh Keng Swee, Toh Chin Chye, and S. Rajaratnam.

The first task of the new PAP government was to instill a sense of unity and loyalty in Singapore's diverse ethnic populace. A new national flag, crest, and anthem were introduced, and the new Ministry of Culture organized open-air cultural concerts and other events designed to bring the three main ethnic groups together. Malay, Chinese, Tamil, and English were all made official languages, but, with its eye on a future merger with Malaya, the government made Malay the national language. Considered the indigenous people and yet the most disadvantaged, Malays were provided with free primary and secondary education.

After national unity, the second most important task facing the new government was that of transforming Singapore from an entrepôt economy dependent on the Malayan commodity trade with no tradition of manufacturing to an industrialized society. A four-year development plan, launched under Minister of Finance Goh Keng Swee in 1961, provided foreign and local investors with such incentives as low taxation rates for export-oriented manufactures, tax holidays for pioneer industries, and temporary protective tariffs against imports. The plan set aside a large area of swamp wasteland as an industrial estate in the Jurong area and emphasized labor-intensive industries, such as textiles. The overhaul of Singapore's economy was urgently needed in order to combat unemployment and pay for badly needed social services. One of the most serious problems was the lack of adequate housing. In 1960 the Housing and Development Board was set up to deal with the problems of slum clearance and resettlement. Under the direction of the banker and industrialist Lim Kim San, the board constructed more than 20,000 housing units in its first three years. By 1963 government expenditures on education had risen to S$10 million from S$600,000 in 1960.

Despite the signs of economic progress, the PAP leaders believed that Singapore's survival depended on merger with Malaysia. "Major changes in our economy are only possible if Singapore and the Federation are integrated as one economy," remarked Goh Keng Swee in 1960. "Nobody in his senses believes that Singapore alone, in isolation, can be independent," stated an official government publication that same year. The procommunists within the party, however, opposed merger because they saw little chance of establishing a procommunist government in Singapore as long as Kuala Lumpur controlled internal security in the new state. Meanwhile, the leaders of the conservative UMNO government in Kuala Lumpur, led by Tengku Abdul Rahman, were becoming increasingly resistant to any merger with Singapore under the PAP, which they considered to be extremely left wing.

Moreover, Malayan leaders feared merger with Singapore because it would result in a Chinese majority in the new state. When a fiercely contested Singapore by-election in April 1961 threatened to bring down the Lee Kuan Yew government, however, Tengku

Abdul Rahman was forced to consider the possibility that the PAP might be replaced with a procommunist government, a "Cuba across the causeway."

Accordingly, on May 27, 1961, in a speech in Kuala Lumpur to the Foreign Correspondents' Association, Tengku Abdul Rahman made a surprise proposal of an association of states that would include the Federation of Malaya, the British Borneo territories, and Singapore. In this proposed Malaysia, the Malay population of Sarawak and North Borneo (now Sabah) would offset numerically the Singapore Chinese, and the problem of a possible "Cuba across the causeway" would be solved.

The proposal, however, led almost immediately to a split between the moderate and procommunist forces within the PAP. In July Lee demanded and received a vote of confidence on the issue of merger from the Legislative Assembly. Following the vote, Lee expelled sixteen rebel PAP assembly members from the party along with more than twenty local officials of PAP. In August the rebel PAP assembly members formed a new opposition party, the Barisan Sosialis (The Socialist Front—see Glossary) with Lim Chin Siong as secretary general. The new party had considerable support among PAP local officials as well as at the grass-roots level. Of the fifty-one branch committees, thirty-five defected to Barisan Sosialis, which also controlled two-thirds of organized labor.

The battle lines were clearly drawn when Lee Kuan Yew announced a referendum on the question of merger to be held in September 1962. Lee launched a campaign of thirty-six radio broadcasts in three languages to gain support for the merger, which was opposed by the Barisan Sosialis as a "sell-out." Of the three merger plans offered on the referendum, the PAP plan received 70 percent of the votes, the two other plans less than 2 percent each, and 26 percent of the ballots were left blank.

Having failed to stop the merger at home, the Barisan Sosialis turned its efforts abroad, joining with left-wing opposition parties in Malaya, Sarawak, Brunei, and Indonesia. These parties were opposed to the concept of Malaysia as a "neocolonialist plot," whereby the British would retain power in the region. President Sukarno of Indonesia, who had entertained dreams of the eventual establishment of an Indonesia Raya (Greater Indonesia) comprising Indonesia, Borneo, and Malaya, also opposed the merger; and in January 1963 he announced a policy of Confrontation (Konfrontasi—see Glossary) against the proposed new state. The Philippines, having revived an old claim to Sabah, also opposed the formation of Malaysia. The foreign ministers of Malaya, Indonesia, and the Philippines met in June 1963 in an attempt to work out some solution. Malaya agreed to allow the United Nations (UN) to survey the people of Sabah and Sarawak on the issue, although it refused to be bound by the outcome. Brunei opted not to join Malaysia because it was unable to reach agreement with Kuala Lumpur on the questions of federal taxation of Brunei's oil revenue and of the sultan of Brunei's relation to the other Malay sultans.

Singapore as Part of Malaysia

The leaders of Singapore, Malaya, Sabah, and Sarawak signed the Malaysia Agreement on July 9, 1963, under which the Federation of Malaysia was scheduled to come into being on August 31. Tengku Abdul Rahman changed the date to September 16, however, to allow the UN time to complete its survey. On August 31, Lee declared Singapore to be independent with the PAP government to act as trustees for fifteen days until the formation of Malaysia on September 16. On September 3, Lee dissolved the Legislative Assembly and called for a new election on September 21, to obtain a new mandate for the PAP government. In a bitterly contested campaign, the Barisan Sosialis denounced the merger as a "sell-out" and pledged increased support for Chinese education and culture. About half of Barisan's Central Executive Committee, including Lim Chin Siong, were in jail, however, following mass arrests the previous February by the Internal Security Council of political, labor, and student leaders who had supported a rebellion in Brunei. The mass arrests, although undertaken by the British and Malayans, benefited the PAP because there was less opposition. The party campaigned on its economic and social achievements and the achievement of merger. Lee visited every corner of the island in search of votes, and the PAP won thirty-seven of the fifty-one seats while the Barisan Sosialis won only thirteen.

On September 14, the UN mission had reported that the majority of the peoples of Sabah and Sarawak were in favor of joining Malaysia. Sukarno immediately broke off diplomatic and trade relations between Indonesia and Malaysia, and Indonesia intensified its Confrontation operations. Singapore was particularly hard hit by the loss of its Indonesian barter trade. Indonesian commandos conducted armed raids into Sabah and Sarawak, and Singaporean fishing boats were seized by Indonesian gunboats. Indonesian terrorists bombed the Ambassador Hotel on September 24, beginning a year of terrorism and propaganda aimed at creating communal unrest in Singapore. The propaganda campaign was effective among Singapore Malays who had hoped that merger with Malaysia would bring them the same preferences in employment and obtaining business licenses that were given Malays in the Federation. When the PAP government refused to grant any economic advantages other than financial aid for education, extremist UMNO leaders from Kuala Lumpur and the Malay press whipped up antigovernment sentiment and racial and religious tension. On July 21, 1964, fighting between Malay and Chinese youths during a Muslim procession celebrating the Prophet Muhammad's birthday erupted into racial riots, in which twenty-three people were killed and hundreds injured. In September Indonesian agents provoked communal violence in which 12 people were killed and 100 were injured. In Singapore, which normally prided itself on the peace and harmony among its various ethnic groups, shock and disbelief followed in the wake of the violence. Both Lee Kuan Yew and Tengku Abdul Rahman toured the island in an effort to restore calm, and they agreed to avoid wrangling over sensitive issues for two years.

The first year of merger was also disappointing for Singapore in the financial arena. No progress was made toward establishing a common market, which the four parties had agreed would take place over a twelve-year period in return for Singapore's making a substantial development loan to Sabah and Sarawak. Each side accused the other of delaying on carrying out the terms of the agreement. In December 1964, Kuala Lumpur demanded a higher percentage of Singapore's revenue in order to meet defense expenditures incurred fighting Confrontation and also threatened to close the Singapore branch of the Bank of China, which handled the financial arrangements for trade between Singapore and China as well as remittances.

Political tensions between Singapore and Kuala Lumpur also escalated as each began getting involved in the politics of the other. UMNO ran candidates in Singapore's September 1963 elections, and PAP challenged MCA Alliance candidates in the Malaysian general election in April 1964. UMNO was unable to win any seats in the Singapore election, and PAP won only one seat on the peninsula. The main result was increased suspicion and animosity between UMNO and PAP and their respective leaders. In April 1965, the four Alliance parties of Malaya, Singapore, Sabah, and Sarawak merged to form a Malaysian National Alliance Party. The following month, the PAP and four opposition parties from Malaya and Sarawak formed the Malaysian Solidarity Convention, most of whose members were ethnic Chinese. Although the Malaysian Solidarity Convention claimed to be noncommunal, right-wing UMNO leaders saw it as a Chinese plot to take over control of Malaysia. In the following months, the situation worsened increasingly, with abusive speeches and writings on both sides. Faced with

Historical Setting

demands for the arrest of Lee Kuan Yew and other PAP leaders by UMNO extremists, and fearing further outbreaks of communal violence, Tengku Abdul Rahman decided to separate Singapore from Malaysia. Informed of his decision on August 6, Lee tried to work out some sort of compromise, without success. On August 9, with the Singapore delegates not attending, the Malaysian parliament passed a bill favoring separation 126 to 0. That afternoon, in a televised press conference, Lee declared Singapore a sovereign, democratic, and independent state. In tears he told his audience, "For me, it is a moment of anguish. All my life, my whole adult life, I have believed in merger and unity of the two territories."

Two Decades of Independence, 1965-85

Reaction to the sudden turn of events was mixed. Singapore's political leaders, most of whom were Malayan-born and still had ties there, had devoted their careers to winning independence for a united Singapore and Malaya. Although apprehensive about the future, most Singaporeans, however, were relieved that independence would probably bring an end to the communal strife and riots of the previous two years. Moreover, many Singaporean businessmen looked forward to being free of Kuala Lumpur's economic restrictions. Nonetheless, most continued to worry about the viability as a nation of a tiny island with no natural resources or adequate water supply, a population of nearly 2 million, and no defense capability of its own in the face of a military confrontation with a powerful neighboring country. Singaporeans and their leaders, however, rose to the occasion.

Under Lee Kuan Yew

The Lee Kuan Yew government announced two days after separation that Singapore would be a republic, with Malay as its national language and Malay, Chinese, English, and Tamil retained as official languages. The Legislative Assembly was renamed the Parliament, and the prominent Malay leader, Yusof bin Ishak, was made president of the republic. The new nation, immediately recognized by Britain, Australia, New Zealand, and the United States, was admitted to the UN in September and the Commonwealth the following month. In the early months following separation, Singapore's leaders continued to talk of eventual reunion with Malaysia. Wrangling between Singapore and Kuala Lumpur over conflicting economic, defense, and foreign policies, however, soon put an end to this discussion, and Singapore's leaders turned their attention to building an independent nation.

The government sought to build a multiracial and multilingual society that would be unified by a sense of a unique "Singaporean identity." The government established a Constitutional Commission on Minority Rights in late 1965, and official policy encouraged ethnic and cultural diversity. Foreign Minister Rajaratnam told the UN General Assembly that year, "If we of the present generation can steadfastly stick to this policy for the next thirty years, then we would have succeeded in creating a Singaporean of a unique kind. He would be a man rooted in the cultures of four great civilizations but not belonging exclusively to any of them." Integrated schools and public housing were the principle means used by the government to ensure a mixing of the various ethnic groups. The government constructed modern high-rise housing estates and new towns, in which the residents of the city's crowded Chinatown slums and the rural Malay kampongs (villages in Malay) were thoroughly intermingled. An English-language education continued to be the preferred preparation for careers in business, industry, and government; English-language pupils outnumbered Chinese-language pupils 300,000 to 130,000 by 1968. Malay-language primary school enrollment declined from 5,000 in 1966 to about 2,000 in 1969. All students, however, were required to study their mother tongue at least as a second language. Many of the country's British-educated leaders, including Lee Kuan Yew, sent their children to Chinese-language schools because they believed that they provided better character training. The government stressed discipline and the necessity of building a "rugged society" in order to face the challenges of nationhood. A government anticorruption campaign was highly effective in combating that problem at all levels of administration.

At the same time that the government addressed the problem of establishing a national identity, it also tackled the serious economic problems facing the new nation. The hopes pinned on establishing a common market with Malaysia were dead, and it was clear that Singapore would not only have to go it alone but also would face rising tariffs and other barriers to trade with Malaysia. Under Goh Keng Swee and other able finance ministers, the government worked hard to woo local and foreign capital. New financial inducements were provided to attract export industries, promote trade, and end the country's dependence on Britain as the major source of investment capital. The generally prosperous world economic situation in the mid-1960s favored Singapore's growth and development. Confrontation with Indonesia had ended by 1966 after Soehárto came to power, and trade between the two countries resumed. Trade with Japan and the United States

Historical Setting

increased substantially, especially with the latter as Singapore became a supply center for the United States in its increasing involvement in Indochina.

A serious problem the government had to deal with in order to attract large-scale investment was Singapore's reputation for labor disputes and strikes. "The excesses of irresponsible trade unions . . . are luxuries which we can no longer afford," stated President Yusof bin Ishak in December 1965, speaking for the government. Two events in 1968 enabled the government to pass stricter labor legislation. In January Britain announced its intention to withdraw from its bases in Singapore within three years. Aside from the defense implications, the news was sobering because British spending in Singapore accounted for about 25 percent of Singapore's gross national product (GNP—see Glossary) for a total of about S$450 million a year, and the bases employed some 21,000 Singapore citizens. The government called an election for April in order to gain a new mandate for facing the crisis. Unopposed in all but seven constituencies, the PAP made a clean sweep, winning all fifty-eight parliamentary seats. With the new mandate, the government passed in August new labor laws that were tough on workers and employers alike. The new legislation permitted longer working hours, reduced holidays, and gave employers more power over hiring, firing, and promoting workers. Workers could appeal actions they considered unjust to the Ministry of Labour, and employers were obligated to increase their contributions to the Central Provident Fund. Workers also were given for the first time sick leave and unemployment compensation. As a result of the new legislation, productivity increased, and there were no strikes in 1969.

With labor relations under control, the government set up the Jurong Town Corporation to develop Jurong and the other industrial estates (see Land Management and Development, ch. 3). By late 1970, 271 factories in Jurong employed 32,000 workers, and there were more than 100 factories under construction. Foreign investors were attracted by the improved labor situation and by such incentives as tax relief for up to five years and unrestricted repatriation of profits and capital in certain government-favored industries. United States firms flocked to invest in Singapore, accounting for 46 percent of new foreign capital invested in 1972. Companies from Western Europe, Japan, Hong Kong, Taiwan, Malaysia, and Australia also invested capital, and by 1972 one quarter of Singapore's manufacturing firms were either foreign-owned or joint-venture companies. Another attraction of Singapore for foreign capital was the region's petroleum resources. Singapore was the natural base for dozens of exploration, engineering, diving, and other support companies for the petroleum industry in nearby Indonesia, as well as being the oil storage center for the region. By the mid-1970s, Singapore was the third largest oil-refining center in the world.

The government turned to advantage the British pullout by converting some of the military facilities to commercial and industrial purposes and retraining laid-off workers for new jobs. The former King George VI Graving Dock was converted to the Sembawang Shipyard, employing 3,000 former naval base workers in ship building and ship repair. Singapore also moved into shipping in 1968 with its own Neptune Orient Line. A container complex built in 1972 made the country the container transshipment center of Southeast Asia. By 1975 Singapore was the world's third busiest port behind Rotterdam and New York.

By the early 1970s, Singapore not only had nearly full employment but also faced labor shortages in some areas. As a result, immigration laws and work permit requirements were relaxed somewhat, and by 1972 immigrant workers made up 12 percent of the labor force (see Manpower and Labor, ch. 3). In order to develop a more highly skilled work force that could command higher wages, the government successfully courted high-technology industries, which provided training in the advanced skills required. Concerned that the country's economic success not be diluted by overpopulation, the government launched a family planning program in 1966 (see Population, ch. 2).

The country's economic success and domestic tranquility, which contrasted so starkly with the impoverished strife-torn Singapore of the late 1940s, was not purchased without cost, however. Although not a one-party state, the government was virtually under the total control of the PAP, and the Lee Kuan Yew administration did not hesitate to block the rise of an effective opposition. Holding a monopoly on power and opportunity in a small state, the party could easily co-opt the willing and suppress dissenters. The traditional bases—student and labor organizations—used by opposition groups in the past were tightly circumscribed. Control of the broadcast media was in the hands of the government, and economic pressures were applied to any newspapers that became too critical. The government leadership had adopted a paternalistic viewpoint that only those who had brought the nation through the perilous years could be trusted to make the decisions that would keep Singapore on the narrow path of stability and prosperity. The majority of Singaporeans scarcely dissented from this view and left the planning and decision making to the political leadership.

*A People's Action Party (PAP) rally during the 1984 election
Courtesy Singapore Ministry of Communications and Information*

Although five opposition parties contested the 1972 elections and won nearly one-third of the popular vote, the PAP again won all of the seats.

Although admired for its success, Lee's government increasingly attracted criticism from the international press for its less than democratic style. Singapore's neighbors also resented the survival-oriented nature of the country's foreign and economic policies. The aggressive defense policy recommended by Singapore's Israeli military advisers irritated and alarmed Muslim Indonesia and Malaysia (see Historical Development, ch. 5). Resentful of the profits made by Singapore in handling their commodities, Malaysia and Indonesia began setting up their own rubber-milling and petroleum-servicing industries. In the early 1970s, Malaysia and Singapore separated their joint currency, stock exchange, and airlines.

A regional political grouping, the Association of Southeast Asian Nations (ASEAN—see Glossary), founded in 1967 by Singapore, Malaysia, Indonesia, Thailand, and the Philippines, had little impact by the early 1970s on the foreign and economic policies of the member nations. However, regional and world developments in the 1970s, including the fall of Indochina to communism and the Vietnamese invasion of Cambodia, steered Singapore and its neighbors toward a new spirit of cooperation.

Toward New Leadership

Singapore successfully pursued its foreign policy goal of improved relations with Malaysia and Indonesia in the early 1980s as Lee Kuan Yew established cordial and productive personal relations with both Soeharto and Malaysian prime minister Mahathir Mohamad. Cooperation agreements were reached between Singapore and Malaysia on joint civil service and military training programs. The economic interdependence of the two countries was reaffirmed as Singapore continued its role as the reexport center for the tin, rubber, lumber and other resources of the Malaysian hinterland, as well as becoming a major investor in that country's economy.

Throughout the early 1980s, Singapore headed the ASEAN drive to find a solution to the Cambodia problem. Beginning in 1979, the ASEAN countries sponsored an annual resolution in the UN calling for a withdrawal of Vietnamese troops and a political settlement on Cambodia. In 1981 Singapore hosted a successful meeting of the leaders of the three Khmer liberation factions, which led to the formation of the Coalition Government of Democratic Kampuchea the following year.

During the first half of the 1980s, the Singapore economy continued to grow steadily, despite a worldwide recession. The economic growth rate of about 10 percent in 1980 and 1981 dipped to 6.3 percent in 1982 but rebounded to 8.5 percent with only 2.7 percent inflation in 1984. In his 1984 New Year's message to the nation, Lee Kuan Yew attributed Singapore's high economic growth rate, low inflation, and full employment during the period to its hardworking work force, political stability and efficient administration, regional peace, and solidarity in ASEAN. Singapore's successful economic strategy included phasing out labor-intensive industries in favor of high-technology industries, which would enhance the skills of its labor force and thereby attract more international investment.

Although Lee Kuan Yew retained a firm grip on the reins of government during the second decade of the country's independence, the shift in leadership had been irrevocably set in motion. By the early 1980s, a second generation of leaders was beginning to occupy the important decision-making posts. The stars of the new team included Goh Chok Tong, Tony Tan, S. Dhanabalan, and Ong Teng Cheong, who were all full ministers in the government by 1980. In that year, the PAP won its fourth consecutive general election, capturing all the seats. Its 75.6 percent vote margin was five points higher than that of the 1976 election. The PAP leadership was shaken out of its complacency the following year, however, when Workers' Party candidate J. B. Jeyaretnam won with 52 percent of the votes the by-election to fill a vacancy in Anson District. In the general election held in December 1984, Jeyaretnam retained his seat and was joined on the opposition benches by Chiam See Tong, the leader of the Singapore Democratic Party, which was founded in 1980.

In September 1984, power in the PAP Central Executive Committee was transferred to the second-generation leaders, with only Lee Kuan Yew, as secretary general, remaining of the original committee members. When Lee hinted in 1985 that he was considering retirement, his most likely successor appeared to be Goh Chok Tong, serving then as first deputy prime minister and defence minister. Speculation also centered on the prime minister's son, Lee Hsien Loong, who had resigned his military career to win a seat in Parliament in the 1984 election. After two decades of the highly successful, but tightly controlled, administration of Lee Kuan Yew, it was difficult to say whether the future would bring a more open and participatory government, yet one with the same knack for success exhibited by the old guard. The answer to that question would only come with the final passing of Lee Kuan Yew from the political scene.

* * *

The early history of Singapore is treated most extensively in works on the Malay peninsula, particularly in the various issues of the *Journal of the Malaysian Branch, Royal Asiatic Society*. Of special interest is a commemorative volume, *150th Anniversary of the Founding of Singapore*, which includes reprints of articles on Singapore from previous issues of the journal. Three monographs that treat Singapore within the Malayan context from prehistory to the modern period are Tan Ding Eing's *A Portrait of Malaysia and Singapore*, N.J. Ryan's *The Making of Modern Malaysia and Singapore*, and K.G. Tregonning's *A History of Modern Malaysia and Singapore*. *Prince of Pirates*, by Carl A. Trocki, gives an interesting glimpse into the world of the early nineteenth-century Malay rulers of Singapore. The forty years during which Singapore was ruled from India as one of the Straits Settlements is well covered in *The Straits Settlements, 1826-67* by Constance M. Turnbull.

Turnbull is also the author of the standard work focusing solely on Singapore, *A History of Singapore, 1819-1975*. Another useful work covering the same period is F.J. George's, *The Singapore Saga*.

Singapore: A Country Setting

Two interesting works, both written in the early twentieth century, view nineteenth-century Singapore from different perspectives. *One Hundred Years of Singapore*, edited by Walter Makepeace, et al., deals with the history of the colonial government, whereas Song Ong Siang's *One Hundred Years' History of the Chinese in Singapore* covers the life and times of prominent Chinese Singaporeans.

For works focused on postwar Singapore, see *Conflict and Violence in Singapore and Malaysia, 1945-1983* by Richard L. Clutterbuck and *Singapore: Struggle for Success* by John Drysdale. An interesting pictorial history is *Singapore: An Illustrated History, 1941-1984*, published by the Singapore Ministry of Culture. (For further information and complete citations, see Bibliography.)

Chapter 2. The Society and Its Environment

Vendor grilling satay, skewered pieces of meat dipped in a spicy peanut sauce.

MIRROR GLASS BANK TOWERS overshadowing Victorian-era government buildings symbolized Singapore's transformation from a colonial port to an independent city-state with the highest standard of living in Southeast Asia in 1989. Singapore's status as a newly industrializing economy (NIE—see Glossary) was signaled by its landscaped complexes of owner-occupied apartments and streets blocked by the private cars of affluent citizens. The citizens increasingly considered themselves Singaporeans rather than Chinese or Indians or Malays, and the multiethnic population increasingly used English as the common speech in schools, offices, and the armed forces. Singapore in the 1980s had become a byword for orderliness and effective administration, a place where stiff fines discouraged littering and citizens of all ethnic groups were subject to common, impartial standards of merit and achievement. Government efforts at social engineering extended beyond slum clearance and the creation of housing estates to such matters as men's hair length, the language families spoke at breakfast, and the number of children born to women with university degrees.

Singapore's leaders reacted to the unanticipated 1965 separation from Malaysia, which left a city without a hinterland, by deciding to "go cosmopolitan." This meant seeking a place in the world rather than in the regional economy; it also meant maintaining a certain social and cultural distance from neighboring countries while deliberately fostering a new and distinctively Singaporean culture and social identity. By late 1989 Singapore was cosmopolitan, prosperous, modernized, and orderly. Its population was educated in English, worked for multinational corporations, and consumed a worldwide popular culture of film, music, and leisure activities. English was, however, a second language for most, and many distinctively Chinese, Indian, and Malay customs, practices, and attitudes continued. In contrast to many countries of the region, Singapore's avowed social values were secular, democratic (within certain limits), and nondiscriminatory.

The content of the distinctive "Singaporean identity" and the proper balance between cosmopolitan and traditional values were issues that both preoccupied the leadership and would continue to shape the society in the 1990s. There was much public discussion of social identity, ethnicity, and the proper relation of Singaporeans to worldwide popular culture. Such discussion, often initiated by political leaders, tended to dichotomize habits and behavior into mutually exclusive "Asian" or "Western" categories. The initial premise was that Singapore should be a modernized but not a Westernized society, and that it would be a mistake for Singaporeans to become so thoroughly Westernized and cosmopolitan as to lose touch with their Asian roots and values. Such concepts as tradition and modernity, local and cosmopolitan, had a distinctively Singaporean meaning as was indicated by the widespread use of such terms as "Asian traditions" and "cultural ballast." The meaning of these concepts, however, remained to be defined more precisely by the discussions and day-to-day decisions of Singapore's citizens.

Physical Setting

Singapore is located at the tip of the Malay Peninsula at the narrowest point of the Strait of Malacca, which is the shortest sea route between India and China. Its major natural resources are its location and its deep-water harbor. Singapore Island, though small, has a varied topography. The center of the island contains a number of rounded granitic hills that include the highest point, the 165-meter Bukit Timah Peak. The western and southwestern regions are composed of a series of northwest to southeast tending ridges, which are low but quite steep. To the east is a large region of generally flat alluvial soils where streams have cut steep-sided valleys and gullies. The island is drained by a large number of short streams, some of which flow into the sea through mangrove swamps, lagoons, or broad estuaries.

The island originally was covered with tropical rain forest and fringed with mangrove swamps. Since the founding of the city in 1819, the natural landscape has been altered by human hands, a process that was accelerated in the 1970s and 1980s. By 1988, Singapore's land area was 49 percent built up, and forest covered only 2.5 percent. Three water reservoirs and their reserve catchment area, which preserves a fragment of the original tropical forest, occupy the center of the island. Extensive land reclamation between 1965 and 1987 increased the size of Singapore Island from 586 square kilometers to 636 square kilometers; further reclamation was planned for the 1990s. Hills have been leveled, swamps drained and filled, and many of the fifty-odd small islets and reefs have been enlarged or joined to form new larger islands suitable for industrial uses. In 1989 three of Singapore's five oil refineries were on offshore islands, and other small islands were used for military gunnery or as bombing ranges. Some of the larger streams were dammed at their mouths to form fresh-water reservoirs, and the major stream courses through built-up areas were lined with concrete to promote rapid drainage. Throughout the 1970s and 1980s, the municipal authorities made great efforts to establish parks and gardens as land became available and to plant tens of thousands of ornamental trees and shrubs, thus completing the transformation of the natural landscape.

Singapore is two degrees north of the equator and has a tropical climate, with high temperatures moderated by the influence of the sea. Average daily temperature and humidity are high, with a mean maximum of 31°C and a relative humidity of 70 to 80 percent in the afternoon. Rain falls throughout the year, but is heaviest during the early northeast monsoon from November through January. The driest month is July in the middle of the southeast monsoon. The intermonsoon months of April–May and October are marked by thunderstorms and violent line squalls locally known as Sumatras. The average annual rainfall is 2,370 millimeters, and much of the rain falls in sudden showers. Singapore is free from earthquakes and typhoons, and the greatest natural hazard is local flash flooding, the threat of which has increased as buildings and paved roads have replaced natural vegetation.

In spite of the high rainfall, Singapore's small size and dense population make it necessary to import water from Malaysia. The water, from reservoirs in upland Johor, comes through an aqueduct under the causeway linking Singapore with the Malaysian city of Johor Baharu. Singapore also supplies treated water to Johor Baharu, which in 1987 took about 14 percent of the 1 million cubic meters treated by Singapore each day. Singapore has responded to this dependence on a foreign country for water by expanding its reservoir capacity and constantly urging household and industrial users to conserve water.

Singapore's rapid economic growth in the 1970s and 1980s was accompanied both by increased air and water pollution and by increasingly effective government efforts to limit environmental damage. The government established an Anti-Pollution Unit under the Prime Minister's Office in 1970, set up the Ministry of the Environment in 1972, and merged the Anti-Pollution Unit with that ministry in 1983 to ensure unified direction of environmental protection. The new unit, subsequently renamed the Pollution Control Department, had responsibility for air and water pollution, hazardous materials, and toxic wastes (see Government Structure, ch. 4). Singapore first moved to limit air pollution, closely monitoring oil refineries and petrochemical complexes and limiting the sulfur content of fuel oil for power plants, factories, and diesel motor vehicles. Because motor vehicles were the main source of air pollution, the government required emissions controls on engines and reduced (but not eliminated) the lead content of gasoline. The government also acted, partly for environmental reasons, to restrict private ownership of automobiles through very high (175 percent) import duties, high annual registration fees, and high charges for the entry of private automobiles to the central business district.

Between 1977 and 1987, the Ministry of the Environment carried out a major program to clean up rivers and streams by extending the sewer system, controlling discharges from small industries and workshops, and moving pig and duck farms to resettlement areas with facilities to handle animal wastes. The success of the program was demonstrated by the return of fish and aquatic life to the lower Singapore and Kallang rivers. Singapore, the world's third largest oil refiner, also acted to prevent the pollution of coastal waters by oil spills or discharges from the many large oil tankers that traversed the Strait of Malacca. The Port of Singapore Authority maintained oil skimmers and other equipment to clean up oil spills, and a comprehensive plan assigned both the oil companies and Singapore's armed forces responsibilities for dealing with major oil spills.

Singapore's environmental management program was intended primarily to ensure public health and to eliminate immediate hazards to citizens from toxins. Protection of the environment for its own sake was a low priority, and the government did not respond to local conservation societies' calls to preserve tropical forests or mangrove swamps. The pollution control laws gave the authorities wide discretion in dealing with offenders, and throughout the 1970s and 1980s penalties usually were light. Enforcement of the laws often reflected an appreciation of the economic benefits of polluting industries and provided time for industrial polluters to find ways to limit or eliminate their discharges.

Population

Population, Vital Statistics, and Migration

Singapore had a population of 2,674,362 in July 1989 and the low birth and death rates common to developed economies with high per capita incomes. In 1987 the crude birth rate (births in proportion to the total population) was 17 per 1,000 and the death rate was 5 per 1,000 for an annual increase of 12 per 1,000. The infant mortality rate of 9.1 per 1,000 in 1986 was quite low by international standards and contributed to a 1987 life expectancy at birth of 71.4 years for males and 76.3 years for females. As in most developed countries, the major causes of death were heart disease, cancer, and strokes. As of 1986, 74 percent of married women of childbearing age practiced contraception, and the total fertility rate (a measure of the number of children born to a woman over her entire reproductive career) was 1.6, which was below the replacement level but comparable to that of many countries in Western Europe (see fig. 5).

Since the city's founding in 1819, the size and composition of Singapore's population has been determined by the interaction of migration and natural increase (see table 2, Appendix). Throughout the nineteenth century, migration was the primary factor in population growth. Natural increase became more important after the 1920s, and by the 1980s immigration and emigration were of minor significance. In the nineteenth and early twentieth centuries, Singapore's population was composed largely of immigrant adult males and grew primarily through immigration. By the 1920s, the proportion of women, the percentage of the population that was Singapore-born, and consequently the relative contribution of natural increase to the population, all were increasing. By the 1947 census, 56 percent of the population had been born in Singapore, and there were 1,217 males for every 1,000 females. The 1980 census showed that 78 percent of the population had been born in Singapore and that the sex ratio had reached 1,042 males for every 1,000 females.

Migration to Singapore dwindled during the Great Depression of the 1930s, ceased during the war years of 1941 to 1945, and resumed on a minor scale in the decade between 1945 and 1955. Most nineteenth-century and early twentieth-century immigrants came from China, India, or Sumatra and the Malay Peninsula. Between 1945 and 1965 immigrants came primarily from peninsular Malaya, which shared British colonial status with Singapore and so permitted the free movement of people between Singapore and the rural areas and small cities of the peninsula. After independence in 1965, Singapore's government imposed strict controls on immigration, granting temporary residence permits only to those whose labor or skills were considered essential to the economy. Most such workers were expected to return to their homelands when their contracts expired or economic downturns made their labor redundant. Illegal immigrants and Singaporeans who employed them were subject to fines or imprisonment. The immigrants of the 1980s fell into two distinct categories. The first category, unskilled labor for factories and service positions, was composed largely of young unmarried people from Malaysia, Thailand, the Philippines, Sri Lanka, and India. Regulations prohibited their marrying without prior official permission and required women to be tested for pregnancy every six months—measures intended to make it difficult

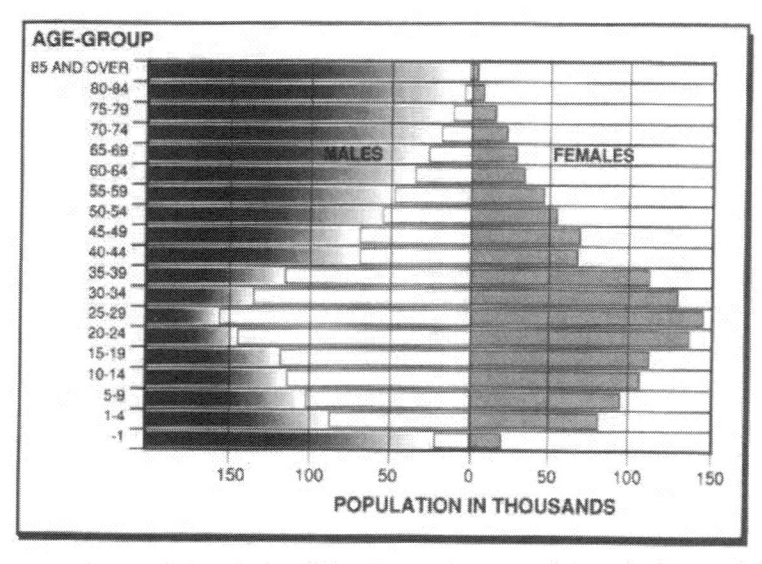

[figure: Age-sex population pyramid of Singapore, 1986, showing males on left and females on right, population in thousands by 5-year age groups from under 1 to 85 and over]

Source: Based on information from United Nations, Department of International Economic and Social Affairs, Statistical Office, *Demographic Yearbook, 1986*, New York, 1988, 210–11.

Figure 5. *Age-Sex Distribution, 1986*

for them to attain Singaporean residence or citizenship by becoming the spouse or parent of a citizen. The second category comprised skilled workers, professionals, and managers, often working for multinational corporations. They came from Japan, Western Europe, North America, and Australia. Predominately middle-aged and often accompanied by their families, they were immigrants only in the strict sense of the government's population registration and had no intention of settling permanently in Singapore.

The 1980 census reported that 9 percent of Singapore's population were not citizens. The aliens were divided into permanent residents (3.6 percent of the population) and nonresidents (5.5 percent). The acquisition of Singapore citizenship was a complex and often protracted process that began with application to the Immigration Department for permanent resident status. After residing in Singapore for two to ten years, depending on skills and professional qualifications, those with permanent resident status could apply to the Registry of Citizens for citizenship. In 1987 citizenship was granted to 4,607 applicants and denied to 1,603 applicants. The 1980 census showed that 85.5 percent of citizens had been born in Singapore, 7.8 percent in China (including Hong Kong, Macao, and Taiwan), 4.7 percent in Malaysia, and 1 percent in the Indian subcontinent (including Pakistan, Bangladesh, and Sri Lanka). Singapore's government, keenly aware of the country's small size and the need to survive by selling the skills of its citizens in a competitive international marketplace, was determined not to permit the city-state to be overwhelmed by large numbers of unskilled rural migrants. In 1989 Singapore mounted a campaign to attract skilled professionals from Hong Kong, offering a Chinese cultural environment with much lower living costs than Hong Kong's. At the same time, however, that the government was attempting to attract skilled professionals, Singaporeans themselves were emigrating. From July 1987 to June 1988, records show that 2,700 Singaporeans emigrated to Australia, 1,000 to Canada, 400 to the United States, and 97 to New Zealand. A large number of the emigrants were university-educated professionals, precisely the category that Singapore wished to keep and attract. In 1989 a special government committee was reported to be devising policies to discourage emigration by professionals and managers.

Population Control Policies

Since the mid-1960s, Singapore's government has attempted to control the country's rate of population growth with a mixture of publicity, exhortation, and material incentives and disincentives. Falling death rates, continued high birth rates, and immigration from peninsular Malaya during the decade from 1947 to 1957 produced an annual growth rate of 4.4 percent, of which 3.4 percent represented natural increase and 1.0 percent immigration. The crude birth rate peaked in 1957 at 42.7 per thousand. Beginning in 1949, family planning services were offered by the private Singapore Family Planning Association, which by 1960 was receiving some government funds and assistance. By 1965 the crude birth rate was 29.5 per 1,000 and the annual rate of natural increase had been reduced to 2.5 percent. Singapore's government saw rapid population growth as a threat to living standards and political stability, as large numbers of children and young people threatened to overwhelm the schools, the medical services, and the ability of the economy to generate employment for them all. In the atmosphere of crisis after the 1965 separation from Malaysia, the government in 1966 established the Family Planning and Population Board, which was responsible for providing clinical services and public education on family planning.

Birth rates fell from 1957 to 1970, but then began to rise as women of the postwar baby boom reached child-bearing years. The government responded with policies intended to further reduce the birth rate. Abortion and voluntary sterilization were legalized in

1970. Between 1969 and 1972, a set of policies known as "population disincentives" were instituted to raise the costs of bearing third, fourth, and subsequent children. Civil servants received no paid maternity leave for third and subsequent children; maternity hospitals charged progressively higher fees for each additional birth; and income tax deductions for all but the first two children were eliminated. Large families received no extra consideration in public housing assignments, and top priority in the competition for enrollment in the most desirable primary schools was given to only children and to children whose parents had been sterilized before the age of forty. Voluntary sterilization was rewarded by seven days of paid sick leave and by priority in the allocation of such public goods as housing and education. The policies were accompanied by publicity campaigns urging parents to "Stop at Two" and arguing that large families threatened parents' present livelihood and future security. The penalties weighed more heavily on the poor, and were justified by the authorities as a means of encouraging the poor to concentrate their limited resources on adequately nurturing a few children who would be equipped to rise from poverty and become productive citizens.

Fertility declined throughout the 1970s, reaching the replacement level of 1.006 in 1975, and thereafter declining below that level. With fertility below the replacement level, the population would after some fifty years begin to decline unless supplemented by immigration. In a manner familiar to demographers, Singapore's demographic transition to low levels of population growth accompanied increases in income, education, women's participation in paid employment, and control of infectious diseases. It was impossible to separate the effects of government policies from the broader socioeconomic forces promoting later marriage and smaller families, but it was clear that in Singapore all the factors affecting population growth worked in the same direction. The government's policies and publicity campaigns thus probably hastened or reinforced fertility trends that stemmed from changes in economic and educational structures. By the 1980s, Singapore's vital statistics resembled those of other countries with comparable income levels but without Singapore's publicity campaigns and elaborate array of administrative incentives.

By the 1980s, the government had become concerned with the low rate of population growth and with the relative failure of the most highly educated citizens to have children. The failure of female university graduates to marry and bear children, attributed in part to the apparent preference of male university graduates for less highly educated wives, was singled out by Prime Minister Lee Kuan

The Society and Its Environment

Yew in 1983 as a serious social problem. In 1984 the government acted to give preferential school admission to children whose mothers were university graduates, while offering grants of S$10,000 (for value of the Singapore dollar—see Glossary) to less educated women who agreed to be sterilized after the birth of their second child. The government also established a Social Development Unit to act as matchmaker for unmarried university graduates. The policies, especially those affecting placement of children in the highly competitive Singapore schools, proved controversial and generally unpopular. In 1985 they were abandoned or modified on the grounds that they had not been effective at increasing the fecundity of educated women.

In 1986 the government also decided to revamp its family planning program to reflect its identification of the low birth rate as one of the country's most serious problems. The old family planning slogan of "Stop at Two" was replaced by "Have Three or More, If You Can Afford It." A new package of incentives for large families reversed the earlier incentives for small families. It included tax rebates for third children, subsidies for daycare, priority in school enrollment for children from large families, priority in assignment of large families to Housing and Development Board apartments, extended sick leave for civil servants to look after sick children and up to four years' unpaid maternity leave for civil servants. Pregnant women were to be offered increased counseling to discourage "abortions of convenience" or sterilization after the birth of one or two children. Despite these measures, the mid-1986 to mid-1987 total fertility rate reached a historic low of 1.44 children per woman, far short of the replacement level of 2.1. The government reacted in October 1987 by urging Singaporeans not to "passively watch ourselves going extinct." The low birth rates reflected late marriages, and the Social Development Unit extended its matchmaking activities to those holding Advanced level (A-level) secondary educational qualifications as well as to university graduates (see The School System, this ch.). The government announced a public relations campaign to promote the joys of marriage and parenthood. In March 1989, the government announced a S$20,000 tax rebate for fourth children born after January 1, 1988. The population policies demonstrated the government's assumption that its citizens were responsive to monetary incentives and to administrative allocation of the government's medical, educational, and housing services.

Population Distribution and Housing Policies

In the early 1950s, some 75 percent of the population lived in very crowded tenements and neighborhoods; these were usually occupied by a single ethnic group in the built-up municipality on the island's southern shore. The remaining 25 percent lived in the northern "rural" areas in settlements strung along the roads or in compact villages, known by the Malay term *kampong*, and usually inhabited by members of a single ethnic group. Many kampongs were squatter settlements housing wage laborers and urban peddlers. Low-cost public housing was a major goal of the ruling People's Action Party (PAP—see Glossary). Vigorous efforts at slum clearance and resettlement of squatters had begun with the establishment in 1960 of the Housing and Development Board, which was granted wide powers of compulsory purchase and forced resettlement. By 1988, Housing and Development Board apartments were occupied by 88 percent of the population and 455,000 of these apartments (74 percent of all built) had been sold to tenants, who could use their pension savings from the compulsory Central Provident Fund for the downpayment (see Forced Savings and Capital Formation, ch. 3). The balance was paid over twenty years with variable rate mortgage loans, the interest rate in 1987 being 3.4 percent. The government envisaged a society of homeowners and throughout the 1980s introduced various measures such as reduced downpayments and extended loan periods to permit low-income families to purchase apartments.

The massive rehousing program had many social effects. In almost every case, families regarded the move to a Housing and Development Board apartment as an improvement in their standard of living. Although high-rise apartment complexes usually are regarded as examples of crowded, high-density housing, in Singapore the apartments were much less crowded than the subdivided shophouses (combined business and residence) or squatter shacks they had replaced. Between 1954 and 1970 the average number of rooms per household increased from 0.76 to 2.15, and the average number of persons per room decreased from 4.84 to 2.52. Movement to a public housing apartment was associated with (although not the cause of) a family structure in which husband and wife jointly made important decisions, as well as with a family's perception of itself as middle class rather than working class. The government used the resettlement program to break up the ethnically exclusive communities and sought to ensure that the ethnic composition of every apartment block mirrored that of the country as a whole. Malays, Indians, and Chinese of various speech groups lived next door to each other, shared stairwells, community centers, and swimming pools, patronized the same shops, and waited for buses together.

A Singaporean Malay family, at home in their Housing and Development Board apartment
Courtesy Singapore Ministry of Communications and Information

Although the earliest public housing complexes built in the 1960s were intended to shelter low-income families as quickly and cheaply as possible, the emphasis soon shifted to creating new communities with a range of income levels and public services. The new complexes included schools, shops, and recreation centers, along with sites on which residents could use their own resources to construct mosques, temples, or churches. The revised master plan for land use called for the creation of housing estates at the junctions of the expressways and the mass transit railroad that were to channel urban expansion out from the old city center (see Land, ch. 3). New towns of up to 200,000 inhabitants were to be largely self-contained and thoroughly planned communities, subdivided into neighborhoods of 4,000 to 6,000 dwelling units. In theory, the new towns would be complete communities providing employment for most residents and containing a mixture of income levels. In practice, they did not provide sufficient employment, and many residents commuted to work either in the central business district or in the heavy industrial area of Jurong in the southwestern quadrant of the island. Public transportation made the journey to the central business district short enough that many residents preferred to shop and dine there rather than at the more limited establishments in their housing estates. Thus, as in other countries that have attempted to build new towns, Singapore's new towns and housing estates have served largely as suburban residences and commuter settlements, the center of life only for the very young and the very old.

Throughout the 1980s, the government and the Housing and Development Board made great efforts to foster a sense of community in the housing estate complexes by sponsoring education and recreation programs at community centers and setting up a range of residents' committees and town councils. The apartment complexes generally were peaceful and orderly, and the relations between residents were marked by civility and mutual tolerance. But social surveys found that few tenants regarded their apartment blocks as communities in any very meaningful sense. Residents' primary social ties were with relatives, old classmates, fellow-workers, and others of the same ethnic group, who often lived in housing complexes some distance away. In the late 1980s, families who had paid off their mortgages were free to sell their apartments, and a housing market began to develop. There were also administrative mechanisms for exchanging apartments of equivalent size and value. Residents used sales, purchases, and apartment exchanges to move closer to kin and friends who belonged to the same ethnic group. The result was a tendency toward the recreation of the ethnic communities that had been deliberately broken up in the initial resettlement.

The government criticized the tendency toward ethnic clustering as contrary to its policy of multiracialism and in March 1989 announced measures to halt it. Although no family would be forced to move from its apartment, new rules prohibited the sale or exchange of apartments to members of other ethnic groups. Although the tendency toward ethnic resegregation apparently stemmed more from personal and pragmatic motivations than from conscious antagonism toward other ethnic groups, the government effort to halt it and to enforce ethnic quotas for apartment blocks demonstrated the continued significance of ethnicity in Singapore's society.

Ethnic and Linguistic Groups

Ethnic Categories

Since the city's foundation in 1819, Singapore's population has been polyglot and multiethnic. Chinese have been in the majority since 1830 but have themselves been divided into sometimes antagonistic segments speaking mutually unintelligible Chinese languages. The colonial society was compartmented into ethnic and

The Society and Its Environment

linguistic groups, which were in turn associated with distinct political and economic functions. Singapore has never had a dominant culture to which immigrants could assimilate nor a common language. This was the foundation upon which the efforts of the government and ruling party to create a common Singaporean identity in the 1970s and 1980s rested.

In July 1989 Singapore's 2,674,362 residents were divided into 2,043,213 Chinese (76.4 percent), 398,480 Malays (14.9 percent), 171,160 Indians (6.4 percent), and 61,511 others (2.3 percent) (see table 3, Appendix). The proportions of the ethnic components had remained substantially unchanged since the 1920s. Although the ethnic categories were meaningful in the Singaporean context, each subsumed much more internal variation than was suggested by the term "race." Chinese included people from mainland China, Taiwan, and Hong Kong, as well as Chinese from all the countries of Southeast Asia, including some who spoke Malay or English as their first language. The Malays included not only those from peninsular Malaya, but also immigrants or their descendants from various parts of the Indonesian archipelago, such as Sumatra, the Riau Islands south of Singapore, Java, and Sulawesi. Those people who in Indonesia were members of such distinct ethnic groups as Acehnese, Minangkabau, Buginese, Javanese, or Sundanese were in Singapore all considered "Malays." Indians comprised people stemming from anywhere in pre-1947 British India, the present states of India, Pakistan, and Bangladesh, and from Sri Lanka and Burma. Singapore's Indian "race" thus contained Tamils, Malayalis, Sikhs, Gujaratis, Punjabis, and others from the subcontinent who shared neither physical appearance, language, nor religion.

The Chinese

Singapore's Chinese residents were the descendants of immigrants from coastal southeastern China, an area of much linguistic and subcultural variation. The migrants spoke at least five mutually unintelligible Chinese languages, each of which contained numerous regional dialects. Singaporean usage, however, following the common Chinese tendency to assert cultural unity, referred to mutually unintelligible speech systems as "dialects." All the Chinese languages and dialects shared common origins and grammatical structures and could be written with the same Chinese ideograms, which represent meaning rather than sound. The primary divisions in the immigrant Chinese population therefore followed linguistic lines, dividing the populace into segments that were called dialect communities, speech groups, or even "tribes" (see table 4,

Appendix). In the nineteenth century, each speech group had its own set of associations, ranging from secret societies to commercial bodies to schools and temples. The groups communicated through leaders conversant with other Chinese languages or through a third language such as Malay or English.

The nomenclature for Chinese speech groups common in Singapore and Southeast Asia is confusing, partly because each group can be referred to by several alternate names. Most of the names refer to places in China with characteristic regional speech or dialects and include the names of provinces, counties, and major cities.

The distribution of Singapore's Chinese speech groups has remained fairly stable since 1900. The largest group were the Hokkien, who came from the area around the trading port of Xiamen (Amoy) in southern Fujian Province. Hokkien traders and merchants had been active in Southeast Asia for centuries before the foundation of Singapore. In 1980 they made up 43 percent of Singapore's Chinese population. The second largest group were the Teochiu (sometimes written Teochew), comprising 22 percent of the Chinese population. Their home area is Chaozhou, in Chao'an County in northeastern Guangdong Province, which has as its major port the city of Shantou (Swatow). Chaozhou is immediately south of the Hokkien-speaking area of Fujian, and both Teochiu and Hokkien are closely related languages of the Minnan group, mutually intelligible to native speakers after sufficient practice. Hainanese, from the island of Hainan south of Guangdong, made up 8 percent of the population. Hainan was settled by people from southern Fujian who arrived by sea, and Hainanese is a Minnan language whose native speakers can understand Hokkien or Teochiu with relatively little difficulty after practice. Speakers of Minnan languages thus made up 72 percent of the Chinese population, for whom Hokkien served as a lingua franca, the language of the marketplace.

The third most numerous group were Cantonese, from the lowlands of central Guangdong Province around the port city of Guangzhou (Canton). They made up 16 percent of the Chinese population. Hakka, a group scattered through the interior hills of southern China and generally considered migrants from northern China, were 7 percent. Other Chinese call them "guest people," and the term *Hakka* (*kejia* in pinyin romanization) is Cantonese for "guest families." There also were small numbers of people from the coastal counties of northern Fujian, called Hokchia, Hokchiu, and Henghua, whose northern Fujian (Minbei) languages are quite distinct from those of southern Fujian and seldom spoken outside of Fujian. A final, residual category of Chinese were the "Three Rivers People," who came from the provinces north of Guangdong

*Wife of Chinese millionaire,
late nineteenth century
Courtesy Library of Congress*

and Fujian. This group included people from northern and central China and more specifically those provinces sharing the word *river (jiang)* in their names—Jiangxi, Jiangsu, and Zhejiang. They would have spoken southern Mandarin dialects or the Wu languages of Shanghai, Ningbo, and Hangzhou. In 1980 they were 1.7 percent of the Chinese population.

A significant category of Chinese, although one not listed in the census reports, were the Baba Chinese (see Glossary) or Straits Chinese (see Glossary). They were Chinese who after long residence in Southeast Asia spoke Malay or English as their first language and whose culture contained elements from China, Southeast Asia, and sometimes Europe as well. An indication of the size of the Baba Chinese community was provided by the 1980 census report that 9 percent of Chinese families spoke English at home. Stereotypically the Baba were the offspring of Chinese migrants and local women. In the nineteenth century, they tended to be wealthier and better educated than the mass of immigrants and to identify more with Singapore and Southeast Asia than with China. In spite of their language, the Baba considered themselves Chinese, retained Chinese kinship patterns and religion, and even when speaking Malay used a distinct Baba dialect of Malay with many loan words from Hokkien. Never a large proportion of Singapore's Chinese population, in the late nineteenth century they took advantage of opportunities for education in English and promoted themselves as loyal to Britain. In Singapore, many Baba families spoke English as a first language and produced many of the leaders of Singapore's independent political movements, including Lee Kuan Yew. Although the Baba, in a sense, provided the model for the current Singaporean who is fluent in English and considers Singapore as home, the community fragmented in the early twentieth century as Chinese nationalism spread. After the 1920s its members gained no advantage, economic or political, from distinguishing themselves from the rest of the Chinese population and tended increasingly to become Chinese again, often learning to speak Chinese as adults. In the 1980s, Baba culture survived largely in the form of a well-known cuisine that mixed Chinese and Malay ingredients and in some families who continued to use English as the language of the home.

As the majority of the population and the ethnic group that dominated the political system and state administrative structure, Singapore's Chinese exhibited the widest range of occupational, educational, and class status. Those with little or no formal education occupied the bottom rungs of the occupational hierarchy and led social lives restricted to fellow members of the same dialect group. The level of formal education and language of education—Chinese or English—divided the Chinese into broad categories. Status for those working in the internationally oriented private sector or in government service depended on command of English and educational qualifications. In the still substantial Chinese private sector, status and security rested on a position in a bounded dialect community and a network of personal relations established over a lifetime. Although the latter exclusively Chinese category was shrinking, by the late 1980s it still contained some quite wealthy men who helped set the international price of rubber, controlled businesses with branches in Malaysia, Indonesia, Hong Kong, and other countries of the region, and supported Singapore's array of Chinese charities, hospitals, and education trusts. Members of Singapore's Chinese society had a high degree of social mobility and their status increasingly was determined by educational qualifications and command of English and Mandarin.

The Malays

The Malay made up 15 percent of Singapore's population and were, like the Chinese and the Indians, descendants of immigrants. They or their ancestors came from peninsular Malaya, Sumatra, Java, and the other islands of the Indonesian archipelago. Throughout the nineteenth and twentieth centuries, Java was much more densely populated than peninsular Malaya, and its people had a

Chinese medicine shop in Chinatown
Courtesy Ong Tien Kwan

significantly lower standard of living. From the mid-nineteenth century to the period just after World War II, many Javanese migrated to Singapore, attracted both by urban wages offering a higher living standard and by freedom from the constraints of their native villages, where they often occupied the lower reaches of the economic and social order. Singapore Malay community leaders estimated that some 50 to 60 percent of the community traced their origins to Java and an additional 15 to 20 percent to Bawean Island, in the Java Sea north of the city of Surabaya. The 1931 census recorded the occupations of 18 percent of the Malays as fishermen and 12 percent as farmers; the remaining 70 percent held jobs in the urban cash economy, either in public service or as gardeners, drivers, or small-scale artisans and retailers. The British colonialists had considered the Malays as simple farmers and fishermen with strong religious faith and a "racial" tendency toward loyalty and deference; they preferentially recruited the Malays to the police, the armed forces, and unskilled positions in the public service. In 1961 more than half of Singapore's Malays depended on employment in the public sector. Although the colonial stereotype of the Malays as rural people with rural attitudes persisted, Singapore's Malay residents were for the most part no more rural

Singapore: A Country Study

than any other residents. Malay identity was couched in religious terms, with Malay being taken almost as a synonym for Muslim and most Malay organizations taking a religious form.

After independence, the government regarded the Malay preponderance in the police and armed forces as disproportionate and a potential threat to security and acted to make the security forces more representative of the society as a whole, which meant in practice replacing Malays by Chinese (see Public Order and Internal Security, ch. 5). The government's drive to break up ethnic enclaves and resettle kampong dwellers in Housing and Development Board apartment complexes had a great effect on the Malays. Evidence of the convergence of Malay patterns of living with those of the rest of the population was provided by population statistics, which showed the Malay birth and death rates, originally quite high, to be declining. In the 1940s, Malay women had married early, had many children, and were divorced and remarried with great frequency. By the 1980s, Malays were marrying later, bearing fewer children (2.05 per woman for mid-1986 to mid-1987), and divorcing less frequently. By the 1980s, a large proportion of Malay women were working outside the home, which was a major social change. Many young women in their late teens and early to mid-twenties were employed in factories operated by multinational corporations, which, unlike the small-scale Chinese shops and workshops that had dominated the economy into the 1960s, paid no attention to ethnicity in hiring. Even Malay fishing communities on the offshore islands, which appeared to preserve the traditional way of life, were in the 1980s losing population as young people moved to Singapore Island, attracted by urban life and unskilled jobs that offered higher and more reliable incomes than fishing.

Although very much a part of Singapore's modernizing society, the Malays conspicuously occupied the bottom rungs of that society; their position illustrated a correlation between ethnicity and class that presented a major potential threat to social stability. With the lowest level of educational attainment of any ethnic group, the Malays were concentrated at the low end of the occupational hierarchy and had average earnings that were 70 percent of those of Chinese. Malays had a higher crime rate than other groups and in 1987 accounted for 47 percent of the heroin addicts arrested. The 1980 census showed that 86 percent of the Malay work force was in the clerical, service, and production sector; 45 percent of all employed Malays worked on assembly lines, largely in foreign-owned electronics factories. Only 8 percent of all professional and technical workers (including schoolteachers), and 2 percent of all administrative and managerial personnel were Malays. Malays dropped out of the competitive school system in large numbers, and those who continued past primary school were concentrated in vocational education programs. In 1980 they made up only 1.5 percent of all university graduates and 2.5 percent of students enrolled in higher education.

In sharp contrast to neighboring Malaysia with its policies of affirmative action for the Malay majority, Singapore's government insisted that no ethnic group would receive special treatment and that all citizens had equal rights and equal opportunities. The potential threat, however, posed by the overlap between Malay ethnicity and low educational achievement and occupational status, was clear. Demonstrating the Singaporean propensity for discussing social affairs in terms of "race," both government spokesmen and Malay intellectuals tended to attribute the Malays' economic position and educational performance to something inherent in the Malay personality or culture, or to their supposed "rural" attitudes. The ways in which lower income and ill-educated Malays resembled or differed from the very many lower income and ill-educated Chinese, who had very different cultural backgrounds, were not addressed.

In 1982 the prime minister defined Malays' educational difficulties as a national problem and so justified government action to improve their educational performance. The colonial government had provided free but minimal education, in the Malay language, to Malays but not to Chinese or Indians, on the grounds that the Chinese and Indian residents of Singapore, even those born there, were sojourners. In the colonial period most English-language schools were run by churches or missionaries, and many Malays avoided them for fear of Christian proselytization. Although after independence schooling in Singapore was not free (fees were generally low, but the government felt that people would not value education if they did not pay something for it), Malays continued to receive free primary education. In 1960 that benefit was extended to secondary and higher education, although the free schooling was offered only to those the government defined as Malay, which excluded immigrant Indonesians whom the Malays regarded as part of their community. Throughout the 1960s and most of the 1970s, most Malay children continued to attend schools that taught only in Malay, or, if they taught English at all, did so quite poorly. Opportunities for secondary and higher education in the Malay language were very limited. Although many Malays were employed in the public service or as drivers or servants for foreign employers, in almost all cases the language used at work was the grammatically and lexically simplified tongue called Bazaar Malay.

Throughout the 1970s, relatively few Malays knew English, a language that became progressively more necessary for high-paying professional and technical jobs. Substantial numbers of the Chinese knew no more English than the Malays, but they found employment in the extensive sector of Chinese commerce and small-scale industry where hiring demanded command of a Chinese regional language and personal recommendation. The former Malay economic niche in the military and police forces was eliminated in the late 1960s and 1970s, and the large number of Malays who had been employed by the British armed forces at British naval and other military facilities lost those secure and well-paying positions when the British withdrew from Singapore from 1970 to 1975. Such factors as poor command of English, limited availability of secondary and postsecondary education in Malay, and the loss of publicsector jobs accounted for much of the low economic position of the Malay community in 1980.

In 1981 Malay community leaders, alarmed by the results of the 1980 census that demonstrated the concentration of Malays in the lower reaches of the occupational hierarchy, formed a foundation called Mendaki, an acronym for Majlis Pendidikan Anak-anak Islam (Council for the Education of Muslim Children). Mendaki (ascent in Malay), devoted itself to providing remedial tuition classes for Malay children in primary and secondary school, offering scholarships for living expenses and loans for higher education, attempting to encourage parents to take a more active role in their children's education, and holding public ceremonies to honor Malay students who excelled in examinations or graduated from academic secondary schools or universities. Government support for Mendaki took the form of financing the organization through a special voluntary checkoff on the monthly contribution of Muslim workers to the Central Provident Fund, and through unspecified other public donations.

Throughout the 1980s, both the number of Malay students in selective secondary schools and institutions of higher education and the proportion of Malays passing and scoring well on standardized examinations slowly increased. As with the changes in birth rates, it was difficult to separate the effects of such government-sponsored programs as those of Mendaki from other factors, including increased female participation in the work force, residence in apartment complexes rather than kampong housing, exposure to television and radio, smaller family size, and better teaching in the schools.

The use of a voluntary checkoff on the monthly Central Provident Fund contribution as a means of raising Malay educational funds was characteristic of Singapore in the 1980s. Malays, like

The Society and Its Environment

other Singaporeans, were assumed to have regular employment and salaries, and their distinctive Malay and Muslim concerns were efficiently and equitably addressed through a computerized government program.

The Indians

The Indians, although a component of Singapore's society since its founding, were in the 1980s its most immigrant-like community. In the nineteenth and early twentieth centuries, Indian men had worked in Singapore, sending money home to families and wives in India, whom they would visit every few years. Indian women and complete Indian families were rare before World War II, and the Indian sex ratio in 1931 was 5,189 men for every 1,000 women. The 1980 census showed 1,323 Indian men for every 1,000 women; most of the surplus males were over age 60. In the 1980s, the "Little India" off Serangoon Road contained many dormitories where elderly single men lived, as well as some shops and workshops whose owners, in the traditional pattern, housed and fed a workforce of middle-aged and elderly men who might or might not have wives and children in India or Sri Lanka. Significant issues for the Indian community included securing residence status, citizenship, or entrance for the Indian families of men who had worked in Singapore for decades and for the Brahman priests who were necessary for Hindu religious life.

Almost two-thirds (64 percent) of the Indian population were Tamils from southeastern India's Tamil Nadu state; some Tamils also came from Jaffna in northern Sri Lanka. The great diversity of the Indian populace was indicated by the census category "other Indians," who made up a substantial 19 percent of the group, followed by Malayalis (8 percent); Punjabis, mostly Sikh (8 percent); and Gujaratis (1 percent). Like the Straits Chinese, some of Singapore's Indians adopted English as a first language, a change facilitated by the widespread use of English in India, where it had become another Indian language. Indians were the most religiously diverse of Singapore's ethnic categories; an estimated 50 to 60 percent were Hindu, 20 to 30 percent Muslim, 12 percent Christian, 7 percent Sikh, and 1 percent Buddhist (see Religion, this ch.). Indian immigrants, like those of other nationalities, had been primarily recruited from among poor farmers and laborers, which meant that they included a large proportion (perhaps one-third) of untouchables. In Singapore untouchables were usually referred to by the more polite Tamil term Adi-Dravidas, meaning pre-Dravidians. Although Tamils made up nearly two-thirds of the Indian population and Tamil was one of the country's four official languages (along with English, Malay, and Mandarin Chinese), by 1978 more Indians claimed to understand Malay (97 percent) than Tamil (79 percent). The 20 to 30 percent of the Indian population who were Muslims tended to intermarry with Malays at a fairly high rate and to be absorbed into the Malay community, continuing a centuries-old process of assimilation of Indian males to Malay society.

The linguistic and religious diversity of the Indian population was matched by their high degree of occupational differentiation. Indians were represented at all levels of the occupational hierarchy in numbers roughly proportional to their share of the total population. Within the Indian category, occupational and education attainment was far from equitably distributed. The untouchables for the most part did unskilled or semiskilled labor, while the Jaffna Tamils and the Chettia caste, who were traditionally moneylenders and merchants, were often professionals and wealthy businessmen. After World War II, caste received no public recognition in Singapore. Untouchables were free to enter Hindu temples, and food was distributed at temple festivals without regard for relative degrees of purity and pollution. Members of the Indian community were reluctant to discuss caste in public, but it continued to play a decisive role in marriage arrangements. The Indians were the most likely of all ethnic groups to attempt to arrange marriages for their children, or at least to restrict the choice of marriage partners to acceptable caste categories. Although the relatively small size of the Indian population and the disparate mixture of local caste groups from large areas of southern India made it difficult for most families to insist on strict caste endogamy (marrying only within the caste), Hindu marriages were made within a tripartite hierarchy. The highest level was occupied by Brahmans and Chettias, who attempted to maintain caste endogamy or at least to marry only members of other high castes. Mid-level caste Hindus intermarried with little difficulty, but the marriages of low-caste or outcaste category of former hereditary washermen, barbers, and untouchables were restricted to their own circle.

Singaporean Identity

The period after Singapore's withdrawal from Malaysia in 1965 saw much public discussion of Singaporean identity. The discussion tended to use terms, categories, and basic assumptions provided by the government and ruling party. One basic assumption was that there was not, at least in the late 1960s and 1970s, a common Singaporean identity, but that there should be. A corollary was that Singaporean identity would not spontaneously emerge from the country's ongoing social, political, and cultural life. Rather, it would have to be consciously created and "built" by policies, directives, and educational campaigns. The content of the identity remained somewhat ill-defined, and it often appeared easier to say what Singaporean identity was not than what it was. The ideal seemed to combine, somewhat uneasily, a self-consciously toughminded meritocratic individualism, in which individual Singaporeans cultivated their talents and successfully competed in the international economy, with an equally self-conscious identification with "Asian roots" and "traditional values," which referred to precolonial India, China, and the Malay world. Singaporeans were to be modern and cosmopolitan while retaining their distinctively Asian traditions.

Singapore's leaders explicitly rejected the ideology of the melting pot, offering rather the vision of a confidently multiethnic society whose component ethnic groups shared participation in such common institutions as electoral politics, public education, military service, public housing, and ceremonies of citizenship; at the same time they were to retain distinct languages, religions, and customs. Singaporeans were defined as composed of three fundamental types—Chinese, Malays, and Indians. These ethnic categories, locally referred to as "races," were assumed to represent self-evident, "natural" groups that would continue to exist into the indefinite future. Singaporean identity thus implied being a Chinese, a Malay, or an Indian, but self-consciously so in relation to the other two groups. The Singaporean model of ethnicity thus required both the denial of significant internal variation for each ethnic category and the highlighting of contrasts between the categories.

Being Singaporean also meant being fluent in English, a language which served both as a neutral medium for all ethnic groups and as the medium of international business and of science and technology. The schools, the government, and the offices of international corporations for the most part used English as their working language. The typical Singaporean was bilingual, speaking English as well as the language of one of the three component ethnic groups. Hence the former English-speaking Baba, Chinese or Indian, would seem to serve as the model of Singaporean identity. The resulting culture would be the type social scientists call "creolized," in which a foreign language such as English or French is adapted to local circumstances and the dominant culture reflects a unique blending of local and "metropolitan" or international elements. In the 1980s, there were signs of the emergence of such a culture in Singapore, with the growth among youth (of all "races") of a distinctive English-based patois called "Singlish" and the attraction of all ethnic groups to international fashions and fads in leisure activities.

Singapore's leaders resisted such trends toward cosmopolitan or creole culture, however, reiterating that Singaporeans were Asians rather than Westerners and that abandoning their own traditions and values for the tinsel of international popular culture would result in being neither truly Western nor properly Asian. The consequence would be loss of identity, which in turn would lead to the dissolution of the society. The recommended policy for the retention of Asian identity involved an ideal division of labor by language. English was to function as a language of utility. The Asian "mother tongues"—Mandarin Chinese, Malay, and Tamil—would be the languages of values, providing Singaporeans with what political leaders and local academics commonly called "cultural ballast" or "moral compasses." Stabilized and oriented by traditional Asian values, the Singaporean would be able to select what was useful from the offerings of "Western" culture and to reject that which was harmful. This theory of culture and identity resulted in the effort to teach the "mother tongues" in the schools and to use them as the vehicle for moral education (see Education, this ch.).

In an extension of the effort to create a suitable national identity, in 1989 Singapore's leaders called for a "national ideology" to prevent the harmful drift toward superficial Westernization. The national ideology, which remained to be worked out in detail, would help Singaporeans develop a national identity and bond them together by finding and encouraging core values common to all the country's diverse cultural traditions. Suggested core values included emphasizing community over self, valuing the family, resolving issues through the search for consensus rather than contention, and promoting racial and religious tolerance.

Language Planning

In colonial Singapore, the nearest thing to a common language had been Bazaar Malay, a form of Malay with simplified grammar and a very restricted vocabulary that members of many ethnic groups used to communicate in the marketplace. The government used English, with translators employed when necessary, as in the courts. Among the Chinese a simplified form of Hokkien served as the language of the marketplace. The Chinese schools, which were founded in large numbers in the early years of the twentieth century and associated with the rise of Chinese nationalism, attempted to teach in Mandarin or Guoyu, the use of which on such formal occasions as weddings and Chinese national holiday celebrations came to carry some prestige. In the terminology of sociolinguistics, Singapore's language system was multilingual and diglossiac, that is, characterized by two languages or dialects, high and low, or classical and vernacular, each used in different social contexts and carrying differential prestige. Bazaar Malay and market Hokkien were the low languages, employed in the streets and market places, and English and Mandarin were the high languages, used in education, government offices, and public celebrations. In addition, such native tongues as pure Malay, Teochiu, Tamil, or Punjabi were used in the home and in gatherings of members of the same speech group. In a 1972 survey asking which language people understood, Hokkien came first, at 73 percent, followed by Malay, with 57 percent. Malay was the most important language for intergroup communication, with almost all the Indians and 45 percent of the Chinese claiming to understand it. English came third, understood by 47 percent of the total population. A follow-up survey in 1978 showed that 67 percent claimed to understand Malay and 62 percent to comprehend English. As the 1990s approached, English was replacing Malay as the common language. It was used not only as the high language but also, in its Singlish variant, as a low language of the streets. Bazaar Malay was declining, and Malay in its full native complexity was increasingly used only by Malays. Even though it was one of the four official languages and the putative "mother tongue" of the Indian community, Tamil was used less often, and literacy in Tamil was reported to be declining.

The most ambitious aspect of Singapore's language planning and attempted social engineering was the campaign to replace the Chinese "dialects" with Mandarin, called the "mother tongue." The Speak Mandarin campaign began in 1979 as a PAP project and was subsequently institutionalized in the Mandarin Campaign Secretariat in the Ministry of Communications and Information. The promotion of Mandarin as a common Chinese language dates back to the early years of the century, when it was associated with the rise of Chinese nationalism and the foundation of Chinese schools. Learning Mandarin would, it was argued, permit all Chinese to communicate in their "mother tongue," be useful for doing business with China, and, perhaps most important, promote traditional Chinese values. All ethnic Chinese were required to study Mandarin through secondary school and to pass examinations in it for university admission. Chinese civil servants took a required 162-hour conversational Mandarin course, and the Mandarin Campaign Secretariat coordinated the annual Speak Mandarin campaigns. Mandarin classes were offered by the Singapore Chinese Chamber of Commerce and Industry and by some native-place and clan associations. All Chinese television broadcasting was in Mandarin, as was most radio broadcasting. Radio programs in

Chinese dialects were limited to 9:00 P.M. to midnight on the same station that broadcast Tamil from 5:00 A.M. to 9:00 P.M. In 1989 members of Parliament complained that some residents were tuning in to Cantonese opera broadcast by television stations in neighboring Malaysia. By late 1988, some 87 percent of the Chinese population claimed to be able to speak Mandarin. People did not agree, however, on the appropriate social contexts for use of what was for everyone a school language. As a result, people tended to use English or their native tongue on most everyday occasions. During the late 1980s, the Speak Mandarin campaign attempted to persuade people to use Mandarin when shopping and targeted taxi drivers, bus conductors, and operators of food stalls as workers who were to use Mandarin.

The goals of the Speak Mandarin campaign included improving communication between Chinese speech groups, teaching people to read Chinese, and promoting Confucianism. Some critics argued that children were expected to learn two foreign languages in school (English and Mandarin) and that for some students the result was fluency in neither. The official response was that the problem would be avoided if people would speak Mandarin at home. Some educators questioned whether a sufficient level of Chinese literacy could be achieved with the amount of time the schools devoted to Chinese, a point that was indirectly supported in August 1988 when Brigadier General Lee Hsien Loong, the minister for trade and industry and son of Prime Minister Lee Kuan Yew, urged Chinese newspapers to use simpler language to attract younger readers. Some academics questioned the restriction of Chinese values to Confucianism and recalled that in the 1950s and early 1960s Chinese was the language of radicalism and revolt rather than of loyalty and conservatism. The necessity of learning Mandarin to conserve traditional Chinese culture was not obvious to those Chinese who felt that Chinese culture had been transmitted for centuries through Hokkien, Teochiu, and Cantonese. They pointed out that the colloquial speech of modern Beijing (upon which Madarin is based) was as distant from the classical Chinese of the Confucian texts as was colloquial Cantonese. Giving up the dialects implied a major transformation of the social structure of the Chinese community, because the associational and commercial structure of Singapore's Chinese-oriented society rested on (and reinforced) dialect distinctions.

The Social System
Ethnicity and Associations

Because Singapore was a small society open to influence from the West through the English language and subject to the homogenizing effects of modernization and industrialization, the persistence of ethnicity as a fundamental element of its social structure was by no means assured. By the late 1980s ethnic affiliations were in many ways less significant than they had been in 1970 or 1940, and the lives of members of distinct ethnic groups had more and more common elements. In Singapore, as elsewhere, the forces of standardized education, impartial application of laws and regulations, common subordination to the impersonal discipline of the factory and the office, common pursuit of leisure activities, and exposure to international mass media resulted in many shared attitudes among ethnic groups. Studies of factory workers in Malaysia and Singapore, for example, found no marked differences in the attitudes and performance of Chinese and Malays. Psychological profiles of a cohort of poorly educated young Chinese who had held a succession of unskilled jobs before induction into the armed forces resembled those of equally poorly educated and unskilled Malays. Foreign popular culture seemed equally tempting or equally threatening to young Singaporeans of all ethnic groups. Ethnic boundaries persisted, especially where they corresponded with religious distinctions, and were evident in the continuing low rate of ethnic intermarriage. In daily life, however, the significance of ethnic affiliation had apparently diminished from the levels of previous generations.

Government policies were a major factor in the continuation of ethnicity as an organizing principle of Singapore's society. On the one hand, the government and the ruling party acted to break up ethnic enclaves, to provide public services to members of all ethnic groups, and to reshape society with the network of People's Association Community Centers, Residents' Committees, and Members of Parliament Constituent Advisory Groups. On the other hand, the government's ideology defined Singaporeans as members of component ethnic groups, and its various ministries listed everyone's "race" on identity cards and all official records, and remained very concerned with such matters as the ethnic mix in apartment complexes. Official statistics usually included breakdowns by "race," indicating an assumption that such categorization was significant. National holidays featured displays of the distinctive traditional cultures of the major ethnic groups, represented by costumes, songs, and dances. Pupils in secondary schools took required courses in the ethics and religion of their designated traditional culture—Confucian ethics for the Chinese, Islamic studies for the Malays, Hindu or Sikh studies for the Indians, and Buddhism or Bible study as options open to all.

Although state policies reinforced ethnic boundaries and the habit of ethnic categorization, they had little effect on the content of the ethnic categories. Ethnic identity was acted out on a daily basis through an extensive network of ethnically exclusive associations. Many Malay and Indian associations took a religious form, such as mosque and endowment management committees, sharia (Muslim law—see Glossary) courts, Hindu temple committees and the high-level Hindu Advisory Board, which represented Hindus to the government. An example of the reinforcement of ethnic identity was provided by the groups of Indian employees in one government department who distinguished themselves from their Malay and Chinese coworkers by jointly sponsoring festivals at a major Hindu temple. All ethnic groups had their own education and charitable associations as well as higher-order federations of such associations whose officers were the recognized community leaders. Singapore law required all associations of ten or more persons to be registered with the government, which supervised and could dissolve them. Trade unions, financial, education, and religious bodies were supervised by the appropriate government departments, and the catch-all Registry of Societies listed all associations that did not come under the authority of a specialized department. In 1987 3,750 associations were under the Registry of Societies.

The most elaborate set of ethnic associations was found among the Chinese, who in 1976 supported over 1,000 clan, locality, occupational, religious, and recreational associations. The membership of each association usually was restricted to those speaking the same dialect or tracing ancestry to the same small region of China. The lowest level associations were clan or district associations, which were in turn grouped into federations based on progressively larger administrative or linguistic regions of China. The Singapore Chinese Chamber of Commerce and Industry, founded in 1906, was the overarching association that represented the entire Chinese community. A federation, its constituent units were not individuals or individual businesses but associations. Its basic structure consisted of representatives of seven regional associations (Fujian, Teochiu, Cantonese, Hakka 1, Hakka 2, Hainan, and "Three Rivers") and ninety-three trade associations, each one usually restricted to speakers of one dialect.

The functions and activities of the associations were multiple, reflecting the concerns of members and leaders. Common activities included mutual aid; insurance benefits; foundation and maintenance of schools, hospitals, or cemeteries; contributions to the same sorts of public projects in the ancestral districts of China; settling disputes between members; acting as spokesman for the community to the government; and promoting good fellowship and continuing identification with the clan or region. Associations were run by committees and met at least once a year for a formal banquet. Association leaders were prosperous businessmen who had played a major part in fundraising and the management of activities. Success in business gave them both the free time to devote to association activities and the funds to contribute to the association and its charities. The associations conferred prestige and public recognition on those who took the burdens of office and community service, but the community so served was restricted to those from the same region and speaking the same dialect. The leadership of the lowest level associations was usually provided by those of moderate means, while the more wealthy belonged to several or many associations and worked for the higher level, more inclusive associations, which conferred more public recognition and prestige. The mechanisms of leadership and prestige and the channeling of much charity and assistance (schools, scholarship funds, hospitals, recommendations for employment or loans from Chinese banks, death benefits) through the associations thus reinforced ethnic and subethnic identification for both poor and rich.

In a pattern common to Chinese urban society in China and in Southeast Asia, groups defined by common place of origin or dialect also tended to specialize in certain trades or monopolies. Exactly which regional group dominated which trade varied from place to place and represented historical accidents and contingencies, but the principle of a regional group also acting as an occupational group was common. As late as the 1980s, the Singapore Hokkien were dominant in banking, insurance, shipping, hardware, real estate, and other lucrative fields. Within the Hokkien community, smaller subgroups controlled particular trades. For example, 96 percent of the merchants dealing in China tea in the 1980s traced their ancestry to Anxi County in southern Fujian. Teochiu dominated the fresh produce trade and the jewelry and antiques business; Cantonese predominated in furniture making, watch and clock repair, and operating drug stores and restaurants; and the Hakka were pawnbrokers, tailors, and dealers in Chinese herbs and medicines. The Henghua people from northern Fujian, a small component of the Chinese population, controlled the very important bicycle, motorcycle, and taxi businesses. Over the years the speech groups competed for the control of trades, and the pattern of dialect-specific occupations was a dynamic one, with, for example, strong competition for shares of the textile trade. In the 1980s, four textile trade associations represented Teochiu, Hokkien, Hakka, and Cantonese traders. The competition between speech groups reinforced both their internal solidarity and the social boundaries between them. Regional associations were, to a certain extent, also trade associations. For the large proportion of the Chinese population employed in regional commerce, service trades, or small-scale manufacturing, there remained a close relation between ethnicity and occupation, each aspect reinforcing the other.

For the proprietors and employees of many small and medium Chinese businesses, continued identification with dialect and subethnic communities provided many benefits and indeed was a precondition for engaging in many lines of trade. Although the dialect communities were not primarily occupational groups, the social solidarities created within the communities were economically useful. Much of the business activity in the extensive Chinese "traditional" sector of the economy depended on credit, personal relations, and the reputation of individuals for trustworthiness. In the final analysis, individuals met their obligations because failure to do so would result in immediate loss of reputation and creditworthiness with their fellows in restricted subethnic communities.

For many members of the Chinese community, economic self-interest reinforced the identification with an ethnic or subethnic community and the continued use of a regional dialect. Such individuals tended to be both more intensely and self-consciously "Chinese" and "Teochiu" or "Anxi Hokkien" than their fellows, who might well be their own brothers, sons, or daughters, who worked for the government or large multinational corporations. For the latter, formal educational certification, command of English, and perhaps skill at golf rather than Chinese finger games and etiquette were associated with economic success.

Social Stratification and Mobility

During the 1970s and 1980s, economic development and industrial growth reduced poverty and income inequity and accelerated upward social mobility. Those with educational qualifications, command of English, and high-level technical or professional skills profited the most from the process.

In the late 1980s, the major indices of social stratification were education level, citizenship status, sector of the economy where employed, and number of employed persons in the household. Residents were sharply differentiated by the amount of education they had completed. In 1980 about 44 percent of the population aged 25 and above had no educational qualifications, 38 percent had completed primary school, 15 percent secondary school, and only 3.4 percent higher education. Those people born after 1970 were on average much better educated than previous generations, but

The Society and Its Environment

throughout the 1990s the work force will contain many individuals with limited education. Wages correlated fairly closely with educational attainment, although education in English brought higher salaries than Chinese education. Many benefits, such as access to a Housing and Development Board apartment, were available only to Singapore citizens, and only citizens and permanent residents were enrolled in the Central Provident Fund. In 1985, a recession year when many foreign factory workers lost their jobs and residence permits, citizens made up 91 percent of the work force. Noncitizens were concentrated in the lower and in the highest wage levels, either as factory or service workers on short-term work permits, or as well-paid expatriate managers and professionals. Wages were relatively higher in government service and government-owned corporations and in the capital intensive and largely foreign-owned export-oriented manufacturing sector. They were lower in the service, retail, and less highly capitalized light industrial, craft, and commercial sector, which was dominated by small Chinese firms (see Wage Policies, ch. 3). Wages for unskilled and semiskilled factory work and for unskilled service jobs were relatively low. Those who held such jobs, often young women in their teens and early twenties, were not entirely self-supporting but parts of households in which several members worked at low-paying jobs. Families of the poorly educated and unskilled improved their standard of living between 1970 and 1990 in part because full employment made it possible to pool the wages of several family members.

Economic growth and the associated increase in the demand for labor from 1960 to 1989 raised living standards and sharply reduced the incidence of poverty. A survey of living costs and household incomes in 1953-54 found 19 percent of all households to be in absolute poverty, meaning that their members did not have enough to eat. Application of the same standard in 1982-83 found 0.3 percent of households in absolute poverty. A measure of moderate poverty, defined as adequate nutrition and shelter but little discretionary income and no savings, was devised by the Amalgamated Union of Public Employees in 1973. By that measure, 31 percent of households in 1972-73 were in moderate poverty, 15 percent in 1977-78, and 7 percent in 1982-83. Compared with other countries in the region, household incomes in Singapore were equitably distributed, with most households falling in the middle or lower middle ranges of the distribution.

The lowest income levels were those of single-person households, representing the elderly, the disabled, and those without kin in Singapore. Apart from the childless elderly and the disabled, those in moderate poverty in the 1980s were overwhelmingly working poor, holding unskilled jobs with no prospects for advancement. Such households typically had only one wage-earner with either primary education or no education and lived in rented housing and often a one-room or two-room Housing and Development Board apartment. Households with two or more members working, even at relatively low-paying jobs, were able to contemplate purchasing a Housing and Development Board apartment, save money for emergencies, and devote more resources to the education of children.

Much of the alleviation of poverty and decrease in income inequality that took place in the 1970s and 1980s resulted from the increased participation of women in the work force. In 1985, 46 percent of all women above the age of fifteen held paid employment; 68 percent of single women and 33 percent of married women worked outside the home. This trend was associated with women marrying later and having fewer children. One reason that more households attained an adequate standard of living in the 1980s was that there were more wives and unmarried daughters at work and fewer young children to be supported and looked after.

Surveys in the 1980s showed that most Singaporeans described themselves as middle class, justifying that status by their ownership of a Housing and Development Board apartment and the substantial and secure savings guaranteed by their Central Provident Fund Account. Families in the middle-income ranges usually occupied two- or three-bedroom apartments that they were buying from the Housing and Development Board, participated in one or more formal associations, took an active part in planning and supervising their children's education, stocked their apartments with a range of consumer appliances, and had money to spend on hobbies, sports, or vacations. Automobile ownership was not common, and most middle-income Singaporeans used public transportation. Their mode of life rested on occupational skills and educational qualifications, secure employment in large, bureaucratic government or private organizations, or ownership of their own small business.

The upper levels of the society were occupied by a tripartite elite of high-level civil servants, local managers and professionals employed by foreign-owned multinational corporations, and wealthy Chinese businessmen who served as leaders in the associational world of the Chinese-speaking communities. The first two categories were marked by fluency in English, university-level education, often in Britain or the United States, and a cosmopolitan outlook reinforced by foreign residence and travel. Many of the

The Society and Its Environment

Chinese businessmen were entrepreneurs who operated in an exclusively Chinese setting and often had minimal educational qualifications. Their sons, however, often were graduates of the best secondary schools and of local or foreign universities and worked either as English-speaking representatives of their fathers' businesses, as civil servants, or as professionals. Few of the elite had inherited their status, and all were aware that they could not directly pass it along to their children. Having themselves been upwardly mobile in a society more open to individual effort than most in the region, they valued that society's stress on competition, individual mobility, and success through hard work. In the domestic sphere, they expressed those values by devoting much effort to the education of their children.

Increased family incomes made possible by full employment and by such government programs as the construction and sale of apartments and the enrollment of nearly everyone in the Central Provident Fund are to be distinguished from upward mobility, in which individuals moved into more highly skilled and highly paid jobs and hence into higher social classes. The expansion of industry, banking, and of the ranks of civil servants created many high and mid-level positions that Singaporeans could aspire to and compete for. Residents from every ethnic community regarded social mobility as a common and accepted goal. Education was regarded as the best channel for upward mobility, and most families tried to encourage their children to do well in school and to acquire educational qualifications and certification. This fact put severe pressure on the school system and the children in it, although, as elsewhere, middle- and upper-income families had an advantage in maneuvering their offspring through the education system.

Individuals approached jobs with a keen appreciation for their potential for further mobility. Most large organizations, whether government or private, provided some training. Some foreign-owned enterprises, such as those in the oil industry, employed large numbers of skilled workers and ran extensive in-house training programs. The electronics assembly factories, in contrast, offered no prospects for advancement to their large numbers of unskilled or semiskilled assembly line workers. Small scale enterprises, which in the late 1980s often recruited along ethnic and subethnic lines, were associated with long working hours and low wages, but sometimes offered the workers opportunity to learn a skill, such as automotive repair. Workers in such establishments commonly advanced by quitting and opening their own small firms, often after years of saving.

In a system that reflected both the great differences in educational attainment in the work force and the great significance attached to educational qualifications, most large organizations, public and private, made a sharp distinction between mental and manual labor, and movement from the lower to the higher was very difficult and rare. Lower level white-collar workers and skilled blue-collar workers often took advantage of opportunities to upgrade their occupational skills, either through training offered by the organization or through night school and short-term courses offered by educational or other government bodies. Unskilled workers in industry and service trades and employees in small Chinese firms saw few prospects for advancement and considered self-employment as their only hope for upward mobility. Vending food and consumer goods on the streets or operating a cooked-food stall, traditional entry points for entrepreneurs, had been practically eliminated by government action to tidy up the environment and to limit the numbers of mobile hawkers who obstructed traffic. Many Singapore economists felt that the successful modernization of the economy and the increases both in government regulation and in rents for shops and small premises had made it more difficult for the ambitious poor to get a start. By the late 1980s, Singapore's academics and political leaders were discussing the perceived shortage of entrepreneurs and suggesting solutions to the problem, although most discussion focused on industrial innovation and growth rather than the commercial fields in which most Singapore entrepreneurs had succeeded (see Policies for the Future, ch. 3).

Family, Marriage, and Divorce

Almost all Singaporeans lived in small nuclear families. Although both Chinese and Indian traditions favored large extended families, such families were always rare in immigrant Singapore where neither the occupational structure, based on wage labor, or the housing pattern, characterized by small, rented quarters, favored such family forms. In the 1980s, families were important in that most individuals as a matter of course lived with their parents until marriage and after marriage maintained a high level of interaction with parents, brothers, and sisters. Probably the most common leisure activity in Singapore was the Sunday visit to the grandparents for a meal and relaxed conversation with brothers, sisters, in-laws, uncles and aunts, cousins, and other assorted kin. Although the age of marriage increased in the 1970s and 1980s, reaching a mean 28.5 years for grooms and 25.8 years for brides in 1987, Singapore remained a society in which it was assumed that everyone would marry, and marriage was a normal aspect of fully adult status.

The Society and Its Environment

Both ethnicity and class affected the form and functioning of families. Chinese and Indian families rested on cultural assumptions of the permanence of marriage and of the household as an ongoing, corporate group whose members, bound by duty, obligation, and subordination, pooled and shared income. The continued efforts of Indian parents to arrange the marriages or at least to influence the marital choices of their offspring and the Tamil obligation to provide daughters with large dowries reflected such cultural definitions of family and household. In a similar manner, some Chinese combined the household with the family enterprise, practicing a traditional entrepreneurial strategy that included mobilizing the savings of all household members and allocating them in accord with a long-term plan for family success. Such a strategy might take the form of a thriving business with branches in the major cities of Malaysia and Indonesia, or of sons and daughters employed in the Singapore civil service, a large foreign bank, or a university in Australia.

Malay families, on the other hand, gave priority to the individual and to individual interests. They viewed relations between siblings as tenuous and saw the household as a possibly short-lived coalition of autonomous individuals linked by sentiments of mutual concern and affection. Malays had traditionally had much higher rates of divorce and adoption than other ethnic groups, and the distinction continued in the 1980s although the divorce rate was lower than in the 1940s or through the 1960s. More significantly, for the Malays divorce was regarded as a realistic and normal, although unfortunate, possibility in all marriages. Because Malays did not define the household as a continuing body, they did not make long-range strategic plans to maximize family income and success. In Malay families, husbands, wives, and children with jobs held separate purses and sometimes separate savings accounts. It was thus difficult for Malays to establish family businesses as the Chinese and the Indians did.

Class affected families in a manner generally similar to many other industrialized societies. In all ethnic groups, lower-class or working-class people tended to be dependent on kin outside the immediate household for a wide range of services, and to operate wide networks of mutual assistance and gift exchange. Throughout the 1980s, kin provided the bulk of child care for married women working in factories. Such relatives were paid for their services, but less than a stranger would have been paid. The possibility of such support often determined whether a woman took a job outside the home, and thus demonstrated the relation between large numbers of kin and material comfort and security. Substantial sums of money were passed back and forth on such occasions as the birthdays of aged parents, the birth of children, or the move into a new apartment. Family members were a major source of information on and referrals to jobs for many unskilled or semiskilled workers. Relations with the extended circle of relatives were not always harmonious or happy, but they were important and necessary to the welfare and comfort of most working-class families.

Middle- and upper-class households were less dependent on kin networks for support. They maintained close ties with parents and siblings, but did not need to rely on them. Indeed their relations with their extended kin often were more amiable than those of the lower-class households, where mutual need often was accompanied by disputes over allocation of such resources as grandparents' childcare services, or of the costs of supporting elderly parents and other dependent kin. Middle- and upper-class households spent more leisure time with people who were not their relatives and gained much of their social support from networks based on common schooling, occupation, and associational memberships. In such families, the bond between husband and wife was close as they shared more interests and activities than most working-class couples and made more decisions jointly.

Marriages across ethnic lines occurred, but not often. Between 1954 and 1984, intermarriage rates remained at a stable 5 to 6 percent of all marriages. None of the traditional cultures encouraged marriage outside the group. The Hindu traditions of caste endogamy and the Malay insistence on conversion to Islam as a condition of marriage were major barriers to intermarriage. Shared religion encouraged intermarriage, with marriages between Malays and Indian Muslims the most common form of ethnic intermarriage. Interethnic marriages included a disproportionate number of divorced or widowed individuals.

Divorce rates in Singapore were low. Interethnic marriages were somewhat more likely to end in divorce than were marriages within an ethnic group. During the 1980s the divorce rate for Malays fell, while it rose for the other ethnic groups. In 1987 there were 23,404 marriages in Singapore, and 2,708 divorces, or 115 divorces for every 1,000 marriages. The figures included 4,465 marriages under the Muslim Law Act, which regulated the marriage, divorce, and inheritance of Muslims, and 796 divorces under the same act, for a Muslim divorce rate of 178 divorces for every 1,000 marriages. Marriages under the Women's Charter (which regulated the marriage and divorce of non-Muslims) totaled 18,939, and divorces under that law were 1,912, for a non-Muslim divorce rate of 100 per 1,000 marriages. The differential rates of divorce for ethnic groups may have suggested greater differences than were in fact the case. Situations that for Malay families resulted in prompt, legal divorce were sometimes tolerated or handled informally by Chinese or Indian families for whom the social stigma of divorce was greater and the barriers to legal separation higher. For all ethnic groups, the most common source of marital breakdown was the inability or unwillingness of the husband to contribute to maintaining the household. This sometimes led to desertion, which was the most common ground for divorce.

Religion
Temples and Festivals

Singapore's immigrants commonly made their religious congregations a form of social organization. From the foundation of the city, colonial authorities had avoided interfering with the religious affairs of the ethnic communities, fostering an atmosphere of religious tolerance. It was characteristic of colonial Singapore that South Bridge Street, a major thoroughfare in the old Chinatown, should also be the site of the Sri Mariamman Temple, a south Indian Hindu temple, and of the Jamae or Masjid Chulia Mosque, which served Chulia Muslims from India's Coromandel Coast. The major religions were Chinese popular religion, commonly although inaccurately referred to as Daoism or Buddhism; Hinduism; Islam; Buddhism; and Christianity. Other religions included smaller communities of Sikhs and of Jains from India; Parsis, Indians of Iranian descent who followed the ancient Iranian Zoroastrian religion; and Jews, originally from the Middle East, who supported two synagogues.

The Chinese practiced Chinese popular religion, a distinctive and complex syncretic religion that incorporates some elements from canonical Buddhism and Daoism but focuses on the worship of gods, ghosts, and ancestors. It emphasizes ritual and practice over doctrine and belief, has no commonly recognized name, and is so closely entwined with Chinese culture and social organization that it cannot proselytize. In Singapore its public manifestations included large temples housing images of deities believed to respond to human appeals for guidance or relief from affliction and use of the common Chinese cycle of calendrical festivals. These occasions included the lunar New Year (in January or February), a festival of renewal and family solidarity; Qing Ming (Ch'ing Ming in Wade-Giles romanization), celebrated by the solar calender on April 5th (105 days after the winter solstice), to remember the ancestors and worship their graves; the fifteenth of the fifth lunar month (April or May), in Singapore known as Vesak Day and celebrated as marking the birth of the Buddah; the festival of the hungry ghosts in the seventh lunar month, a major Hokkien holiday, marked by domestic feasting and elaborate public rituals to feed and placate the potentially dangerous souls of those with no descendants to worship them; and the mid-autumn festival on the fifteenth of the eighth lunar month, an occasion for exchanging gifts of sweet round mooncakes and admiring the full moon. All Chinese temples held one or more annual festivals, marked by street processions, performances of Chinese traditional operas, and domestic banquets to which those who supported the temple, either because of residential propinquity, subethnic affiliation with a particular temple and its deity, or personal devotion to the god, invited their friends and business associates. To prevent the disruption of traffic and preserve public order, the government limited the length and route of street processions and prohibited the use of the long strings of firecrackers that had previously been a component of all Chinese religious display. Some festivals or customs that had little religious significance or were not practiced by the southeastern Chinese migrants were promoted by the government's Singapore Tourist Promotion Board for their spectacular and innocuous content. These included the summer dragon boat races, originally held only in China's Chang Jiang (Yangtze) River Valley, and the lantern festival in which paper lanterns in the shape of animals or other objects are carried through the streets by children or, if especially impressive, displayed in parks and temples. In China the lantern festival is celebrated in the first lunar month at the end of the New Year season, but in Singapore it is combined with the mid-autumn festival.

Canonical Buddhism was represented in Singapore as Sinhalese Theravada Buddhism. This form of Buddhism prevails in Sri Lanka and mainland Southeast Asia and differs from the Mahayana Buddhism of China, Korea, and Japan in both doctrine and organization. Theravada Buddhism was brought by Sinhalese migrants from Ceylon (contemporary Sri Lanka), who also influenced the architectural style of Thai and Vietnamese Theravada temples. These latter were staffed by Thai or Vietnamese monks, some of whom were originally members of the overseas Chinese communities of those countries and served a predominantly Chinese laity, using Hokkien, Teochiu, Cantonese, or English. Singapore was also home to a number of Chinese sects and syncretic cults that called themselves Buddhist but taught their own particular doctrines and lacked properly ordained Buddhist monks.

Sri Mariamman Hindu temple in Chinatown
Courtesy Ong Tien Kwan

Hindus have been part of Singapore's population since its foundation in 1819, and some of the old Hindu temples, such as the Sri Mariamman Temple, were declared national historical sites in the 1980s and so preserved from demolition. Singapore's Hindus adapted their religion to their minority status in two primary ways—compartmentalization and ritual reinterpretation. Compartmentalization referred to the Hindus' tendency to distinguish between the home, in which they maintained a nearly completely orthodox Hindu pattern of diet and ritual observance, and the secular outer world of work, school, and public life, where they did not apply categories of purity and pollution. Singapore lacked the tightly organized caste groups of communities found in India but replaced them in large-scale temple festivals with groups representing those of the same occupation or place of employment. The major Hindu holidays were the Hindu New Year, in April or May; Thaipusam, a festival during which penitents fulfilled vows to the deity Lord Subramanya by participating in a procession while carrying *kavadi*, heavy decorated frameworks holding offerings of milk, fruit, and flowers; and Deepavali, the Festival of Lights. Deepavali, a celebration of the victory of light over darkness and hence of good over evil, was a national holiday.

Seven of the ten national holidays were religious festivals; two of them were Chinese, two Muslim, two Christian, and one Hindu.

The festivals were the Chinese New Year; Vesak Day; Hari Raya Haji, the Muslim pilgrimage festival; Hari Raya Pusa, which marked the end of the fasting month of Ramadan and was a time of renewal; Christmas; Good Friday; and Deepavali. Citizens were encouraged to learn about the festivals of other religious and ethnic groups and to invite members of other groups to their own celebrations and feasts. Public ceremonies such as National Day or the commissioning of military officers were marked by joint religious services conducted by the Inter-Religious Organization, an ecumenical body founded in 1949 to promote understanding and goodwill among the followers of different religions.

Religion and Ethnicity

In the 1980s, members of all ethnic groups lived and worked together, dressed similarly, and shared equal access to all public institutions and services. Religion, therefore, provided one of the major markers of ethnic boundaries. Malays, for instance, would not eat at Chinese restaurants or food stalls for fear of contamination by pork, and a Chinese, in this case, could not invite a Malay colleague to a festive banquet. Funerals of a traditional and ethnically distinctive style were usually held even by families that were not otherwise very religiously observant. The community associations and the Singapore Tourist Promotion Board encouraged the public celebration of such ethnically distinctive and appropriately colorful and noncontroversial festivals as the Chinese lantern festival and the dragon boat races.

The marriages, divorces, and inheritances of members of religious communities and the management of properties and endowments dedicated to religious purposes were of concern to the government, which interacted with some religious bodies through advisory boards dating back to the colonial period. The Hindu Advisory Board, established in 1917, advised the government on Hindu religion and customs and on any matters concerning the general welfare of the Hindu community. It assisted the Hindu Endowments Board, which administered the four major Hindu temples and their property, in organizing the annual festivals at the temples. The Sikh Advisory Board acted in the same way for the Sikhs.

The Singapore Muslim Religious Council (Majlis Ugama Islam Singapura) played a very important role in the organization of Islamic affairs and therefore of the Malay community. Authorized by the 1966 Administration of Muslim Law Act, the council, composed of members nominated by Muslim societies but appointed by the president of Singapore, was formally a statutory board that advised the president on all matters relating to the Muslim religion.

*Entrance to Sultan Mosque
Courtesy Ong Tien Kwan*

It acted to centralize and standardize the practice of Islam. The council administered all Muslim trusts (*wafs*); organized a computerized and centralized collection of tithes and obligatory gifts (*zakat harta* and *zakat fitrah*); and managed all aspects of the pilgrimage to Mecca, including registering pilgrims, obtaining Saudi Arabian visas, and making airline reservations. The council also helped the government reorganize the mosque system after redevelopment. Before the massive redevelopment and rehousing of the 1970s and 1980s, Singapore's Muslims were served by about ninety mosques, many of which had been built and were funded and managed by local, sometimes ethnically based, communities. Redevelopment destroyed both the mosques and the communities that had supported them, scattering the people through new housing estates. The council, in consultation with the government, decided not to rebuild the small mosques but to replace them with large central mosques. Construction funds came from a formally voluntary contribution collected along with the Central Provident Fund deduction paid by all employed Muslims. The new central mosques could accommodate 1,000 to 2,000 persons and provided such services as kindergartens, religious classes, family counseling, leadership and community development classes, tuition and remedial instruction for school children, and Arabic language instruction.

The government had regulated Muslim marriages and divorces since 1880, and the 1957 Muslim Ordinance authorized the establishment of the centralized Sharia Court, with jurisdiction over divorce and inheritance cases. The court, under the Ministry of Community Development, replaced a set of government-licensed but otherwise unsupervised *kathi* (Islamic judges) who had previously decided questions of divorce and inheritance, following either the traditions of particular ethnic groups or their own interpretations of Muslim law. The court attempted to consistently enforce sharia law, standard Islamic law as set out in the Quran and the decisions of early Muslim rulers and jurists, and to reduce the high rate of divorce among Malays. In 1989 the Singapore Muslim Religious Council took direct control of the subjects taught in Islamic schools and of the Friday sermons given at all mosques.

Religious Change

Modernization and improved education levels brought changes in religious practice. The inflexible work schedules of industrialism, which tended to restrict communal ritual to evenings and Sundays, and the lack of opportunity or inclination to devote years to mastering ceremonial and esoteric knowledge, both contributed to a general tendency toward ritual simplification and abbreviation. At the same time, prosperous citizens contributed large sums to building funds, and in the 1980s a wave of rebuilding and refurbishing renewed the city's mosques, churches, Chinese temples, Buddhist monasteries, and Hindu temples. Ethnic affiliation was demonstrated by public participation in such annual rituals as processions, which did not require elaborate training or study.

Immigrants tended to drop or modify religious and ritual practices characteristic of and peculiar to the villages they had come from. Hindu temples founded in the nineteenth century to serve migrants of specific castes and to house deities worshipped only in small regions of southeastern India became the temples patronized by all Hindu residents of nearby apartment complexes. They offered a generic South Indian Hinduism focused on major deities and festivals. Many Chinese became more self-consciously Buddhist or joined syncretic cults that promoted ethics and were far removed from the exorcism and sacrificial rituals of the villages of Fujian and Guangdong. The movement away from village practices was most clearly seen and most articulated among the Malays, where Islamic reformers acted to replace the customary practices (*adat*) of the various Malay-speaking societies of Java, Sumatra, and Malaya with the precepts of classical Islamic law—sharia.

In 1988 the Ministry of Community Development reported the religious distribution to be 28.3 percent Buddhist, 18.7 percent

Buddhist temple
Courtesy Ong Tien Kwan

Christian, 17.6 percent no religion, 16 percent Islam, 13.4 percent Daoist, 4.9 percent Hindu, and 1.1 percent other religions (Sikhs, Parsis, Jews). The Christian proportion of the population nearly doubled between 1980 and 1988, growing from 10 percent to nearly 19 percent. The growth of Christianity and of those professing no religion was greatest in the Chinese community, with most of the Christian converts being young, well-educated people in secure white-collar and professional jobs. Most converts joined evangelical and charismatic Protestant churches worshiping in English. About one-third of the members of Parliament were Christians, as were many cabinet ministers and members of the ruling party, which was dominated by well-educated, English-speaking Chinese. The association of Christianity with elite social and political status may have helped attract some converts.

By the late 1980s, some Buddhist organizations were winning converts by following the Protestant churches in offering services, hymnbooks, and counseling in English and Mandarin. A Buddhist Society at the National University of Singapore offered lectures and social activities similar to those of the popular Christian Fellowship. Some Chinese secondary students chose Buddhism as their compulsory religious studies subject, regarding Confucianism as too distant and abstract and Bible study as too Western and too difficult. They then were likely to join Buddhist organizations, which offered congenial groups, use of English, and a link with Asian cultural traditions. In the late 1980s, other Chinese white-collar and skilled workers were joining the Japan-based Sōka Gakkai (Value Creation Society, an organization based on Nichiren Buddhism), which provided a simple, direct style of worship featuring chanting of a few texts and formulas and a wide range of social activities. The more successful religious groups, Christian and Buddhist, offered directly accessible religious practice with no elaborate ritual or difficult doctrine and a supportive social group.

In the 1980s, the government regarded religion in general as a positive social force that could serve as a bulwark against the perceived threat of Westernization and the associated trends of excessive individualism and lack of discipline. It made religious education a compulsory subject in all secondary schools in the 1980s. The government, although secular, was concerned, however, with the social consequences of religiously motivated social action and therefore monitored and sometimes prohibited the activities of religious groups. The authorities feared that religion could sometimes lead to social and implicitly political action or to contention between ethnic groups. Islamic fundamentalism, for example, was a very sensitive topic that was seldom publicly discussed. Throughout the 1980s, the authorities were reported to have made unpublicized arrests and expulsions of Islamic activists. The government restricted the activities of some Christian groups, such as the Jehovah's Witnesses who opposed military service, and in 1987 the government detained a group of Roman Catholic social activists, accusing them of using church organizations as cover for a Marxist plot. The charismatic and fundamentalist Protestant groups, though generally apolitical and focused on individuals, aroused official anxiety through their drive for more converts. Authorities feared that Christian proselytization directed at the Malays would generate resentment, tensions, and possible communal conflict. As early as 1974 the government had "advised" the Bible Society of Singapore to stop publishing materials in Malay. In late 1988 and early 1989, a series of leaders, including Prime Minister Lee Kuan Yew, condemned "insensitive evangelization" as a serious threat to racial harmony. Official restatements of the virtue of and necessity for religious tolerance were mixed with threats of detention without trial for religious extremists.

Health and Welfare
Medical Services and Public Health

As indicated by their long life expectancy and low death rates, Singaporeans generally enjoyed good health. Standards of nutrition

The Society and Its Environment

and environmental sanitation were high. The Ministry of the Environment's Vector Control and Research Department was responsible for controlling mosquitoes, flies, rats, and other disease-bearing animals; the Food Control Department and the Hawkers Department inspected food producers and outlets for cleanliness and sanitation. The Ministry of the Environment's Public Affairs Department conducted educational campaigns on such topics as environmental sanitation, control of mosquito-breeding sites, proper disposal of refuse, and food handling. Educational efforts were backed up by sanctions, which included fines of up to S$500 for spitting or failing to flush public toilets.

The population was served by nine government hospitals with 7,717 beds and by twelve private hospitals with 2,076 beds. In 1987 the Ministry of Health certified 2,941 physicians, 9,129 nurses, 653 dentists, and 487 pharmacists. Five of the nine government hospitals were general hospitals, providing a complete range of medical services and twenty-four hour emergency rooms, and the other four each had a specialty: obstetrics and gynecology, dermatology and venereology, psychiatry, or infectious diseases. In 1987 the Ministry of Health's Community Health Service operated twenty-four clinics in major housing complexes, offering primary medical treatment for injuries and common diseases. The Maternal and Child Health Service provided preventive health care for mothers and preschool children at twenty-three clinics, while school children were served by the School Health Service.

Government hospitals and clinics charged fees for their services, although the fees were generally low and the medical services were heavily subsidized. The fees were intended to discourage frivolous use of the medical system and to demonstrate that residents were responsible for their own health costs, as Singapore was not a welfare state. After 1984 Singaporeans could pay for their medical expenses through the Medisave Scheme, under which 6 percent of the monthly income of every contributor to the Central Provident Fund could be set aside for the medical expenses of the contributor and the contributor's spouse, parents, grandparents, and children in all government or private hospitals.

Mortality and Morbidity

The major causes of death in 1986 were heart disease, accounting for 24 percent of all deaths; cancer, 23 percent; cerebrovascular disease (stroke), 11 percent; and pneumonia, 8 percent. In 1988 two minor outbreaks of dengue fever took place but were halted through prompt control of arthropod-borne microorganisms, and a minor cholera epidemic broke out among the inmates of a mental institution. In 1982 the World Health Organization (WHO) declared Singapore malaria-free, and 161 of the 165 cases of malaria reported in 1987 were determined to be imported. In 1987 the most serious epidemic disease was hepatitis; 752 cases of acute viral hepatitis and 11 deaths were reported. Noise-induced deafness and industrial-related skin disease were the major occupational diseases; there was also some concern over exposure of workers to toxic and carcinogenic substances and to asbestos. The health authorities paid special attention to patients with kidney failure, a condition that killed some 200 people a year. The number of deaths reflected inadequate dialysis facilities and a shortage of organ donors. The 1987 Human Organ Transplant Law gave doctors the right to remove the kidneys of those killed in accidents unless the victim had objected in writing or was a Muslim.

AIDS Policy

At the end of 1988, the Ministry of Health reported thirty-four cases of acquired immune deficiency syndrome (AIDS) among Singaporeans; four of these cases resulted in death. The first two cases were identified in 1985. Thereafter the incidence increased; five new cases were reported in December 1988 alone. In 1987 the Ministry of Health established an AIDS Task Force to inform health professionals of research on and treatment programs for the disease. A National Advisory Committee, also formed in 1987, with representatives from the Ministry of Health, other ministries, the public media, hotels, and travel agencies concentrated on educating the public about the disease. The Ministry of Health worked with WHO, adapting its information and strategies to local circumstances. All blood donors were routinely screened for AIDS, and blood screening could be done at designated government clinics. In 1989 the Ministry of Health was sponsoring education programs on AIDS and offering confidential counseling to people worried that they might be infected. The ministry was trying to reach members of high-risk groups, but many of them refused counseling from fear of being identified and stigmatized.

Education

The School System

The government frequently referred to Singapore's population as its only natural resource and described education in the vocabulary of resource development. The goal of the education system was to develop the talents of every individual so that each could contribute to the economy and to the ongoing struggle to make

Singapore productive and competitive in the international marketplace. The result was an education system that stressed the assessment, tracking, and sorting of students into appropriate programs. Educators forthrightly described some students and some categories of students as better "material" and of more value to the country than others. In the 1960s and 1970s the education system, burdened with large numbers of children resulting from the high birth rates of the previous decades and reflecting the customary practices of the British colonial period, produced a small number of highly trained university graduates and a much larger number of young people who had been selected out of the education systems following secondary schooling by the rigorous application of standards. The latter entered the work force with no particular skills (see table 5, Appendix). Major reforms in 1979 produced an elaborate tracking system, intended to reduce the dropout rate and to see that those with low academic performance left school with some marketable skills. During the 1980s, more resources were put into vocational education and efforts were made to match the "products" of the school system with the manpower needs of industry and commerce. The combination of a school system emphasizing testing and tracking with the popular perception of education as the key to social mobility and to the source of the certifications needed for desirable jobs led to high levels of competition, parental pressure for achievement, and public attention and concern.

In 1987 some 4 percent of the gross domestic product (GDP—see Glossary) was devoted to education. The government's goal for the 1990s was to increase spending to 6 percent of GDP, which would match the levels of Japan and the United States. Education was not compulsory, but attendance was nearly universal. Primary education was free, and Malays received free education through university. Students' families had to purchase textbooks and school uniforms, but special funds were available to ensure that no student dropped out because of financial need. Secondary schools charged nominal fees of S$9.50 per month. Tuition at the National University of Singapore for the 1989-90 academic year ranged from S$2,600 per year for students in the undergraduate arts and social sciences, business administration, and law courses to S$7,200 per year for the medical course. The university-level tuitions were intended to induce prosperous families to bear a share of the cost of training that would lead to a well-paying job, but a system of loans, need-based awards (bursaries), and scholarships for superior academic performance meant that no able students were denied higher education because of inability to pay.

The schools operated a modified British-style system in which the main qualifications were the Cambridge University-administered General Common Entrance (GCE) Ordinary level (O level) and Advanced level (A level) examinations. Singapore secondary students took the same examinations as their counterparts in Britain or in British system schools throughout the world. All instruction was in English, with supplementary teaching of the students' appropriate "mother tongue"—Malay, Tamil, or Mandarin. The basic structure was a six-year primary school, a four-year secondary school, and a two-year junior college for those preparing to enter higher education. As part of the effort to reduce the dropout rate, some students progressed through the system more slowly than others, spending more time in primary and secondary school but achieving similar standards. The goal was that every student achieve some success and leave school with some certification. Both primary and secondary schools operated on double sessions. Plans for the 1990s called for converting secondary schools to single-session, all-day schools, a measure that would require construction of fifty new schools.

As of June 1987, there were 229 government and government-aided primary schools enrolling 266,501 students. Government-aided schools originally were private schools that, in return for government subsidies, taught the standard curriculum and employed teachers assigned by the Ministry of Education. There were 157 secondary schools and junior colleges, enrolling 201,125 students, and 18 vocational training schools, enrolling 27,000 students. The 15 junior colleges operating by late 1989 enrolled the "most promising" 25 percent of their age cohort and were equipped with computers, laboratories, and well-stocked libraries. Some represented the elite private schools of the colonial period, with their ancient names, traditions, and networks of active alumni, and others were founded only in the 1980s, often in the centers of the housing estates (see Land Management and Development, ch. 3). In 1989 the government was discussing the possibility of permitting some of the junior colleges to revert to private status, in the interest of encouraging educational excellence and diversity.

Singapore had six institutions of higher education: National University of Singapore (the result of the 1980 merger of Singapore University and Nanyang University); Nanyang Technological Institute; Singapore Polytechnic Institute; Ngee Ann Polytechnic; the Institute of Education; and the College of Physical Education. In 1987 these six institutions enrolled 44,746 students, 62 percent male and 38 percent female. Enrollment in universities and colleges increased from 15,000 in 1972 to nearly 45,000 in 1987,

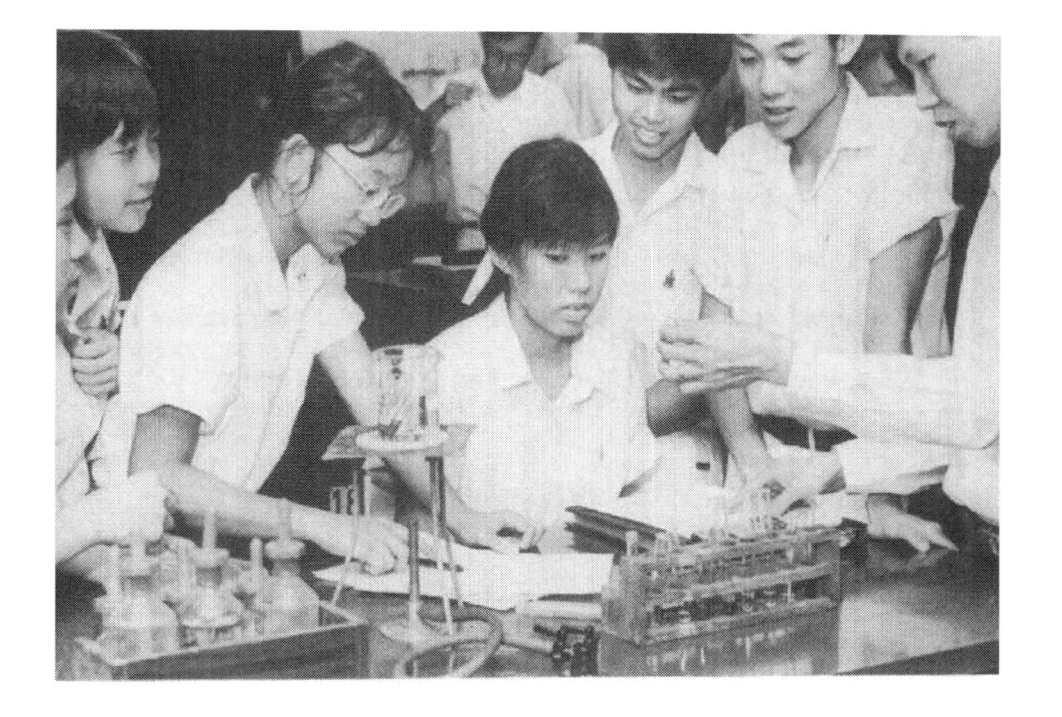

Raffles Junior College chemistry laboratory
Courtesy Singapore Ministry of Communications and Information

tripling in fifteen years. The largest and most prestigious institution was the National University of Singapore, enrolling 13,238 undergraduates in 1987. Only half of those who applied to the National University were admitted, a degree of selectivity that in 1986 brought parliamentary complaints that the admission rate was inconsistent with the government's objective of developing every citizen to the fullest potential.

The Ministry of Education tried to coordinate enrollments in universities and polytechnic institutes and specific degree and diploma courses with estimates of national manpower requirements. At the university level, the majority of the students were enrolled in engineering, science, and vocationally oriented courses. The Ministry of Education and the government clearly preferred an education system that turned out people with vocational qualifications to one producing large numbers of general liberal arts graduates. The ministry attempted to persuade students and their parents that enrollment in the three polytechnic institutes, which offered diplomas rather than the more prestigious degrees (a common distinction in the British system of higher education), was not necessarily a second choice. In promoting this choice, the ministry pointed to the good salaries and excellent career prospects of polytechnic graduates who were employed by large multinational corporations. Similar arguments were used to persuade those who left secondary school with respectable O level scores to enroll in short courses at vocational and technical training institutes and to qualify for such positions as electronics technicians or word processors that were beyond the capabilities of those who had been directed into vocational schools after the primary grades. Almost all of the graduates of the demanding four-year Honors Degree Liberal Arts and Social Science program at the National University of Singapore were recruited into the upper levels of the civil service. Many graduates of the ordinary three-year arts, social science, and science programs were steered into teaching in secondary schools.

Education and Singaporean Identity

More clearly than any other social institution, the school system expressed the distinctive vision of Singapore's leadership, with its stress on merit, competition, technology, and international standards, and its rejection of special privileges for any group. Singaporeans of all ethnic groups and classes came together in the schools, and the education system affected almost every family in significant and profound ways. Most of the domestic political issues of the country, such as the relations between ethnic groups, the competition for elite status, the plans for the future security of the nation and its people, and the distribution of scarce resources were reflected in the schools and in education policy. Many of the settled education policies of the 1980s, such as the use of English as the medium of instruction, the conversion of formerly Malay or Chinese or Anglican missionary schools to standard government schools, or the attempted combination of open access with strict examinations, were the result of long-standing political disputes and controversy. In the determination of families and parents that their children should succeed in school, and in the universally acknowledged ranking of primary and secondary schools and the struggle to enroll children in those schools that achieved the best examination results, families expressed their distinctive values and goals. The struggle for achievement in the schools, which often included tutoring by parents or enrollment of young children in special private supplementary schools to prepare for crucial examinations, also demonstrated the system of social stratification and the struggle for mobility that characterized the modern society. It was in the schools, more than in any other institution, that the abstract values of multiracialism and of Singaporean identity were given concrete form.

* * *

The Information Division of the Ministry of Communications and Information produces useful and informative annual volumes and monthly journals, such as *Singapore 1988, Singapore Facts and Pictures 1988, Mirror,* and the *Singapore Bulletin.* The Department of Sociology of the National University of Singapore and the Institute of Southeast Asian Studies both publish social science and historical research on Singapore's society. Maurice Freedman's *Chinese Family and Marriage in Singapore* and Judith Djamour's *Malay Kinship and Marriage in Singapore,* both based on field research conducted in 1949–50, provide a baseline for assessing subsequent social change. Cheng Lim-Keak's *Social Change and the Chinese in Singapore* analyzes the associations and economic organization of the Chinese-speaking community, a topic not covered in government reports. Janet W. Salaff's *State and Family in Singapore,* which concentrates on Chinese families, and Tania Li's *Malays in Singapore* both analyze family structure in the context of economic growth and modernization. Although somewhat dated, the essays in *Singapore: Society in Transition,* edited by Riaz Hassan, provide a good introduction to major aspects of Singapore society. Some of the flavor of life in Singapore is conveyed in Tan Kok Seng's autobiographical *Son of Singapore* and in the fiction of Philip Jeyaretnam, such as *First Loves* and *Raffles Place Ragtime.* The *Far Eastern Economic Review* regularly covers events and trends in Singapore, sometimes illuminating topics such as religious change that are not treated in official publications. (For further information and complete citations, see Bibliography.)

Chapter 3. The Economy

Harbor workboats at mooring

A FORMER COLONIAL TRADING PORT serving the regional economies of maritime Southeast Asia, Singapore in the 1990s aspired to be a "global city" serving world markets and major multinational corporations. A quarter century after independence in 1965, the city-state had become a manufacturing center with one of the highest incomes in the region and a persistent labor shortage. As one of Asia's four "little dragons" or newly industrializing economies (NIEs—see Glossary), Singapore along with the Republic of Korea (South Korea), Taiwan, and Hong Kong was characterized by an export-oriented economy, relatively equitable income distribution, trade surpluses with the United States and other developed countries, and a common heritage of Chinese civilization and Confucian values. The small island had no resources other than its strategic location and the skills of its nearly 2.7 million people. In 1988 it claimed a set of economic superlatives, including the world's busiest port, the world's highest rate of annual economic growth (11 percent), and the world's highest savings rate (42 percent of income).

Singapore lived by international trade, as it had since its founding in 1819, and operated as a free port with free markets. Its small population and dependence on international markets meant that regional and world markets were larger than domestic markets, which presented both business managers and government policymakers with distinctive economic challenges and opportunities. In 1988 the value of Singapore's international trade was more than three times its gross domestic product (GDP—see Glossary). The country's year-to-year economic performance fluctuated unpredictably with the cycles of world markets, which were beyond the control or even the influence of Singapore's leaders. In periods of growing international trade, such as the 1970s, Singapore could reap great gains, but even relatively minor downturns in world trade could produce deep recession in the Singapore economy, as happened in 1985–86. The country's dependence on and vulnerability to international markets shaped the economic strategies of Singapore's leaders.

The economy in the 1980s rested on five major sectors: the regional entrepôt trade; export-oriented manufacturing; petroleum refining and shipping; production of goods and services for the domestic economy; and the provision of specialized services for the international market, such as banking and finance, telecommunications, and tourism. The spectacular growth of manufacturing in the 1970s and 1980s had a major impact on the economy and the society, but tended to obscure what carried over from the economic structure of the past. Singapore's economy always depended on international trade and on the sale of services. An entrepôt was essentially a provider of services such as wholesaling, warehousing, sorting and processing, credit, currency exchange, risk management, ship repair and provisioning, business information, and the adjudication of commercial disputes. In this perspective, which focused on exchange and processing, the 1980s assembly of electronic components and manufacture of precision optical instruments were evolutionary steps from the nineteenth-century sorting and grading of pepper and rubber. Both processes used the skills of Singaporeans to add value to commodities that were produced elsewhere and destined for consumption outside the city-state.

The dependence on external markets and suppliers pushed Singapore toward economic openness, free trade, and free markets. In the 1980s, Singapore was a free port with only a few revenue tariffs and a small set of protective tariffs scheduled for abolition in the 1990s. It had no foreign exchange controls or domestic price controls. There were no controls on private enterprise or investment, nor any limitations on profit remittance or repatriation of capital. Foreign corporations were welcome, foreign investment was solicited, and fully 70 percent of the investment in manufacturing was foreign. The government provided foreign and domestic enterprises with a high-quality infrastructure, efficient and graft-free administration, and a sympathetic concern for the problems of businesses.

The vulnerability inherent in heavy dependence on outside markets impelled Singapore's leaders to buffer their country's response to perturbations in world markets and to take advantage of their country's ability to respond to changing economic conditions. Unable to control so much that affected their nation's prosperity, they concentrated on those domestic institutions that could be controlled. The consequence was an economy characterized by a seemingly paradoxical adherence to free trade and free markets in combination with a dominant government role in macroeconomic management and government control of major factors of production such as land, labor, and capital. The extraordinarily high domestic savings rate provided reserves to weather such economic storms as trade recessions and generated a pool of domestically controlled capital that could be invested to serve the long-term interests of Singapore rather than of foreign corporations. The high savings rate, however, was the result of carefully formulated government

Singapore River in the mid-1960s
Courtesy Daniel Regan

programs, which included a compulsory contribution of up to 25 percent of all salaries to a government-controlled pension fund. The government held about 75 percent of the country's land, was the largest single employer, controlled the level of wages, and housed about 88 percent of the population in largely self-owned apartments. It also operated a set of wholly-owned government enterprises and held stock in additional domestic and foreign firms. Government leaders, deeply aware of Singapore's need to sell its services in a competitive international market, continually stressed the necessity for the citizens to master high levels of skills and to subordinate their personal wishes to the good of the community. The combination of devotion to free-market principles and the need for internal control and discipline in order to adapt to the demands of markets reminded observers of many family firms, and residents of the country commonly referred to it as Singapore Inc.

Patterns of Development

Modern Singapore, founded as a trading post of the British East India Company in 1819, achieved its initial economic success as an entrepôt because of the island's location, harbor, and free port status (see Founding and Early Years, 1819–26, ch. 1). Although

Singapore at first served only as a center for trade and transshipment, by the early twentieth century, primary goods, mainly rubber and tin from the neighboring Malay Peninsula, were being imported for processing. Singapore also became a regional center for the distribution of European manufactured goods. After World War I, when the British established a naval base on the island, Singapore became a key element of the British Commonwealth of Nations (see Glossary) military defense east of India, thus adding the naval support industry to the island's economy.

In the period immediately after World War II, Singapore faced enormous problems, including labor and social unrest, a decaying, war-ravaged infrastructure, inadequate housing and community facilities, a slow economic growth rate, low wages, and high unemployment made worse by a rapidly expanding population (see Aftermath of War, 1945-55, ch. 1). As late as 1959, the unemployment rate was estimated at 13.5 percent. The struggle for survival in the postwar period deeply affected the economic decision making of Singapore's first generation leaders.

Mounting political pressure for independence from Britain culminated in 1963 in the merger of Malaya, Singapore, and the British northern Borneo territories of Sabah and Sarawak into the new nation of Malaysia. A combination of political and ethnic differences between Singapore and the national government, however, led in 1965 to Singapore's separation from Malaysia and establishment as an independent nation. The economic prospects of the new city-state at first appeared bleak. Upon separation from Malaysia, Singapore lost its economic hinterland and jeopardized its hopes for an enlarged domestic market to absorb the goods produced by a small but growing manufacturing sector. Moreover, Indonesia's policy of Confrontation (Konfrontasi—see Glossary) with Malaysia between 1963 and 1966 had substantially reduced Singapore's entrepôt trade (see Road to Independence, 1955-65, ch. 1).

Britain's announcement in 1968 of its intention to withdraw military forces from Singapore by the early 1970s marked the beginning of a greatly expanded, more intrusive role for the government in the economy. From then on, the government no longer confined itself to such traditional economic pursuits as improving the infrastructure, but instead began to engage in activities that were or could have been the domain of private enterprise (see fig. 6). Britain's departure meant the loss, directly or indirectly, of 38,000 jobs (20 percent of the work force) at a time of already rising unemployment and rapid population growth; a consequent reduction in the GDP; and an increase in Singapore's own budgetary defense allocation to compensate for the British withdrawal. Even so, the

S$1,616 (for value of the Singapore dollar—see Glossary) per capita income of Singapore in 1965 already was quite high by developing country standards, an indication that subsequent high growth rates were not merely a result of beginning at a low base.

The period from 1965 to 1973 witnessed unprecedented economic growth for the island nation, during which the average annual growth of real GDP was 12.7 percent. Major credit for this development must be given to the effective implementation of soundly conceived government policies, which from the outset took full account of Singapore's strengths and weaknesses. Furthermore, the time was right for structural change in the economy. Enough capital had been accumulated to permit the domestic production of goods that were more capital intensive. The government's economic response to separation from Malaysia and the withdrawal of British military forces included efforts to increase industrial growth and solve the domestic problems of unemployment, population growth, and housing. Growth was achieved because workers were added to the payroll and provided with better machinery with which to work. Even more remarkable, this growth was accomplished with an outstanding record of price stability. Inflation was kept low by the government's conservative fiscal policies, which included the maintenance of strict control over the money supply.

Industrialization promised the most economic progress. The strategic question was whether to rely principally on domestic entrepreneurs or to make a conscious effort to attract foreign direct investment. The decision to encourage the latter resulted both in a large share of Singaporean manufacturing being foreign-owned and a high degree of export-led growth. Singapore's reliance on multinational corporations of the world to provide the necessary investment meant less dependence on the Southeast Asian region generally and neighboring countries particularly.

The 1973 oil shock with the collapse of prices and the worldwide recession it triggered brought the end of the super growth period. Even so, Singapore's growth rate averaged 8.7 percent from 1973 to 1979, which was high compared with other countries during that same period. Manufacturing continued to grow as did transportation and communications. Although the second worldwide oil crisis, beginning in 1979, set off the longest and deepest recession in the industrialized countries since the Great Depression of the 1930s, Singapore was seemingly untouched. If anything, its economy grew in 1980–81 while the world economy was contracting. The real average GDP growth rate between 1979 and 1981 was 8.5 percent. Financial and business services joined manufacturing as the major economic engines. During this period, Singapore's

Singapore: A Country Study

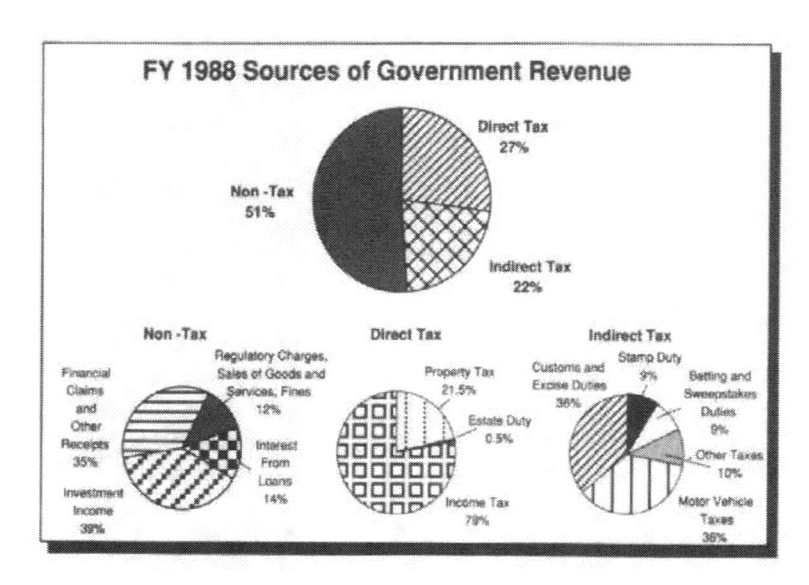

Source: Based on information from "Country Watch: Singapore," *Asian Finance*, Hong Kong, 15, No. 9, September 15, 1989, 83.

Figure 6. Sources of Government Revenue, Fiscal Year (FY) 1988

function as a petroleum-servicing entrepôt made it more like an oil producer than an oil consumer.

For the first two decades of its independence, Singapore enjoyed continuous high economic growth, largely outperforming the world economy. Its GDP growth rate never fell below 5 percent and rose as high as 15 percent. At the same time, Singapore managed to maintain an inflation rate below world averages.

Given Singapore's dependence on the world economy, however, the consequences of declining foreign demand were inevitable. The 1985 recession was the worst in the nation's history. Singapore staggered under a year of negative growth (−1.5 percent), then recovered slightly in 1986 (+1.9 percent). The causes lay both outside and within the country. Externally, worldwide slumps in petroleum-related and marine-related sectors were reflected in reduced demand for Singapore's goods and services and raised the specter of worldwide overcapacity in shipbuilding and shiprepairing. Furthermore, the slowdown in demand for semiconductors and electronics in the United States sharply reduced demand for Singaporean components and parts.

Internally, the construction boom—which had produced a glut of hotels, shopping centers, and apartments—began to be reversed.

Domestic demand also weakened as a result of a rise in domestic savings, which was not matched by a rise in productive domestic investment. The situation was complicated by a loss of international competitiveness and a profit squeeze attributed to labor costs rising faster than productivity.

The government responded promptly and firmly by lowering employer contributions to the Central Provident Fund, freezing overall wage levels for 1986 and 1987, reducing corporate income taxes from 40 to 30 percent, reducing personal income taxes in line with corporate taxes, and introducing an across-the-board investment allowance of 30 percent to encourage greater investment in equipment and machinery (see Forced Savings and Capital Formation; Finance, this ch.). These measures were highly successful; costs dropped 30 percent and productivity climbed. By 1988 Singapore's economy had rebounded.

Economic Roles of the Government

Budgeting and Planning

Although Singapore billed itself as a free-enterprise economy, the economic role of government was pervasive. As governing body for both the nation and the city, the government was responsible for planning and budgeting for everything from international finance to trash collection. The government owned, controlled, regulated, or allocated land, labor, and capital resources. It set or influenced many of the prices on which private investors based business calculations and investment decisions.

State intervention in the economy had a positive impact not only on private business profitability but also on the general welfare of the population. Beyond the jobs created in the private and public sectors, the government provided subsidized housing, education, and health and recreational services, as well as public transportation. The government also managed the bulk of savings for retirement through the Central Provident Fund and Post Office Savings Bank. It also decided annual wage increments and set minimum fringe benefits in the public and private sectors. State responsibility for workers' welfare won the government the support of the population, thus guaranteeing the political stability that encouraged private investment. In general, state intervention in the economy managed to be probusiness without being antilabor, at least regarding material welfare.

Budgeting and taxation were frequently used for attaining economic goals. In the postrecession period, budgetary changes primarily benefited business. For example, the fiscal year (FY—see Glossary)

Singapore: A Country Study

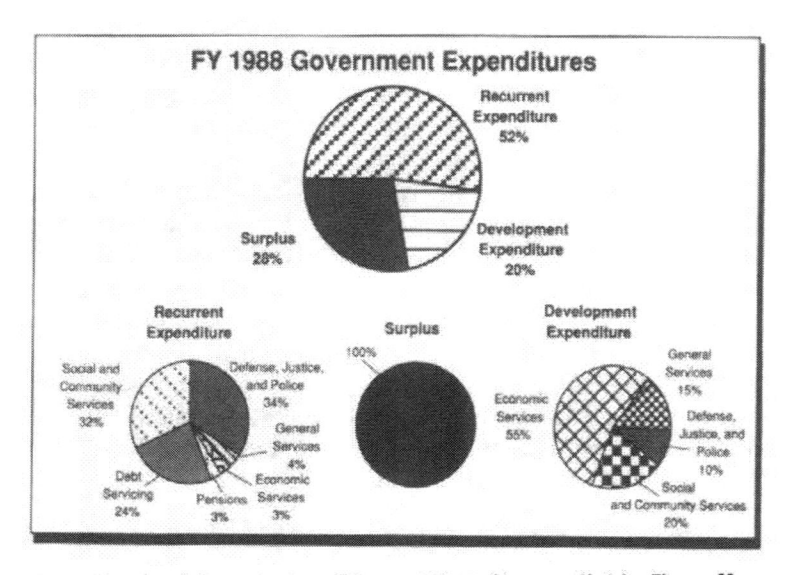

Source: Based on information from "Country Watch: Singapore," *Asian Finance*, Hong Kong, 15, No. 9, September 15, 1989, 83; and Singapore, Ministry of Trade and Industry, *Economic Survey of Singapore, Second Quarter 1989*, Singapore, 1989, 53.

Figure 7. *Government Expenditures, Fiscal Year (FY) 1988*

1988 budget included an overseas investment incentive program, administered by the Economic Development Board, allowing tax write-offs for losses from approved overseas investments (see fig. 7). Other concessions such as suspension of taxes on utilities and a 50 percent rebate on property taxes were in effect between 1985 and 1988 to counteract the economic slump.

Budgeting and taxation also were often used to achieve or reinforce social goals such as population control. Until 1984 the government encouraged limiting of families to two children by levying higher medical and education costs for additional children. In 1986, however, tax rebates were introduced to encourage college-educated women to have third and fourth children.

Economic Boards

Under the appropriate government ministries, statutory boards—a concept carried over from colonial days—were established to manage specific parts of the economy and foster overall and sectoral development. Each worked somewhat autonomously, using a hands-on approach to the problems in the areas in which it operated.

Economic Development Board

The Economic Development Board was established in 1961 to spearhead Singapore's industrialization. Initially its function was to promote industrial investment, develop and manage industrial estates, and provide medium- and long-term industrial financing. The latter function was taken over in 1968 by the newly created Development Bank of Singapore (see Financial Center Development, this ch.). When the limits of import substitution became evident, given the small domestic market, policy was redirected toward promoting an export-oriented, labor-intensive industrialization program. After 1986 the board's portfolio was enlarged to include the promotion of services in partnership with other government agencies responsible for the various service sectors and the development of local small- and medium-sized enterprises. In the first two decades following independence, the board evolved industrial strategies in response to changes in the international and domestic business environments, and negotiated the public-private consensus necessary for implementing them. The board was not an economic czardom but, rather, a consensus maker among agencies and corporations that commanded larger financing. In 1989 the Economic Development Board focused its attention on attracting investments in manufacturing and other high value-added services, which met the technological skills and employment needs of Singapore's future economic development.

Small Enterprise Bureau

The Small Enterprise Bureau was established in 1986, following the economic slump, when the government realized the importance of developing and upgrading local small- and medium-sized enterprises. The bureau worked closely with the Economic Development Board and managed a number of assistance programs, some of which predated the bureau. Emphasis was placed on helping local firms to improve and modernize their plants and technology, product design, management skills, and marketing capabilities. Launched in 1976, the Small Industry Finance Scheme provided low-cost financing to local small- and medium-sized enterprises in manufacturing and related support services. In 1985 this program was extended to the nonmanufacturing sector, and in 1987 some 1,125 loans amounting to S$297 million were approved by the Economic Development Board under the plan. The Small Industry Technical Assistance Scheme, introduced in 1982, provided grants to defray part of the cost of engaging short-term consultants and increasing or establishing in-service training for employees.

National Productivity Board

The National Productivity Board was established in 1972 to improve productivity in all sectors of the economy. Increasing individual and company productivity at all levels was a government priority, given Singapore's full employment picture and relatively high wages. Greater worker productivity than the country's neighbors and competitors was viewed by the government as a necessity as well as one of Singapore's major advantages.

The National Productivity Board followed a "total productivity" approach, which emphasized productivity measurement, product quality, a flexible wage system, worker training, and assistance to small- and medium-sized enterprises. In order to promote productivity in both the public and private sectors, the board used mass media publicity, seminars, conventions, and publications to remind Singaporeans that productivity must be a permanent pillar of the economy. The board sponsored a productivity campaign each year with such slogans as the one for 1988, "Train Up—Be the Best You Can Be."

The National Productivity Board offered management guidance services to small- and medium-sized enterprises to assist them in improving their productivity and efficiency, as well as referring companies to private management consultancy services available in Singapore. Beginning in the early 1980s, the board also spearheaded campaigns to introduce productivity management techniques used extensively by Japanese business and industry, such as quality control circles.

Trade Development Board

Changes in world trade patterns and in what the government viewed as an increasingly protectionist international trade environment prompted the establishment of the Trade Development Board in 1983 as a national trade promotion agency. Based on the recommendations of specialists, the board formulated policies reflecting the needs of traders in general, as well as the specific needs of particular trade sectors. Initial areas of focus were trade facilitation of electronics, printing and publishing, textiles, and timber products. The Trade Development Board reviewed existing marketing policies, strategies, and techniques and explored new opportunities in both traditional and nontraditional markets. The board assisted both local and foreign companies interested in using Singapore as a base for such trading activities as warehousing and distribution. The Trade Development Board also helped

Singapore companies market their products by assisting them in improving their product designs.

Land Management and Development

One of the government's most important roles was the oversight of land use and development. This was a particularly critical issue given the country's minute size and dense population; a total land area of 636 square kilometers and a population density of 4,166 per square kilometer made Singapore one of the most densely populated countries in the world (see Population, ch. 2). As pressure for economic growth increased, optimization of land use became more critical.

Housing and Development Board

Central to the issue of land management was another statutory board, the Housing and Development Board, established in 1960. Between 1960 and 1985, the government-owned board completed more than 500,000 high-rise, high-density public housing apartments—known as housing estates—along with their related facilities. By comparison, the British colonial government's Singapore Improvement Trust had completed only 23,000 apartments in its thirty-two years of existence (1927-59). From 1974 to 1982, the Housing and Development Board built and marketed middle-income apartments, an activity that became a function of the board after 1982.

By 1988 the Housing and Development Board was providing housing and related facilities for 88 percent of Singaporeans, or some 2.3 million people—a feat that has been called urban Singapore's equivalent of "land reform." Government encouragement of apartment ownership was both an economic and a "nation building" goal because individual ownership would ultimately pay for the program while giving citizens a "stake in Singapore." The board also provided estate management services and played an active role in promoting the advancement of construction technology. As one of the country's major domestic industries, housing construction served as an important economic pump primer.

Home owners were encouraged to use their Central Provident Fund savings to pay for the apartments. The factors determining the selling prices of apartments included location, construction cost, ability of the applicants to pay, and the practical limits to government subsidies. Resettlement policies aimed at equitable payments, minimal readjustment, and real improvement in housing conditions. In social terms, attention was paid to providing an environment conducive to community living, integrating the population, preserving the traditional Asian family structure, and encouraging upward social mobility by providing opportunities for home upgrading.

Starting with a capital expenditure of S$10 million in 1960, the Housing and Development Board's annual capital expenditures rose to about S$4 billion by 1985. The board's capital budget, with funds obtained in the form of low-interest government loans, represented 40 percent of the government's capital budget. Selling prices, rent rates, and maintenance charges were determined by the government, and the board received an annual subsidy of 1 to 2 percent of the government's main operating expenditure.

Urban Renewal Authority

In 1974 the Housing and Development Board's Urban Renewal Department was made a statutory board and named the Urban Renewal Authority. Responsible for slum clearance and comprehensive development of the city's Central Area, the authority was to plan, guide, and implement urban renewal. The Urban Renewal Authority drew up long-term land-use plans, which it implemented through its own development projects as well as the Sale of Sites Programme. The latter, a key instrument in the government's comprehensive redevelopment plans, represented a partnership between the public and private sectors. The public sector provided initiative, expertise, and infrastructural services; the private sector contributed financial resources and entrepreneurship to facilitate the completion of projects. Between 1967 and 1983, some 166 parcels of land were turned into 143 projects for residential, office, shopping, hotel, entertainment, and industrial developments.

Jurong Town Corporation

The primary responsibility for acquiring, developing, and managing industrial sites, however, belonged to the Jurong Town Corporation, established in 1968. The corporation provided manufacturers with their choice of industrial land sites on which to build their own factories or ready-built factories for the immediate start-up of manufacturing operations. In the 1950s, when the idea of establishing an industrial estate was first conceived, Jurong was an area of dense tropical forests and mangrove swamps on the southwestern quadrant of the island, and it was not until 1960 that the government decided to undertake the project. During the first few years, entrepreneurial response was disappointing, but after independence the pace of development accelerated. By 1989 Jurong had quadrupled its original size, and the corporation also managed twenty-three other industrial estates, including the Singapore Science Park, a research and development park adjacent to the National University of Singapore. Although the emphasis in the 1970s had been on the development of labor-intensive industries, in the 1980s priority was given to upgrading facilities to make them more attractive for the establishment of high value-added and high technology industries.

The industrial estates were designed to be self-contained urban centers and included such facilities as golf courses, banks, shopping centers, restaurants, child-care centers, and parks. As of 1988, they contained some 3,600 factories employing a total of 216,000 workers. The Jurong Town Corporation also provided infrastructure and support facilities, including the Jurong Industrial Port, which was the country's main bulk cargo gateway, and the Jurong Marine Base, which serviced offshore petroleum operations.

The Jurong Town Corporation shared responsibility for coastal planning and development control with the Housing and Development Board, the Urban Renewal Authority, and the Port of Singapore Authority. The coastal zone, dominated by its entrepôt facilities, was the traditional foundation on which Singapore's economy was built. Between 1965 and 1987, the coastal zone was enlarged by about fifty square kilometers through reclamation of tidal flats, shallow lagoons, and wetlands. The two largest landfill operations were the East and the West Coast Reclamation schemes adjoining the Central Business District. The former was the Housing and Development Board's largest project, in which a "sea city" almost the size of the present-day downtown area had been developed by both the private and public sector. Experts estimated that in the 1980s Singapore, including the offshore islands, had the potential of increasing its existing land resources by about 10 percent.

Forced Savings and Capital Formation

Singapore's much-vaunted savings rate—and much of the funding for development, particularly public housing—resulted in large measure from mandatory contributions to the Central Provident Fund, as well as voluntary deposits in the Post Office Savings Bank. The Central Provident Fund was set up in 1955 as a compulsory national social security savings plan to ensure the financial security of all workers either retired or no longer able to work. Both worker and employer contributed to the employee's account with the fund. The rate of contribution, which had gradually risen to 50 percent of the employee's gross wage (coming equally from employer and employee), was lowered to 35 percent in 1986. In 1987 new long-term contribution rates were set calling for 40 percent for employees below fifty-five years of age, 25 percent for those fifty-five to fifty-nine, 15 percent for those sixty to sixty-four, and 10 percent for those over sixty-five, with equal contributions coming from employee and employer. A series of transition rates leading to the new long-term rates were first applied in 1988. The contributions were tax-exempt and subject to maximum limits based on a salary ceiling. Beginning in 1986, the government paid a market-based interest rate on Central Provident Fund savings (3.19 percent per year in June 1988).

Every employed Singaporean or permanent resident was automatically a member of the Central Provident Fund, although some self-employed people were not. Membership grew from 180,000 in 1955 to 2.08 million in 1989. At the end of 1988, the 2.06 million members of the fund had S$32.5 billion to their credit. That same year, a total of S$2,776 million was withdrawn to purchase residential properties; S$9.8 million was paid under the Home Protection Insurance Scheme; S$1,059 million was paid under the Approved Investments Scheme; and S$13.7 million was withdrawn for the purchase of nonresidential properties.

Each member actually held three accounts with the Central Provident Fund: Ordinary, Special, and, since the mid-1980s, Medisave Accounts. The first two were primarily for old age and contingencies such as permanent disability. The Ordinary Account, in addition, could be used at any time to buy residential properties, under various Housing and Development Board programs, and for home protection and dependents' protection insurance. Two further programs were established in 1987: a Minimum Sum Scheme, which established a base amount to be retained in the account against retirement, and a Topping-up Extension under which, as well as adding to their own, members could demonstrate "filial piety" by adding to their parents' accounts. Since the late 1980s, members could use their accounts to buy approved shares, loan stocks, unit trusts, and gold for investment. Part of the rationale for the latter was to allow Singaporeans to diversify their savings and to gain experience in financial decision making.

Although comparable to social security programs in some Western countries, the Central Provident Fund's concept and administration differed. Rather than having the younger generation pay in while the older generation withdrew, whatever was put into the Central Provident Fund by or for a member was guaranteed returnable to that person with interest.

Thus, at the individual level, Central Provident Fund savings promoted personal and familial self-reliance and financial protection, an economic attitude constantly encouraged by government leaders. Collectively, the Central Provident Fund savings assured the government of an enormous, relatively cheap "piggy bank" for funding public-sector development; the savings also served as a mechanism for curtailing private consumption, thereby limiting inflation. The result, according to some critics, was that the city-state had become overendowed with buildings, with too few productive businesses to put in them. They also noted that the bloated size of the Central Provident Fund (S$32.5 billion in 1988, equivalent to 82 percent of the GDP) was the most important factor behind the unwieldiness of public savings. Some analysts advised that the fund was beginning to outlive its usefulness and should be dismantled and replaced by private pension funds and health insurance plans. As a result, they stated, savings would be channeled to private businessmen rather than to bureaucrats.

State-Owned Enterprises

Over time, the statutory boards not only became major actors in the economy but also formed subsidiary companies to add flexibility to their own operations. For example, in 1986 the Singapore Broadcasting Corporation formed a subsidiary to produce commercials on a fee-for-service basis. The government entered other areas of the economy that it considered appropriate, exerting leadership, assuming risk, and not hesitating to withdraw its support or close down unprofitable companies.

Numerous state and quasi-state companies were created either directly by ministries or, more often, organized under three wholly owned government holding companies (Temasek Holdings (Private) Limited, MND Holdings, and Sheng-Li Holding Company), which provided a wide range of goods and services. Joint ventures between the government and both domestic and foreign partners produced several industrial products, including steel and refined sugar. In addition, the National Trades Union Congress (NTUC), which was closely tied to the government, ran many cooperative businesses, including supermarkets, taxis, and a travel agency.

Although these companies collectively contributed significantly to the growth of the economy, neither their total amount of profits nor their rate of return on investment could be documented. In 1983 some 450 such companies, excluding subsidiaries of the statutory boards, employed 58,000 workers, or 5 percent of the labor force. In 1986 there were approximately 500 such companies still active. These different institutional forms permitted versatility.

Public Utilities

The Public Utilities Board, established in May 1963, was responsible for providing the country's utility services. At the turn of a faucet, potable water was available throughout the country. All parts of the main island and several offshore islands were supplied with electricity. About one in three households used piped gas.

In its early years, Singapore depended on wells for its water supply. By the mid-nineteenth century, however, wells were inadequate to supply the needs of a booming seaport and the ships that called there, and a series of reservoir and waterworks projects were undertaken. By the late 1980s, the water supply system consisted of eighteen raw water reservoirs, twelve service reservoirs, eleven waterworks, and about 4,000 kilometers of pipeline. Although some water came from rainfall trapped in catchment basins, much of the country's supply was imported from Malaysia and piped into the reservoir system. Consequently, water was a precious resource, and domestic and commercial consumers were constantly advised to use it efficiently.

Electricity was made available to the public for the first time in 1906. It was purchased from Singapore Tramway Company and distributed to consumers in the main town areas. The demand escalated from 39,613 kilowatt-hours in 1906 to about 13 billion kilowatt-hours in 1988. The first power station, commissioned in 1926, had a generating capacity of two megawatts. In 1988 electricity was generated at four power stations with a total installed generating capacity of 3,371 megawatts. From these stations, electricity was distributed to consumers through more than 4,900 substations and a network of more than 23,000 kilometers of main cables. To meet the increasing demand, a second stage was required for the Pulau Seraya Power Station, the first power station to be sited on an offshore island. Its Stage II, having a generating capacity of 750 megawatts, was scheduled to have its first 250-megawatt generating unit operational in early 1992 and to be completed in 1993. Because all fuel oil used for electricity generation had to be imported, energy conservation was encouraged.

The first gasworks started in Kallang in 1862 using coal as feedstock. In the late 1980s, gas was manufactured from naphtha, a pollution-free fuel, by six gas-making plants at the Kallang Gasworks. To meet the increasing demand, a S$4.3 million plant was scheduled for completion in 1989 to replace an older, smaller plant. Gas was piped to consumers through about 1,800 kilometers of gas main extending over major areas of Singapore. Of the total gas production in 1988 of 681 million units, about 46 percent

Singapore coffee plantation, late nineteenth century
Courtesy Library of Congress

of gas sales went for domestic and 54 percent for commercial consumption.

Policies for the Future

Although the Singapore government took a long-range economic view, it steadfastly refused to draft five-year economic plans of fixed targets and objectives. Rather, its leaders preferred the freedom to change and adapt—coping with unforeseen crises or reacting to sudden global opportunities—a system that worked more often than it failed. As needed, detailed plans were formulated, policies reorganized, and programs implemented. According to the 1986 Report of the Economic Committee, however, economic planning for the 1990s and beyond would require new strategies. Certain fundamental goals, including "good government, efficient infrastructure, education, free enterprise, and flexibility," would remain, but long-term competitiveness would depend on new initiatives. As a result of the report, Singapore announced plans to become an "international total business center for manufacturing and services" and a major exporter of services, focused on information technology (see Information Technology, this ch.).

To lay further groundwork for the next century, the National Productivity Board in 1989 instituted Productivity 2000, a plan for adjusting management styles and work attitudes to deal with a variety of factors expected to exert pressure on the economy in the coming decades. These anticipated factors included slower economic growth resulting from stiffening trade barriers and increasing world competition for foreign investors and markets, slower productivity growth and pressure to tie wage increases to productivity increases, the need to increase capital investments for technology and machinery, the changing labor force profile, and increased standards of living resulting in higher expectations for improvement in the quality of work-life (see Manpower and Labor, this ch.).

In planning for the economic future, the government placed the ultimate burden for continued sacrifice on all Singaporeans: "It is true," an article published in the national magazine *Mirror* in 1988 informed citizens, "that in the past few decades we have all been too easy in choosing the soft options. We gave in to demands without insisting on responsibilities... specifically responsibilities of productivity. This is true both domestically and internationally. It is not possible anymore."

Privatization

Privatization was the long-term government policy that ultimately could have the most effect on the structure of the economy and the lives of Singaporeans. At one level, privatization represented the government's decision, articulated in the 1986 Report of the Economic Committee, that the economy had sufficiently matured for the private sector to become the primary engine. Since government-owned enterprises had "been successful in their respective areas of endeavor and should continue to be so," the government no longer needed to continue running them. In 1987 a government-appointed committee, the Private Sector Investment Committee, issued a report recommending the sale of shares in 41 of the approximately 500 state-backed firms, ranging from Singapore Airlines (SIA) to the national lottery, while retaining more than half the value of the share. SIA shares subsequently went public, although the government retained control. Sale of four statutory boards, including the telecommunications monopoly, was also recommended in the proposed ten-year divestment plan.

At another level, privatization meant that, over time, Singapore intended to divest itself of the loss-making functions of government—chiefly the responsibility for subsidizing housing and health care—the burden of which would increasingly be shifted to private employers and the workers themselves. Examples of the likely trend were the addition of Medisave and the topping-up plans to the Central Provident Fund package. The government was increasingly unable, given escalating costs, to provide subsidized social services to match the ever-rising demands and expectations of the population. The result might be called a shift from "state welfarism" to "company welfarism."

Singapore's younger leaders seemed particularly in favor of privatization. Although they approved of the near-monopoly on political life maintained by the People's Action Party (PAP), they expressed fear that Singaporeans were growing far too dependent on the government and expected it to solve their problems.

Through privatization the state was changing its role from that of direct provider of social and business amenities to that of director and overseer of a much wider range of private, social, and business institutions. The strategy was not without problems, however. One of the most difficult questions was what effect privatization would have on the management of the divested companies and on the statutory boards. Since the government had absorbed the "best and brightest" into the civil service, there was a critical shortage of private-sector top-level entrepreneurial talent. Moreover, even if the plan were carried out fully, the government would still maintain control in many areas of industry and services because more than half the value of shares of state firms would remain under government control, a partial divestment at best.

Economist Linda Y.C. Lim had suggested in 1983 that, despite the success of its state development policies, the government itself had succumbed to the free-market ideology and believed that its so-called Second Industrial Revolution in the mid-1970s—upgrading technology and moving upmarket—required dismantling much of the state apparatus rather than divesting itself of its profit-making functions. She also warned that the shift would likely also mean more interference by the government in companies' internal production and employment decisions. The new policy, Lim contended, could also inhibit rather than enhance free-market adjustments in the labor market: labor and management would be locked into benefits derived from a particular company, which in turn could adversely affect productivity. Singapore's spectacular economic success, Lim asserted, was the result more of state intervention than of the free market. "Privatization—the reduction of the state's responsibility for social welfare—will further limit free market adjustments and personal freedoms, and possibly pose a threat to continued economic success while undermining the government's political support on which both political stability and labor

Singapore: A Country Study

peace—the strongest investment attractions of Singapore—were based."

Economist Lawrence B. Krause suggested in 1987 that Singapore needed less government control of the economy, which could come about through the government's restraining itself from absorbing new investment opportunities and encouraging local private entrepreneurs to undertake the new investing. In time, this would likely produce a more vibrant economy.

Manpower and Labor

Singaporeans themselves were universally viewed as the nation's best natural resource. In 1989, however, the work force was a shrinking resource (see table 6, Appendix). The high rate of economic growth combined with an increasing number of Singaporeans over the retirement age of fifty-five (nearly 12 percent) and a lower-than-replacement birth rate had resulted in a significant labor shortage. By the end of the century, the labor market was projected to be even tighter. According to the Ministry of Health, the fifteen to twenty-nine age-group would decline 25 percent, from 816,000 in 1985 to 619,000 in the year 2000.

In 1987 and 1988, slightly more than six Singaporeans out of ten were working or looking for work. Men's rate of participation, 79 percent, remained steady. Women, however, responding to job opportunities in the manufacturing and commercial sectors, were increasingly entering the labor market (48 percent in 1988, up from 47 percent in 1987, 40 percent in 1978, and 24.6 percent in 1970). Job-switching was rampant, particularly in manufacturing, where a 1988 survey showed that three out of four new workers quit within the month they were hired. Higher wage and input costs, as well as job-switching, resulted in a decline in the growth of manufacturing productivity (2.4 percent in 1988 compared with 3.7 percent in 1987 and 13.6 in 1986). The labor market, then, was at the center of challenges facing the Singaporean economy. The nature of the concern about the labor market had been almost totally reversed since independence. The early 1960s were a time of labor unrest, and unemployment was still about 10 percent by 1965. By the late 1960s, however, there was substantial industrial peace, which had continued through the 1970s and 1980s. With unemployment at a very manageable 3.3 percent in 1988, the government's attention was focused on other aspects of the labor market.

Industrial Relations and Labor Unions

Industrial relations in Singapore reflected the symbiotic relationship between the labor movement and the dominant political party, the People's Action Party (PAP), a relationship rooted in a political history of confrontation that evolved into consensus building. Trade unions were a principal instrument in the anticolonial struggle used by both the democratic socialist PAP and the communists with whom they cooperated uneasily. In 1961 the Singapore Trade Union Congress split into the left-wing Singapore Association of Trade Unions (SATU) and the noncommunist National Trades Union Congress (NTUC). The NTUC quickly became the leading trade union organization, largely because of its effectiveness and government support. Moreover, in 1963, when SATU led a general strike against the government, the procommunist trade organization was banned and many of its leaders were arrested.

Strong personal ties between leaders of the PAP and the NTUC formed the background of the symbiotic relationship, which was institutionalized by formal links. In 1980 NTUC Secretary General Ong Teng Cheong was made a minister-without-portfolio, and a NTUC-PAP Liaison Committee comprising top leaders of both organizations was established. As the "second generation" political leaders assumed more government leadership following the 1984 election, Ong was named second deputy prime minister. Following the September 1988 general elections, the NTUC reaffirmed its close relationship with the PAP by expelling officers of NTUC-affiliated unions who had run for Parliament on opposition tickets. The NTUC and the PAP shared the same ideology, according to NTUC officials, so that active support of the opposition was inconsistent with membership in NTUC-related institutions. Workers who did not support the PAP were advised to form their own unions.

The legal-institutional framework also exerted control over labor conditions. In mid-1968, in an attempt to woo private foreign investment, Prime Minister Lee Kuan Yew successfully pushed through Parliament a new employment bill and amendments to the 1960 Industrial Relations Act. In order to make factors such as working hours, conditions of service, and fringe benefits predictable, and thus make businesses sufficiently attractive for investors, trade unions were barred from negotiating such matters as promotion, transfer, employment, dismissal, retrenchment, and reinstatement, issues that accounted for most earlier labor disputes. To spread work and help alleviate the effects of unemployment, overtime was limited and the compulsory retirement age was set at fifty-five. Lee's actions, which the militant unions opposed but could do little about, were part of the government's efforts to create in Singapore the conditions and laissez-faire atmosphere that had enabled Hong Kong to prosper. Such measures, in the government's view, were necessary to draw business to the port. Lee stressed survival, saying: "No one owes Singapore a living."

Rapid economic growth in the late 1960s and early 1970s reduced unemployment and resulted in the amendment of these laws. A National Wages Council was formed in 1972 and many of its recommendations adopted (see Wage Policies, this ch.). By 1984 a twelve-hour shift was permitted. In order to enlarge the limited labor pool, in 1988 changes were introduced in Central Provident Fund policies reducing payment rates for those over fifty-five, thereby encouraging employers to raise the retirement age to sixty. The discipline imposed on, and expected of, the labor force was accompanied by provisions for workers' welfare. The Industrial Arbitration Court existed to settle disputes through conciliation and arbitration. The court, established in 1960, played a major role in settling labor-management disputes through binding decisions based on formal hearings and through mediating voluntary agreements. Adjudication of disputes between employers and nonunion workers came under the separate jurisdiction of the Labour Court. To help job seekers, the government maintained a free employment service serving both job seekers and employers. A comprehensive code governed the safety and health of workers and provided a system of workers' compensation. Under the Ministry of Labour, the Factory Inspectorate enforced these provisions in factories, where more than 35 percent of Singapore's workers were employed in 1988.

The trade unions' role and structure also had been modified. In the 1970s, the NTUC began establishing cooperatives in order to promote the welfare of its members. In the 1980s, omnibus unions were split along industry lines and further split into house unions to facilitate better labor-management relations and promote company loyalty. In the 1982 Amendment to the Trade Union Act, the role of trade unions was defined as promoting good industrial relations between workers and employers; improving working conditions; and improving productivity for the mutual benefit of workers, employers, and the country.

Union membership declined steadily beginning in the late 1970s. In 1988 there were some 83 registered unions, with about 1,000 branch locals, representing one-quarter of the organizable work force. This number was down from ninety unions in 1977. Increasing emphasis on developing white-collar, capital-intensive, and service-oriented industries was partly responsible for the union membership decline. The unions were countering the decline by offering attractive packages to bring in new members.

Wage Policies

Following the rapid economic growth of the late 1960s and early 1970s, signs of a tight labor market emerged along with a concern that wages might escalate. In response, the government in 1972 established the National Wages Council, a tripartite forum with representation from the employers' federations, trade unions, and the government. As a government advisory body, the council recommended annual wage increases for the entire economy; ensured orderly wage development so as to promote economic and social progress; and assisted in the development of incentive schemes to improve national productivity.

The wage guidelines were not mandatory but were followed by the public sector (by far the largest employer) and widely implemented in the private sector. The influence of these recommendations generally was not applicable to private-sector professional and managerial workers, whose wages were determined more by international forces, but was more important for non-professional white-collar workers. For blue-collar workers, who constituted about 40 percent of the labor force in both the public and private sector, union influence was more crucial than the National Wages Council's recommendations, but market forces were even more important.

Between 1973 and 1979, actual wage increases followed the council recommended wage increases closely. In 1979 the "wage correction policy," in which there were three years of high-wage recommendations, was designed to force an increase of the productivity of higher value-added operations, to reduce the reliance on cheap unskilled foreign labor, and to rise labor productivity. From 1980 to 1984, however, actual wage increases exceeded the recommendations by an average of 2.4 percentage points per year, as the increasingly heavy demands for labor apparently outstripped its supply. Additionally, collective agreements for unionized workers lasted for two or three years with built-in wage increases. Although starting pay was relatively low, large gaps in wages were institutionalized through longevity of employment and annual raises.

The effect of wage increases, compounded by a further rise in the mandatory Central Provident Fund component of wages, was to price Singapore out of the market. High wages were a major contributor to Singapore's 1985 recession. Consequently, in 1986 and 1987 the government instituted a wage restraint policy: wages were frozen and the employer's contribution to the fund substantially reduced. The policy's relative success could be attributed to close government-labor ties and to the tripartite forum of the National Wages Council.

Proposals for wage reform—a "flexi-wage policy"—were announced in mid-November 1986 and became effective with the enactment of the 1988 Employment (Amendment) Act. Under this plan, the basic wage remained relatively stable with adjustments for good or bad years made by increasing or reducing the annual bonus. Negotiating the size of the bonus—frozen to the equivalent of one month's salary since 1972—was left to employers and unions, who would be able to bargain for its retention, abolition, or modification. Profit-sharing, productivity incentive, and employee share plans were encouraged to ensure that high wage payments awarded in fat years were not perpetuated in lean years and that individual as well as company productivity, growth, profitability, competitiveness, and prospects for the industry were taken into account. The government was anxious that wages not increase precipitously. This concern was shared by management, which worried about shrinking profit margins resulting from higher operating costs. Workers, on the other hand, wanted to share in the benefits of the economic boom after giving up wage increases to help cope with the 1985 recession.

Foreign Labor

Two groups comprised foreign nonresident labor in Singapore. The majority were unskilled work-permit holders who could only enter and work in the country if their prospective employers applied for work permits for them. Skilled workers and professionals on employment passes comprised the other group.

Work permits were for a short duration with no guarantee of automatic renewal. Malaysia, particularly the southernmost state of Johor, was the traditional source of such workers. Singapore's tight immigration policy was relaxed as early as 1968 to allow in these workers. At the peak of the economic boom in 1973, noncitizen work-permit holders reportedly accounted for about one-eighth of the total work force. Large numbers of these "guest workers" were repatriated during the 1974–75 world recession because of retrenchments, particularly in the labor-intensive manufacturing industries.

With the tightening of the labor market in 1978–79, it became more difficult to fill less desirable jobs with domestic labor or labor from Malaysia, which also had a tight job market. Foreign workers were then recruited from Indonesia, Thailand, Sri Lanka, India, Bangladesh, and the Philippines. By 1984 workers from South Korea, Hong Kong, Macao, and Taiwan were being allowed in, on the basis that their Confucian cultural background might enable them to adapt more readily than immigrants from other cultures.

Serving up roti canai *(Indian pancakes) near Arab Street*
Courtesy Ong Tien Kwan

The increase in foreign workers was remarkable; by 1980 they comprised 7 percent of the total labor force compared with 3 percent a decade earlier. No figures on foreign labor were published after 1980. According to the 1980 census, 46 percent of the foreign workers were in manufacturing, 20 percent in construction, and 9 percent in personal and household services. The recession led to a repatriation of some 60,000 foreign workers in 1985, two-thirds of the total employment decline. The foreign worker levy was raised to S$250 per month in July 1989, and the maximum foreign worker dependency at the firm level was reduced from 50 percent to 40 percent. Both measures were designed to encourage firms to speed up automation of labor-intensive operations in order to reduce reliance on foreign workers.

Manpower Training

The main goals of manpower training were to increase the average skill level of the labor force and, at the same time, provide sufficient numbers of workers with the specialized skills necessary to meet future industrial needs. Beginning in the late 1970s, the government placed increased stress on education in order to achieve the objective of industrial restructuring. As of 1987, however,

Singapore's work force was less educated than that of some of the countries with which it competed. Five percent of the work force had university educations compared with 19 percent for the United States and Japan and 6 percent for Taiwan. Some 11 percent had received post-secondary schooling other than in universities, compared with 46 percent for Japan, 23 percent for Taiwan, and 16 percent for the United States.

In the early 1980s, government studies showed that about half of the work force had primary-level education or less, and many older workers had low levels of English language skills. To remedy this situation, the Basic Education for Skills Training (BEST) program was introduced in 1984 to provide opportunities for workers who had not completed primary education to improve their English and math. By 1989 some 116,300 workers (half the target group) had had some BEST training. Time was also solving the problem as younger people received more education and the older, less-educated workers passed out of the work force; between 1979 and 1984, entrants to the work force with only primary-level education or less declined from 43 percent to 26 percent. The government needed, however, to ensure that this better-educated work force was trained in the necessary skills to complete the transformation of Singapore from a labor-intensive economy to a high-technology city-state—a "technopolis."

A further problem in achieving this transition resulted from "government brain drain." Each year 50 to 60 percent of new university graduates were absorbed by the government, including government-owned companies and the statutory boards. A system of awarding undergraduate scholarships, which often tied the awardees to eight years of government service, assured that the public sector absorbed many of the top-ranking students. Some critics thought that this concentration of the country's valuable human resources in the public sector might be to the long-run detriment of entrepreneurial and private-sector development.

Industry

Industrialization Policy

The manufacturing sector was a mainstay of Singapore's economic growth despite the absence of natural resources or an agricultural base (see table 7, Appendix). By the mid-1970s, the country had undergone a quarter-century of rapid industrial advance based on low-cost labor, low- to middle-level technology, and a rapid increase in exports. At that time, Singapore's planners settled on a policy emphasizing high technology, particularly information technology. In 1988 Singapore's 3,694 manufacturing establishments, employing 352,600 workers, were responsible for 29 percent of the GDP (see fig. 8). Industrial production, valued at S$14,509.7 million, was fractionally higher than earnings from financial and business services, double those from commerce, and nearly equal to the total of commerce and transport and communications. This represented a 20-percent increase over 1987. The manufacturing sector's continuing success was largely a function of Singapore's ability to attract foreign investment through a favorable business climate and then provide investors with an educated, trained, and disciplined labor force.

Singapore entered nationhood with a mixed legacy. The industrial sector was small, its productivity low. Manufacturing in 1960 was a mere 11.4 percent of the GDP; commerce, far and away the largest sector, accounted for 32 percent. The industrial policy in 1959 sought to promote industrialization as a way of diversifying from Singapore's traditional role as an entrepôt. Reliance was placed on private enterprises whose basic decisions were determined on the expectation of a common market with the neighboring Federation of Malaya. A system of import quotas was introduced for a limited number of goods, along with controls on how many enterprises could enter a particular field. Circumstances altered strategies. After separation from Malaysia in 1965, quotas were mainly replaced by a low level (for developing countries) of protective import tariffs. A traditional import substitution strategy was implemented.

In 1968, when the British announced their intention to withdraw from their Singapore bases, import substitution was succeeded by a strategy promoting export-oriented, labor-intensive industrialization. At that time, the government began its central role in formulating and implementing the industrialization program through the Economic Development Board.

The new approach became official policy in 1967 with the government's proclamation of the Export Expansion Incentives (Relief from Income Tax) Act and was further enhanced by the 1968 Employment Act. Direct foreign investment was welcomed both to help Singapore penetrate export markets and to bring in advanced technology. As early as 1970, when full employment was attained, there was some thought given to upgrading the industrial structure in order to provide more higher paying jobs. By 1979 efforts to upgrade the overall industrial structure and to accelerate the trend toward skill- and technology-intensive, higher value-added economic activity were intensified. The government implemented the large, three-year wage increases recommended by the National Wages

Singapore: A Country Study

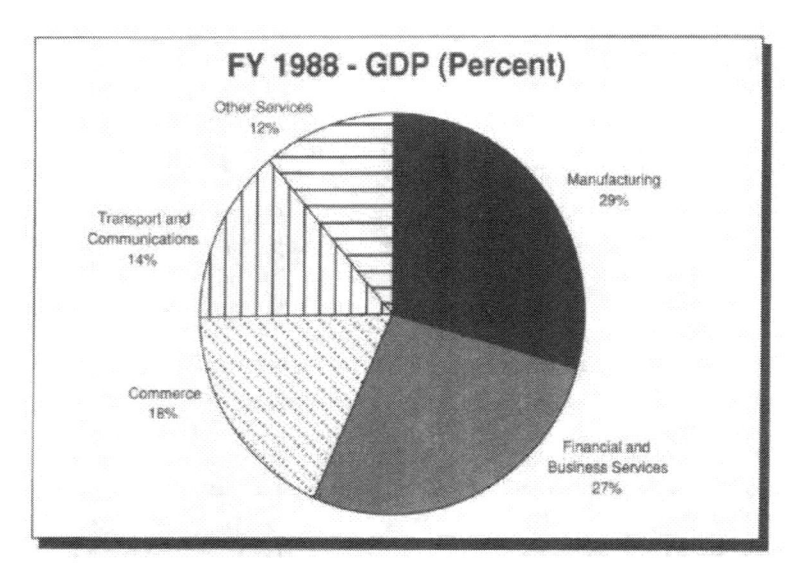

FY 1988 - GDP (Percent)

- Other Services 12%
- Manufacturing 29%
- Transport and Communications 14%
- Commerce 18%
- Financial and Business Services 27%

Source: Based on information from Singapore, Ministry of Trade and Industry, *Economic Survey of Singapore, Second Quarter 1989*, Singapore, 1989, 24.

Figure 8. Gross Domestic Product (GDP), by Sector, Fiscal Year (FY) 1988

Council, which began the easing out of labor-intensive, low value-added activities in Singapore.

The machinery industry was increasingly in the forefront of technological innovation as a result of the Economic Development Board's promotion of computer-controlled production, industrial robots, and flexible manufacturing systems. The industry's output increased by 17 percent in 1987 and 20 percent in 1988.

Domestic enterprises played a lesser role in industrialization. The government argued that the emphasis on large industry was a more effective stimulus to increased productivity and long-range economic development. Major promotional efforts sponsored by the government were focused on high-productivity projects, creating industries that officials claimed would not otherwise have been established in Singapore. Although institutional assistance for small-scale local industry, the majority of enterprises, was provided through a subsidiary of the Economic Development Board, the effectiveness of this aid was limited until after the mid-1980s recession, when greater emphasis was placed on encouraging and upgrading small-scale local industry.

Following a decline in the textile industry in the mid-1980s resulting from increased international competition, automation and the upgrading of product lines were encouraged. What had originally been a textile industry and then a mass-market clothing industry was encouraged to target high-fashion markets. A 10 percent growth in the fashion industry in 1987 reflected both the new trend and a strong market among Western trading partners.

Information Technology

After 1979 there was a single-minded emphasis among policy makers on escalating the level of technology in order to implement the succeeding phases of Singapore's industrial revolution. They relied on information technology as the strategy's principal instrument. The Telecommunications Authority of Singapore (Telecoms) was a key to the strategy because of the high caliber of its services and products and because Telecoms and the telecommunications industry had an important role in the progress of every industry in Singapore (see Telecommunications, this ch).

A second key was computers and related electronics, which in the late 1980s constituted Singapore's largest industry, measured both in numbers of jobs and in value added by manufacturing. In 1981 the 65,000 to 70,000 electronics workers comprised about 7 percent of the labor force; gross production of electronics at about S$5.9 billion was about 15 percent of total manufacturing output. By 1987 electronics accounted for 28 percent of manufacturing employment and contributed 31 percent or S$11 billion in output. By 1989, Singapore had become the world's largest producer of disk drives and disk drive parts. Other related products included integrated circuits, data processing equipment, telecommunications equipment, and radio receivers.

The electronics industry began a calculated transition away from labor-intensive products toward higher technological content and worker-skilled products in 1974. Potential investors were encouraged to look elsewhere for low-wage, unskilled labor. Aside from producing high value-added exports, the computer and electronics industries played a vital role in raising manpower productivity in other technology-intensive industries through computerization and computer communications. The National Computer Board was formed in 1981 to establish Singapore as an international center for computer services, to reduce the shortage of trained computer professionals, and to assure standards of international caliber at all levels.

Copyright and "intellectual property" issues served as an impediment to computer and other industrial development in the early 1980s, when Singapore, as well as other Asian countries, was known for producing pirated versions of everything from computers and computer software to designer handbags. Following threats by their major Western trading partners to impose trade sanctions and by international computer and software companies not to do business, Singapore passed its first copyright law in 1986. There was fairly rigorous enforcement in areas in which Western pressure was applied (computer software, films, and cassette tapes), and nearly full compliance in the book trade, which had not been as serious a problem. The Asian "copyright revolution" (Singapore's was one of several such laws enacted in the region) was significant as a realization by those countries that they had joined the international knowledge network as producers as well as consumers.

By the mid-1980s, the small but growing printing and publishing industry had entered the high-technology world with computerized typesetting, color separation, and book binding. Its high-quality printing facilities and sophisticated satellite telecommunications network made Singapore a regional publishing and distribution center in 1989.

Petroleum

Petroleum and petrochemicals were another base of Singapore's industrial and economic life. In the late 1980s, Singapore was the world's third largest oil-trading center and also the third largest center for petroleum refining. It was the second largest builder of drilling rigs, and its facilities for repairing and maintaining rigs and tankers were the most competitive in East Asia.

When oil prices began eroding in 1981 and collapsing toward the end of 1985, Singapore felt both negative and positive consequences. The collapse of oil prices dealt a severe blow to oil exploration. The impact was felt widely and immediately in everything from reduced orders for rig construction to lowered occupancy of luxury apartments as foreign petroleum workers returned home. With both of its immediate neighbors, Indonesia and Malaysia, heavily dependent on oil and gas exports for revenue, Singapore had a resulting loss of trade in both goods and services.

Singapore benefited, however, from the availability of cheaper energy, which in 1986 amounted to a savings of about S$2.5 billion (US$1.12 billion). Furthermore, Singaporean refineries invested in the equipment and technology necessary to enable them to refine a wide variety of crude oils and obtain a greater proportion of high-valued products from the refining process. Petroleum refining alone made up 28 percent of Singapore's manufacturing output in 1985, although by 1988 it had dropped by half as a result of a decline in petroleum production and growth in other industries. Singapore also benefited indirectly when large oil importers such as Japan and the United States obtained higher real incomes from lower oil prices, enabling them to increase their imports from Singapore and other countries.

Trade, Tourism, and Telecommunications
Foreign Trade

Trade in goods and services was Singapore's life blood as truly in 1989 as it was in the early twentieth century or a century earlier when the British East India Company first began business there. Trade, along with domestic savings and foreign investment, remained key to the country's growth. Singapore traditionally had a merchandise-trade balance deficit (in part at least because food was imported), which it customarily offset with a surplus on the services account (see table 8, Appendix). It was one of the world's few countries where total international trade (domestic exports and reexports plus imports) was greater than total GDP. In 1988 trade (S$167.3 billion) was more than three times GDP (S$48 billion), and two-thirds of the goods and services Singapore produced were exported.

Singapore, however, was more than simply a trade and manufacturing center in the late 1980s. Trade and manufacturing were closely tied to the country's expanding business services and international financial market; each enhanced the other. In addition to the more than 650 multinational companies that had set up manufacturing plants and technical support facilities, several thousand international financial institutions, service companies, and trading firms also maintained a presence in Singapore. The increasing internationalization of the economy and the continuing centrality of external trade meant that world trade fluctuations and the state of the global economy were significant factors—largely out of the country's direct control—in what happened to Singapore's trade and wider economy.

As a British colony in the nineteenth and early twentieth centuries, Singapore was an entrepôt for the exchange of raw materials from Southeast Asia—mainly present-day Indonesia and Malaysia—for European merchandise. Newly independent Singapore's decision in 1965 to emphasize industrial development and the growing success of that plan gradually resulted in a significant change in the nature of trade. By the mid-1970s, the proportion of reexports and domestic exports had been roughly reversed, with reexports accounting for less than 41 percent.

In the 1980s, the somewhat diminished entrepôt trade remained important, and Singapore continued to act as a regional processing and distribution center. Reexports' share of total exports averaged 35 percent from 1980 to 1987. Although primary commodities (crude rubber, nonferrous metals, and to a lesser extent palm and coconut oil) were still a factor in trading activities, machinery and transportation equipment dominated (see table 9, Appendix). Singapore also served as a back door to trade with Asian communist countries for third countries, such as Indonesia.

Between 1980 and 1984, total exports grew an average of 5.5 percent per year. The strongest impetus came from the newer electrical and electronics industries. The trade deficit declined steadily after 1982, reflecting lower commodity prices paid to foreign producers, greater levels of internal efficiency, and industrial upgrading. In 1985, however, total exports decreased by 2.26 percent. Higher value-added exports declined, both as a function of weaker demand and a worldwide saturation in many areas, such as computer peripherals. Petroleum exports, still a major sector, virtually stagnated.

Trade, along with the rest of the economy, reasserted itself by 1987, resulting partly from government economic decisions and partly as a reflection of rising world commodity prices. In 1988 Singapore's total trade amounted to about S$167.3 billion (US$80.8 billion), with a global trade deficit of about S$8.18 billion. Singapore's GDP grew by 10.8 percent in 1988, the best growth rate in fifteen years. Disk drives were the largest non-oil item exported, worth S$4.89 billion. Other major exports were integrated circuits, data processing equipment and parts, telecommunications equipment, radio receivers, clothing, and plastics.

By early 1989, signs of slowing down and leveling off had appeared with the first export declines in eighteen months. Analysts agreed the weak external demand for electronics and computer parts resulted, in part, from an oversupply on the world market of disk drives, semiconductors, and related items. Imports surged, however, widening the trade deficit sharply (see table 10, Appendix).

Although their volume was not large, food products were a significant aspect of Singapore's trade. The urban nation produced only a small proportion of its own food (see Agriculture, this ch.), requiring it to import large quantities. Some food products, such as soy sauce and juices, were processed in Singapore for export, and Singapore continued its historical role as the regional center for the spice trade.

Trading Partners

Along with the changes in the composition of trade that had taken place since independence, there also were changes in direction.

The Keppel Wharves handled mainly noncontainerized general cargo.
Courtesy Singapore Ministry of Communication and Information
Container handling facilities at the Tanjong Pagar Terminal
Courtesy Singapore Ministry of Communication and Information

The preeminence of Britain as supplier of manufactures declined after independence, and by the early 1970s the United States and Japan had become Singapore's two leading sources of industrial products. Malaysia and Indonesia remained the principal sources of such primary imports as crude rubber, vegetable oils, and spices and an important destination for manufactured exports, including both the products of Singapore and of the entrepôt trade.

Singapore did not report trade with Indonesia. The omission dated from the period of the Indonesian Confrontation in the mid-1960s and continued, according to some observers, because Singapore was afraid that if the Indonesian government knew the volume of the trade, it might try to curtail it. Estimates were difficult because a substantial part of the trade was viewed by Indonesia as smuggling and was, therefore, unlisted, although in Singapore's open export market it was legal. Nevertheless, trade with Indonesia could be presumed, based partly on Indonesian trade figures, to have assumed a gradually larger role starting in the mid-1970s.

As Singapore became more export oriented, its trading patterns became increasingly complex and interdependent. By the late 1980s, Singapore's trade links were strongest with the countries of the Organisation for Economic Co-operation and Development (OECD—see Glossary), especially the United States, Japan, and the countries of the European Economic Community (EEC—see Glossary) or of the Association of Southeast Asian Nations (ASEAN—see Glossary; see table 11, Appendix). Singapore's drive to industrialization had drawn it increasingly towards the OECD countries for foreign investment, technology, and markets. To a large extent, this shift had meant decreasing reliance on its ASEAN neighbors, particularly for markets and supplies (see table 12, Appendix). The other Asian NIEs, Hong Kong, Korea, and Taiwan, were sometimes viewed as Singapore's competitors. On the other hand, Singapore engaged in considerable and growing trade with them, particularly with Taiwan, and all three were a source of skilled labor.

United States

By the 1980s, the United States had become Singapore's most important trading partner and, as such, crucial to the country's welfare. Singaporean officials often stated that a 1 percent drop in the United States economy had a 1.4 percent effect on Singapore's gross national product (GNP—see Glossary). Consequently, in the 1980s Singapore was critically concerned about protectionist policies and budget deficits in the United States. In 1988 Singapore's total exports to the United States amounted to S$18.8 billion, up 28 percent over the previous year, and accounted for 24 percent of the nation's total exports. Of that total, about 80 percent were Singaporean manufactures, including disk drives, integrated circuits, semiconductors, parts for data processing machines, television sets, radios and radio cassette players, and clothing. Reexports to the United States also were an important part of the trade. Singapore's exports to the United States outstripped its imports from there, although the United States was, after Japan, Singapore's second largest supplier.

Until 1989 Singapore and the three other NIEs enjoyed trade preferences with the United States under the United States Generalized System of Preferences (GSP—see Glossary). This system was originally instituted to aid developing economies, but in 1989, the four Asian NIEs were removed from the program because of what some observers have seen as their major advances in economic development and improvements in trade competitiveness. The United States had been trying for some time to wrest trade and currency concessions from all four countries (but primarily South Korea), which had not been forthcoming. Although Washington presented the decision more as an economic graduation ceremony, observers noted that the move reflected United States frustration over its continuing trade deficit despite considerable devaluation in the United States dollar.

The removal of the GSP affected less than 15 percent of Singapore's exports to the United States, among them telephones, office machines, wood furniture, and medical instruments, which faced duties of 5 to 10 percent. Ironically, United States firms based in Singapore were among the hardest hit. More than 50 percent of Singapore's exports to the United States came from American firms with operations there, such as AT&T, Digital Equipment, Hewlett-Packard, Rockwell International, and Travenol Laboratories. Singaporean companies, as well as Japanese and European firms with operations in Singapore, were also affected by the removal of the GSP. In early 1988, some 4,000 NTUC members gathered outside the United States Embassy in Singapore to protest the decision, and the Singaporean government expressed regret.

Japan

Japan's place in Singapore's business picture was underscored by the fact that, in the 1980s, Japanese were the largest resident expatriate community in the city. Japan was the country's single largest supplier, accounting in 1987 for 25.3 percent of total imports, and Singapore's largest trade deficit was with Japan. Buyback arrangements for products manufactured by Japanese firms in Singapore also accounted for a significant part of the trade. Oil accounted for 40 percent of Singapore's exports to Japan in 1988. Singaporean observers noted by 1989 a significant difference in the market orientation between Japanese firms and United States-owned multinationals. Japanese firms in Singapore were producing primarily for the United States and other third-country markets, rather than for the Japanese home market. The United States-controlled multinationals, on the other hand, produced mainly for their own home market. Many of these same observers, both official and unofficial, also expressed the sentiment that the world export market in the 1990s, would "belong to Japan."

Association of Southeast Asian Nations

The Association of Southeast Asian Nations (ASEAN) was founded in 1967 primarily as a forum for discussing issues of mutual concern among neighboring Southeast Asian countries rather than as a trading union similar to the EEC. In part, this orientation was because, other than Singapore, most of the ASEAN countries had similar products, tending to make them more competitive than cooperative. Although trade relations among the ASEAN countries remained largely bilateral, there was some informal economic cooperation, including joint representations to foreign governments on economic issues of common concern. In 1989 the possibility of a more formalized economic entity was at least being considered by the ASEAN members.

In 1988 Malaysia was Singapore's largest ASEAN trading partner and third largest overall trading partner, after the United States and Japan. The Malaysian market was the single largest ASEAN destination for Singapore's exports and its second largest export market overall. In the late 1980s, Singapore established increasingly close economic and industrial ties with Malaysia's Johor state, which had served as Singapore's hinterland in colonial times. To alleviate its land shortage as well as its labor shortage and high labor costs, Singapore began to transfer labor-intensive industries to sites across the causeway connecting it to Malaysia's southernmost state. Johor, in turn, hoped "economic twinning" with Singapore would boost its long-term development. By early 1987, there were 217 Singaporean companies or Singapore-based multinationals in Malaysia, having total investments of slightly more than S$200 million.

Singapore's much smaller markets with the other ASEAN countries also were growing. In 1989 Singapore recorded its highest growth in bilateral ASEAN trade with Thailand, which replaced Taiwan as its fifth largest trading partner. Intra-ASEAN trade generally might have been underestimated, partly because of the

The Economy

volume of informal trade, including smuggling, and partly because so much of it was controlled by the Chinese community in each country. Keeping business within the family, clan, or dialect group was a central Chinese business practice that persisted across national boundaries.

Other Trading Partners

Beginning in the mid-1980s, Singapore—which for two decades had sharply curtailed many forms of contact with China—began promoting itself as an alternative to Hong Kong as a "Gateway to China." In 1989 Singapore was estimated to be the fourth-largest foreign investor in the special economic zones of southern China and that country's fifth-largest trading partner; Singapore's companies were estimated to have about S$1 billion directly invested in China. Since most such investments were made in conjunction with Hong Kong-based companies, the real extent of Singapore's exposure to China may have been considerably higher.

Non-oil trade with the various EEC countries, which had been steady during the early 1980s, strengthened in 1987 and 1988. Nearly three-quarters of this increase was in exports of disk drives and integrated circuits, particularly to the Federal Republic of Germany (West Germany), Great Britain, and the Netherlands. Overall, however, Singapore had a small trade deficit with Western Europe in 1988.

Tourism

Tourism had been an important sector of Singapore's economy for more than a decade, averaging 16 percent of total foreign exchange earnings and 6 percent of GDP between 1980 and 1985. Tourist arrivals had dropped sharply in 1983, however, the first decline in over twenty years. The decrease resulted both from the regional and world economic downturn at that time and from travel restrictions instituted by neighboring countries to preserve their own foreign exchange. Observers noted also that Singapore was losing its "oriental mystique and charm." In its effort to build a modern city, it had torn down old buildings and curtailed traditional street activities, aspects considered by tourists to be part of Singapore's attraction. In 1984 the government established a Tourism Task Force to recommend ways to attract more visitors, and the following year the budget of the Singapore Tourist Promotion Board was increased by 60 percent. Steps were taken to preserve areas of special architectural, historical, or cultural interest. Sentosa Island, off the southern coast, was developed as a resort and recreation center, complete with museums, parks, golf courses, lagoons, beaches, trails, and gardens, all connected by monorail. Singapore also began billing itself as the "hub of Southeast Asia" and marketing sidetrips to destinations in neighboring countries. As with other economic activities, tourism was viewed as a high value-added industry. Although increasing the absolute number of visitor arrivals was the main target, a further aim was to attract the high-spending, business visitors attending conventions and trade exhibitions, which Singapore hosted in large numbers.

Tourist arrivals recovered quickly from the 1983 downturn, reaching 3 million in 1985. In 1987 tourist arrivals reached 3.7 million, a 15 percent increase over the previous year. In 1988 arrivals rose another 14 percent to nearly 4.2 million. Singapore's top tourist-generating markets in 1987 were ASEAN (29 percent), Japan (15 percent), Australia (9 percent), India (7 percent), the United States (6 percent), and Britain (5 percent). Although a building boom had caused a glut of hotel rooms in the mid-1980s, by early 1989 occupancy was running at about 80 percent.

Telecommunications

The Singaporean government, which had inherited a fairly good telecommunications system from the British at independence, assigned telecommunications a high priority in economic planning. By the late 1980s, Singapore had one of the world's most advanced telecommunications infrastructures, developed under the guidance of Telecoms, a statutory board. Its mission was to provide high quality communications for domestic and international requirements, and to serve the business community as well as the public. Telecoms offered a comprehensive range of products and services at rates among the lowest in the world. Information services accounted for an estimated 2 percent of Singapore's GDP in 1988.

Chartered to function commercially, Telecoms received no subsidies. Aside from an initial loan, Telecoms paid for its capital needs out of its earnings. In lieu of taxes, it made an annual payment to the Treasury comparable to a business tax. This financial autonomy was a major factor in Telecom's ability to respond to user demand. During the early 1980s, as the drive for high technology got underway, Telecom's capital budget rose by 20 to 30 percent a year, the highest growth of any public agency in Singapore. Although the rate of increase dropped to about 15 to 20 percent in the late 1980s, the capital budget remained high and continued to increase.

Telecoms offered a large and growing number of services, including radio paging, mobile phones, facsimile, electronic mail, and telepac, a system for linking computers locally and internationally. By 1987 Singapore's domestic telephone network was completely push-button, and all twenty-six telephone exchanges were linked by an optical fiber network. The country had more than 1.2 million telephones in 1988, or 48.5 telephones for every 100 Singaporeans, providing virtually 100 percent coverage in homes and offices.

Satellite links with the world were provided by satellite earth stations at Bukit Timah and on Sentosa Island. Submarine cables connected Singapore to all of its ASEAN neighbors except Brunei, which was scheduled to be linked with Singapore by fiber-optic cable in 1991. In 1988 Singapore installed the region's first dedicated digital data network, providing up to two megabits per second (Mbps) high-speed data transmission and voice communications. Intelsat Business Service was available for a wide range of applications, including corporate data communications, financial services, and remote printing via satellite. A video conferencing service also was offered by 1988.

Finance

The country's rapid development was closely linked to the government's efficient financial management. Conservative fiscal and monetary policies generated high savings, which, along with high levels of foreign investment, allowed growth without the accumulation of external debt. In 1988 Singapore had foreign reserves worth about S$33 billion, which, per capita, put it ahead of Switzerland, Saudi Arabia, and Taiwan. That same year, the domestic savings rate rose to one of the highest in the world (42 percent), as gross national savings, comprising public and private savings, totaled S$20.9 billion, 19 percent higher than in 1987. By the mid-1980s, however, domestic demand had been so stunted that it became increasingly difficult to find productive areas for investment. In the recession year of 1986, for the first time, gross national savings exceeded gross capital formation. This was in spite of a 15 percent cut in the employers' contribution to the Central Provident Fund. As a result, already depressed domestic demand was depressed even further, falling by 1 percent in 1986 after a decline of 3 percent the previous year.

Singapore's foreign reserves were, in fact, the country's domestic savings held overseas. Since the source of the domestic savings was in large measure the compulsory savings held by the Central Provident Fund, Singapore had a huge domestic liability. The fund claims, standing in 1988 at S$32 billion, almost equalled Singapore's foreign reserves. But since they were fully funded and denominated in Singapore dollars, the country was relieved of the problems of showing either a budget deficit or an external debt.

Indeed, for many years, the government had pointed out that its foreign reserves, managed by the Government of Singapore Investment Corporation, were larger than that of wealthier, more populous countries. The reserves issue became politicized after 1987 when Lee Kuan Yew proposed a change in the country's government to an executive presidency in which the president (presumably Lee himself) would have veto power over Parliament's use of the reserves. In 1986 the government-sponsored Report of the Economic Committee admitted that "over saving" was a problem. Not until 1988, however, were some tentative steps taken to invest the surpluses directly in productive resources. This process included a one-time transfer to government revenue of S$1.5 billion from the accumulated reserves of four statutory boards.

The country's public sector financial system was structurally complex and difficult to follow owing to different accounting practices. Funds essentially were derived from three sources: tax revenue (directly on income, property, and inheritance; indirectly as excise duties, motor vehicle taxes; stamp duties, and other taxes); nontax revenue (regulatory charges, sales of goods and services, and interest and dividends); and public sector borrowing (see fig. 6). The statutory boards had separate budgets, although they played a major role in infrastructure creation. Government companies also were not included in public finance reporting.

After 1975 the government consistently had substantial current as well as overall surpluses. From 1983 to 1985, total government expenditure averaged 59.8 percent of current revenue. In fact, the overall surplus exceeded even the net contributions to the Central Provident Fund. The seven major statutory boards also had consistent current surpluses. Economic theoretician and member of Parliament Augustine Tan suggested that Singapore's public spending and public savings were much too large. According to Tan, the government tended to err on the side of financial surplus, despite frequent forecasts of deficit, because the government consistently underestimated tax revenues and overestimated expenditures. These surpluses then put upward pressure on the exchange rate and eroded manufacturers' competitiveness.

Currency, Trade, and Investment Regulation

Singapore had an exceptionally open economy. Fundamentally strong, the currency reflected a sound balance of payments position, large reserves, and the authorities' conservative attitude. From 1967 until June 1973, the Singapore dollar was tied to the

United States dollar, and thereafter the currency was allowed to float.

The Monetary Authority of Singapore, the country's quasi-central bank, pursued a policy of intervention both domestically and in foreign exchange markets to maintain a strong currency. This multifaceted strategy was designed to promote Singapore's development as a financial center by attracting funds, while inducing low inflation by preventing the erosion of the large Central Provident Fund balances. Furthermore, the strong currency complemented the high wage industrial strategy, forcing long-term quality rather than short-term prices to be the basis for export competition.

Given Singapore's dependency on imports, however, setting an exchange rate always generated controversy. The 1986 Report of the Economic Committee did not clarify official thinking. It recommended that the exchange rate should "continue to be set by market forces, but its impact on [Singapore's] export competitiveness and tourist costs should be taken into account. The [Singapore] dollar should, as far as possible, be allowed to find its own appropriate level, reflecting fundamental economic trends."

After 1978, when the government abolished all currency exchange controls, Singaporean residents (individuals and corporations) were free to move funds, import capital, or repatriate profits without restriction. Likewise, trade regulations were minimal. Import duties applied only to a few items (automobiles, alcohol, petroleum, and tobacco), and licenses were required only for imports originating from a few Eastern bloc countries. There were no export duties. As the government played an active part in promoting exports, there was an extensive system of supports including an export insurance plan.

The government promoted investment vigorously through a whole range of tax and investment allowances and soft loans aimed at attracting new investment or at helping existing businesses upgrade or expand. There was no capital gains tax. Special incentives existed for foreigners, including concessionary tax arrangements for some nonresidents, relief from double taxation, and permission to buy commercial and certain residential property. In 1985 extensive tax reductions were introduced to reduce business costs.

Financial Center Development

As a result of its strategic location and well-developed infrastructure, Singapore traditionally had been the trade and financial services center for the region. In the 1970s, the government identified financial services as a key source of growth and provided incentives for its development. By the 1980s, the focus was on further diversification, upgrading, and automation of financial services. Emphasis was placed on the development of investment portfolio management, securities trading, capital market activities, foreign exchange and futures trading, and promotion of more sophisticated and specialized fee-based activities.

Consequently, by the mid-1980s, Singapore was the third most important financial center in Asia after Tokyo and Hong Kong. The financial services sector, having sustained double digit growth over the previous decade, accounted for some 23 percent of GDP and employed approximately 9 percent of the labor force. In 1985, however, growth in the sector slowed to just 2.6 percent, and in December of that year the Stock Exchange of Singapore suffered a major crisis, which forced it to close for three days. In view of the troubled domestic economy, observers worried that Singapore's future as a financial center looked somewhat problematic. Furthermore, international financial market deregulation threatened to create an environment in which it would be more difficult for Singapore to thrive, especially given its high cost structure and somewhat heavy-handed regulatory environment. The government took steps to correct some of the problems, and by 1989 Singapore's financial service sector could again be described as "booming."

The financial sector included three types of commercial banks (full license, restricted, and offshore), representative offices, merchant banks, discount houses, and finance companies. In 1988 there were 13 local, 64 merchant, and 134 commercial banks. All banks in Singapore were administered by the Monetary Authority of Singapore and were required to hold a statutory minimum cash balance against their deposit and other specified liabilities with the authority.

The Development Bank of Singapore was established in 1968 to provide financial services supporting industrialization and general economic development. Owned jointly by the government (49 percent) and private sector shareholders, it had evolved from a long-term financing institution to a multiservice bank. The largest Singaporean commercial bank in terms of assets in 1989, the Development Bank was listed on the stock exchanges of both Singapore and Malaysia. Through its subsidiaries, it also provided specialized financial and insurance services, factoring, stockbroking, merchant banking, and venture capital investment management services. The Development Bank was the city-state's largest source of long-term finance, including equity and venture capital financing, medium- and long-term loans, and guarantees.

The Economy

The Singapore Foreign Exchange Market had grown remarkably since the 1985 recession. As an international financial center, the country had benefited from the worldwide increase in business as well as from the related expansion in the financially liberated Japanese market. Major currencies—the United States dollar, the Japanese yen, the West German deutsche mark, and the British pound sterling—were actively traded. Volumes in such other currencies as the Australian dollar had risen as well. Average daily turnover was US$45 billion in 1988 compared with US$12.5 billion in 1985.

Singapore established the Asian dollar market as the Asian equivalent of the Eurodollar market in 1968 when the local branch of the United States-based Bank of America secured government approval to borrow deposits of nonresidents, mainly in foreign currencies, and use them to finance corporate activities in Asia. At the time, expanding economic development in Southeast Asia was rapidly increasing the demand for foreign investment funds, and the desirability of a regional center able to carry out the necessary middleman function was apparent. Singapore offered the ideal location. The Asian dollar market was essentially an international money and capital market for foreign currencies, and its assets grew from US$30 million in 1968 to US$273 billion in November 1988. To operate in the market, financial institutions were required to obtain approval from the Monetary Authority of Singapore and to set up separate bookkeeping entities called Asian currency units for transactions in the market. Funds were obtained mainly from external or nonresident sources—central banks, foreigners seeking a stable location such as Singapore to deposit cash, multinational corporations, and commercial banks outside Singapore.

In 1973, to stimulate the expansion of the Asian dollar market, the Monetary Authority of Singapore established the so-called offshore banking system, designed to concentrate on that market and its foreign exchange operations. Beginning in 1983, funds managed in Singapore on behalf of nonresidents and invested offshore or in the local stock market were exempt from tax. The fees earned for managing such offshore funds were taxed at a concessionary rate of 10 percent.

Inaugurated in 1973, the Stock Exchange of Singapore was governed by a committee comprising four elected stockbroker members and five appointed nonbroker members. In late 1988, the 327 companies listed on the main board of the exchange were classified into six groups: industrial and commercial, finance, hotel, property, plantation (farming), and mining. The market underwent a major, prolonged reorganization following the December

1985 collapse of a Singaporean company, Pan Electric, which revealed a massive web of forward share dealings based on borrowed money. The collapse resulted in a tighter regulation of the financial futures market and the securities industry. In 1986 the Securities Industry Council was established to advise the minister for finance on all matters relating to the securities industry.

In 1987 the government introduced tax incentives to encourage the trading of international securities in Singapore. The National Association of Securities Dealers (NASDAQ) in the United States and the Stock Exchange of Singapore established a link to facilitate the trading of NASDAQ stocks in Singapore by providing for the exchange of price and trading information on a selected list of NASDAQ stocks between the two exchanges. A move by the Singapore exchange to a new, spacious location in 1988 brought a transformation in trading methodology, including partial automation of the trading system, which until then had adhered to the traditional outcry auction system.

By 1987 Singapore's stock market, fuelled by bullish sentiments sent indices soaring to new highs—a recovery from the December 1985 crisis. All gains, however, were wiped out by the crash of world stock markets in October 1987, a crash from which the Singapore exchange had made substantial recovery by mid-1989.

Singapore also expanded other international financial markets in the late 1980s. Trading in gold futures originally was undertaken in the Gold Exchange of Singapore, which was established in 1978 and reorganized in 1983. The scope of its activities was widened to include financial futures trading, and it was renamed the Singapore International Monetary Exchange (SIMEX). Starting in 1984, the financial futures market featured a mutual offset arrangement between SIMEX and the Chicago Mercantile Exchange, which allowed contracts executed on one exchange to be offset on the other without additional transactional cost for market participants. The linkage was the first of its kind in the world and greatly facilitated round-the-clock trading in futures contracts. In 1988 six forms of futures contracts were traded: international gold futures; the Eurodollar time deposit interest rate; the Nikkei Average Stock Index; and three currency exchange rates—US dollar/West German deutsche mark, US dollar/Japanese yen, and US dollar/British pound sterling. Trading volume on the SIMEX had grown steadily.

The restructured Government Securities Market was launched in May 1987, auctioning at market rates taxable Singapore government securities ranging in maturity from three months to five years. Previously, long-term government stock was sold to a captive

The Economy

market of banks, insurance companies, and a few individuals and nonprofit organizations.

International Financial Organizations

In 1966 Singapore became a member of the International Monetary Fund (IMF—see Glossary), the World Bank (see Glossary), and the Asian Development Bank (see Glossary). Two years later, Singapore joined the International Finance Corporation, an affiliate of the World Bank. Singapore's loans from the World Bank and the Asian Development Bank had been used to finance development projects relating to water supply, electric power generation and distribution, sewerage, telephone services, educational services, and environmental control. A total of fourteen loans were secured from the World Bank between 1963 and 1975 and fourteen from the Asian Development Bank between 1969 and 1980. There were no further loans in the 1980s. Singapore's estimated outstanding borrowings from the World Bank and the Asian Development Bank in late 1988 totalled US$35.1 billion and US$45.4 million, respectively. Its 1988 quota of IMF special drawing rights (SDR)—related to its national income, monetary reserves, trade balance and other economic indicators—was SDR 92.4 million.

Transportation

Singapore as a modern city came into being because of its location and its harbor. Both assets remained major sources of its economic vitality as the island nation continued to serve as a major transportation and communications hub.

Sea

In 1988 the port of Singapore was the world's busiest in terms of shipping tonnage (396.4 million gross registered tons), just ahead of Rotterdam. Singapore was also a major transshipment hub and a global warehousing and central distribution center. In 1988 more than 36,000 vessels arrived in Singapore, up 6 percent from the previous year. The 150 million freight tons of cargo handled by the wharves and oil terminals represented an increase of 16 percent over the previous year.

Ships of more than 700 lines linked Singapore and the region to some 600 ports worldwide. The port area was administered by the Port of Singapore Authority, a statutory board responsible for the provision and maintenance of facilities and services and for the control of navigational traffic in the port. Operations were continuous, round the clock and year round. As a member of the International Maritime Organization since 1966, Singapore kept abreast of international developments in shipping and adhered to international conventions adopted under the organization's auspices. The five port terminals operated by the port authority had about fifteen kilometers of wharf, which could accommodate vessels of all sizes. The Tanjong Pagar Terminal was the port's main gateway for containerized cargo. It had ten container berths, supported in 1988 by a fleet of twenty-six quay cranes, sixty-seven transtainers (straddle carrier cranes), seventeen van carriers, and other types of heavy moving equipment. The seven container freight stations were all equipped with closed-circuit television to enhance fire safety and cargo security. A new billion-dollar container terminal with five container berths, four multipurpose berths, support facilities, and storage space for 8,500 twenty-foot equivalent units (TEUs) was being developed on a nearby island. The first berth was scheduled to be operational by 1992.

Keppel Wharves, the oldest conventional gateway, handled mainly containers and bulk cargo, such as cement, vegetable oil, and rubber. With four kilometers of sheltered deep-water berths, Keppel Wharves could accommodate twenty-two ocean-going vessels and three coasters at any one time. Pasir Panjang Wharves was also a conventional gateway with facilities for coasters, lighters, barges, and ocean-going vessels. It had three deep-water, ten coastal, and forty-six lighterage berths. Sembawang Wharves handled primarily high-volume homogeneous cargo such as timber and rubber. Equipped with five berths, Sembawang also handled containerized and bulk cargo. Jurong Port, developed principally to serve the industries in the Jurong Industrial Estate, had twelve berths.

Singapore's merchant fleet ranked fifteenth among the principal merchant fleets of the world. In late 1988, its 1,243 vessels totaled 7.33 million gross registered tons and included 156 general cargo ships, 150 oil tankers, 74 bulk carriers, 49 container ships, and 12 passenger vessels. There were two vessels above 100,000 gross registered tons: a very-large crude carrier and an ultra-large crude carrier.

Singapore also was noted for its ship-repair industry, the beginnings of which dated to colonial times. In 1968 the government turned the former British dockyard into the Sembawang Shipyard and built it into a commercial success.

Three major yards—Keppel, Sembawang, and Jurong—in which the government held a controlling stake dominated the industry, accounting for about 90 percent of the S$1.1 billion business in 1988. Many privately owned yards, of which the largest was Hitachi Zosen, split the remaining 10 percent of the business.

In 1989 the four major shipyards employed some 70,000 workers, about 40 percent from overseas, mainly from Malaysia, Thailand, and Bangladesh. Despite the booming business of the late 1980s, the shipyards faced problems of rising labor costs and government restrictions on importation of labor. As a result, a joint venture between Keppel and a shipyard near Madras, India, was given government approval in 1989, and the industry was exploring the possibility of joint-venture projects in other neighboring countries. Government strategists reportedly favored an eventual merger between Sembawang and Jurong—which would overtake Keppel to become the largest ship-repairing group—as part of a move to consolidate the industry and begin directing it toward a less labor-intensive future.

Land

In line with its goal of providing fast, convenient, and affordable transport for its population and visitors and a transportation infrastructure that supported its economic position, the government gave top priority to investments in public transport and the highway system. Beginning in the early 1970s, Singapore engaged in a systematic program of road building that led to the development of a network that was considered to be one of the best among developing countries. By late 1988, Singapore had 2,789 kilometers of roads occupying some 11 percent of the country's land area. In the previous decade, the government had spent some S$1.9 billion on building and maintaining roads.

In 1989 five expressways—the thirty-five-kilometer Pan Island Expressway (PIE), the nineteen-kilometer East Coast Parkway, the eleven-kilometer Bukit Timah Expressway, the fourteen-kilometer Ayer Rajah Expressway, and the sixteen-kilometer Central Expressway—were complete, and work was underway on four more (see fig. 9). The highway building program called for a network of nine expressways, for a total of 141 kilometers, to be completed by 1991. Access to the Central Business District was limited during rush hour to holders of special passes sold on a day-to-day basis, and a one-way street pattern further facilitated traffic movement. A computerized traffic control system, introduced in 1981, monitored some 200 major road junctions. The Public Works Department planned to put the remaining 800 signals on-line in the 1990s, making Singapore's one of the largest traffic control systems in the world.

At the end of 1988, 491,808 motor vehicles were registered, an increase of 20,000 over the previous year. Nearly half of registered vehicles were automobiles. In order to implement a government

Singapore: A Country Study

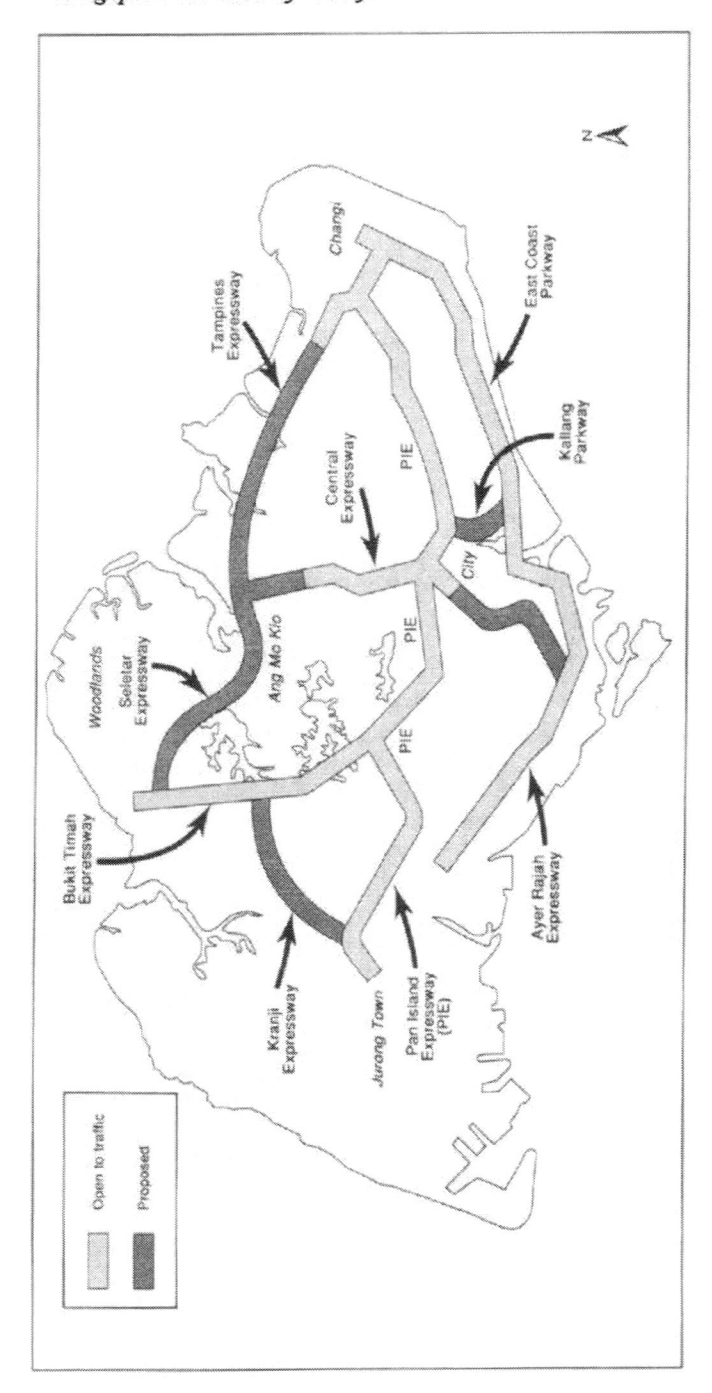

Figure 9. *Expressway System, 1989*

policy of limiting the number of private automobiles, a number of monetary disincentives were employed, including heavy annual road taxes, fuel taxes, ad valorem registration fees, and other licenses and fees.

Taxi fares also were kept reasonable in order to reduce traffic flow into and out of congested areas during rush hour. By late 1988, Singapore's 10,500 taxis were mostly air-conditioned and equipped with electronic taximeters. Most taxis were driven twenty-four hours a day by a succession of drivers. The largest company, NTUC Comfort, was affiliated with the union. A fleet of nearly 2,800 buses also helped to alleviate the need for private automobiles. The Singapore Bus Service and the Trans-Island Bus Service provided fullday service throughout the island.

In 1987 land transportation was propelled into a new era with the opening of the S$5 billion Mass Rapid Transit (MRT) system, which formed the backbone of the country's public transport network (see fig. 10). The entire MRT system, spanning 67 kilometers, was expected to be fully operational by 1990—two years ahead of schedule—when it would serve 800,000 passengers daily. The bus routes were being progressively redesigned to dovetail with the expanding system. Some 40 percent of all businesses and industrial areas were located near stations, and some 50 percent of all Singaporeans lived within one kilometer of an MRT station. The infusion of MRT construction funds into the economy beginning in the early 1980s helped offset downturns in other sectors of the construction industry during the recession.

Overland connections to the Malay Peninsula, across the causeway spanning the Johore Strait, included a highway and a Malaysian-owned railroad. These, in turn, were connected with the Thai railroad system.

Air

Singapore's supermodern Singapore Changi Airport, a travel and shipping hub, had connections to all parts of the world in keeping with Singapore's "open skies" policy. In 1988 forty-eight scheduled international airlines—twelve more than in 1983—linked the country to 101 cities in fifty-three countries. These carriers offered a total of 1,500 scheduled flights per week to and from Singapore; a total of 12.6 million passengers used the airport in 1988—a 12.4 percent increase over the previous year and the highest passenger volume recorded in any one year since the airport opened in 1981. Nearly half of those passengers came from or went to other destinations in Southeast Asia. A second passenger terminal scheduled for completion in 1990 would increase Changi's passenger

Singapore: A Country Study

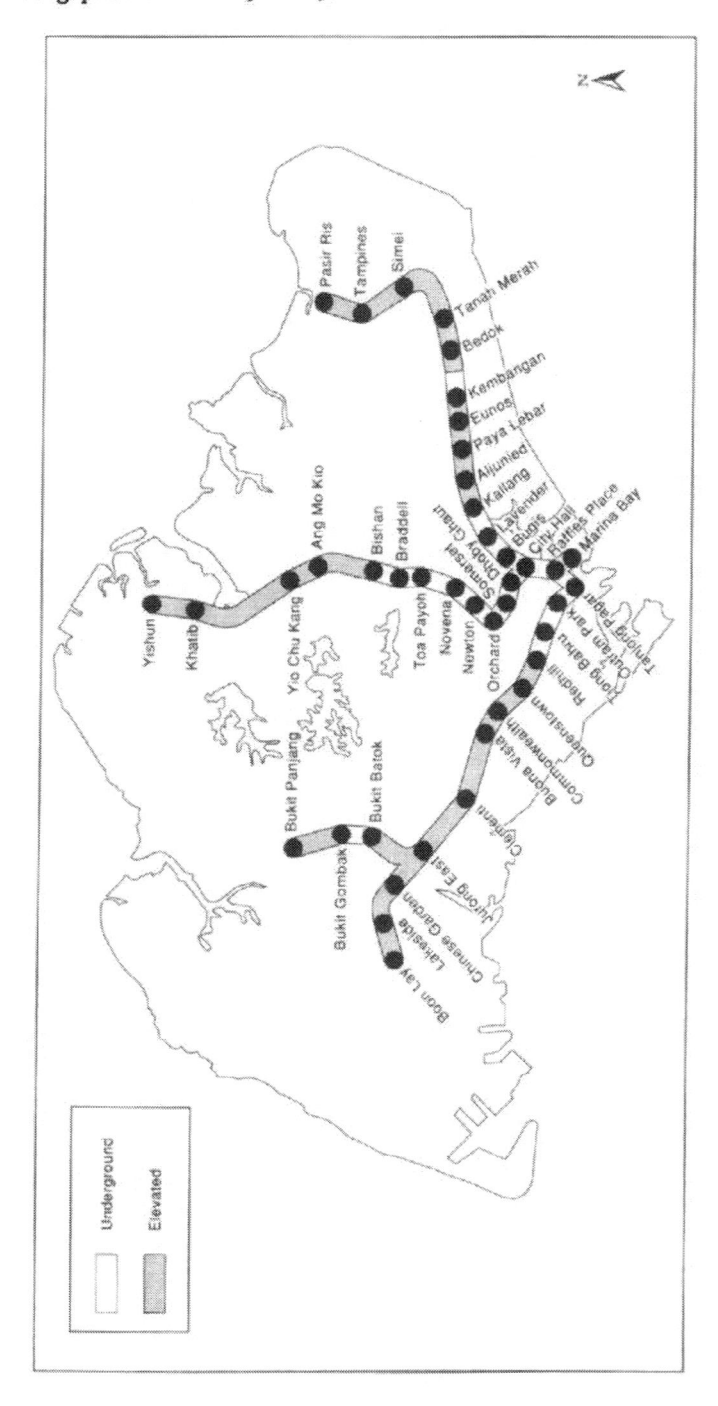

Figure 10. *Mass Rapid Transit System, 1989*

The Economy

handling capability to 20 million annually. The Civil Aviation Authority of Singapore managed the facility, which was consistently rated by the travel industry as one of the best airports in the world.

Changi also was noted for its air cargo facilities. The total volume of air cargo surged to 511,541 tons in 1988, an increase of 22.3 percent over the previous year and more than double the volume handled in 1983. Seletar Airport was used for charter and training flights. Additionally, Singapore was one of the most comprehensive airline maintenance and overhaul centers in the Asia-Pacific region, having more than fifty approved airline organizations in 1987.

Singapore Airlines (SIA) emerged from its humble beginnings in 1972 to become one of Asia's, if not the world's, leading airlines with an unparalleled reputation for service and efficiency. Following the division of Malaysia-Singapore Airlines, the airline owned jointly by Malaysia and Singapore between 1965 and 1972, SIA inherited the company's limited international routes and an aging fleet of ten airplanes. By 1988 SIA operated with one of the youngest fleets in the airline industry—twenty-two Boeing 747s, four Boeing 757s, six Airbus 310s, and twenty Boeing 747-400s on order. SIA flew to fifty-seven cities in thirty-seven countries around the globe, carrying 5.6 million passengers in 1988 and filling 74.8 percent of its seats. The airline ranked fourteenth worldwide in the number of passenger-kilometers and twelfth in terms of air freight-kilometers in 1987.

In economic terms, SIA's earnings accounted for 3.6 percent of the 1987 GNP. The airline was one of the country's major employers, providing jobs for one out of every eighty-nine workers in the country in 1987. As part of the government's move toward privatization, shares of its stock were sold to the public in 1985, leaving the government holding 63 percent of the shares, foreign investors 20 percent, and the public, including SIA employees, 17 percent. Another public sale of stock in 1987 brought the government-owned holdings down to 55 percent.

Agriculture

Orchard Road, now one of Singapore's most up-scale thoroughfares, got its name because it originally was lined with fruit orchards and vegetable gardens. Although contemporary Singapore still maintained a tiny agricultural base, by 1988 urbanization had reduced the land area used for farming to only about 3 percent of the total. Nonetheless, with intensive production, the farming sector met part of the domestic demand for essential fresh farm produce: poultry, eggs, pork, some vegetables, and fish. In 1988 there were 2,075 licensed farms occupying only 2,037 hectares of land, with a total output of some S$362 million worth of farm produce. A decade earlier farm holdings had covered 10,280 hectares.

The Primary Production Department, under the Ministry of National Development, ensured an adequate and regular supply of fresh produce and provided support for agro-industries, including research and development aimed at improving commercial and high-technology farming. The department projected in 1988 that a total of 2,000 hectares of land in ten agro-technology parks would be developed and rented out for long-term farming over the next decade.

The government began phasing out pig farming in 1984 because of odor and environmental pollution. Some 200 pig farms raising about 500,000 pigs in 1987 were scheduled to be reduced to 22 farms with 300,000 pigs by 1990. Imports from Malaysia, Indonesia, and Thailand would be increased to meet domestic needs. Some 1,000 poultry farms kept a total of about 2.2 million layers, 1.6 million broilers, 245,000 breeders, and 645,000 ducks. Singapore remained free of major animal diseases.

Singapore grew 5.6 percent of its total supply of 180,000 tons of fresh vegetables in 1988 and imported the rest from Malaysia, Indonesia, China, and Australia. The main crops cultivated locally included vegetables, mushrooms, fruit, orchids, and ornamental plants. About 370 vegetable farms produced an estimated 10,000 tons of vegetables, and mushroom cultivation expanded rapidly after the mid-1980s. The Mushroom Unit of the Primary Production Department conducted research on mushroom cultivation and advised commercial mushroom growers, who produced a variety of mushrooms for the local market.

Noted for its orchids, Singapore exported flowers worth S$13.8 million in 1988, mainly to Western Europe, Japan, Australia, and the United States. Singapore's 153 orchid farms produced another S$2.2 million worth of flowers for the domestic market.

Local fishermen provided about 13 percent of the country's 110,000-ton fresh fish supply in 1988, using three major fishing methods—trawling, gill-netting, and long-lining. There were about 1,170 licensed fishermen operating nearly 400 fishing vessels, most of which were motorized. The Jurong Port and Market Complex was a major fish landing point for both domestic and foreign vessels and handled 84 percent of the total fresh fish supply in 1988. Many foreign vessels brought their catches there for processing and reexport. Fresh fish arrived also by truck from Malaysia and Thailand and by sea and air from other neighboring countries.

The Ayer Rajah Expressway
Courtesy Singapore Ministry of Communications and Information

Mass Rapid Transit train passing a Housing and Development Board apartment complex
Courtesy Singapore Ministry of Communications and Information

Fish farming was a small but growing field. In 1988 seventy-four licensed marine fish farms raised mainly high-value fish such as grouper and sea bass in a total of forty hectares of coastal waters. Many of the farms had also introduced prawn farming in floating cages. Exports of ornamental fish for aquariums amounted to S$60 million in 1988. Some 400 licensed aquarium fish farms operated in Singapore in 1988, including 36 commercial farms operating in the Tampines Aquarium Fish Farming Estate.

* * *

Lawrence B. Krause, et al. present an interesting and readable background analysis in *The Singapore Economy Reconsidered*. For a summary of Singaporean economic development between 1959 and 1984, see *Singapore: Twenty-Five Years of Development* edited by You Poh Seng and Lim Chong Yah. The 1986 Report of the Economic Committee *The Singapore Economy: New Directions* (Singaporean Ministry of Trade and Industry) is vital for understanding the 1985 recession and the government's strategies for overcoming it and entering the 1990s. Analysis on this same subject is provided in *Policy Options for the Singapore Economy* by Lim Chong Yah, et al. Margaret W. Sullivan's *"Can Survive, La": Cottage Industries in Highrise Singapore* presents a sidewalk-level view of Singapore's small-scale manufacturing and economic and social psychology. The weekly *Far Eastern Economic Review* [Hong Kong] provides up-to-date information on economic events and developments. Statistical information from the Singapore government abounds in the form of annual yearbooks from the various ministries—Culture, Trade and Industry, and the Department of Statistics—and the very useful, although promotional, *Singapore 1989* and its annual equivalents. (For further information and complete citations, see Bibliography.)

Chapter 4. Government and Politics

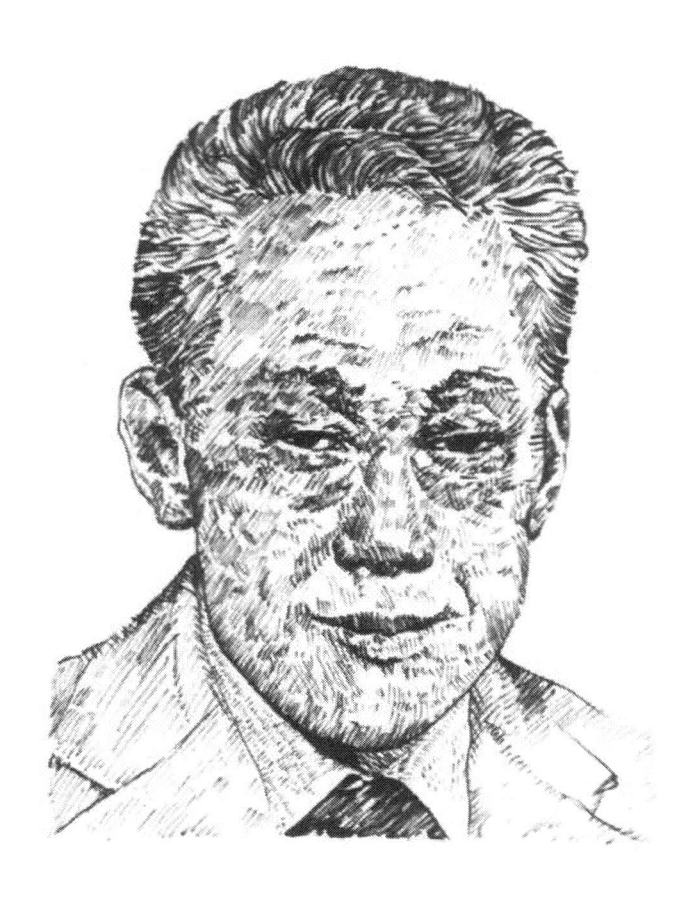

Lee Kuan Yew, prime minister of Singapore, 1959-90

AFTER TWENTY-FIVE YEARS OF INDEPENDENCE, Singapore enjoyed a reputation for political stability and honest, effective government. Probably the world's only ex-colony to have independence forced upon it, Singapore responded to its unanticipated expulsion from Malaysia in August 1965 by concentrating on economic development and by fostering a sense of nationhood. Though the survival of the miniature state was in doubt for a time, it not only survived but also managed to achieve the highest standard of living in Southeast Asia. The country also enjoyed a rare political continuity; its ruling party and prime minister triumphed in every election from 1959 to 1988. Singapore's government had an international reputation for effective administration and for ingenious and successful economic policies. It was also known for its authoritarian style of governance and limited tolerance for opposition or criticism, qualities the government deemed necessary to ensure survival in a hostile world and which its domestic and foreign critics claimed indicated a refusal to consider the opinions of its citizens or anyone outside the closed circle of the aging leadership. In the early 1990s, the leadership would face the issues of political succession and of modifying the relationship between the state and the increasingly prosperous and well-educated society it had created.

Government Structure

Form of Government

The Republic of Singapore is a city-state with a governing structure patterned on the British system of parliamentary government (see fig. 11). In 1989 legislative power was vested in a unicameral Parliament with eighty-one members who were elected for five-year terms (or less if the Parliament was dissolved prematurely). Members of Parliament were elected by universal adult suffrage from forty-two single-member constituencies and thirteen group representation constituencies. Voting was compulsory for all citizens above the age of twenty-one. The group representation constituencies elected a team of three members, at least one of whom had to be Malay, Indian, or a member of one of Singapore's other minorities. The group representation constituencies, introduced in the 1988 general election, were intended to ensure multiracial parliamentary representation to reflect Singapore's multiracial society. In another

Singapore: A Country Study

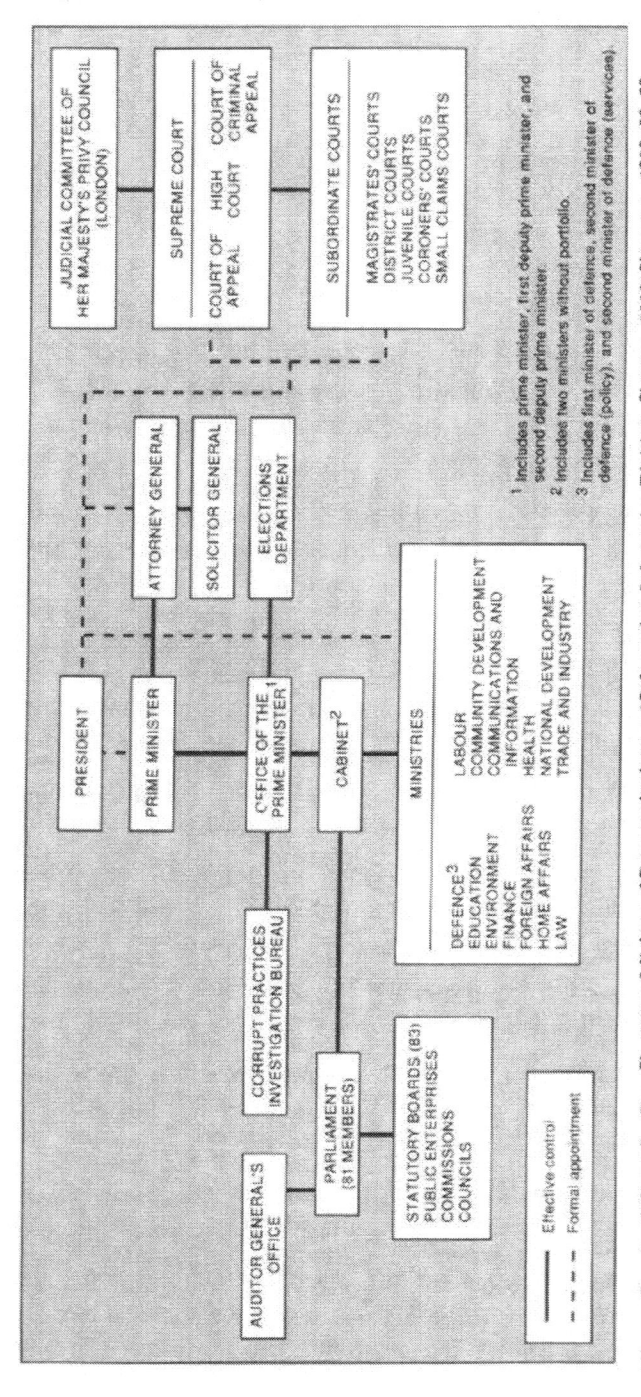

Source: Based on information from Singapore, Ministry of Communications and Information, Information Division, *Singapore, 1989*, Singapore, 1989, 53–63.

Figure 11. *Governmental Structure, 1989*

Government and Politics

departure from the British model, members of Parliament elected on a party ticket had to resign if they changed parties. A 1984 amendment to the Parliamentary Elections Act provided for the appointment to Parliament of up to three nonconstituency members if the opposition parties failed to win at least three seats in the general election. The nonconstituency members were chosen from the opposition candidates who had polled the highest percentage of votes. The seventh Parliament, elected on September 3, 1988, and meeting for the first time on January 9, 1989, included one elected opposition member and one nonconstituency member.

Singapore had only one level of government—national government and local government were one and the same. The form of the government reflected the country's unusually small area and modest total population of 2.6 million. Below the national level, the only recognized territorial divisions were the fifty-five parliamentary constituencies. Members of Parliament thus performed some of the same functions as municipal aldermen in foreign cities and often won political support by helping to find jobs for constituents or doing other favors requiring intercession with the powerful civil bureaucracy. The single-member constituencies varied in population from 11,000 electors to as many as 55,000; some of the variability reflected population movement away from the old urban core and out to new housing developments.

As in all British-style polities, the government was headed by a prime minister who led a cabinet of ministers of state selected from the ranks of the members of Parliament. The cabinet was the policy-making body, and its members directed the work of the permanent civil servants in the ministries they headed. In 1989, the cabinet comprised fifteen members. Below the prime minister were a first deputy prime minister and a second deputy prime minister. They were followed by the ministers in charge of such functional departments as the Ministry of Finance or the Ministry of Defence and by two ministers without portfolio. The prime minister could reassign his cabinet members to new portfolios or drop them from the cabinet, and successful ministers headed several progressively more significant ministries in their careers. There were thirteen ministerial portfolios in 1989: defence, law, foreign affairs, national development, education, environment, communications and information, home affairs, finance, labour, community development, trade and industry, and health. Some portfolios were split between different ministers. The first deputy prime minister (Goh Chok Tong) was also first minister for defence. The minister for communications and information (Yeo Ning Hong) also served as second minister for defence (policy). The minister for trade and industry (Brigadier General (Reserve) Lee Hsien Loong) was concurrently second minister for defence (services). The foreign affairs and law portfolios were similarly divided.

The cabinet met once or twice a week; its meetings were private and confidential. Administrative and staff support to the prime minister and cabinet was provided by the Office of the Prime Minister, the officials of which included a senior minister of state, a political secretary, a secretary to the prime minister, and a secretary to the cabinet. The Office of the Prime Minister coordinated and monitored the activities of all ministries and government bodies and also directly supervised the Corrupt Practices Investigation Bureau and the Elections Department. Each minister was assisted by two secretaries, one for parliamentary or political affairs and the other for administrative affairs. The latter, the permanent secretary, was the highest ranking career civil servant of the ministry.

The constitutional head of state was the president, who occupied a largely powerless and ceremonial role. The president was elected by the Parliament for a four-year term. He could be reelected without limit and removed from office by a two-thirds vote of Parliament. In turn, the president formally appointed as prime minister the member of Parliament who had the support of the majority of Parliament. On the advice of the prime minister, the president then appointed the rest of the ministers from the ranks of the members of Parliament. The president, acting on the advice of the prime minister, also appointed a wide range of government officials, including judges and members of advisory boards and councils.

In 1988 the government discussed amending the Constitution to increase the power of the president. A white paper introduced in Parliament in July 1988 recommended that the president be directly elected by the people for a six-year term and have veto power over government spending as well as over key appointments. It also proposed an elected vice president with a six-year term of office. The proposed changes originated as a device intended to permit Prime Minister Lee Kuan Yew, who had been prime minister since 1959, to retain some power should he retire, as he had hinted, and assume the presidency. No specific dates for the proposed constitutional change were given in the white paper. As of late 1989, no action had been taken.

Constitutional Framework

Singapore became an autonomous state within Malaysia, with its own constitution, on September 16, 1963. It separated from Malaysia on August 9, 1965. On December 22, 1965, the Legislative Assembly passed a Singapore Independence Bill and a

Constitutional Amendment. The Constitutional Amendment provided for a parliamentary system of government, with a president, whose duties were largely ceremonial, elected every four years by the Parliament.

The Constitution can be amended by a two-thirds vote of Parliament. A 1966 amendment allowed appeal from the Court of Appeal in Singapore to the Judicial Committee of Her Majesty's Privy Council (see Glossary) in Britain. In 1968 an amendment created the office of vice president and liberalized the requirements of citizenship. A 1969 amendment established the Supreme Court in place of the High Court and Court of Appeal as the highest appeal tribunal. A 1972 amendment entitled "Protection of the Sovereignty of the Republic of Singapore" introduced a measure to ensure the sovereignty of the city-state. It prohibited any merger or incorporation with another sovereign state, unless approved in a national referendum by a two-thirds majority. Under the same terms, it also prohibited the relinquishment of control over Singapore police forces and armed forces. In 1978 the Fundamental Liberties section of the Constitution (Part IV, Articles 9–16) was amended; the amendment extended government powers by establishing that arrests to preserve public safety and good order and laws on drug abuse would not be inconsistent with liberties set forth in that section of the Constitution.

Major Governmental Bodies

The President

The Constitution states that the president shall be elected by Parliament for a term of four years. In consultation with the prime minister, the president appoints to his personal staff any public officers from a list provided by the Public Service Commission. In the exercise of his duties, the president acts in accordance with the advice of the cabinet or of a minister acting under the authority of the cabinet. The president may use his discretion in the appointment of the prime minister and in withholding consent to a request for the dissolution of Parliament.

The Executive

The Constitution stipulates that the executive authority of Singapore is vested in the president and exercised by him or the cabinet or any minister authorized by the cabinet, subject to the provisions of the Constitution. The cabinet directs and controls the government and is responsible to Parliament. The president appoints a member of Parliament as prime minister and, in accordance with the advice of the prime minister, appoints an attorney general. The attorney general advises the government on legal matters and has the discretionary power to initiate, conduct, or terminate any proceedings for any offense.

The Legislature

The legislature consists of the president and Parliament. Members must be citizens of Singapore, twenty-one years of age or older, on the current register of electors, able to communicate in either English, Malay, Mandarin Chinese, or Tamil, and of sound mind. Membership ceases with the dissolution of a Parliament, which takes place every five years or at the initiative of the president. A general election must be held within three months of the dissolution of Parliament. Parliament convenes at least once a year, scheduling its meetings after the first session is summoned by the president. Members may speak in English, Malay, Mandarin Chinese, or Tamil, and simultaneous translation is provided. Parliamentary procedure follows the British pattern: all bills are deliberated in three readings and passed by a simple majority. Only the government may introduce money bills, those that allocate public funds and so provide for the ongoing operations of the state. Once passed, bills become laws with the assent of the president and publication in the official *Gazette*.

The final step in the passage of laws is the examination of bills by the Presidential Council for Minority Rights. The council, established by the Constitution (Amendment) Act of 1969, must determine if bills or other proposed legislation discriminate against any religious or ethnic community or otherwise contravene the fundamental liberties guaranteed by the Constitution. It also renders advisory opinions on matters affecting ethnic and religious communities that are referred to the council by the Parliament or government. The council is composed of ten members appointed for life and ten members and a chairman appointed for three-year terms by the president on the advice of the cabinet. Any bill on which the council renders an adverse opinion may not become law unless modified to its satisfaction or passed by two-thirds of the Parliament. The council has no jurisdiction over money bills or over any bill certified by the prime minister as affecting the defense or security of Singapore or the country's "public safety, peace, or good order." In addition, bills certified by the prime minister as so urgent that it is not in the public interest to delay their enactment are also exempted from review by the council.

Singapore Supreme Court
Courtesy Ong Tien Kwan
Singapore Parliament House
Courtesy Singapore Ministry of Communications and Information

Elections

The electoral system is based on single-member constituencies. The law (amendments to the Constitution and to the Parliamentary Elections Act) providing for group representation constituencies also stipulated that the total number of members of Parliament from group representation constituencies had to total less than half the total number of members. Slightly more than half the constituencies would remain single-member constituencies. The candidate receiving the largest number of votes wins the election in that constituency. The consequence of this electoral rule, common to most British-style constitutions, is to eliminate parliamentary representation for minority parties and to encourage the organization of parties whose candidates can win pluralities in many constituencies. In theory it is possible for a party to win every seat in parliament by receiving a plurality in every constituency.

The Judiciary

Singapore's judicial power is vested in the Supreme Court, consisting of a chief justice and an unspecified number of other judges. All are appointed by the president, acting on the advice of the prime minister. The judiciary functions as the chief guardian of the Constitution through its judicial review of the constitutionality of laws. The Supreme Court of Judicature Act of 1969, and various subsequent acts ensured judicial independence and integrity by providing for the inviolability of judges in the exercise of their duties and for safeguards on their tenure.

The Constitution establishes two levels of courts—the Supreme Court and the subordinate courts. The subordinate courts are the magistrates' courts, trying civil and criminal offenses with maximum penalties of three years' imprisonment or a fine of S$10,000 (for value of the Singapore dollar—see Glossary); the district courts, trying cases with maximum penalties of ten years' imprisonment or a fine of S$50,000; the juvenile courts, for offenders below the age of sixteen; the coroners' courts; and the small claims courts, which hear civil and commercial claims for sums of less than S$2,000. The Supreme Court consisted of the High Court, which has unlimited original jurisdiction in all civil and criminal cases and which tries all cases involving capital punishment; the Court of Appeal, which hears appeals from any judgment of the High Court in civil matters; and the Court of Criminal Appeal, which hears appeals from decisions of the High Court in criminal cases. The final appellate court is the Judicial Committee of Her Majesty's Privy Council in London. According to Article 100 of the Constitution, the president may make arrangements for appeals from the Supreme Court to be heard by the Judicial Committee of the Privy Council. In May 1989, Parliament abolished the right to appeal to the Privy Council except for criminal cases involving the death sentence and civil cases in which the parties had agreed in writing to such an appeal at the outset. The judicial system reflected British legal practice and traditions, except for trial by jury. Singapore abolished jury trials except for capital offenses in 1959; all jury trials were abolished by the 1969 amendment of the code of criminal procedure.

The chief justice and other judges of the Supreme Court are appointed by the president on the advice of the prime minister. The prime minister, however, is required to consult the chief justice on his recommendations for the Supreme Court. Judges of the subordinate courts are appointed by the president on the advice of the chief justice. Singapore's judges and superior courts repeatedly demonstrated their independence from the government by ruling against the government in cases involving political opponents or civil liberties. The government response in such cases was to amend the law or to pass new laws, but it did not attempt to remove or to intimidate judges. Although internal political struggle in Singapore from the 1950s through the 1980s was often intense, and the ruling government was quite willing to intimidate and imprison its political opponents, it always followed legal forms and procedures.

The attorney general is appointed by the president, on the advice of the prime minister, from persons qualified to become judges of the Supreme Court. A judge may be removed from office only for misbehavior or incapacitation, which must be certified by an independent tribunal. The attorney general, who is assisted by the solicitor general, is the principal legal advisor to the government, serves as the public prosecutor, and is responsible for drafting all legislation. The office of the attorney general, the Attorney General's Chambers, is divided into the legislation, civil, and criminal divisions.

The Public Service

The public services included the Singapore Armed Forces, the Singapore Civil Service, the Singapore Legal Service, and the Singapore Police Force. A Public Service Commission, consisting of a chairman and no less than five nor more than nine other members, was appointed by the president, with the advice of the prime minister. The Public Service Commission acted to appoint, confirm, promote, transfer, dismiss, pension, and impose disciplinary control over public officers. The Public Service Division, established within the Ministry of Finance in 1983, managed civil service personnel. It was headed by a permanent secretary who was responsible to the minister for finance.

A Legal Service Commission, with jurisdiction over all officers in the Singapore Legal Service, was composed of the chief justice as president, the attorney general, the chairman of the Public Service Commission, a judge of the Supreme Court nominated by the chief justice, and not more than two members of the Public Service Commission nominated by that commission's chairman. The Legal Service Commission acted to appoint, confirm, promote, transfer, dismiss, pension, and exercise disciplinary control over officers in the Singapore Legal Service.

The investigation of corruption in both the public and private sectors was under the sole authority of the Corrupt Practices Investigation Bureau, part of the prime minister's office. The Auditor General's Office, an independent agency functioning without interference from any ministry or department, monitored Parliament to ensure its compliance with laws and regulations and to identify irregularities in its disbursement of government resources.

The Public Bureaucracy

The government played an active role in managing the society and developing the economy and was the country's largest single employer. Government bodies and their employees fell into two distinct categories. The regular ministries and their civil service employees concentrated on recurrent and routine administrative tasks. The three ministries of education, health, and home affairs (including police, fire, and immigration) employed 62 percent (43,000) of the 69,700 civil servants in 1988. Members of the civil service in the strict sense of the term were those public employees who were appointed by the Public Service Commission and managed by the Ministry of Finance's Public Service Division. Active projects in economic development and social engineering were carried out by a large number of special-purpose statutory boards and public enterprises, which were free from bureaucratic procedures and to which Parliament delegated sweeping powers. As of 1984, there were eighty-three statutory boards employing 56,000 persons. About 125,000 members (10 percent) of the 1987 total work force were public employees (see Manpower and Labor, ch. 3).

The two branches of the public service served different functions in the political system. The civil service proper represented institutional continuity and performed such fundamental tasks as the

Government and Politics

collection of revenue, the delivery of such goods as potable water, and the provision of medical and educational services. The various quasigovernmental bodies, such as statutory boards, public enterprises, commissions, and councils represented adaptability, innovation, and responsiveness to local conditions. The constitutional framework of Singapore's government, with its Parliament, cabinet, courts, and functional ministries, resembled that of its British model and its peers in other countries of the British Commonwealth of Nations (see Glossary). The particular collection of boards and councils, which included everything from the Central Provident Fund to the Sikh Advisory Board, reflected the successful adaptation of the British model to its Southeast Asian environment.

Public service employment carried high prestige, and there was considerable competition for positions with the civil service or the statutory boards. Civil servants were appointed without regard to race or religion, and selected primarily on their performance on competitive written examinations. The civil service had four hierarchical divisions and some highly ranked "supergrade" officials. On January 1, 1988, there were 493 supergrade officers, who included ministerial permanent secretaries and departmental secretaries and constituted less than 1 percent of the 69,700 civil servants. Division one consisted of senior administrative and professional posts and contained 14 percent of the civil servants. The mid-level divisions two and three contained educated and specialized workers who performed most routine government work and who made up the largest group of civil servants, 33 and 32 percent of all civil servants, respectively. Division four consisted of manual and semiskilled workers who made up 20 percent of employees. In 1987, there were 3,153 appointments from the 9,249 applicants for positions in divisions one through three; 2,200 (some 70 percent) of the appointees were women.

The Singapore public service was regarded as almost entirely free from corruption, a fact that in large part reflected the strong emphasis the national leadership placed on probity and dedication to national values. The Corrupt Practices Investigation Bureau enjoyed sweeping powers of investigation and the unreserved support of the prime minister. Official honesty was also promoted by the relatively high salaries paid to public officials; the high salaries were justified by the need to remove temptations for corruption. In a system with clear echoes of the Chinese Confucian tradition, and the British administrative civil service, which recruited the top graduates of the elite universities, Singapore's public service attempted, generally successfully, to recruit the most academically talented youth. The Public Service Commission awarded scholarships to promising young people for study both in Singapore and at foreign universities on the condition that the recipients join the civil service after graduation. Young recruits to the development-oriented statutory boards were often given substantial responsibilities for ambitious projects in industrial development or the construction of housing estates. Officials had greater social prestige than their peers in business; power and official title outranked money in the local scale of esteem.

Statutory Boards

The eighty-three statutory boards were a distinctive feature of Singapore's government. In law, a statutory board was an autonomous government agency established by an act of Parliament that specified the purpose, rights, and powers of the body. It was separate from the formal government structure, not staffed by civil servants, and it did not enjoy the legal privileges and immunities of government departments. It had much greater autonomy and flexibility in its operations than regular government departments. Its activities were overseen by a cabinet minister who represented Parliament to the board and the board to Parliament. Statutory boards were managed by a board of directors, whose members typically included senior civil servants, businessmen, professionals, and trade union officials. The chairman of the board of directors, who was often a member of Parliament, a senior civil servant, or a person distinguished in some relevant field, was appointed by the cabinet minister who had jurisdiction over the board. The employees of the board were not civil servants, as they were not appointed by the Public Service Commission. The salary scales and terms of service of employees differed from board to board. Statutory boards did not receive regular allocations of funds from the public treasury, but were usually expected to generate their own funds from their activities. Surplus funds were invested or used as development capital, and boards could borrow funds from the government or such bodies as the World Bank (see Glossary). Statutory boards included the Housing and Development Board, the Central Provident Fund, the Port of Singapore Authority, the Industrial Training Board, the Family Planning and Population Board, and the Singapore Muslim Religious Council (Majlis Ugama Islam Singapura).

The statutory boards played the major role in the government's postindependence development strategy, and their activities usually served multiple economic and political goals. The Housing and Development Board provided a good example. The board was established by the first People's Action Party (PAP) government on

February 1, 1960, to provide low-cost public housing. The Lands Acquisition Act of 1966 granted the board the power of compulsory purchase of any private land required for housing development. The prices paid by the board were about 20 percent of the estimated market value of the land, which was, in fact if not in form, being nationalized. Between 1960 and 1979, the percentage of land owned by the government rose from 44 to 67 percent, increasing the government's control over that scarce resource and benefiting low-income voters, who supported the PAP, at the expense of the much smaller number of private landowners. Rents for Housing and Development Board apartments were subsidized, and selling prices for the apartments were set below construction costs and did not include land acquisition costs. Purchase prices for board apartments in the 1980s were 50 to 70 percent below those of privately owned apartments. By 1988 Housing and Development Board apartment complexes were home to 86 percent of the population, and construction of new apartments continued.

The Housing and Development Board succeeded in its primary goal of building large numbers of high-quality apartments. Its success depended on several factors, among them: access to large amounts of government capital; sweeping powers of land acquisition; the ability to train its own construction workers and engineers; the freedom to act as a building corporation and develop its own quarries and brick factory; the opportunity to enter into partnerships and contracts with suppliers of construction materials; and the ability to prevent corruption in contracting and allocation of apartments to the public. The government raised the capital for housing construction from the Central Provident Fund, a compulsory savings plan into which all Singapore workers contributed up to 25 percent of their monthly incomes, and from low-interest, long-term loans from such international development agencies as the World Bank.

By providing adequate housing at low cost to low-paid workers in the 1960s, the PAP delivered a highly visible and concrete political reward to the electorate and laid the foundations for its unbroken electoral success. In the 1960s and early 1970s, before the growth of export-oriented industry, housing construction provided much employment and an opportunity for workers to learn new skills. By controlling the pace and scale of housing construction, the government was able to better regulate the economy and smooth out cycles of economic activity. The result of rehousing practically the entire population was to make the government either the landlord or the mortgage holder for most families and so bring them into closer contact with the state. The government used resettlement to break up the ethnic enclaves and communities that had characterized colonial Singapore. It put its policy of multiracialism into practice by seeing that all apartment buildings contained members of all ethnic groups in numbers that reflected their proportion of the national population (see Population Distribution and Housing Policies, ch. 2). The program kept the cost of housing in Singapore relatively low and helped to avert pressure to raise wages. Because access to subsidized housing was a benefit extended only to citizens, it served to promote identification with the new state. Providing most of the population with low-cost housing gave the government and ruling party much favorable publicity, won public support, and was used as evidence for the correctness of the government's policies of centralized planning and social engineering implemented by experts on behalf of a passive public.

In a similar fashion, the Central Provident Fund (see Patterns of Development, ch. 3) benefited the citizens by providing them with secure savings for their old age and the satisfaction of having their own account, which could be used as security for the purchase of a Housing and Development Board apartment, for such expenses as medical bills, for college tuition, or to finance a pilgrimage to Mecca. The government benefited by gaining control of a very large pool of capital that it could invest or spend as it would and by removing enough purchasing power to limit inflationary tendencies. Furthermore, the proportion of the wage contributed to the fund by both workers and their employers could be adjusted at any time, enhancing the government's ability to control the economy. In 1988 the fund took 36 percent of all wages up to S$6,000 per month; 24 percent was paid by the worker and 12 percent by the employer. Among its other functions, the Central Provident Fund was one of the major instruments used by the government to control wages.

Public Enterprises

Apart from the statutory boards, which met general development and infrastructure goals, the government owned or held equity in many businesses that operated in the private sector. The government asserted that such businesses received no special subsidies and would be liquidated if they proved unprofitable. The wholly government-owned Temasek Holdings (Private) Limited was the country's largest corporation. Operated as an investment and holding corporation, its offices were in the Ministry of Finance, which provided the corporation with free accounting and secretarial services. Some government enterprises included former government departments, such as the Government Printing Office, which in

1973 became the Singapore National Printers Limited and offered its services to the private sector at market rates. Most government enterprises either provided key and potentially monopolistic services, such as Singapore International Airline or Neptune Orient Line, an ocean shipping firm, or they met strategic and defense needs. The Ministry of Defence wholly owned or had large equity shares in a range of companies engaged in weapons production, electronics, computer software, and even food production. In some cases the government banks, holding companies, or corporations were partners or had shares in local operations of multinational corporations. In such cases, the goal was both to attract the corporations to Singapore by offering investment funds and the promise of cooperation from government departments and to ensure that the corporations transferred proprietary technology and training to Singapore. The strategic nature of much government enterprise was acknowledged by the January 20, 1984, passage of the Statutory Bodies and Government Companies (Protection of Secrecy) Act. The law barred the unauthorized disclosure of confidential information by anyone associated with a statutory board or government enterprise and was considered necessary because the Official Secrets Act did not cover those bodies.

Parapolitical Institutions

After independence, Singapore's rulers perceived the population as uncommitted to the new state and as lacking a common identity. Accordingly, the government devoted much effort to fostering popular identification with the nation and commitment to the government's goals. In 1985 the Ministry of Community Development was formed by combining the former Ministry of Social Affairs with activities previously administered by the Office of the Prime Minister and by the Ministry of Culture. The new ministry coordinated a network of grassroots agencies intended to promote community spirit and social cohesion. These were the People's Association, the Citizens' Consultative Committees, the Residents' Committees, and the Community Center Management Committees. The People's Association was a statutory board established in 1960 and until 1985 a part of the Office of the Prime Minister. Its primary activity was to manage a system of 128 community centers, which offered recreational and cultural programs, along with such services as kindergartens and a limited number of daycare centers for children of working parents. The members of the various consultative and management committees were volunteers who received prestige but no salary. Each parliamentary constituency had a Citizens' Consultative Committee, whose members were in frequent contact with their member of Parliament. All Housing and Development Board apartment complexes had Residents' Committees, headed by volunteers and intended to promote neighborliness and community cohesion. The committees' activities included organization of neighborhood watch programs and tree-planting campaigns, in which the committees were assisted by the civil servants of the Residents' Committees Group Secretariat. In 1986 the government began organizing Town Councils in the larger housing estates. Although not official government bodies, the councils' immediate purpose was to take over some responsibilities for management of the complexes from the Housing and Development Board. Their larger purpose was to promote a greater sense of community and public involvement in the residents of the clusters of high-rise apartment buildings. In March 1985, the government inaugurated a Feedback Unit, a body intended to collect public opinion on proposed government policies and to encourage government departments to respond quickly to public suggestions or complaints.

The various advisory committees and the Feedback Unit provided functions that in many countries are provided by political parties. In Singapore the parapolitical institutions, which had the clearly political goal of generating public support for government policies, were presented as apolitical, inclusive, community-oriented bodies, headed by people motivated by a selfless desire for public service. Such an approach reflected a decision made by the country's rulers in the 1960s to avoid trying to organize a mass political party, in part because many less-educated citizens tended to shy away from partisan and overtly political groups. Others habitually avoided government offices and officers but would participate in community-oriented and attractive programs. The ruling elite had had serious problems both with opposition parties and with left-wing opposition factions within the PAP and apparently found the controlled mobilization offered by the parapolitical institutions more to its liking. Members of all the advisory and consultative boards were appointed by the government and were carefully checked by the security services before appointment. The government closely watched the performance of the leaders of the community organizations and considered the organizations a pool of talent from which promising individuals could be identified, promoted to more responsible positions, and perhaps recruited to the political leadership.

Political Parties

In 1989 the government of Singapore had been led since 1959 by one political party, the PAP, and one man, Prime Minister Lee

Government and Politics

Kuan Yew. In the 1988 parliamentary elections, opposition candidates challenged the ruling party in an unprecedented seventy contests, but the PAP still won eighty of the eighty-one seats in Parliament with 61.8 percent of the popular vote, 1 percent less than in 1984, and 14 percent less than in 1980.

The PAP was founded in 1954, and in the mid- and late 1950s acted as a left-wing party of trade unionists, whose leadership consisted of English-educated lawyers and journalists and Chinese-educated and pro-communist trade union leaders and educators. It won control of the government in the crucial 1959 election to the Legislative Assembly, which was the first election with a mass electorate and for an administration that had internal self-government (defense and foreign relations remained under British control). The PAP mobilized mass support, ran candidates in all fifty-one constituencies, and won control of the government with forty-three of the fifty-one seats and 53 percent of the popular vote (see People's Action Party, ch. 1). After a bitter internal struggle the English-educated, more pragmatic wing of the party triumphed over the pro-communists in 1961 and went on to an unbroken string of electoral victories, winning all the seats in Parliament in the 1968, 1972, 1976, and 1980 general elections.

With a single party and set of leaders ruling the country for thirty years, Singapore had what political scientists called a dominant party system or a hegemonic party system, similar to that of Japan or Mexico. There were regular elections and opposition parties and independent candidates contested the elections, but after the early 1960s the opposition had little chance of replacing the PAP, which regularly won 60 to 70 percent of the popular vote. The strongest opposition came from the left, with union-based parties appealing to unskilled and factory workers. In the early 1960s, the union movement split between the leftist Singapore Association of Trade Unions and the National Trades Union Congress (NTUC), which was associated with Lee Kuan Yew's pragmatic wing of the PAP. In 1963 the Singapore Association of Trade Unions was banned and its leaders arrested as pro-communist subversives. The NTUC was controlled by the PAP and followed a government-sponsored program of "modern unionism," under which strikes were unknown and wages were, in practice, set by the government through the National Wages Council.

The dominance of the PAP rested on popular support won by economic growth and improved standards of living combined with unhesitating repression of opposition leaders, who were regularly arrested on charges of being communist agents or sympathizers. In the mid-1980s, eighteen other political parties were registered, although many of them were defunct, existed only on paper, or were the vehicles of single leaders. Much of the electoral support for opposition parties represented protest votes. Those voting for opposition candidates did not necessarily expect them to win or even wish to replace the PAP government. They used their votes to express displeasure with some or all PAP policies.

At the top of the PAP organization was the Central Executive Committee (CEC). In 1954 the PAP constitution provided for a CEC of twelve persons directly elected by party members at the annual general meeting. The CEC then elected its own chairman, vice chairman, secretary, assistant secretary, treasurer, and assistant treasurer. This practice continued until August 1957, when six pro-communist members of the party succeeded in being elected. In 1958 the party revised its constitution to avoid a recurrence. The document called for CEC members to be elected at biennial party conferences by party cadre members, who in turn were chosen by a majority vote of the committee. The CEC was the most important party unit, with a membership overlapping the cabinet's. The two bodies were practically indistinguishable. Chairmanship of the CEC was a nominal post. Actual power rested in the hands of a secretary general, a post held by Lee Kuan Yew since the party's founding. He was assisted by a deputy secretary general who was charged with day-to-day party administration.

Subordinate to the CEC were the branches, basic party units established in all electoral constituencies. The branches were controlled by individual executive committees, chaired in most cases by the local delegate to Parliament. As a precaution against leftist infiltration, the CEC approved all committee members before they assumed their posts. One-half of the committee members were elected and one-half nominated by the local chairman. Branch activities were monitored by the party's headquarters through monthly meetings between members of the party cadre and the local executive committee. The meetings provided a forum for party leaders to communicate policy to branch members and a means to maintain surveillance over local activities.

The party's cadre system was the key to maintaining discipline and authority within the party. Individual cadres were selected by the CEC on the basis of loyalty, anticommunist indoctrination, education, and political performance. Cadre members were not easily identified but were estimated to number no more than 2 percent of the party's membership. As of 1989 a list of cadres had never been published.

Although clearly the dominant party, the PAP differed from the ruling parties of pure one-party states in two significant ways.

Government and Politics

Unlike the leaders of communist parties, the leaders of the PAP made no effort to draw the mass of the population into the party or party-led organizations or to replace community organizations with party structures. Singapore's leaders emphasized their government roles rather than their party ones, and party organizations were largely dormant, activated only for elections. Compulsory voting brought the electors to the polls, and the record of the government and the fragmented state of the opposition guaranteed victory to most if not all PAP candidates. In many general elections, more than half of the seats were uncontested, thus assuring the election of PAP candidates. The relatively weak party organization was the result of the decision of the leaders to use government structures and the network of ostensibly apolitical community organizations to achieve their ends. By the 1970s and 1980s, the leaders had confidence in the loyalty of the public service and had no need for a separate party organization to act as watchdog over the bureaucracy. The government was quite successful at co-opting traditional community leaders into its system of advisory boards, committees, and councils, and felt no need to build a distinct organization of party activists to wrest power from community leaders. Second-echelon leaders were recruited through appointment and co-optation and were preferentially drawn from the bureaucracy, the professions, and private enterprises, typically joining the PAP only when nominated for a parliamentary seat. The path to Parliament and the cabinet did not run through constituency party branches or the PAP secretariat. In the view of the leadership, political parties were instruments used to win elections and could be dispensed with if there was little prospect of serious electoral competition.

Political Dynamics
Power Structure

In 1989 political power in Singapore had largely passed from the hands of the small group of individuals who had been instrumental in Singapore's gaining independence. The successors of the independence generation tended to be technocrats, administrators, and managers rather than politicians or power brokers. The PAP leaders, convinced that a city-state without natural resources could not afford the luxury of partisan politics, acted after 1965 to "depoliticize" the power structure. Economic growth and political stability would be maintained instead by the paternal guidance of the PAP. Politics, as a result, was only exercised within very narrow limits determined by the PAP. Singapore was thus administered by bureaucrats, not politicians, in a meritocracy in which power was gained through skill, performance, and demonstrated loyalty to the leaders and their policies.

At the top of the hierarchy in 1989 were fifteen cabinet ministers, who were concurrently members of Parliament and the CEC, the PAP's highest policy-making body. Among these ministers was an inner core of perhaps five members. Below this group was a tier of senior civil servants who, in addition to their official duties, filled managerial and supervisory roles as directors of public corporations and statutory bodies. PAP members of Parliament without cabinet or government portfolios also tended to function at this level of the power hierarchy, providing links between the government and the populace.

Rifts within the leadership were rare. Although minor differences over policy may have existed, the top leaders presented a united front once decisions were made. The mode of decision making was consensus, and the style of leadership was collective, but in 1989 Prime Minister Lee Kuan Yew was by far the first among equals on both counts. The leaders identified themselves with the nation, were convinced that they knew what was best for the nation, and interpreted opposition to themselves or their policies as a threat to the country's survival.

The overwhelming majority of the leadership were not propertied or part of the entrepreneurial class. They did not appear particularly motivated by profit, gained lawfully or through corruption (which was almost nonexistent), or by the perquisites of their office (which although increasing, remained less than could be achieved in the private sector). Their reward, instead, derived from their access to power and their conviction that they were working for the nation and its long-term survival. Prime Minister Lee Kuan Yew and his close associates were highly conscious of their roles as founders of the new city-state.

The power structure was extremely centralized. It was characterized by a top-down style, featuring appointment rather than election to most offices; the absence of institutional restraints on the power of the prime minister and cabinet; and more effort devoted to communicating the government's decisions and policies to the public than to soliciting the public's opinion. The high degree of centralization was facilitated by the country's relatively small size and population. Although members of Parliament were elected by the public, the candidates were selected by the core leadership, often ran unopposed, and regarded their positions as due to the favor of the prime minister rather than the will of the voters. At the highest levels, the distinction between the bureaucracy and the political offices of Parliament was only nominal, and many members of

Parliament were selected from the upper ranks of the civil service and the public enterprises. Many high-level civil servants had direct access to the prime minister, who consulted them without going through their nominally superior cabinet minister.

Political Culture

Singapore possessed a distinct political culture, which fit into no simple category formulated by political scientists. It was centralized, authoritarian, and statist. It was also pragmatic, rational, and legalistic. In spite of possessing the superficial trappings of British institutions such as parliamentary procedure and bewigged judges, Singapore was, as its leaders kept reiterating, not a Western country with a Western political system. Although elections were held regularly, the electoral process had never led to a change of leadership, and citizens did not expect that political parties would alternate in power. Nor was there a tradition of civil liberties or of limits to state power. The rulers of an ex-colony with a multi-ethnic population, and a country independent only by default, assumed no popular consensus on the rules of or limits to political action. Singapore was a city-state where a small group of guardians used their superior knowledge to advance the prosperity of the republic and to bring benefits to what they considered a largely ignorant and passive population.

Singapore's leaders were highly articulate and expressed their principles and goals in speeches, books, and interviews. Their highest goal was the survival and prosperity of their small nation. They saw this as an extremely difficult and risk-filled endeavor. Conscious of the vulnerability of their state and aware of many threats to its survival, they justified their policy decisions on the grounds of national survival. They viewed government as an instrument intended to promote national ends and recognized no inherent limits on government concerns or activities. They prized intellectual analysis and rational decision making, and considered their own decisions the best and often the only responses to problems. The senior leadership prided itself on its ability to take the long view and to make hard, unpopular decisions that either responded to immediate dangers or avoided problems that would become apparent one or two decades into the future. They valued activism and will, and tried to devise policies, programs, or campaigns to deal with all problems. In a characteristic expression of Singapore's political culture, the rising young leader Brigadier General (Reserve) Lee Hsien Loong, when discussing the threat to national survival posed by declining birth rates, said, "I don't think we should . . . passively watch ourselves going extinct."

Passivity and extinction were linked and identified as trends the government's policies must counter.

The leadership's conviction of the state's vulnerability to manifold dangers and of the self-evident correctness of its analysis of those dangers resulted in very limited tolerance for opposition and dissent. According to Singapore's leaders, their opponents were either too unintelligent to comprehend the problems, too selfish to sacrifice for the common good, or maliciously intent on destroying the nation. Although by the 1980s Singapore had the highest standard of living in Southeast Asia, its leaders often compared it with generalized Third World countries. They saw such countries suffering from widespread corruption and demagogic politics, both reflecting concentration on immediate payoffs at the expense of long-term prosperity and the common good. For Singapore's leaders, politics connoted disruptive and completely negative activities, characterized by demagoguery, factionalism, and inflammatory appeals to communal, ethnic, or religious passions. When they spoke of "depoliticizing" Singapore's government, they had this view of politics in mind.

Key Political Issues
Succession

Prime Minister Lee Kuan Yew marked his sixty-fifth birthday in October 1988 and celebrated thirty years as prime minister in May 1989, and the question of political succession received increasing attention. The prime minister and his long-time associates devoted a good deal of their attention to the issue during the mid- and late 1980s. They continued their efforts to identify promising younger leaders and bring them into the cabinet. The process of selection was an elaborate one, which began by identifying well-educated administrators from the public service or private sector. Those people selected would be promoted to managerial positions, often when in their thirties; those who succeeded would be considered for appointment to a government position, often by being designated a parliamentary candidate. In addition to identifying good administrators, the older leaders tried to select persons of integrity and good character who were able to work as members of a team. Second-generation leaders were then tested by being given ministerial portfolios and encouraged to go out and meet the common people. The selection favored technocrats and administrators and rewarded those able to defer to senior leaders and get along smoothly with their peers. The senior leaders were aware that the process did not test the ability of the second-generation leaders to cope with a severe political crisis, but apparently could find no way to select for that skill.

The first-generation leaders were confident of their own rectitude and ability to use their very extensive powers for the common good, but they were not confident that their successors would be so self-restrained. Throughout the 1980s, they considered various limits on executive power that would minimize the possibility of arbitrary and corrupt rule. These included constitutional changes such as a popularly elected president with significant powers. The leaders claimed, perhaps with hindsight, that their refusal to build up the PAP as a central political institution and their efforts to bring a wide range of low-level community leaders into the system of government advisory bodies reflected a deliberate effort to disperse power and, in this sense, to "depoliticize" the society. The effort to encourage the circulation of elites between the government and the private sectors and between the military and the civilian structures served the same end. In so centralized a system, much depended on the decisions of the prime minister and undisputed leader, who was reluctant to appoint a designated heir or to approve any measure that would diminish his authority. The expectation clearly was that a much more collective leadership would replace the old guard.

An important member of the next generation of leaders was Lee Kuan Yew's son, Lee Hsien Loong. A brigadier general in the army, he first attained prominence in mid-1984 when he was cited as a possible candidate for the December 1988 general election. His prominence soared when, as minister for trade and industry and second ministor for defence (services), he was appointed head in 1986 of the critical Economic Committee assigned to redraft Singapore's economic strategy.

Lee Hsien Loong's ascendancy and his consolidation of administrative and political power assisted the political fortunes of bureaucrats who formerly had served in the Ministry of Defence (known as the "Min-def mafia") and ex-army officers who had served with Lee when he was a brigadier general. The ascendancy of the so-called "Min-def/ex-army officer group" under Lee initially was suggested by some observers when Singapore's armed forces appeared to assume new importance in government policy decisions. In March 1989, when the government announced a substantial pay raise for the civil service, the military received an even larger raise with guarantees that future raises would be consistently higher than those allotted for the civil service. The government also announced that the policy of assigning military officers to two-year rotations in civil service positions would continue. The policy ensured that the Singapore armed forces would be represented in all branches of the government and that the distinction between the civilian and military bureaucracies would be less clear.

The younger Lee's ascendancy to positions of greater power both in the PAP and the cabinet demonstrated his increased political stature. He was elected second assistant secretary general of the party in 1989, a post that had been vacant since 1984. This position placed him second in line in the party hierarchy behind his father and Goh Chok Tong, who was first assistant secretary general of the party and deputy prime minister and minister for defence in the cabinet. Lee enhanced his position in the cabinet when, as minister for trade and industry, he was named chairman of a special economic policy review committee. In this capacity, he gained the power to review the policies of all the ministries for their economic impact on Singapore. Previously such reviews were conducted only by the Ministry of Finance. Some Singapore observers speculated in 1989 that Lee would one day be appointed minister for finance and add control of Singapore's purse to his influence over the armed forces.

Generational ties supplemented the institutional links. Lee Hsien Loong and his associates were in their mid- to late thirties in 1989. Lee's nearest rival for power was Goh, who was forty-seven years old and for the past five years had been carefully groomed to serve as Lee Kuan Yew's immediate successor. For those with a military background, the military connection remained important even though they had resigned from the military before undertaking their civilian posts. The obligation of all males to periodically undergo reservist training assured that the military connection was not severed. If the army became a source of future cabinet ministers, some political observers expected that ethnic Malays and Indians would find it even more difficult to gain access to senior government positions. Ironically, the army in pre-independent Singapore was predominantly Malay and Indian. After independence, however, the government changed this bias by increasing Chinese representation through universal conscription.

Relations Between State and Society

By the late 1980s, Singapore's leaders generally agreed that the extensive economic and social transformation achieved after independence required a changed pattern of relations between the government and society. Government policies and practices devised to deal with the much simpler economy and less educated and prosperous citizenry of the 1960s were becoming increasingly

Goh Chok Tong, first deputy prime minister and minister for defence
Courtesy Singapore Ministry for Communications and Information

Brigadier General Lee Hsien Loong, minister for trade and industry and second minister for defence
Courtesy Singapore Ministry for Communications and Information

ineffective in the 1980s. The major issues were economic, involving debate over the optimal form of government involvement in the economy, and political, centering around highly contentious questions of the limits of government efforts to regulate the lives of citizens and to suppress dissent and criticism.

The Government's Economic Role

Singapore had achieved economic success with an economy that was heavily managed by the government (see Budgeting and Planning, ch. 3). The state owned, controlled, or regulated the allocation of capital, labor, and land. It controlled many of the market prices on which investors based their investment decisions and was the exclusive provider of social services and infrastructure. The 1985-86 recession, however, stimulated discussion of impediments to economic performance and of dysfunctional aspects of the government's role in the economy. A 1987 report by the government-appointed Private Sector Divestment Committee recommended that the state dispose of most of its interest in private companies over a ten-year period. It recommended privatizing forty-one of ninety-nine government-controlled companies and investing the proceeds in high-technology companies.

Throughout the 1970s and 1980s, the government controlled wages through the annual wage guidelines set by the National Wages Council, a body in which representatives of employers, trade unions (which were controlled by the PAP), and the government reached a consensus on wage levels for the coming year. The council's wage guidelines were in the form of macroeconomic projections and were applied across the board in all sectors of the economy. In December 1986, the cabinet approved a National Wages Council report calling for a revised wage system that permitted greater flexibility (the flexi-wage policy), with more use of bonuses and wage increases linked to increases in productivity. It was, however, not clear how the productivity of white-collar workers and civil servants, who constituted an increasing proportion of the work force, was to be measured. The call for wages to reflect the productivity and profitability of particular industries and firms implied more bargaining between workers and employers and a diminished role for the government, which could not impose a single rate on hundreds of distinct firms.

Although there was general agreement on the need for changed economic policies and modes of administration, significant tensions remained between those who favored greater flexibility and liberalization and those who wanted government direction of the economy. For Singapore's leaders, the challenge was to devise more

Singapore courtesy campaign
Courtesy Ong Tien Kwan

sophisticated means of ensuring overall control while permitting greater autonomy and flexibility at lower levels.

The Limits of Government Control

The highly ordered quality of life in Singapore itself became a political issue. Many citizens felt that they were over-regulated, governed by too many laws that were too easy to break. Singapore's leaders attributed the cause of the assumed decline of Western societies to the excessive individualism fostered by Western culture and warned that Singapore would suffer a similar fate unless saved by a national ideology (see Singaporean Identity, ch. 2).

The perceived need for an ideology was a phenomenon of the 1980s. Previously, Singapore's leaders had been concerned with physical survival more than cultural survival and had dismissed official ideologies as contrary to Singapore's status as an open port unfettered by conventional wisdom or fashionable orthodoxies. In the 1980s, as peace prevailed in the region, the government shifted its focus to the cultural sphere. Cultural preservation replaced physical survival as the major concern of leaders who feared being overrun by foreign cultures.

Looking ahead, senior leaders identified two major dangers to the nation: the failure of the nation to reproduce itself and the loss of national identity. The first threat was manifested in steadily falling birth rates, particularly among the nation's best educated citizens, many of whom failed even to marry (see Population, Vital Statistics, and Migration, ch. 2). The second threat, loss of identity, it was feared, would lead to loss of cohesion and hence to the destruction of the nation.

Singapore's leaders addressed these problems by proposing a series of policies intended to encourage citizens to marry and reproduce and to create a distinct Singaporean identity. The programs addressing the population problem included extensive publicity and exhortation, along with material incentives for giving birth to third and fourth children. Women university graduates were singled out for special attention because of their failure, in general, to marry and pass on their supposedly superior genes. The efforts to foster a Singaporean identity involved defending positive traditional Asian values against the perceived threat from Western culture. Both the schools and the society at large emphasized mastering Asian languages, such as Mandarin Chinese, and promoting Confucianism. Such programs, which attempted to modify the personal and intimate behavior of citizens but did not clearly reflect the demands of economic development, aroused a good deal of opposition, especially from younger and better educated citizens. The leadership's paternalistic style and its intolerance of criticism became political issues and were blamed by some observers for the increased vote for opposition candidates in the 1984 and 1988 elections.

Opponents of programs relating to Singapore identity claimed that the leaders' purpose was to shift support for a national ideology into support for the government and the ruling PAP. Promoting Confucianism, for example, was a convenient means of convincing individuals to subordinate their interests to those of society. Others held that the government's real fear was not that Singapore would lose its culture or values but that continued Westernization of the society would mean more pressure for real democracy, more opposition candidates, and the possibility of a change in government.

The electoral vote for the PAP dropped considerably, going from 75.6 percent in 1980 to 62.9 percent in 1984 and by a lesser amount to 61.8 percent in 1988. In 1988 the PAP campaign slogan was "More Good Years" and the opposition had no solid issues with which to attract support. The election resulted in another landslide victory for the PAP and the winning of eighty out of eighty-one parliamentary seats.

The PAP's style of leadership emphasized control by a strong bureaucratic leadership intolerant of political opposition. The PAP mind-set has been traced to its battle for political preeminence with its communist rivals in the 1950s and 1960s. In the late 1980s,

Government and Politics

Singapore had one of Asia's highest standards of living and was not regarded as fertile ground for a communist insurrection. The PAP maintained that Singapore was too small for a two-party system to work effectively and did not anticipate sharing power. It stymied the development of a legitimate opposition by a range of political tactics, such as using the provision of public services to induce citizens to vote for PAP candidates. Critics also charged that the party controlled the press, preventing the free flow of ideas. Although there was no direct censorship of the press, newspapers were closely monitored and radio and television stations were owned by the government (see The Media, this ch.).

Political Opposition

In the elections of September 1988, the only opposition member to win election was Singapore Democratic Party candidate Chiam See Tong who repeated his 1984 victory. However, in the contest over eight additional seats—two representing single-seat constituencies, and six representing two newly formed three-member group representation constituencies—the PAP received less than 55 percent of the vote. Furthermore, under a constitutional amendment passed in 1984, the opposition was to be allotted three parliamentary seats, whether it won them or not. Thus, as a result of the 1988 election, in addition to Chiam, the opposition was permitted to seat two additional, nonconstituency, nonvoting members of Parliament in the new Parliament.

In the 1988 elections, Lee Siew Choh, a candidate of the Workers' Party and one of the two opposition members chosen to sit in Parliament as nonvoting members, was forced on the campaign's opening day to go to court and pay damages for comments he made about PAP during the 1984 election. The other opposition member, Francis Seow, faced trial for alleged tax evasion and, if convicted, faced disqualification from Parliament. Shortly afterwards, Prime Minister Lee threatened to bring a defamation suit against Workers' Party leader J.B. Jeyaretnam. Another Workers' Party candidate, Seow Khee Leng, was threatened by the government with bankruptcy proceedings. All three had been successfully sued by Lee for slander in earlier elections.

The state of the opposition was rooted in the PAP's drive, beginning in 1963, to suppress all communist and leftist influence in Singapore. The government discouraged opposition political activity through the use of open-ended laws such as the Internal Security Act, which was originally intended to deal with armed communist insurrection during the Malayan Emergency of 1948-60. This law permitted the indefinite detention by executive order of any person suspected of leftist or procommunist activity. Amnesty International frequently cited Singapore for using the act to suppress legitimate, nonviolent political opposition. That organization also cited Singapore's use of deprivation of citizenship and banishment as means of repression. The government often associated opposition with foreign manipulation, which compounded its fear of dissent of any kind.

There were few issues on which the PAP could be challenged. Under PAP rule, Singapore had achieved unprecedented economic prosperity as well as marked social progress in racial harmony, education, health care, housing, and employment. The PAP's achievements had created a popular confidence in the party that was difficult to overcome. The opposition parties themselves were divided along racial and ideological lines and unable to compete with the PAP as a common front.

In May and June 1987, twenty-two people were detained without trial under the Internal Security Act for alleged involvement in a communist conspiracy. All detainees were released by the end of the year with the exception of Chia Thye Poh, who was held for more than two years. A virulent critic of the government and former member of Parliament representing the Barisan Sosialis (The Socialist Front—see Glossary), he was finally released in May 1989 after having been detained since October 1986. Although Chia was never charged, the government alleged that he was a member of the outlawed Communist Party of Malaya (CPM—see Glossary), assigned to infiltrate the Barisan Sosialis in order to destabilize the government. In 1987 amendments were made to the Parliament Privilege, Immunities, and Powers Act of 1962, giving Parliament the power to suspend any parliamentary member's immunity from civil proceedings for statements made in Parliament and to imprison and fine a member if he or she were found guilty of dishonorable conduct, abuse of privilege, or contempt.

The Workers' Party, led by J.B. Jeyaretnam in 1989, was the principal opposition party. The Workers' Party stood for a less regimented society, constitutional reforms, less defense spending, and more government social services. It was supported by lower income wage earners, students, and intellectuals. Next was the United People's Front, founded in December 1974 as a confederation of the Singapore Chinese Party, the Singapore Islamic Party, and the Indian-supported Justice Party. It campaigned for a more democratic political system. A third party, ideologically to the left of both the United People's Front and the Workers' Party, was the People's Front, established in 1971. In 1972 its campaign platform advocated a democratic socialist republic and no foreign military ties. In 1973 the party's secretary general, Leong Mun Kwai, received a six-month prison sentence for inciting the people of Singapore to seize government leaders. Seventeen other opposition parties were registered in 1989, including the Barisan Sosialis, once the primary target of the government's political surveillance activities because of its former role in antigovernment street demonstrations, student protests, and industrial strikes. Lee Siew Choh, a nonvoting member of Parliament in 1989, was the leader of the party's moderate wing.

Foreign Policy

Governing Precepts and Goals

Minister for Foreign Affairs Suppiah Dhanabalan described the governing precepts of the country's foreign policy in 1981 as a willingness to be friends with all who sought friendship, to trade with any state regardless of ideology, to remain nonaligned, and to continue to cooperate closely with Association of Southeast Asian Nations (ASEAN—see Glossary) members (see fig. 12). These precepts, while consistent with the thrust of foreign policy from the 1960s to the mid-1980s, failed to account for the basic role that the survival of the nation played in determining foreign policy goals. A primary foreign policy consideration until the mid-1980s, survival became an issue because of Singapore's size and location and Indonesia's Confrontation (Konfrontasi—see Glossary) campaign against Malaysia in the 1960s. It was further linked to the concept of the "global city" first proposed in 1972 by then Deputy Prime Minister for Foreign Affairs Sinnathamby Rajaratnam. This concept suggested that Singapore's survival depended on its ability to create a continuing demand for its services in the world market. By implementing a policy of international self-assertion, Singapore would shift from a reliance on entrepôt trade and shipping to export-oriented industries.

The focus on survival was evidenced in Singapore's reaction to Vietnam's invasion of Cambodia in 1978. Of the many issues surrounding the event, one of particular interest to Singapore was Vietnam's blatant disregard for the sovereignty of a small nation. Singapore's decision to draw international attention to the situation was based, in part, on the need for international recognition of its own sovereignty. Following the invasion, Singapore heightened its international profile by expanding diplomatic representation abroad and attending international forums. Singapore was a member of ASEAN, the Nonaligned Movement (see Glossary), the Asian Development Bank (see Glossary), the Group of 77 (see

Singapore: A Country Study

Figure 12. Association of Southeast Asian Nations (ASEAN), 1989

Glossary), the International Telecommunications Satellite Organization (Intelsat—see Glossary), and the United Nations and its affiliated organizations.

With the passing of the first generation of leaders in the late 1980s, foreign policy was shaped less by the old fears produced by the events of the 1960s and 1970s and more by the experience of regional stability that prevailed during the formative years of the new guard or second generation of leaders. The self-assertion of a decade earlier was no longer required, and Singapore could afford to be less abrasive in its foreign policy style. Foreign policy objectives in the late 1980s were far more subtle than simple survival.

In March 1989, Singapore announced that it was charting a new course of "economic diplomacy" to meet future international challenges. It sought expanded economic ties with China, the Soviet

Union, several East European nations, and the three nations of Indochina: Laos, Cambodia, and Vietnam. In a speech to Parliament on March 17, 1989, Minister of Foreign Affairs Wong Kan Seng announced that Singapore was hoping to reverse its previous staunchly anticommunist posture and normalize relations with several communist countries to promote more compatible relationships based on mutual economic interests.

Foreign policy also had to accommodate the views of predominantly Islamic neighbors who were viewed by Singapore's leaders as possible threats to its existence. As a gesture toward its neighbors and in recognition of its own regional roots, Singapore maintained its membership in the Nonaligned Movement, although it consistently rejected neutrality as a foreign policy option. Singapore's leaders had reasoned that avoiding entanglements with the great powers would leave Singapore far too vulnerable to threats from regional neighbors, as Indonesia's Confrontation campaign had demonstrated. Neutrality also was perceived to be inconsistent with the Total Defence (see Glossary) style of defensive vigilance that the PAP attempted to instill in the citizenry following the Soviet invasion of Afghanistan and the Vietnamese occupation of Cambodia. The guiding concept of Total Defence was known as national integration and was meant to unify a population made up of immigrants and a mix of racial groups into a people with the "human will" to be "unconquerable."

Foreign policy, therefore, stressed maintaining a balance of power in the region. Singapore promoted the regional involvement of all great powers because it feared aggravating a neighbor by relying on any one power. Although it would have preferred relying upon the United States to guarantee its security, such dependence would not have been tolerated by the other ASEAN states. Singapore also remained suspicious of the ability of the United States to pursue a consistent foreign policy following its withdrawal from Vietnam.

Retaining its developing nation status was another foreign policy goal of the 1980s. In 1989, however, Singapore lost the concessions enjoyed under the United States government's Generalized System of Preferences (GSP—see Glossary) on imports from developing countries and the ability to borrow from the World Bank and the Asian Development Bank at concessional rates (see Trade, Tourism, and Telecommunications, ch. 3).

Regional

Association of Southeast Asian Nations

Cooperation with ASEAN, which included Indonesia, Malaysia, Thailand, the Philippines, and Brunei, was the center of Singapore's foreign policy after 1975. Before 1975, Singapore's interests were global rather than regional, and its policy toward ASEAN was characterized by detachment. As the wealthiest country in Southeast Asia, it was criticized for failing to help its neighbors. After 1975, however, Singapore was criticized for being too ASEAN oriented, too active, and too vocal in the organization for its size, particularly where matters of regional security were concerned. The shift in Singapore's stance toward ASEAN followed the communist victory in Vietnam in 1975, the waning of a United States military presence in Asia, and new signs of Soviet interest in the region. Furthermore, the other ASEAN states permitted Singapore to assume a leading role in regard to the issue of Vietnam's invasion of Cambodia in 1978. The situation in Cambodia, in fact, became the unifying force for the diverse countries belonging to ASEAN. Singapore's minister for foreign affairs, Wong Kan Seng, commented in March 1989 that, if the situation were resolved, some other force would be required to unite the member nations. The resolution of the Cambodian conflict would also raise the possibility of Vietnam being considered for membership, although in 1989 Singapore was not prepared to support Vietnam's immediate entry.

ASEAN provided Singapore with a means of improving its bilateral relations with Indonesia and Malaysia, two neighbors who were potential threats to Singapore's security. Singapore's leaders never identified the external enemy Singapore's armed forces were trained to deter (see Strategic Perspectives, ch. 5). When asked in 1984 who was Singapore's biggest threat, Prime Minister Lee responded only that "the biggest threat . . . is that any threat will come from someone bigger than us."

Malaysia

The acrimony that once characterized Singapore's relationship with Malaysia began to change in the 1980s when the two countries adopted a course of reconciliation. The improvement in relations began when Mahathir Mohamad became prime minister of Malaysia. Lee Kuan Yew and Mahathir achieved a personal rapport that established the tone for a rapprochement, but Singapore's expulsion from Malaysia in August 1965 continued to color the relationship. Singapore's primary concern was that Malaysia maintain a political system that tolerated multiracialism. In Singapore's view, the undermining of this political principle in Malaysia would have regional ramifications. Regional tolerance of multiracialism, for example, might be reduced if an Islamic revival in Malaysia led to the establishment of an Islamic state and the status of Malaysia's Chinese population were subsequently endangered.

Government and Politics

Singapore was linked with Malaysia militarily through the 1971 Five-Powers Defence Agreement (see Glossary), an arrangement under which the security of Singapore and Malaysia was guaranteed by Britain, Australia, and New Zealand. Singapore cooperated with both Malaysia and Indonesia in maintaining the security of the Malacca and Singapore straits. Another link with Malaysia was the Inter-Governmental Committee, a forum established in 1980 for the informal discussion of bilateral issues by delegations headed by each country's minister for foreign affairs.

Indonesia

Singapore's relationship with Indonesia, like its relationship with Malaysia, was built on a foundation of past discord, specifically Indonesia's Confrontation campaign against Malaysia from 1963 to 1966. After President Sukarno (1945-67) was deposed, relations were based to a large degree on Lee Kuan Yew's personal relationship with President Soeharto. Because bilateral relations lacked an institutional foundation, they were vulnerable to the departure of either leader.

Indochina

Singapore's relationship with the countries of Indochina in 1989 permitted the conduct of normal commercial transactions, but discouraged aid, training, infrastructural development, and trade in strategic goods. In April 1989, the Ministry of Home Affairs and the Ministry of Foreign Affairs informed Singaporean companies that they could not invest in Vietnam until the Vietnamese had withdrawn their troops from Cambodia. The companies were allowed to conduct negotiations with Vietnam but could not commit any investments until the Vietnamese withdrawal was complete. A few Singaporean companies had invested in Vietnam while normal commercial transactions were still going on, before the government had a clear policy concerning investments. Minister for Foreign Affairs Wong Kan Seng indicated in 1989, however, that Singapore was looking beyond the Cambodian problem to its future relations with Indochina.

Superpowers

The United States

Relations between Singapore and the United States became strained in 1988 after the United States was accused of meddling in Singapore's internal affairs and a United States diplomat was expelled as a result of the charge. The United States had objected to the government's policy of restricting the circulation of several Hong Kong-based publications, including the *Asian Wall Street Journal* and the *Far Eastern Economic Review*, and to the use of the Internal Security Act to detain indefinitely dissidents or those deemed a threat to the existing order. The expelled diplomat was accused of instigating members of the opposition to contest the 1988 elections. The essence of a speech on United States-Singapore relations, given by Lee Hsien Loong before the Asia Society in Washington, D.C., on May 16, 1989, was that the relationship was strong but that the United States should refrain from interfering in Singapore's internal affairs.

The United States was Singapore's largest trading partner in the 1980s. It also was viewed as a benevolent power whose military presence in the region kept Soviet influence in check, balanced China's increasing military strength, and obviated Japan's rearming. Singapore was concerned, however, that the United States eventually would tire of its role in the Asia-Pacific region. This concern was somewhat allayed in 1989 when President George Bush, demonstrating his commitment to maintain American interests in the area, both dispatched Vice President Dan Quayle on an Asian tour and visited the region himself in the first few months of his administration.

China

In 1989 Singapore had not yet established diplomatic relations with China, largely out of deference to Indonesia, the ASEAN state most concerned about China's intentions in the region. Indonesia's move to initiate diplomatic relations with Beijing in February 1989, however, was expected to clear the way for Singapore to follow. Regarding Indonesia's announced intentions, Singapore's First Deputy Prime Minister Goh Chok Tong stated in February 1989 that it was "logical" for Singapore "to follow suit"; however, he saw no need to move hastily because Singapore already had a cordial trading relationship with China. Singapore's trade with China in 1988 amounted to US$2.98 billion, a 27 percent increase over 1987. Reexports to China were up by 108 percent over the same period.

The other side of improving relations with China was maintaining good relations with Taiwan. Although Singapore lacked diplomatic ties with Taiwan in 1989, the two enjoyed a flourishing economic exchange. Trade with Taiwan in 1988 reached S$6.9 billion, exceeding that with China (S$5.7 billion). Some analysts suspected, however, that once serious negotiations to establish diplomatic ties began with Beijing, China was likely to pressure Singapore to end its

Queen Elizabeth II visiting Prime Minister Lee Kwan Yew in 1989
Courtesy Singapore Ministry of Communications and Information

relationship with Taiwan, particularly in matters of military cooperation such as the training in Taiwan of Singaporean troops. Others speculated that the relationship would not be affected. Lee Kuan Yew said in March 1989 that he did not expect Singapore's relationship with Taiwan to change because both countries had been aware for some time of Singapore's intention to follow Indonesia in normalizing relations with China and both had taken such a development into consideration. A visit by Taiwan's President Li Teng-hui shortly after Indonesia's diplomatic initiative was interpreted as a sign of continuing warm relations between Taiwan and Singapore.

The Soviet Union

In 1989 Singapore maintained both economic and diplomatic relations with the Soviet Union. From the mid-1960s until the mid-1970s, Singapore's leaders promoted trade relations with Moscow in the belief that a Soviet role in Southeast Asia would ensure the permanent interest of the United States in the region. The Soviet Union was viewed as a major power and as a counterweight to China and, therefore, as a significant factor in maintaining the regional power balance. This view changed when the Soviets established a military presence at Cam Ranh Bay in Vietnam, following the signing of the Soviet-Vietnamese Treaty of Friendship and Cooperation in November 1978, and actively supported the Vietnamese invasion of Cambodia a month later. At that time, according to Singapore, Moscow became a threat to regional stability.

Soviet diplomacy toward the region changed, however, in the mid-1980s under the leadership of new General Secretary Mikhail Gorbachev. Beginning with a milestone foreign policy address in Vladivostok in July 1986, he initiated extended ties with the ASEAN states and committed the Soviet Union to playing a more constructive role in resolving the Cambodian issue. His interest in improving ties with the region and his new emphasis on Soviet economic development acted to modify regional perceptions. Singapore, as well as many of its ASEAN partners, became increasingly receptive to upgrading their bilateral relations with Moscow.

Trade, banking, and shipping were the three critical areas of Singapore's economic ties with Moscow. Singapore's exports were mainly in the form of repairs to Soviet vessels in Singapore shipyards. Other exports included rubber, coconut oil, and fuel oil. In return, the Soviets exported fish and fish products, cast iron, light machinery, and crude oil. Beginning in the mid-1980s, the Soviets encouraged Singaporean firms to invest in joint ventures in the Soviet Union. Singapore's shipyards were reported in 1988 to be interested in reconstructing and developing the port of Nakhodka, the second largest port in the Soviet Far East after Vladivostok.

The Media

The government did not normally censor the press, but it owned the radio and television stations and closely supervised the newspapers. Under the Newspapers and Printing Presses Act, passed in 1974 and amended in 1986, the government could restrict—without actually banning—the circulation of any publication sold in the country, including foreign periodicals, that it deemed guilty of distorted reporting. These laws provided the legal justification for restrictions placed on the circulation of such foreign publications as the *Asian Wall Street Journal* and *Time* magazine's Asian edition in 1987. The government also restricted the circulation of *Far Eastern Economic Review* and *Asiaweek* in 1987 for "engaging in the domestic politics of Singapore."

Singapore had seven daily newspapers at the end of 1987: two in English, *The Straits Times* and *The Business Times;* three in Chinese, *Lianhe Wanbao, Shin Min Daily News,* and *Lianhe Zaobao;* one in Malay, *Berita Harian;* and one in Tamil, *Tamil Murasu.* With the exception of the *Tamil Murasu*, all were published by Singapore Press Holdings Ltd, a group that comprised Singapore News and Publications Ltd, the Straits Times Press Ltd, and the Times Publishing Company. Daily newspaper circulation in 1988 totaled 743,334 copies, with Chinese language newspapers accounting for the highest number (354,840), followed by English (340,401) and Malay (42,458) newspapers.

The Singapore Broadcasting Corporation operated five radio stations and three television channels. Established in 1980, it provided programming in Singapore's four official languages—Malay, Chinese, Tamil, and English—and was supported by revenue from radio and television licensing fees and commercial advertising. Each of four of the five radio stations broadcast in one of the four official languages, while the fifth alternated between English and Mandarin. The television stations, which provided a total of about 163 hours of programming a week, also broadcast in separate languages. Channel Five's programming was in Malay and English, Channel Eight's in Mandarin and Tamil, and Channel Twelve's in English. In many cases, programs also were subtitled in several languages.

By 1989 Singapore's leadership had been in place for three decades, during which it guided an extraordinarily successful program of economic development and physical rebuilding. In the 1990s, a new generation of leaders would take over, and the debate over the need to change the political system that had been so successful in the past would grow. Some elements of an increasingly prosperous and well-educated population, who took Singapore's national viability and survival for granted, questioned the elderly leaders' assertions that a host of pressing dangers justified their authoritarian and paternalistic style of governance. To the leaders, however, the country's prosperity and their continued electoral victories demonstrated the correctness of their policies and methods of rule. They envisioned a new generation of leaders who would continue the proven practices established by the country's founding fathers. The inherent tensions between generations and between the advocates of change and those of continuity were likely to mark the politics of the 1990s.

* * *

Basic information on Singapore's form of government is provided by the annual volumes published by the Information Division of the Ministry of Communications and Information, such as the annual editions of *Singapore* and *Singapore Facts and Pictures*. The same division's monthly *Singapore Bulletin* provides brief coverage of a wide range of events in the country, and its sister publication, *Mirror*, publishes longer articles on selected topics, focusing on industry and education. Singapore's internal politics attracted little attention from foreign scholars in the late 1980s; the basic sources were produced by local scholars affiliated with the National University of Singapore and the Institute for Southeast Asian Studies. The most comprehensive is *Government and Politics of Singapore*, edited by Jon S.T. Quah, Chan Heng Chee, and Seah Chee Meow. This is complemented by Peter S.J. Chen's *Singapore: Development Policies and Trends*. Raj K. Vasil's *Governing Singapore* takes a more analytical perspective and includes information based on interviews with senior leaders. The annual country summaries published in the February issue of *Asian Survey* and the *Far Eastern Economic Review*'s annual *Asia Yearbook* provide authoritative coverage of politics and foreign relations. The quarterly and annual *Country Reports* for Singapore, published by the Economist Intelligence Unit, contain timely and succinct political reporting. The weekly *Far Eastern Economic Review* and *Asiaweek* regularly cover Singapore's politics and social trends. (For further information and complete citations, see Bibliography.)

Chapter 5. National Security

Singaporean preparedness

THE TOTAL DEFENCE CONCEPT, the cornerstone of Singapore's national security policy in 1989, called for the deterrence of aggression through the maintenance of a small but well-trained and well-equipped military backed by a committed population proficient in civil defense. During the late 1960s and early 1970s, the Singapore government under Prime Minister Lee Kuan Yew laid the foundation for a national security system based on total preparedness, which involved more than 10 percent of the adult population in some type of national service. After 1967 all males were required to register at age sixteen for two years of national service. By 1989 almost all males under the age of fifty had received military training in the armed forces, or training in the police force or in a public service related to civil defense.

Singapore's national security perceptions under Lee were influenced by the country's size and geographic location and by changes in the regional military balance. The nation's military planners acknowledged that if it were attacked by a larger power, Singapore could not defend itself with its own resources for more than a few weeks. However, they believed that the total preparedness for war of the country's military and civilian populace would deter potential adversaries from regarding Singapore as an easy target for aggression. Singapore's foreign policies were carefully planned to accommodate national security considerations. In 1989, for example, Lee stated that Singapore would consider normalizing its relations with China only after Indonesia had completed its plan to do the same. This position was consistent with Singapore's national security policy of deferring to the foreign policy concerns of its larger neighbors. After the Republic of Vietnam (South Vietnam) fell to communist forces in 1975, Singapore viewed the growth of communist influence in the region, and the reduced American military presence in Southeast Asia, as a potential threat to its national security. Singapore's leaders feared that a militaristic Vietnam, supported by the Soviet Union, would promote communist movements in Thailand, Malaysia, and Singapore. Throughout the 1980s, the Lee government supported the Association of Southeast Asian Nations (ASEAN—see Glossary) in opposing Vietnam's occupation of Cambodia; the government also promoted the improvement of bilateral military cooperation with its ASEAN partners as part of its national security strategy. In 1989 Singapore was continuing to strengthen its military relations with its neighbors, although the threat of Soviet and Vietnamese-supported aggression against any one of the six ASEAN members appeared on the decline (see Foreign Policy, ch. 4).

From 1965 to 1989, subversive groups posed no threat to Singapore's political system, and there was no recurrence of the ethnic and communist-inspired riots of the 1950s and early 1960s. British statutes that had allowed the indefinite incarceration of persons accused of advocating the violent overthrow of the government were still in force in 1989 under the Internal Security Act of 1960. Although the government continued to use this statute to discourage radical political movements, by the late 1980s it had established a policy of releasing most persons detained under the Internal Security Act within a few months of their arrest unless they were referred to the court for trial.

In the 1970s, while the numbers for most types of crime remained relatively stable, there was an increase in crime related to the sale and use of illegal drugs. Although drugs continued to be a factor in crime in 1989, the occasional use of capital punishment for drug trafficking and the introduction of new law enforcement and rehabilitation programs for addicts reportedly were proving effective in controlling the problem.

The Civil Defence Act of 1986 defined the mission and responsibilities of the Civil Defence Force, which had been established in 1982. By the early 1980s, the armed services had a surplus of conscripts, and the government decided to expand the national service system to include civil defense organizations. By 1989 Singapore had ten operational civil defense divisions and had organized civil defense programs in each of the country's fifty-five legislative districts.

The Armed Forces

In 1989 Singapore's armed forces comprised the army, navy, and air forces, their reserves, and the People's Defence Force, which was the country's national guard. There were 55,000 personnel in the regular armed services, 182,000 in the reserves, and 30,000 in the national guard. All males were required to register for service at age sixteen and became eligible for conscription when they turned eighteen. Most conscripts served in one unit during their twenty-four to thirty months of active duty, and they continued with the same unit until they completed their duty in the reserves. The 1970 Enlistment Act required enlisted men to remain in the reserves until they turned forty and officers until the age of fifty.

The Constitution was amended in 1972 to prohibit the armed forces from being subordinated to any foreign power without the approval of the voters in a national referendum. The amendment, Article Six of the Constitution, states that defense treaties and collective security agreements negotiated by the government are to be approved by a two-thirds majority of the electorate. This amendment did not preclude Singapore's participation in the 1971 Five-Powers Defence Agreement (see Glossary), which was primarily intended to provide support by Australia, Britain, and New Zealand for Malaysia and Singapore should either nation be attacked. In 1989 the members of the Five-Powers Defence Agreement maintained an air defense network for the protection of Singapore and Malaysia and organized military exercises to improve the interoperability of their armed forces.

The Armed Forces Act of 1972 defines the organization and mission of the armed forces. The Armed Forces Council in 1989 was chaired by the minister for defence and included as members the commanders of the army, navy, and air force; it was the top military policymaking body, subordinate only to the prime minister. In 1989 the minister for defence was a civilian, as had been his predecessors although military officers were not legally prohibited from holding a ministerial appointment.

Historical Development

Until Singapore's separation from Malaysia in August 1965, responsibility for national security matters had always resided either in London or Kuala Lumpur. In the two decades following the end of World War II (1939-45), Britain spent billions of dollars to rebuild its military bases in Singapore in order to honor its defense commitments to Malaysia and Singapore. Between 1963 and 1966, several thousand British troops were deployed to protect the two countries during the Indonesian Confrontation (Konfrontasi—see Glossary). By 1967 the British Labour and Conservative parties had reached a consensus that Britain could no longer afford to pay the cost of maintaining a military presence in Southeast Asia. In January 1968, London informed the Singapore government that all British forces would be withdrawn by 1971, ending 152 years of responsibility for the defense of Singapore.

After the 1963 merger of Malaya, Singapore, Sabah, and Sarawak to form the Federation of Malaysia, Singapore ceded control over its armed forces to the federal government in Kuala Lumpur. For a time, Malaysian army and air force units were stationed in Singapore, and Lee Kuan Yew's refusal to allow Malaysia to retain control over Singapore's military establishment after separation was one reason political relations between the two nations remained strained well into the 1970s.

British Military Involvement, 1819-1942

In the years preceding the founding of Singapore in 1819, neither the British government nor the British East India Company was eager to risk the establishment of new settlements in Southeast Asia. From 1803 to 1815, London was preoccupied with war with France and, after Napoleon's abdication in October 1815, with establishing a stable peace in Europe. Britain administered the Dutch colonies in Malaya and Indonesia from 1795 to 1815 when the Netherlands was under French occupation. The British government returned control of these territories to the Dutch in 1816 over the objections of a small minority of British East India Company officials, including Sir Thomas Stamford Raffles. Raffles, in London from 1816 to 1818, failed to convince the company's directors to support a plan to challenge Dutch supremacy in the Malay Archipelago and Malaya. Enroute from London to Malaya, however, Raffles stopped in India and gained the support of Lord Hastings, the British East India Company's governor general of India, for a less ambitious plan. They agreed to establish a trading post south of Britain's settlement in Penang, Malaya.

From 1819 to 1867, when Singapore was administered by the British East India Company, Britain relied on its navy to protect its interests there and in Malaya. The Netherlands was the only European country to challenge the establishment of Singapore. In 1824, however, the Dutch ceded Malacca on the Malay Peninsula to Britain and recognized the former's claim to Singapore in exchange for British recognition of Amsterdam's sovereignty over territories south of the Singapore Strait. Two years later, the British East India Company united Singapore with Malacca and Penang to form the Presidency of the Straits Settlements (see Glossary). With no threat to its interests, the British employed the policy of allowing Singapore to assume responsibility for its own defense, although British naval vessels called in Singapore to show the flag and to protect shipping in the Singapore Strait (see fig. 3). By the mid-nineteenth century, London was recognized as the supreme naval power in the region, despite the fact that it deployed only about twenty-four warships to patrol an area extending east from Singapore as far as Hong Kong and west from Singapore as far as India.

Between 1867 and 1914, London contributed little to the establishment of permanent armed forces in Singapore. Units of the British Army's Fifth Light Infantry Regiment, which included infantry units brought from India, were stationed on the island. More often than not, however, these forces were deployed in the Malay states to protect British citizens there during periods of domestic violence. In 1867 when the strategic value of Singapore influenced London's decision to make the Straits Settlements a crown colony, the local governments were required to pay 90 percent of their own defense expenditures. The issue of collecting taxes from the residents of Singapore for defense remained controversial until 1933, when the Colonial Office finally agreed that the city should not be required to pay more than 20 percent of its revenue for defense costs.

Following World War I (1914-18), London attempted to integrate Singapore into a unified defense plan for all of the Straits Settlements and Malay states under British control. London had replaced the Indian elements of the Fifth Light Infantry Regiment with regular British Army units following the mutiny of Singapore's Indian troops in February 1915 (see Crown Colony, 1867-1918, ch. 1). As late as 1937, London had not deployed more than a few hundred British army regulars in the Straits Settlements and Federated Malay States. As there was no overt threat from neighboring countries or Britain's European rivals, the War Office believed that these units, aided by local militias trained by the British army, could adequately protect British interests on the Malay Peninsula. Singapore's militia, known as the Volunteer Rifle Corps, comprised infantry, artillery, and support units with a total personnel strength of about 1,000. The Volunteer Rifle Corps was integrated into the newly established Straits Settlements Volunteer Force in 1922. London believed that in the unlikely event that the Straits Settlements were attacked, regular and militia forces could hold out until reinforcements arrived from Hong Kong, India, and other British outposts in Asia.

In June 1937, Britain began to prepare for the possibility of war with Japan. Three British army battalions stationed in Singapore, one Indian battalion at Penang, and one Malay regiment at Port Dickson in the Malayan state of Negri Sembilan were the only regular forces available at the time for the defense of Singapore and the Malay Peninsula. Although the British military leaders had warned London in 1937 that the defense of Singapore was tied to the defense of Malaya and that any Japanese attack on the island would likely be made from the Malay Peninsula, their assessment was rejected by the British War Office, which was convinced that the impenetrable rain forests of the peninsula would discourage any landward invasion. Air bases were established in northern Malaya but were never adequately fortified. A new naval base was constructed on the northern coast of the island, but few ships were deployed there. Military strategists in London believed that the

Singapore garrison could defend the island for about two months, or the time it would take for a relief naval force to arrive from Britain.

In December 1941, British and Commonwealth of Nations (see Glossary) forces committed to the defense of the Malay Peninsula and Singapore comprised four army divisions supported by small numbers of aircraft and naval vessels that had been sent from other war zones to provide token support to the ground forces. Lieutenant General Arthur E. Percival, commander of these forces, deployed most units in the northern Malayan states of Kedah, Perak, Kelantan, and Terengganu. Fortified defensive positions were established to protect cities and the main roads leading south to Kuala Lumpur, Malacca, and Singapore. The British had no armor and very little artillery, however, and air bases that had been constructed in the Malayan states of Kelantan, Pahang, and Johore and in Singapore at Tengah, Sembawang, and Seletar were not well fortified. The attention of the War Office was focused on the fighting in Europe, and appeals to London for more aircraft went largely unanswered.

A small fleet, comprising the aircraft carrier *Unsinkable*, the battleship *Prince of Wales*, the battle cruiser *Repulse*, and four destroyers, represented the only naval force deployed to Singapore before the outbreak of war in the Pacific. The *Unsinkable* ran aground in the West Indies enroute to Singapore, leaving the fleet without any air protection.

Japanese Invasion, December 1941–February 1942

By the summer of 1941, Japan's relations with the Western powers had deteriorated so much that Japanese leaders saw no point in delaying plans for military operations in Southeast Asia and the Pacific. Japan's short-term goal was to secure the necessary supplies to complete its conquest of China by occupying the Southeast Asian territories controlled by France, Britain, the United States, and the Netherlands. Japan's long-term plans called for further expansion south to Australia and north from Manchuria into Mongolia and the Soviet Union.

Japanese air and naval attacks on British and United States bases in Malaya and the Philippines were coordinated with the December 7, 1941, assault on the United States Pacific Fleet Headquarters at Pearl Harbor, Hawaii. Japan's Southern Army, headquartered in Saigon, quickly moved from bases in southern Indochina and Hainan to attack southern Thailand and northern Malaya on December 8 and the Philippines on December 10. The

National Security

Japanese easily captured British air bases in northern Malaya and soon controlled the air and sea-lanes in the South China Sea as far south as the Strait of Malacca. Naval landings were made on the Thai coast at Singora (present-day Songkhla) and Patani and on the Malayan coast at Kota Baharu. Also on December 10, the Japanese located and destroyed the *Prince of Wales* and the *Repulse*, thereby eliminating the only naval threat to their Malaya campaign. The Thai government capitulated to a Japanese ultimatum to allow passage of Japanese troops through Thailand in return for Japanese assurances of respect for Thailand's independence. This agreement enabled the Japanese to establish land lines to supply their forces in Burma and Malaya through Thailand.

The prediction that Japan would conquer the Malay Peninsula before attempting an invasion of Singapore proved to be correct. Lieutenant General Yamashita Tomoyuki was placed in command of the Twenty-fifth Army comprising three of the best Japanese divisions. The Japanese used tactics developed specifically for the operation in northern Malaya. Tanks were deployed in frontal assaults while light infantry forces bypassed British defenses using bicycles or boats, thereby interdicting British efforts to deliver badly needed reinforcements, ammunition, food, and medical supplies (see fig. 13). Cut off from their supply bases in southern Malaya and Singapore, demoralized by the effectiveness of Japan's jungle warfare, and with no possibility that additional ground or air units would arrive in time to turn the tide of battle, the British withdrew to Singapore and prepared for the final siege. The Japanese captured Penang on December 18, 1941, and Kuala Lumpur on January 11, 1942. The last British forces reached Singapore on January 31, 1942, and on the same day a fifty-five-meter gap was blown in the causeway linking Singapore and Johore.

In January 1942, London had provided an additional infantry division and delivered the promised Hurricane fighter aircraft, although the latter arrived in crates and without the personnel to assemble them. In the battle for Singapore, the British had the larger ground force, with 70,000 Commonwealth forces in Singapore facing 30,000 Japanese. The Japanese controlled the air, however, and intense bombing of military and civilian targets hampered British efforts to establish defensive positions and created chaos in a city whose population had been swollen by more than a million refugees from the Malay Peninsula. Yamashita began the attack on February 8. Units of the Fifth and Eighteenth Japanese Divisions used collapsible boats to cross the Johore Strait, undetected by the British, to Singapore's northwest coast. By February

Singapore: A Country Study

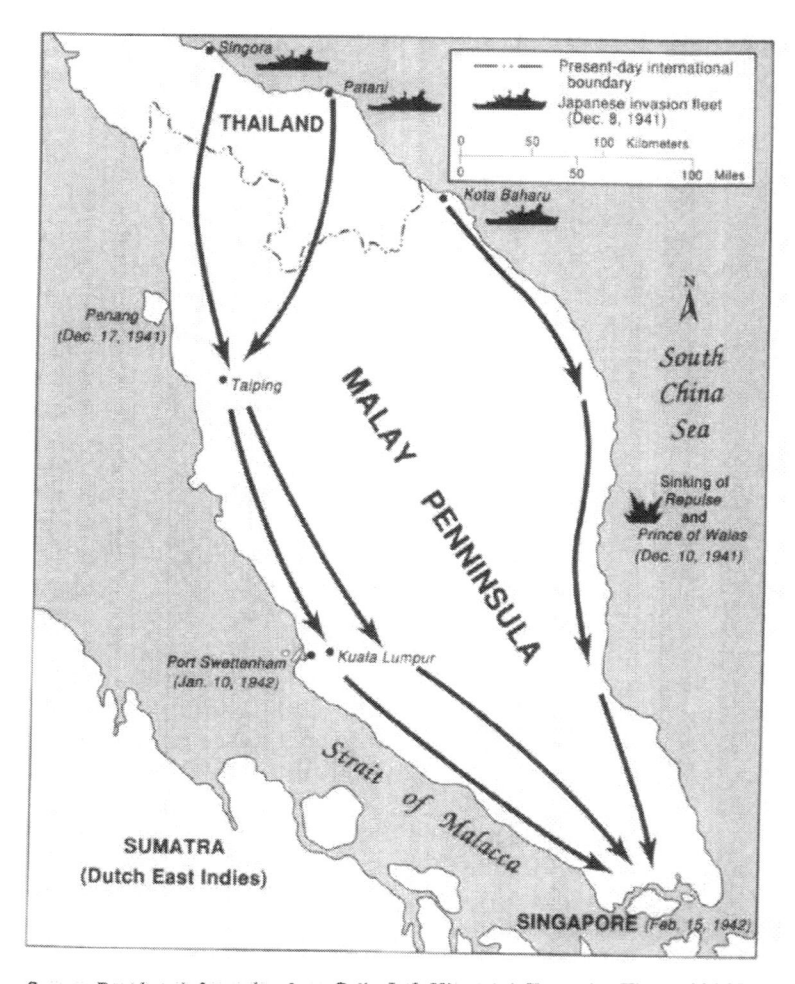

Source: Based on information from Colin Jack-Hinton, *A Sketch Map History of Malaya, Sarawak, Sabah, and Singapore*, London, 1966, 62; and N.J. Ryan, *The Making of Modern Malaysia and Singapore*, Kuala Lumpur, 1969, 221.

Figure 13. Japanese Campaign on Malay Peninsula, 1941–42

13, the Japanese controlled all of the island except the heavily populated southeastern sector. General Percival cabled Field Marshal Sir Archibald Wavell, British Supreme Commander in the Far East, informed him that the situation was hopeless, and received London's permission to surrender. On February 15, one week after the first Japanese troops had crossed the Johore Strait and landed in Singapore, Percival surrendered to Yamashita.

National Security

Decline of British Military Influence, 1945-75

British military influence in Singapore was reestablished at the end of World War II and declined at a slower pace than London's political influence. Singapore was made the headquarters for British forces stationed in the East Asia. The local population's resentment of British rule was tempered by the magnitude of the social and economic problems remaining after the Japanese occupation. Britain's military expenditures provided jobs and promoted support for its political objectives in the region. From 1948 to 1960, Malaya and Singapore were under Emergency rule as a result of the threat posed by the Communist Party of Malaya (CPM—see Glossary). Throughout this period, the majority of Singapore's political and business leaders were strong supporters of the British military presence. As Singapore moved from being a crown colony, to becoming a state in the Federation of Malaysia, and finally to independence in 1965, the British armed forces continued to be viewed as the protector of Singapore's democratic system of government and an integral part of the island's economy.

By 1962 the British were questioning the strategic necessity and political wisdom of stationing forces in Singapore and Malaya. At that time London was spending about US$450 million annually to maintain four infantry battalions, several squadrons of fighter aircraft, and the largest British naval base outside the British Isles, even though Southeast Asia accounted for less than 5 percent of Britain's foreign commerce.

In January 1968, the British government informed Prime Minister Lee that all British forces would be withdrawn from the country within three years. By then Singapore already had begun to organize its army and to plan for the establishment of an air force and navy. The British left behind a large military infrastructure and trained personnel of the newly formed Air Defence and Maritime commands. London formally ended all responsibility for Singapore's defense in 1972 when it turned over control of the Bukit Gombak radar station to Singapore.

Growth of the Armed Forces

Singapore's separation from Malaysia in August 1965 forced government leaders to begin thinking about the new nation's defense strategy and what armed forces would be needed to make that strategy a viable deterrent to potential adversaries. The task was made all the more difficult because of Singapore's strained relations with Malaysia and Indonesia (see Two Decades of Independence, 1965-85, ch. 1). Lee appointed Goh Keng Swee to head the newly established Ministry of the Interior and Defence. By June 1966, the government had decided that instituting compulsory conscription was the best way to build up the armed forces. Government leaders were impressed with Israel's successful use of a small regular army supported by a large citizen reserve and believed that the development of this type of armed forces would encourage national pride and self-reliance.

Between 1967 and 1970, the army was expanded from two infantry battalions to two brigades comprising one tank regiment, six infantry battalions, and one artillery battalion. The first classes of officers and noncommissioned officers (NCOs) graduated from the Armed Forces Training Institute in June 1967. This group of about 500 men was trained by Israeli instructors and provided the army with a core of leaders for both regular and reserve battalions. Under the system developed by the army's general staff, officers and NCOs were assigned to stay with newly formed national service battalions for the two-and-a-half years the conscripts remained on active duty. During this period, qualified enlisted men were selected for training as section and platoon leaders so that when a battalion was transferred to the reserves, a stable leadership would remain with the unit until its demobilization. In 1970 the government divided the Ministry of Interior and Defence into two separate ministries responsible for home affairs and defense, respectively. By December of that year, the army's reserve brigade comprised three infantry battalions.

The evolution of the air force and navy occurred at a slower pace than was the case with the army. In 1968 British air force commanders and pilots began assisting the newly formed Air Defence Command to establish its own air units. The British helped to establish an air force pilot training program at the Flying Training School located at Tengah Air Base. The first class of pilots received basic military training and general flying instruction in Singapore and then was sent to Britain for fighter aircraft training. These pilots returned to Singapore in 1971 and were assigned to the Air Defence Command's two fighter squadrons comprising one ground attack squadron with sixteen Strikemaster and four Hawker Hunter jet aircraft, and one interceptor squadron with sixteen Hawker Hunters. In 1969 the Maritime Command established temporary headquarters on Sentosa Island where it remained until a permanent base was completed on Pulau Brani (*pulau* means island). The government had negotiated agreements with two private companies—Lürssen Werft of the Federal Republic of Germany (West Germany) and Vosper Thornycroft of Britain—for the joint production of the navy's first naval vessels. Two gunboats produced

Japanese officer handing over maps to British officers and discussing troop positions, 1945
Courtesy National Archives

in Britain were delivered to Singapore in 1969 and were followed by Singapore-produced models of the same design, which entered service in 1970.

In the 1970s, the army, air force, and navy were expanded, new weapon systems were acquired from abroad, local defense industries were established, and military logistical systems were improved. In 1970 the army had 14,000 personnel on active duty and 6,000 in the reserves. Infantry training and equipment were considered adequate. However, the army's newly formed armored regiment was not yet operational, and the single artillery battalion was underequipped. The engineer and signal branches also were in the early stages of development. In 1967 the government had established the Sheng-Li Holding Company under the Ministry of Defence to promote state-owned-and-operated defense industries. By the mid-1970s, Singapore was producing ammunition, small arms, mortars, and artillery for the army and for export. In most cases, a Singapore manufacturer purchased the design and marketing rights for a weapon from European and American firms and then built the necessary plant for assembling the weapon. Tanks, armored vehicles, aircraft, and some surplus United States Navy amphibious craft and minesweepers were purchased to fill critical equipment shortages. Military logistical organizations established in the 1960s evolved into an efficient network of supply and maintenance facilities. These concerns included both interservice ordnance and transportation supply bases and intraservice facilities responsible for the procurement and repair of weapons and equipment used by only one of the service.

By 1980, the armed forces had 42,000 personnel on active-duty, and the reserves had expanded to 50,000. The army had become a well-balanced force with regular units organized into one armored and three infantry divisions under the operational control of a single division commander. The navy's twelve patrol craft, which were equipped with guns and missiles, gave Singapore a coastal defense force, and its six landing ships provided a limited capability to support the army in an amphibious operation. The air force, with 131 fighter aircraft and 2 surface-to-air missile battalions, was now large enough to fulfill both its air defense and ground support missions. Additionally, the air force had one transport squadron capable of airlifting a fully equipped infantry battalion anywhere in Southeast Asia and one helicopter squadron available for counterinsurgency or search-and-rescue operations.

In the 1980s, the number of army reservists more than tripled, although expansion of the regular armed services was constrained for budgetary reasons. By 1989 there were 170,000 army reservists. Only about 70,000 reservists, however, served in combat or combat support units subject to immediate mobilization. These units comprised one armored brigade equipped with AMX-13 tanks and M-113 armored personnel carriers, six infantry brigades, ten artillery battalions, one commando battalion, and an unknown number of combat support battalions. Most of the remaining 100,000 reservists probably either were assigned to units that would be used as fillers during wartime or served in the People's Defence and Civil Defence Forces. In the army, the number of engineer and signal battalions were increased by five and two, respectively, but the number of combat units remained basically the same throughout the decade. The air force added one squadron of F-5E interceptors, one early warning and reconnaissance squadron with four E-2Cs, and one transport helicopter squadron. Most growth in the navy occurred in combat support organizations. In 1989 the navy was in the process of establishing a new unit that would eventually comprise six missile-equipped corvettes.

Organization and Mission of the Armed Forces

In 1989 Prime Minister Lee continued to make most policy decisions concerning defense strategy and to approve the military budget. However, Goh Chok Tong, who served concurrently as first deputy prime minister and minister for defence, no doubt had the authority to decide most policy questions relating to the armed forces. He was assisted by two deputy defence ministers, one responsible for policy and the other for the organization of combat and combat support organizations. According to the Armed Forces Act of 1972, the minister for defence was to serve as the chairman of the Armed Forces Council and, in this capacity, was to assume responsibility for organizing and administering the armed forces and those government agencies having jurisdiction over military installations and defense industries.

In 1989, the Ministry of Defence was organized into a general staff for the army and six divisions responsible for the air force, navy, security and intelligence, logistics, manpower, and finance (see figure 14). The air force and navy were largely autonomous and were commanded by a brigadier general and commodore, respectively. In wartime, the air force and navy would come under the operational control of the chief of the general staff, an army lieutenant general.

Army

The combat units of the army were organized into infantry and armored brigades and antiaircraft artillery battalions. Although there was one division headquarters for the regular army and two division headquarters for the reserves, these arrangements undoubtedly were established for administrative purposes. Because of the scarcity of open land in Singapore, most unit training was conducted at the battalion and lower levels. Combat support was provided by engineer, signal, transportation, maintenance, and medical units.

In 1989 there were three infantry brigades in the regular army and six infantry brigades in the reserves comprising approximately thirty infantry battalions. Three of these battalions were trained in airmobile operations for rapid deployment to trouble spots and two others for commando operations. The primary offensive mission assigned to the infantry included moving into populated and rural areas occupied by an enemy force and retaking territory. Defensive missions included deployment to strategic points on the main island and surrounding islands to protect areas inaccessible to armored and artillery units; protection of tank and artillery units during enemy assaults; and movement behind enemy lines to harass combat units, interdict lines of communication and supply, and collect intelligence. Each infantry battalion was organized into a headquarters company, four rifle companies, and a support

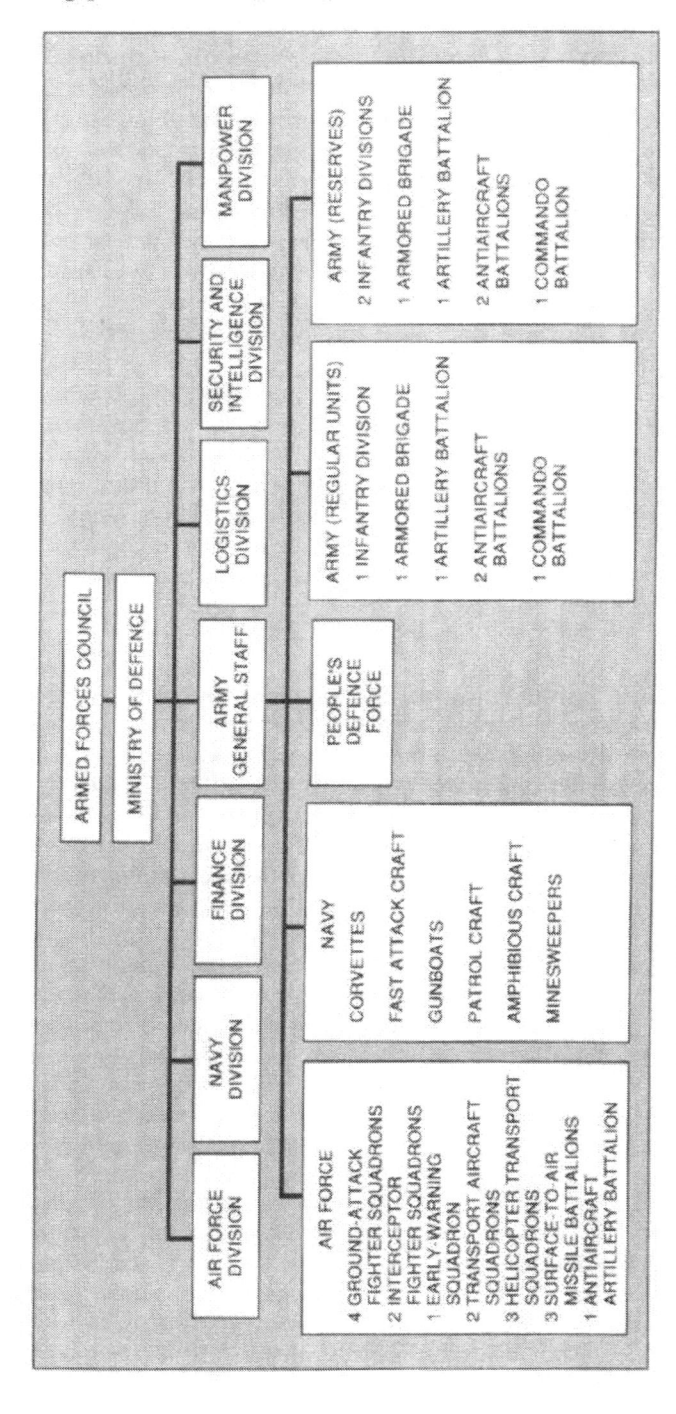

Singapore: A Country Study

```
                    ARMED FORCES COUNCIL
                    MINISTRY OF DEFENCE
     ┌──────────┬──────────┬──────────┬──────────┬──────────┬──────────┐
AIR FORCE    NAVY      FINANCE    ARMY       LOGISTICS  SECURITY AND  MANPOWER
DIVISION   DIVISION    DIVISION   GENERAL    DIVISION   INTELLIGENCE  DIVISION
                                  STAFF                 DIVISION
                                    │
                            PEOPLE'S DEFENCE FORCE
```

AIR FORCE
- 4 GROUND-ATTACK FIGHTER SQUADRONS
- 2 INTERCEPTOR FIGHTER SQUADRONS
- 1 EARLY-WARNING SQUADRON
- 2 TRANSPORT AIRCRAFT SQUADRONS
- 3 HELICOPTER TRANSPORT SQUADRONS
- 3 SURFACE-TO-AIR MISSILE BATTALIONS
- 1 ANTIAIRCRAFT ARTILLERY BATTALION

NAVY
- CORVETTES
- FAST ATTACK CRAFT
- GUNBOATS
- PATROL CRAFT
- AMPHIBIOUS CRAFT
- MINESWEEPERS

ARMY (REGULAR UNITS)
- 1 INFANTRY DIVISION
- 1 ARMORED BRIGADE
- 1 ARTILLERY BATTALION
- 2 ANTIAIRCRAFT BATTALIONS
- 1 COMMANDO BATTALION

ARMY (RESERVES)
- 2 INFANTRY DIVISIONS
- 1 ARMORED BRIGADE
- 1 ARTILLERY BATTALION
- 2 ANTIAIRCRAFT BATTALIONS
- 1 COMMANDO BATTALION

Source: Based on information from International Institute for Strategic Studies, *The Military Balance 1988–89*, London, 1989, 176; and Singapore, Ministry of Defence, *The Singapore Armed Forces*, Singapore, 1985.

Figure 14. Organization of the Armed Forces, 1989

company. Most rifle companies were equipped with indigenously produced SAR-80 assault rifles and Ultimax-100 machine guns. The support company included a reconnaissance platoon, 81mm mortar platoon, 106mm recoilless gun platoon, engineer platoon, and a sniper section. Unit training emphasized conventional and unconventional tactics for urban and jungle warfare, marksmanship, marching, concealment, and survival techniques. The three airmobile battalions and two commando battalions were given airborne and ranger training in addition to their infantry training.

The army had one active-duty armored brigade and an additional armored brigade in the reserves. Each brigade comprised one tank battalion and two mechanized infantry battalions. The French-produced AMX-13 light tank was used by both tank brigades. Mechanized infantry units used either M-113, V-150, or V-200 armored personnel carriers. In wartime, armored units would have the mission of assaulting and defending against heavily armed enemy units. Unit training focused on combined arms operations, assaults on fortified and soft targets, and tactics for countering enemy antitank guns and missiles.

There were seventeen field artillery, mortar, and antiaircraft artillery battalions in the army. Two battalions were equipped with American-produced and Israeli-produced 155mm howitzers. Each howitzer was operated by a twelve-man crew and could be used in wartime for long-range (ten to twenty kilometers) artillery support for infantry and armored units. The equivalent of twelve battalions of mortar-equipped troops provided direct support to infantry units during assaults on enemy positions. Most of these units were equipped with indigenously produced 120mm mortars that could be towed into combat on a light two-wheeled trailer attached to a jeep. Some mortar units also had M-113 armored personnel carriers that were modified to serve as the firing platform for 120mm mortars. In offensive operations, these units would follow closely behind armored forces to provide counterfire against enemy artillery and tanks. There were also the equivalent of three battalions of antiaircraft artillery in the army. Most of these units were equipped with either the Swedish-produced single-barrelled 40mm automatic gun or the Swiss-produced Oerlikon twin-barrelled 35mm automatic gun.

Responsibility for various types of combat support was delegated to several army commands, which were responsible for providing engineer, signal, transportation, and other services. The army had the equivalent of eleven battalions of combat engineers, five in the regular army and six reserve units. Engineer companies and platoons were attached to the combat units and during wartime would be responsible for clearing minefields, breaching obstacles, building bridges, supporting amphibious operations, and preparing defensive positions. There were the equivalent of four signal battalions. Signal units also were attached to the combat units, probably down to company level. Most transportation units were deployed to army bases located throughout the country and supported both regular and reserve units assigned to that base. In wartime, the army's Transportation Headquarters would quickly acquire civilian vehicles through its civil resources mobilization center. Weapons and military matériel that required maintenance usually were delivered to designated stations where they were exchanged or repaired. Each army base had a hospital and medical units that were deployed with combat units during military exercises. During wartime, the medical units would establish field hospitals to accommodate personnel wounded in battle until they could be transported to military or civilian hospitals.

Air Force

Fighter aircraft were organized into intercept and ground-attack squadrons. There were additional aircraft squadrons for long-distance troop and equipment transport and early warning; surface-to-air missile and antiaircraft gun units for air defense; and helicopter squadrons for transporting airmobile infantry into battle or search-and-rescue operations.

Air defense missions were controlled from the ground by the Air Defence Command at Bukit Gombak and from the air by Grumman E-2C early warning and control aircraft. Ground control included a number of radar stations strategically deployed throughout the country. The first of the air force's four Grumman E-2Cs were acquired by Singapore in 1987. Sophisticated long-range radar and tracking equipment aboard these aircraft enabled air defense controllers to detect possible enemy aircraft long before they entered the range of Singapore's ground-based defense radar system. Together the two systems provided an effective air defense warning system.

Two squadrons with thirty-five Northrop F-5E and F-5F interceptors based at Tengah Air Base provided the nation's first line of air defense. The first squadron of F-5s was formed in 1979 and the second in 1985. The F-5, equipped with AIM-9J air-to-air missiles, would perform well in combat against most other types of fighter and bomber aircraft. If necessary, aircraft assigned to the ground-attack squadrons could be used for air intercept missions.

The air force operated four surface-to-air missile systems and deployed antiaircraft guns to protect air bases and radar stations.

National Security

One unit equipped with British-produced Bloodhound 2 missiles provided long-range and high-altitude protection within an eighty-kilometer range. Another unit equipped with United States-produced improved HAWK missiles provided defense against medium- to high-flying aircraft at distances up to forty kilometers. Two missile systems were intended for close-range air defense: the British-produced Rapier, with radar and optical tracking modes, had a twelve-kilometer range; and the Swedish-produced RBS-70, which usually was transported on domestically modified V-200 armored personnel carriers, had a five-kilometer range. The air force was equipped with the same types of antiaircraft guns as the army.

Two models of fighter aircraft were imported by the air force for ground-attack missions in the 1970s and continued to be utilized for that role in 1989. Three squadrons with sixty-three McDonnell Douglas A-4S/S1 Skyhawks comprised the largest component of the ground-attack force. The Skyhawks could be used for bombing missions and close air support. Some of these aircraft were modified by Singapore Aircraft Industries for antishipping and antisubmarine warfare. In 1989 one squadron of thirty British-produced Hawker Hunter fighter aircraft was still flying. However, these aircraft were scheduled to be replaced by twenty F-16 fighter-bombers in the early 1990s.

Two models of helicopters were used by the air force for joint service operations with the army and for search-and-rescue missions. Two squadrons of Bell UH-1H helicopters, each having a complement of twenty helicopters, were formed in the late 1970s to enable the air force to transport specially trained infantry anywhere on the island during combat. If both squadrons were used, the air force could airlift a lightly armed battalion into battle within hours of receiving its orders. In 1986 the air force began to import French-produced AS-332B helicopters to augment its force of UH-1H helicopters for troop transport and to provide an improved search-and-rescue capability. The AS-332B had the advantage of a larger troop capacity and a greater combat radius. In 1989 the air force had taken delivery of six AS-332Bs and deployed them for search-and-rescue operations. An additional sixteen AS-332Bs were scheduled to be delivered to the air force in the early 1990s and would be used primarily for troop transport.

Navy

The navy had one missile gunboat squadron, one patrol craft squadron, one amphibious transport squadron, and additional ships for minesweeping and support operations. The West German Lürssen Werft model and the indigenously produced missile gunboats provided the navy with a limited, but effective, capability to patrol Singapore's international boundaries with Indonesia and Malaysia as well as the seaplane approaches to the island, which were vital to the nation's shipping interests. The six Lürssen-designed Sea Wolf fast-attack craft could, if necessary, conduct operations several hundred kilometers out to sea, and their Gabriel and Harpoon surface-to-surface missiles would be effective against enemy naval craft within a ninety kilometer range. They also were equipped with 57mm and 40mm guns. The six British Vosper Thornycroft, which were indigenously produced patrol craft, were effective for patrolling coastline and inlets. These vessels were equipped with 40mm and 20mm guns. The six landing ships that comprised the amphibious transport squadron could transport up to two fully equipped army battalions to landing areas in Singapore and neighboring countries. The age and slowness of these craft, however, would make them easy targets for hostile aircraft and naval vessels during wartime. Similarly, Singapore's two obsolescent minesweepers would be inadequate to clear all of the sea-lanes around Singapore should a hostile foreign power attempt to control the Strait of Malacca and other strategic channels in the area.

People's Defence Force and National Cadet Corps

In the late 1980s, the People's Defence Force, with 30,000 members organized under two commands, and the National Cadet Corps, with an enrollment of 20,000 high school and university students, were Singapore's only paramilitary organizations. The People's Defence Force was established in 1965 to absorb former members of several paramilitary organizations that, prior to independence, had been part of the Singapore Volunteer Corps. By 1980, however, fewer than 200 volunteers remained in the volunteer force, and most of its personnel were national servicemen who had completed their twenty-four to thirty months of active duty. These personnel were assigned to units of the People's Defence Force to complete their reserve obligation. The ministries of defence and education were jointly responsible for the administration of the voluntary National Cadet Corps, which had army, air force, and naval components. Approximately 10 percent of the nation's high school students participated in this extracurricular program. The legal framework for the People's Defence Force and National Cadet Corps was provided by parliamentary acts passed in 1965 and 1971, respectively.

The Army General Staff had operational responsibility for the People's Defence Force. The specific organization and missions of units of the two People's Defence Force commands undoubtedly

Jungle warfare military training
Courtesy Singapore Ministry of Communications and Information

were similar to those found in the army reserves. Guarding coastal areas and local administrative jurisdictions against possible sabotage and other military actions during wartime or a national emergency were the most likely assignments for battalions. Unit training was said to have been limited to physical fitness, weapons familiarization, and infrequent mobilization exercises.

Military Establishment

The military system was designed to provide an effective fighting force that could be partially or fully mobilized in emergencies and yet would maintain a low profile during peacetime. Because the reserves were viewed as the backbone of the armed forces, particular emphasis was placed on mobilization training. In a 1985 mobilization exercise that involved four army reserve brigades, 97 percent of 7,000 reservists reported to their assigned bases within a six-hour period. Selected units were equipped and deployed only twelve hours after the initial order to mobilize. By 1989 more than two decades of effective planning had promoted a well-trained and well-equipped military establishment that was adequately prepared for its defense mission.

The armed forces occasionally were asked to provide assistance to disaster relief efforts in Singapore and abroad. In 1986 several hundred reservists belonging to sixteen army and air force units assisted efforts to rescue 100 persons trapped when a six-story hotel collapsed in one of Singapore's commercial districts. In 1987 the Ministry of Defence had army reserve logistics units assemble food, clothing, and medical supplies from storage depots for Philippine typhoon victims. An air force transport unit delivered the supplies to the Philippines less than sixteen hours after the relief effort was organized.

Defense Spending

Defense expenditures, which accounted for between 25 and 38 percent of the national budget in the 1960s and 1970s, gradually decreased to less than 10 percent in the 1980s. One of the reasons government leaders chose to establish a citizen's army in the 1960s was to enable the growth of the armed forces to keep pace with the growth of the economy. The pay-as-you-go principle worked well for Singapore. In the 1960s and early 1970s, the government raised taxes in order to pay for purchases of foreign military equipment. The largest increases occurred between 1968 and 1972. Defense budgets increased from US$100 million to US$249 million during this period, with the largest part of the budget allocated for the acquisition of tanks and naval vessels.

In 1971 defense was the largest component of the budget. Defense would have been a still larger portion of the budget if Britain had not provided US$94 million in grants and US$281 million in loans as part of a compensation package for the withdrawal of its armed forces. Singapore's takeover of British military installations enabled the government to focus most of its spending on matériel, operations, and training. By 1973 when defense spending peaked at 38.9 percent of the national budget, the army was adequately equipped, and military planners began to focus more attention on the long-term needs of the armed forces, particularly the air force. In that year, military expenditures were less than 17 percent of the budget. In 1988 an estimated US$1 billion was spent on defense, which amounted to 7.5 percent of that year's total budget.

In response to the economic recession of 1985, the government instituted a five-year freeze on the size of the armed forces but continued to acquire new types of weapons and training equipment that were part of its ongoing modernization program. In 1986 the defense budget was reduced by US$175 million from the record high US$1.2 billion figure spent in 1985, with the cuts being apportioned throughout the armed forces. The five-year freeze did not affect national service. As new army units were formed and began their active service, other units were transferred to the reserves, and the longest serving reserve units were deactivated. The remainder of the cuts was absorbed through reduced spending on nonessential military supplies and certain types of training (see table 13, Appendix).

In the 1970s, the government established a number of education programs and increased military pay to encourage officers and NCOs to remain in the service. Officers were required to serve three years on active duty, after which most left to pursue more lucrative professions. In 1971 the government began to offer scholarships to promising officers who agreed to reenlist for at least one additional tour of duty. The Overseas Training Awards, the first such program to be implemented, enabled qualified officers to earn undergraduate and postgraduate degrees in management and other disciplines needed by the armed forces at prestigious universities and colleges in Western Europe and the United States. Many of the officers trained through this program accepted managerial and technical positions in the civil service after they completed their military obligation. Other officers were given scholarships to the National University of Singapore, Singapore Polytechnic Institute, and other local schools. In the early 1980s, more officers and NCOs opted for longer service because of pay increases and the tighter labor market resulting from the economic downturn in the civil sector. In 1982 the salaries of 19,000 NCOs were raised an average of 26 percent at a cost to the government of US$25 million annually. Officer salaries no doubt were increased proportionally, and the government continued to increase military pay, albeit at lower levels, in subsequent years.

In 1987 the ruling People's Action Party agreed to the establishment of a parliamentary committee to review military spending and provide a forum for public debate on defense issues. Prior to that, the government had closely monitored the press and discouraged the publication of articles critical of the government's defense policies on the pretext that national security was the prerogative of the small number of government officials responsible for policy-making and budget decisions. In 1989 the committee's primary function was to review the decisions of the executive branch on defense issues and to advise the government concerning public opinion about military spending. However, the committee lacked the power to change the government's defense policy or to amend the defense budget.

Role in Society

Government efforts to enhance the status of the military profession, particularly in the Chinese community, were only partially successful. During the colonial period, the Confucian tradition that valued scholarship over military service and parental influence discouraged young Singaporeans of Chinese descent from choosing a career in the military. In the 1960s and 1970s, the government attempted to overcome opposition to the conscription system through a media campaign that emphasized the important role of the armed forces. By the late 1970s, the draft and compulsory service no longer were controversial, but soldiers still were not held in high esteem by the general population. Although military service was generally viewed as acceptable within the Malay community, government concerns about ethnic and religious loyalties of Malays in the armed forces made it difficult for them to become officers or to be assigned to sensitive positions.

Uniforms and Insignia

In 1989 there were four categories of uniforms worn by all three services of the armed forces. The ceremonial uniform for officers consisted of a cap, white tunic, white shirt, trousers with service braids and color, black boots for the army and air force, and white shoes for the navy. The mess kit uniform was worn by sergeants and higher ranking NCOs for ceremonies. The basic work and parade uniform was a white shirt worn with the appropriate trousers: olive drab for the army, light blue for the air force, and dark blue for the navy. Air Force, navy, and army personnel assigned to armored units were issued a one-piece jump suit as a second work uniform. The combat uniform for army officers and enlisted personnel included camouflage fatigues with a helmet and black boots. Uniforms for women included skirts for ceremonies and work but otherwise were similar to those provided for male personnel.

Rank insignia were standardized for all three services, except that the air force used silver whereas the army and navy used gold. Generals in the army and air force and commodores in the navy wore one, two, or three stars. Field grade officers wore the appropriate number of crests on shoulder tabs. Enlisted personnel wore chevrons, in their service color, on both sleeves (see fig. 15).

Recruitment and Training of Personnel

All male citizens were eligible for the draft on their eighteenth birthday. Prospective draftees reported to the central manpower base operated by the Ministry of Defence with their birth certificate, identity card, educational record, and medical records. In the 1970s, the Ministry of Defence computerized the registration process. The Integrated Manpower Information System maintained at the central manpower base enabled the government to match more efficiently the skills and educational capabilities of draftees to the staffing needs of the services. Exemptions were granted only if a person was medically unfit for service, had a criminal record, or could prove that his enlistment was a hardship for his family. Deferments were granted to students who were enrolled or had been accepted for admission at an accredited college or other education institution.

Singapore's declining rate of population was partially responsible for government efforts to recruit more women for noncombatant duties. In 1980 about 50 percent of all women in the armed forces served in clerical positions in which promotion and career opportunities were limited. By 1989, however, military regulations had been changed to allow women to be considered for assignment to a number of military occupation specialties previously reserved for men. Women with high school diplomas and those with specialized skills, such as computer programming or office management, were offered professional and technical positions in support units. Many women found the medical and fringe benefits that came with a military career to be equivalent or better than those in the civilian job market. The recruitment of women for noncombatant duties enabled the Ministry of Defence to maintain manpower levels in combat units without changing length of service requirements or extending the length of reserve duty.

Because of the scarcity of open land on the main island, Singapore established training bases and firing ranges on offshore islands and sometimes sent army units abroad for training that could not be provided in the country. The Military Maneuvers Act—passed in 1963 while Singapore was a part of Malaysia, and amended in 1983—strengthened restrictions on civilian access to several islands located northwest and south of the main island of Singapore. Each of the services conducted live firing exercises in the restricted areas, and the army used some of the islands for basic military training and various types of field training. Operational exercises, such as amphibious landings and training conducted with Brunei and other countries, took place on these islands. The use of unpopulated islands for military training enabled the armed forces to avoid endangering the city and other heavily populated areas on the main island. Large scale exercises involving several battalions, however, were considered too dangerous even on the deserted islands. After 1975 the army used bases in Taiwan for military training that included combined arms exercises involving infantry, artillery, and armored units. These exercises, engaging as many as 10,000 troops at one time, provided officers a chance to simulate wartime

Singapore: A Country Study

COMMISSIONED OFFICERS

SINGAPORE RANK	SECOND LIEUTENANT	LIEUTENANT	CAPTAIN	MAJOR	LIEUTENANT COLONEL	COLONEL	BRIGADIER	MAJOR GENERAL	LIEUTENANT GENERAL
ARMY, AIR FORCE, AND NAVY							COMMODORE[4]	REAR ADMIRAL[4]	VICE ADMIRAL[4]
U.S. RANK TITLES [1,2]	SECOND LIEUTENANT	LIEUTENANT	CAPTAIN	MAJOR	LIEUTENANT COLONEL	COLONEL	BRIGADIER GENERAL	MAJOR GENERAL	LIEUTENANT GENERAL
U.S. RANK TITLES [3]	ENSIGN	LIEUTENANT JUNIOR GRADE	LIEUTENANT	LIEUTENANT COMMANDER	COMMANDER	CAPTAIN	COMMODORE ADMIRAL	REAR ADMIRAL	VICE ADMIRAL

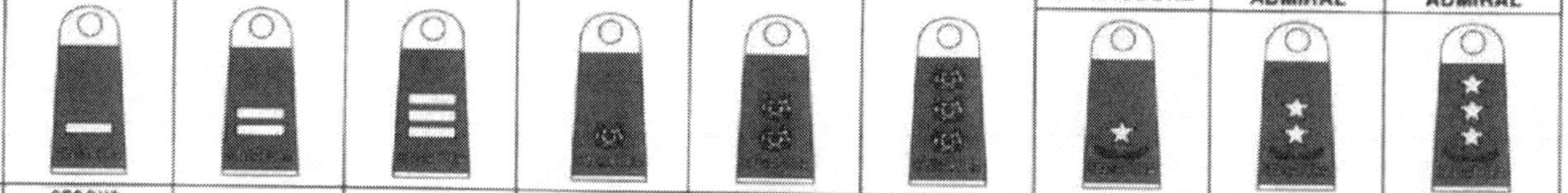

WARRANT OFFICERS AND ENLISTED PERSONNEL

SINGAPORE RANK	PRIVATE	NO RANK	LANCE CORPORAL	CORPORAL	CORPORAL 1ST CLASS	SERGEANT	STAFF SERGEANT	WARRANT OFFICER CLASS II	WARRANT OFFICER CLASS I
ARMY, AIR FORCE, AND NAVY		NO INSIGNIA 							
U.S. RANK TITLES [1]	BASIC PRIVATE	PRIVATE	PRIVATE 1ST CLASS	CORPORAL	SERGEANT	STAFF SERGEANT	SERGEANT 1ST CLASS	SERGEANT MAJOR	COMMAND SERGEANT MAJOR
U.S. RANK TITLES [2]	AIRMAN BASIC	AIRMAN	AIRMAN 1ST CLASS	SERGEANT	STAFF SERGEANT	TECHNICAL SERGEANT	MASTER SERGEANT	SENIOR MASTER SERGEANT	CHIEF MASTER SERGEANT
U.S. RANK TITLES [3]	SEAMAN RECRUIT	SEAMAN APPRENTICE	SEAMAN	PETTY OFFICER 3D CLASS	PETTY OFFICER 2D CLASS	PETTY OFFICER 1ST CLASS	CHIEF PETTY OFFICER	MASTER CHIEF PETTY OFFICER	FLEET FORCE MASTER CHIEF PETTY OFFICER

NOTES— [1] Army. [2] Air Force. [3] Navy. [4] Navy.

Figure 15. Military Rank Insignia, 1989

conditions more closely and gain experience in the command and control of operations involving several battalions.

In each of the three services, male inductees were given three months and female inductees three weeks of basic military training at the basic military training camp on Pulau Tekong. For the men, the program included daily physical exercise to build stamina, classroom and field instruction in handling small arms, and day and night combat operations. Particular emphasis was placed on learning to function as members of a combat team. Infantry personnel usually remained with their basic training company throughout their military careers. In this way the army hoped to strengthen the efficiency of units during combat by encouraging the loyalty of the individual soldier to his unit. Basic training for female military personnel emphasized military discipline, physical training, and an introduction to military skills, including handling small arms, marching, and survival techniques.

Following basic training, conscripts selected for the army's combat units were given additional training that familiarized them with military procedures, weapons and equipment, tactics, and a unit's offensive and defensive missions during wartime. Infantry unit members were assigned specific duties. Those assigned to rifle platoons learned assault tactics at their home base, while those selected for the weapons platoon were sent to the School of Infantry Weapons at Pasir Laba Camp where they received instruction in how to fire and care for mortars and recoilless rifles. Artillery training was provided first at the Artillery School at Khatib Camp, where recruits learned to locate and fire accurately at targets, and then at their home base, where the emphasis was on weapons deployment in battle. The courses at the Artillery School lasted from eight to thirteen weeks. In the eight-week gunner course, artillery personnel were trained to fire 155mm howitzers. There were additional courses for those assigned to heavy mortar units and for artillery specialists such as the technical assistants responsible for computing target engagement data. Base training was conducted in two phases. During the first phase, field artillery and mortar units practiced what they had learned at the Artillery School and participated in cross-training, through which personnel were trained to perform the duties of other members of their unit. The second phase involved field deployment drills and battalion or brigade exercises. Tank crews were given an eight-week course at the Armor School located at Sungai Gedong Camp. A three-man crew comprised a commander, driver, and gunner. Training included familiarization with the tank, cross-training, and the use of computers and visual aids to simulate combat conditions. Most field exercises involving tanks were limited to small units, usually at the company or platoon level, again because of the limited space available for such training.

Outstanding army recruits were selected for training as NCOs and sent to Pasir Laba Camp to attend the School of Infantry Section Leaders. This program emphasized toughness and endurance during combat. Trainees were taken to various parts of the main island and Pulau Tekong and given extensive instruction in leading a small group and taking responsibility for its survival in combat. Additional training included conventional and unconventional unit tactics, discipline, and communication with the platoon and company headquarters.

The Armed Forces Training Institute located at Jurong Camp provided officer training and instruction for army personnel enrolled in advanced programs designed to improve leadership and military skills. Officer candidates, including university graduates and other recruits considered to have the aptitude and physical capabilities to command a platoon, took a nine-month course at the Officer Cadet School of the Armed Forces Training Institute. Classroom instruction included lectures on unit administration, tactics, planning operations, command and communications, and assessing unit capabilities in combat. During field exercises, cadets were presented with both urban and rural battle scenarios in which they took turns performing the duties of officers and enlisted men in order to improve their understanding of the role of subordinates. Graduates of the course were commissioned as second lieutenants and assigned to command active-duty or reserve units. The army's Advanced Training School and Command and Staff College also were located at the Armed Forces Training Institute.

The air force provided pilot training at the Flying Training School at Paya Lebar Air Base. Pilot trainees were required to complete the army's basic training and nine-month officer cadet courses before being accepted into the flight training program. The introduction to flying began with a one-month orientation course in advanced aerodynamics and aircraft instruments. This course was followed by sixteen weeks of training in Italian-produced SF-260 turboprop and S-211 jet trainer aircraft. Following this basic flying course, cadets were assigned to fighter aircraft squadrons for forty weeks of advanced training that included sight and instrument control of flight, air-to-air and air-to-ground combat tactics, flying in formation, night flying, and other subjects. Those who failed to qualify were reassigned to transport or rotary aircraft units, or given ground assignments.

Urban warfare military training
Courtesy Singapore Ministry of Communications and Information

The air force also operated schools to train air traffic controllers, air defense controllers, and aircraft maintenance personnel. Air traffic controllers, trained at the Air Traffic Control School at Seletar Air Base, were taught how to distinguish commercial and military aircraft, to regulate military air traffic, and to provide emergency services. Air defense controllers learned to identify enemy aircraft on radar screens, to guide fighter aircraft to the enemy, and to operate surface-to-air missiles. The Air Engineering Training Institute offered a wide range of courses to train mechanics and technicians in the maintenance of the various types of aircraft, engines, radar, and communications equipment used by the air force.

Naval officer training was provided in the Midshipman School at Sembawang. This school had separate eighteen-month courses to train navigation, gunnery, communications, and logistics officers. Advanced officer training was not available, but most ship commanders received additional training in Australia, Britain, or the United States. The navy also operated a Technical Training School for ship maintenance personnel at Pulau Brani and a school to train seamen for duties as gunners, radar operators, and communications specialists.

Training for army reserves included weekend duty at army bases, field and mobilization exercises, and occasional assignments to schools and training bases. Reserve military personnel were required to spend a minimum of forty days a year with their military unit or in an individual training program. Regularly scheduled weekend duty usually included physical fitness exercises, instruction in individual and unit military skills, and occasional travel for shooting practice to one of the army's indoor firing ranges or to a training area for field exercises. Every few years, reserve units were sent to the Basic Combat Training Center at Pasir Laba Camp for a ten-day refresher course in unit tactics. During mobilization exercises, selected units were required to assemble at their home base and deploy to their assigned field positions to test the readiness of personnel to respond to an alert. Most branch schools had some on-site and correspondence courses that reservists could take in order to fulfill part of their annual service requirement. The Armed Forces Training Institute offered courses for reservists chosen for officer training.

Defense Industries

Singapore's defense industries were established in the late 1960s because the government believed that the country should not become too dependent on foreign countries to resupply the armed forces during wartime. By 1975 three government-owned corporations were involved in assembling, rebuilding, overhauling, and designing small arms, artillery, armor, military aircraft, and naval vessels. In 1979 the government started a defense marketing effort to promote the sale of Singapore-designed weapons to foreign countries. In addition to government-owned defense industries, a number of foreign-owned producers of military equipment operated in Singapore. These firms were attracted by government incentives designed to promote employment in high technology industries, to lower production costs, and to explore the possibility of using Singapore as a base for promoting the sale of their products in Asia.

In 1989 three divisions of the state-owned and -operated Singapore Technology Corporation were producing various types of ammunition, weapons, and vehicles used by the army. In addition, the divisions were responsible for rebuilding or adapting some types of foreign military matériel to army specifications. The first division, commonly known as Chartered Industries, was established in 1967 and produced various types of ammunition and small arms. Ammunition manufactured included 5.56-, 7.62- and 12.7-caliber shells used in pistols, rifles, and machine guns; 60-, 81- and 120mm

National Security

mortars; 75mm armor-piercing rounds for the main gun of the AMX-13 tank; and 155mm high-explosive artillery ammunition. In 1970 Chartered Industries began licensed production of the M16 assault rifle. More than 80,000 M16s were manufactured for the army between 1970 and 1979. In 1976 Chartered Industries purchased the rights to the SAR-80 assault rifle from Britain's Sterling Armament Company. Engineers at Chartered Industries worked with a team of weapons experts at the Armed Forces Training Institute to improve the Sterling design. An estimated 100,000 indigenously designed SAR-80s were produced between 1980 and 1989 for domestic use and for export. The second division of Singapore Technology Corporation—Ordnance Development and Engineering—was established in 1973 to design and produce mortars and 155mm howitzers for the army. Three indigenously designed mortars based on designs provided to the division by a Finnish manufacturer were still in production in 1989 and fired 60-, 81- and 120mm ammunition. The indigenously designed FH-88 155mm howitzer was based on the Israeli-produced M-68 that was exported to Singapore in the 1970s. Soltam Limited of Israel no doubt assisted Ordnance Development and Engineering in the development and initial assembly of the FM-88. Automotive Engineering, the third division of Singapore Technology Corporation involved in military production, was established in 1971. The division received a number of foreign-produced vehicles, including three-ton Mercedes transport trucks and the AMX-13 tank, and modified them to army specifications. Additionally, the division modified V-150, V-200, and M-113 armored personnel carriers to serve as platforms for weapons such as the Bofors RBS-70 surface-to-air missile system and indigenously produced 120mm mortars.

Singapore Aerospace Corporation, established in 1981, comprised four state-owned divisions that were involved in the assembly of foreign-produced trainer aircraft for the air force and the overhaul and maintenance of various types of military aircraft, aircraft engines, and avionics equipment. Between 1984 and 1987, the Maintenance Division assembled at least twenty-six Italian-produced SIAI-Marchetti S-211 trainer aircraft for the air force. The Maintenance Division also overhauled and refurbished A-4S Skyhawk fighter aircraft and performed depot-level maintenance on C-130 transport aircraft for both the Singapore and United States air forces. Singapore Aerospace Corporation could manufacture spare parts for the Skyhawks, handle routine maintenance on 6,000 types of civil and military aircraft components, and overhaul various types of jet engines.

The state-owned Singapore Shipbuilding and Engineering Company produced naval vessels under technology transfer agreements negotiated with Lürssen Werft of West Germany. In 1974 and 1975, the company constructed four TNC-45 missile-equipped gunboats for the navy based on Lürssen-designed Zobel-class torpedo gunboats. The West German design was modified to allow for the installation of Israeli-produced Gabriel missiles and a larger gun. The agreement with Lürssen Werft included marketing rights, and Singapore Shipbuilding and Engineering constructed lightly armed gunboats for at least two Asian countries. In 1976 and 1977, the company built three TNC-45s for the Thai navy. These vessels had the same armament as the TNC-45s produced for the Singapore navy. In 1986 Singapore Shipbuilding and Engineering negotiated an agreement with the Indian government that provided for joint construction of six TNC-45s for the Indian Coast Guard. Two of these craft were to be built in Singapore and four in India. In 1989 Singapore Shipbuilding and Engineering constructed the first of five corvettes for the navy. Again, Lürssen Werft provided the design and one prototype vessel, and Singapore Shipbuilding and Engineering modified the design to navy specifications. The modification involved replacing surface-to-surface missiles with American-produced Harpoon ship-to-ship missiles. Both the Singapore and West German models of this craft were equipped with one 76mm gun (see table 14, Appendix).

Between 1983 and 1987, Singapore exported US$311 million worth of weapons and military equipment to other countries. According to the Stockholm International Peace Research Institute, Singapore was the fifteenth largest exporter of military hardware to Third World nations during the period. These weapons and equipment sales increased from only US$1 million in 1983 to US$125 million in 1987 and were believed to have been limited to the same types of ammunition, small arms, and mortars that were produced for the army. The government marketed its military equipment through its own brokerage firm, Unicorn International.

Strategic Perspective

From 1959 to 1989, Singapore developed a defensive security outlook that emphasized the maintenance of strong military and civil defense organizations, cooperative military relations with other members of ASEAN, the Five-Powers Defence Agreement; and other noncommunist states. In 1989 more than 90 percent of Singapore's population was under the age of fifty and could not recall the Japanese invasion and occupation. Although Singapore had not had to combat an insurgency or defend itself against a hostile neighbor since the Indonesian Confrontation ended in 1966, the government frequently addressed such issues as Vietnam's 1978 invasion of Cambodia in order to highlight the vulnerability of small countries. Public opinion polls taken in the 1980s indicated that, although most citizens supported having some form of national service, many questioned the need for their leaders' "siege mentality." By 1989, as Lee Kuan Yew prepared for what he hoped would be a smooth transfer of power to a younger generation, Singapore's strategic perspective appeared to place increasing emphasis on regional developments that augured well for improved regional security rather than on any threat to the country posed by communist expansion in Southeast Asia (see Foreign Policy, ch. 4).

Total Defence Concept

Singapore's leaders defined Total Defence (see Glossary) as the capability of the nation to deter or overcome aggression by maintaining small, well-equipped regular armed forces backed up by a large, well-trained military reserve and a civil sector that could be quickly mobilized to provide support to the armed forces. By 1989 Singapore had each of these components in place. The air force was recognized as one of the best in the region, and the army continued to make steady progress in improving its capability to react, albeit on a limited scale, to repel an invasion. The addition of six corvettes strengthened the navy's ability to defend territorial waters and conduct limited operations farther out to sea. More than 50 percent of Singapore males had received formal military training, and more than 10 percent of them belonged to a reserve unit. The Ministry of Defence monitored the combat capabilities of reserve units through frequent training and mobilization exercises. The country was believed to have adequate stockpiles of fuel and ammunition. Its military logistics and maintenance capabilities were excellent. Finally, the national Civil Defence Force, established in 1982, had gradually been expanded to coordinate military, police, and civilian organizations involved in efforts to maintain internal security and to restore vital services quickly during wartime and other emergencies.

In 1989 the most apparent weakness in Singapore's Total Defence system was the friction between the government and business community over the financial and social costs of sustaining the defense sector. As the birth rate declined after 1967, the percentage of males drafted for service increased each year. Concurrently, the number of persons available to Singapore's expanding export industries also decreased. Thus, some business leaders were critical of government policies that perpetuated the national service system and argued that the armed forces had grown too large and that new weapons, increased army pay, and other military programs were unnecessary. The same business leaders were reluctant to grant workers leave for reserve training. Government-sponsored public opinion polls confirmed that a large segment of the general population questioned the need for national service. A poll taken in 1983 indicated that 40 percent of Singaporeans thought that national service was a waste of time and money. Government officials defended the system by arguing that even small countries must maintain credible defenses or risk disaster. They also noted that a large percentage of personnel trained by the armed forces in various technical and professional fields were well prepared to compete for skilled jobs in the private sector when they completed the active-duty portion of their national service. In the mid-1980s, the government began a variety of public relations programs to overcome opposition to its defense policies and, as of 1989, had no intention of reducing manpower levels or proposing cuts in military spending.

Military Relations with Other Countries

After Singapore separated from Malaysia in 1965, the government actively sought to establish a broad-based international network of military contacts as part of its overall strategic plan to strengthen recognition of its existence as a sovereign state. In the 1960s, Britain, Israel, New Zealand, and France were among the nations that were approached for assistance as Singapore's military planners began to formulate doctrine and evaluate which aircraft, artillery, naval vessels, and tanks would be affordable and appropriate for the country's armed forces. In the 1970s, hundreds of officers, pilots, and technical specialists were sent to Australia, Britain, Japan, the United States, West Germany and other countries for advanced training that could not be provided in Singapore. Programs in the United States included flight training and live-firing exercises for air force personnel selected to pilot F-5E and F-5F interceptors, special forces training for infantrymen from the army's commando battalions, and command training for officers who earned government scholarships offered through the Overseas Training Awards fund.

In the 1980s, as the ASEAN countries became increasingly concerned about Vietnam's occupation of Cambodia and the possibility of war between Vietnam and Thailand, Singapore began to participate in annual military exercises with Brunei, Indonesia, and Malaysia. In 1979 the Singapore and Brunei navies conducted the first in a series of annual naval exercises (code-named Pelican), and in 1983 the two countries initiated annual infantry maneuvers (code-named Termite) involving selected battalions from both armies. Singapore infantry units were frequently deployed to Brunei for commando and helicopter-borne training. In 1980 the Singapore and Indonesian air forces began annual exercises (code-named Indopura) that were gradually expanded to include joint air maneuvers. Between 1987 and 1989, the two nations shared the costs of constructing the Siabu Air Weapons Range in northern Sumatra. Singapore's use of this range reduced the need for costly deployment of interceptor and ground-attack squadrons to Taiwan or the United State for live-firing exercises. In 1989 Indonesia also agreed to allow the Singapore army to use its Baturaja training base in southern Sumatra. In 1984 the Singapore and Malaysian navies began annual joint exercises (code-named Malapura). These exercises usually were held in the Strait of Malacca to improve the cooperation between the two nations in patrolling that important sea-lane. In 1989 Singapore and Malaysia also initiated joint training for army units: the first exercise was held in Singapore in May; the second exercise was held in Malaysia in October. Although there were no indications that Singapore, Malaysia, and Indonesia were interested in negotiating a multilateral defense agreement, each country viewed increased bilateral cooperation as beneficial to its national security and to regional stability.

Singapore has maintained good military relations with the United States and has supported the stationing of United States forces in Asia as necessary to counter both Vietnamese military expansion in the region and the establishment of the Soviet military presence in Indochina. The 1975 communist victory in Vietnam and the subsequent reevaluation of the United States' role in Asia and the Pacific worried Singapore's military leaders. In 1979 Prime Minister Lee expressed concern that Vietnam would become a Soviet proxy for the proliferation of a new wave of communist guerrilla movements in Thailand, Malaysia, Indonesia, and Singapore. Lee admitted that American reluctance to become involved in another Southeast Asian war was understandable, but he observed that the ASEAN states lacked the military capability to reverse the trend alone. By 1988, however, the scenario of a domino-like progression of communism south through Thailand and Malaysia and into Singapore had lost much of its credibility. Singapore viewed the Soviet Union's decision to withdraw its forces from Afghanistan and Vietnam's promise to follow Moscow's lead and withdraw its troops from Cambodia as actions that would enhance the security of ASEAN states, particularly Thailand. Although further

Vietnamese and Soviet-sponsored military incursions in the region were considered unlikely for the foreseeable future, Singapore viewed the stationing of United States forces in Asia and the Pacific as advantageous to ASEAN.

By 1988 improved relations between Singapore and Malaysia had facilitated a revitalization of the Five-Powers Defence Agreement. Britain also began to demonstrate renewed interest in the pact. In 1970 approximately 12,000 British troops were sent to Malaysia for a joint military exercise that included contingents from the members of the Five-Powers Defence Agreement. Throughout the rest of the 1970s, however, the British limited their participation in military exercises conducted to promote the agreement. In 1971 Australia assumed primary responsibility for managing the Integrated Air Defence System, which was the only functional organization maintained under the pact for the protection of Singapore and Malaysia. Air defense exercises were conducted annually after 1971. During the 1970s and 1980s, New Zealand and Australia also deployed some army and air force units to Malaysia and Singapore. In 1981 the five states party to the agreement began to hold annual ground and naval exercises, which gradually grew in size and importance. The 1988 joint naval maneuvers (codenamed Lima Bersatu) were the largest and most complex military exercise organized by the five nations since 1970. They involved 20 naval vessels, including a British aircraft carrier and a British submarine, and more than 100 fighter and reconnaissance aircraft. Fighter aircraft from the five countries were assigned to multinational flight teams, and Singapore's E-2C reconnaissance aircraft were used along with P-3C maritime reconnaissance aircraft belonging to the Australian and New Zealand air forces. Singapore air and naval units gained valuable combat experience from their participation in exercises with other members of the agreement. Britain, Australia, and New Zealand displayed their readiness to respond to any military contingency affecting Malaysia and Singapore. Thus, in 1989 the Five-Powers Defence Agreement continued to contribute to Singapore's security and the overall stability of Southeast Asia.

Public Order and Internal Security

Between 1819 and 1867, the British East India Company worked closely with citizens' councils that represented the European, Chinese, Malay, and Indian communities to maintain law and order in Singapore. The British civil service comprised a small and overworked staff that often tried unsuccessfully to enforce British laws in the Straits Settlements. The resident councillor for Singapore was responsible for adjudicating most criminal and civil cases. More serious cases were referred to the governor of the Straits Settlements in Penang, or, on rare occasions, to the governor general in India. Chinese secret societies flourished, and violent crime was a fact of life. Thomas Dunman, Singapore's first superintendent of police, was a young British merchant who was respected by leaders of the European community and supported by influential Malays and Indians, who felt powerless to prevent Chinese gangs from roving into their districts, assaulting people, and robbing homes and businesses. In 1843 Dunman recruited a small group of itinerant workers and single-handedly trained and organized them into an effective police force. By 1856 gang robberies no longer were a major problem, but the secret societies continued to control lucrative gambling, drug, and prostitution operations.

From 1867 to 1942, the Straits Settlements had unified law enforcement and criminal justice systems. However, colonial authorities in Singapore continued to respect religious and cultural customs in the Chinese and Malay communities as long as local practices were peaceful and residents respected British authority. In 1868 Governor Sir Harry Ord established a circuit court, and its jurisdiction over criminal and civil matters gradually expanded in Singapore during the period up to World War II. Leaders of the Chinese community appreciated the cooperative nature of British government officials and helped to promote respect for the law. By the 1880s, government efforts to reduce the criminal elements of the Chinese secret societies had succeeded in making the city a safer place to live. Europeans and Indians dominated the police force. Colonial authorities rarely hired Chinese for police work for fear the secret societies would infiltrate the force. After World War I, an increase in political violence was attributed to the growth of communist influence within the Chinese community. In 1919 a special branch was established in the police force to combat the communist-inspired anticolonial activities, which were increasing in Chinese schools and businesses. In 1931 a special branch operation resulted in the arrest and deportation of leaders of the newly formed Communist Party of Malaya (CPM). By the end of the decade, however, communist influence and political subversion were once again a problem for law enforcement officials.

During the period that Singapore was a crown colony, militia groups trained by the British army occasionally assisted the police force in maintaining civil order and promoted citizen involvement in protecting the city from foreign invasion. Even before Singapore became a crown colony, concerned citizens in the European community had formed a citizens' militia. In 1854 about sixty

European expatriates established the Volunteer Rifle Corps to protect citizens from violent riots. Although most riots occurred because of factional fighting between Chinese secret societies, some disturbances also disrupted the commercial activities of the city. By 1910 there were 700 volunteers in six organizations that were collectively called the Singapore Volunteer Corps. Europeans comprised four groups, including two infantry companies, one artillery company and one engineer company. The Chinese and Malay communities each contributed one company. In February 1915, the Volunteer Corps was mobilized to help restore order following a rebellion by Singapore's Indian troops (see Crown Colony, 1867–1918, ch. 1). Approximately 800 Punjabi Muslim soldiers, who comprised most of the British garrison in Singapore at that time, were deceived by German prisoners of war into believing that they were about to be redeployed to the front lines in Europe. The Punjabis killed their officers and went on a rampage through the city before dispersing in small groups to the northern section of the island. For a two-week period, the Singapore Volunteer Corps, along with the police and the crews from British, French, Japanese, and Russian warships, rounded up the Punjabis and protected the city while the colonial government restored order. In 1922 the Straits Settlements Volunteer Force was established, and the British army became more active in training the volunteers. Mobilized on December 1, 1941, six days before the Japanese Malayan campaign began, Singapore's volunteers manned bunkers and artillery positions along the south coast to defend the city from an invasion from the sea that never came.

In response to communal riots in December 1950, the British reorganized the Singapore Police Force and established links between the police and the British army that effectively prevented subsequent civil disturbances from getting out of hand. The 1950 riots occurred when Malay police officers, who comprised 90 percent of the police force, failed to control a demonstration outside Singapore's Supreme Court. The demonstration occurred following a decision by the court to return to her natural parents a Dutch Eurasian girl who had been raised in a Malay foster home during the Japanese occupation. Incensed by the court's decision, large groups of Malays randomly attacked Europeans and Eurasians killing 18 and wounding 173. The British army had to be called in to restore order.

The British reorganization of the police force included the hiring of large numbers of Europeans, Chinese, and Indians to improve the ethnic balance; the establishment of riot control teams; and the modernization of police command and communication

Victory parade and demonstration, September 1945
Courtesy National Archives

channels. The riot control teams belonged to a new organization known as the Police Reserve Unit. Members of the unit had to be politically reliable and had to pass a rigorous training course. The first riot control teams were deployed in December 1952. In May 1955, these units were effective in containing communist-inspired rioters during a transportation workers' strike, although four people were killed and thirty-one injured over a three-day period.

In July 1956 the Singapore government under Chief Minister Lim Yew Hock's administration prepared an internal security plan that simplified arrangements for cooperation between the police and the British army during serious civil disturbances. The new plan provided for a joint command post to be set up as quickly as possible after the police recognized the possibility of a riot. The Police Reserve Unit was to assume responsibility for riot control operations within clearly defined sectors while army units were deployed to control the movement of civilians in the immediate area. The plan was tested and proved effective during communist-inspired riots in October 1956, when five army battalions supported the police and five helicopters were used for aerial surveillance of the demonstrators. Police and army cooperation succeeded in breaking up large groups of rioters into smaller groups and preventing the spread of the violence to neighboring communities. Police and army restraint kept deaths and injuries to a minimum and improved the confidence of the public in the government's capability in handling incidents of domestic violence. The British role was a stabilizing factor that facilitated the demise of the CPM in Singapore and a smooth transition of power to the People's Action Party (PAP).

Subversive Threats

Communist-inspired subversion and violence was a serious problem in Malaya and Singapore in the post-World War II period. In June 1948, the British colonial government declared a state of emergency in Malaya and Singapore and passed tough security laws to cope with the threat. After Lee Kuan Yew led the PAP to victory in the 1959 election, the influence of the communists quickly declined and citizens known or alleged to have contacts with the CPM or other groups that advocated the overthrow of the government were closely monitored by the police.

The Communist Threat, 1945-63

The CPM was legal in Singapore during the first thirty months of post-war British colonial rule. The communist-controlled Malayan People's Anti-Japanese Army, formed during the Japanese occupation, had several hundred Chinese members, including the commander, Chin Peng. In 1945 and 1946, many poorly educated Chinese Singaporeans sympathized with the communists because they seemed to offer a program of labor reforms that would benefit the common person. Additionally, most of the better educated Chinese resented British policies that limited participation in politics to Straits-born British subjects who were literate in English. A large segment of the Chinese community also supported the Chinese Communist Party as it moved closer to gaining control in China. Chin Peng was elected secretary general of the CPM in March 1947. At that time, the communists had an estimated 300 members in Singapore who were committed to the party's goal of destabilizing the British regime by promoting civil unrest in the trade unions. In 1947 communist fronts were influential in organizing over 300 strikes involving more than 70,000 workers. Economic concessions by the colonial government and business community reduced but did not destroy communist influence, and communist leaders gradually became more militant. They recruited former guerrillas of the Malayan People's Anti-Japanese Army and members of various secret society gangs to form the underground

National Security

Workers' Protection Corps. When the communists were unsuccessful in penetrating targeted trade unions, small groups belonging to the Workers' Protection Corps used various methods of intimidation in an effort to have moderate leaders replaced by communists or communist sympathizers.

The party's chance to take over Singapore from the British through legal means ended in 1948 when the communist leaders decided to adopt a strategy of insurrection and terrorism in Malaya and Singapore, which led to the period known as the Emergency (see Glossary). The CPM was declared illegal and was subjected to countermeasures by the government; its membership in Singapore dropped precipitously, and all of the members of the Singapore Town Committee, which was the CPM's central committee for Singapore, were arrested in December 1950. The communist effort was crippled until the mid-1950s, when a new strategy of collaboration with legal political organizations was adopted by the government. The communist movement survived in Singapore largely in the Chinese-language middle schools, whose students were particularly susceptible to propaganda because their employment and political opportunities were much more limited than those of English-speaking Chinese. After 1949 the success of the communists in China also attracted students to the party. The organizing force behind student activity was the Singapore Chinese Middle School Students Union. Because of the unpopularity of the 1954 National Service Ordinance, which required males between the ages of eighteen and twenty to register for conscription or face jail or a fine, the communists had little difficulty in organizing violent student demonstrations. No popular uprising in support of the communists ever materialized, however.

In 1956 when it had become clear that the British were going to leave Singapore, the communists moved to obtain control of an independent government by legal means while continuing to foster disorders. In October 1956, after more rioting by students and laborers, Singapore's police raided labor unions and schools and rounded up large numbers of communists and communist supporters. The concurrent effort by the communists to find a legal route to power focused on the party's alliance with the PAP. Organizers of the PAP had deliberately collaborated with the communists in order to broaden the PAP's organizational base among the Chinese majority, and the communists saw in the leftist orientation of the PAP an ideologically acceptable basis for an alliance. When the communists attempted to seize control of the PAP Central Executive Committee in 1957, however, they were defeated by supporters of Lee Kuan Yew. Lee went on to lead the PAP to victory in the 1959 election. As prime minister, Lee gradually eliminated communists from influential positions within the party and government and later used provisions of the Internal Security Act to prevent alleged communists from participating in politics.

In February 1963, the Singapore and Malaysian police forces organized a joint operation that resulted in the arrest of 111 suspected communists in the two countries. This large-scale police action targeted suspected CPM members in Singapore and successfully destroyed the party's underground political organization in Singapore. In 1989 there were no reports of the CPM's having reestablished a base of operations in the country.

Indonesia's Destabilization Attempts, 1963-66

Indonesia's opposition to the 1963 establishment of the Federation of Malaysia presented the only known external threat to Singapore since Japanese occupation. The opposition of Indonesian President Sukarno to the incorporation of Sabah and Sarawak on the island of Borneo into the Federation of Malaysia set up the early stages of a low-intensity conflict called Confrontation, which lasted three years and contributed to Sukarno's political demise. In August 1963, Indonesia deployed several thousand army units to the Indonesian-Malaysian border on Borneo. Throughout the latter part of 1963 and all of 1964 the Indonesian army dispatched units, usually comprising no more than 100 troops, to conduct acts of sabotage and to incite disaffected groups to participate in an insurrection that Djakarta hoped would lead to the dissolution of the Federation. In June and July 1964, Indonesian army units infiltrated Singapore with instructions to destroy transportation and other links between the island and the state of Johor on the Malay Peninsula. Indonesia's Kalimantan Army Command also may have been involved in the September 1964 communal riots in Singapore. These riots occurred at the same time Indonesian army units were deployed to areas in Johor in an attempt to locate and encourage inactive communists in the Chinese communities to reestablish guerrilla bases destroyed by British and Malaysian military units during the Emergency. After September 1964, Indonesia discontinued military operations targeting Singapore. In March 1965, however, a Singapore infantry battalion deployed on the southern coast of Johor was involved in fighting against a small Indonesian force that was conducting guerrilla operations in the vicinity of Kota Tinggi. Indonesia supported Singapore's separation from Malaysia in 1965 and used diplomatic and economic incentives in an unsuccessful effort to encourage the Lee administration to sever its defense ties with Malaysia and Britain. In March 1966, General Soeharto,

Collecting water during Civil Defence Force exercises
Courtesy Singapore Ministry of Communications and Information

who until October 1965 was deputy chief of the Kalimantan Army Command, supplanted President Sukarno as Indonesia's de facto political leader. Soeharto quickly moved to end the Confrontation and to reestablish normal relations with Malaysia and Singapore.

Subversive Political Groups, 1965 to the Present

From 1965 to 1989, the government occasionally reported police actions targeting small subversive organizations. However, at no time were any of these groups considered a significant threat to the Lee government. From 1968 to 1974, a group known as the Malayan National Liberation Front carried out occasional acts of terrorism in Singapore. In 1974 the Singapore Police Force's Internal Security Department arrested fifty persons thought to be the leading members of the organization. After police interrogation, twenty-three of the fifty persons arrested were released, ten were turned over to Malaysia's police for suspected involvement in terrorist activities there, and seventeen were detained without trial under the Internal Security Act. One leader subsequently was executed in 1983 for soliciting a foreign government for weapons and financial support. The government alleged the Malayan National Liberation Front had been a front organization of the CPM, which in the late 1980s was still operating in the border area of northern Malaysia and southern Thailand.

In 1982 a former Worker' Party candidate for Parliament and fourteen of his associates were arrested for forming the Singapore People's Liberation Organization. Zinul Abiddin Mohammed Shah, who had run unsuccessfully for Parliament in the 1972, 1976, and 1980 elections, was accused of distributing subversive literature calling for the overthrow of the government. Shah was tried and convicted on this charge in 1983 and was sentenced to two years in jail. His associates were not prosecuted.

In 1987 twenty-two English-educated professionals were arrested under the Internal Security Act for their alleged involvement in a Marxist group organized to subvert the government from within and promote the establishment of a communist government. For reasons unknown, the Marxist group had no name or organizational structure. The government accused those arrested of joining student, religious, and political organizations in order to disseminate Marxist literature and promote antigovernment activities. Although twenty-one of the twenty-two persons arrested were released later that year after agreeing to refrain from political activities, eight were rearrested in 1988 for failing to keep this pledge. According to a 1989 Amnesty International report, two persons were being detained in prison without trial under Section 8 of the 1960 Internal Security Act. This number represented a significant reduction from the estimated fifty political prisoners held in 1980 (see Political Opposition, Ch. 4).

In January 1974, four terrorists belonging to the Japanese Red Army detonated a bomb at a Shell Oil Refinery on Singapore's Pulau Bukum and held the five-man crew of one of the company's ferry boats hostage for one week. The incident tested Singapore's capability to react to a terrorist attack by a group based outside the country and one having no direct connection with antigovernment activities. The counterterrorist force mobilized by the government after the bombing and hijacking comprised army commando and bomb disposal units and selected air force, navy, and marine police units. Negotiations with the terrorists focused on the release of the hostages in return for safe passage out of the country. Apparently the government's primary consideration was to end the incident without bloodshed if at all possible. The Japanese government became involved when five other members of the Japanese Red Army attacked the Japanese embassy in Kuwait and threatened to murder the embassy's staff unless they and the four terrorists in Singapore were allowed to travel to Aden in the People's Democratic Republic of Yemen (South Yemen). Singapore refused

A neighborhood police post
Courtesy Singapore Ministry of Communications and Information

to provide transportation for the terrorists but allowed a Japanese commercial airliner to land in Singapore, pick them up, and fly from Singapore to Kuwait. The hostages were released unharmed, and no deaths or serious injuries resulted from the incident.

Crime and Law Enforcement

In 1984, the most recent year for which complete statistics were available on crime in Singapore, the country reported 35,728 arrests. The incidence of serious violent crime in that year was considered low and included 69 murders, 677 assaults, and 1,620 armed robberies. In comparison to the eighty-two other countries that reported criminal statistics to the International Criminal Police Organization (Interpol) in 1984, Singapore had a low rate of assaults and was close to the median for three other types of crime: murder, sexual offenses, and thefts. Although Singapore did not report figures on drug arrests to Interpol, the sale and use of illegal drugs was known to be one of the country's most serious criminal problems.

In the 1980s, police instituted several new schemes designed to reduce the time required to dispatch officers to the scene of a crime and to improve the investigation capabilities of the force. In 1983 the Neighborhood Police Force System was introduced as an experimental project in one of Singapore's police divisions. This system, based on a successful Japanese program, placed small police substations in residential neighborhoods. The police officers assigned to those stations instituted crime prevention programs through their association with community organizations, and they assisted the criminal investigation department by soliciting residents of the neighborhood for information on specific cases. By 1989 the experimental project's success led to the establishment of neighborhood police posts in all ten police divisions.

A new crime report computer network was completed in 1987 enabling officers in their patrol cars to be notified minutes after a crime had been reported. The computer network maintained a record of the call and the status of the police units dispatched to the scene of the incident. During the 1980s, police routinely took blood and urine samples from all criminal suspects to determine if there was a possible link between the use of drugs and the suspect's behavior at the time of his arrest. This program enabled police and the courts to improve procedures for dealing with drug addicts who resorted to crime to support their habit.

Any citizen indicted for a crime had the right to obtain legal counsel and to be brought to trial expeditiously, unless the government determined that the person was involved in subversion, drug trafficking, or was a member of a criminal organization. Trials were conducted by magistrates or judges without a jury, and in most cases defendants could appeal their verdicts to a higher court. The death penalty could be imposed for individuals convicted of murder, kidnapping, trafficking in arms, or importing and selling drugs; between 1975 and 1989, twenty-four prisoners were executed for various drug offenses. Mandatory beating with a cane and imprisonment were required for most serious crimes, including rape, robbery, and theft. Government interference in the judicial process was prohibited by the Constitution. The chief justice of the Supreme Court and the attorney general were responsible for guaranteeing the impartiality of the courts and the protection of the rights of the accused, respectively (see Major Governmental Bodies, ch. 4).

Trends in Criminal Activities

Singapore's criminal code included seven classes of offenses. Class one covered serious crimes against persons, including murder, rape, and assault with a deadly weapon. Classes two through four were concerned with arson, robbery, theft, and abuse of another's property. Class five crimes included forgery, counterfeiting, and fraud. Classes six and seven covered violations of the penal code

National Security

in matters of public safety and violations of special criminal ordinances, particularly those related to drugs, firearms, gambling, vagrancy, vandalism, and petty crime.

A high percentage of murder cases were solved each year by police. In 1988 only ten of fifty-four murders had not been solved by police at the end of the year. The percentage of murder cases solved had steadily increased since the 1960s. In 1969 police solved 44 percent of seventy-eight murders. This number improved to 68 percent of fifty-seven murders in 1983, and in 1988 to 81 percent of the total.

Police were less successful in solving other types of crimes. In 1984, there were 677 incidents reported to police that included sexual and other types of assaults on persons, including robberies and beatings. Police solved approximately 50 percent of these crimes. In 1984 only 20 percent of the reported 1,620 armed robbery cases had been solved at the time statistics for that year were reported to the INTERPOL. Persons under the age of sixteen were classified as juveniles and given special treatment under the law. In 1984, few juveniles were charged with committing serious crimes. Juveniles were involved in no murders, 8 percent of the sexual assaults, and 10 percent of the armed robberies.

Most of the crimes for which statistics were available in 1984 involved various types of theft. Sixty percent of the crimes reported that year were classified as thefts that did not involve a dangerous weapon. Police solved 18 percent of the almost 23,000 reported cases of theft, and juveniles were believed to be responsible for 12 percent of these crimes. Between 1971 and 1983, police were successful in substantially reducing the number of car thefts. In 1971 almost 9,000 vehicles were stolen, compared with only 470 in 1984. In 1983, juveniles were responsible for 77 percent of all car thefts.

In the early 1970s, the government determined that the misuse of illegal drugs, particularly heroin, cannabis, and such psychotropic tablets as methaqualone, was a major problem. In 1973 Parliament passed the Misuse of Drugs Act, which mandated imprisonment for drug dealers and instituted new programs to rehabilitate users. The act also enabled the government to monitor the problem more accurately because most of the persons arrested each year on drug charges already had a criminal record. In the 1980s, more than 5,000 persons were arrested annually on drug charges. Only 10 percent of those arrested were newly identified users, however, and another 10 percent were found to be involved in selling illegal drugs.

Organization, Recruitment, and Training of Police

In 1989 Singapore's police force had 7,000 constables and inspectors,

Singapore: A Country Study

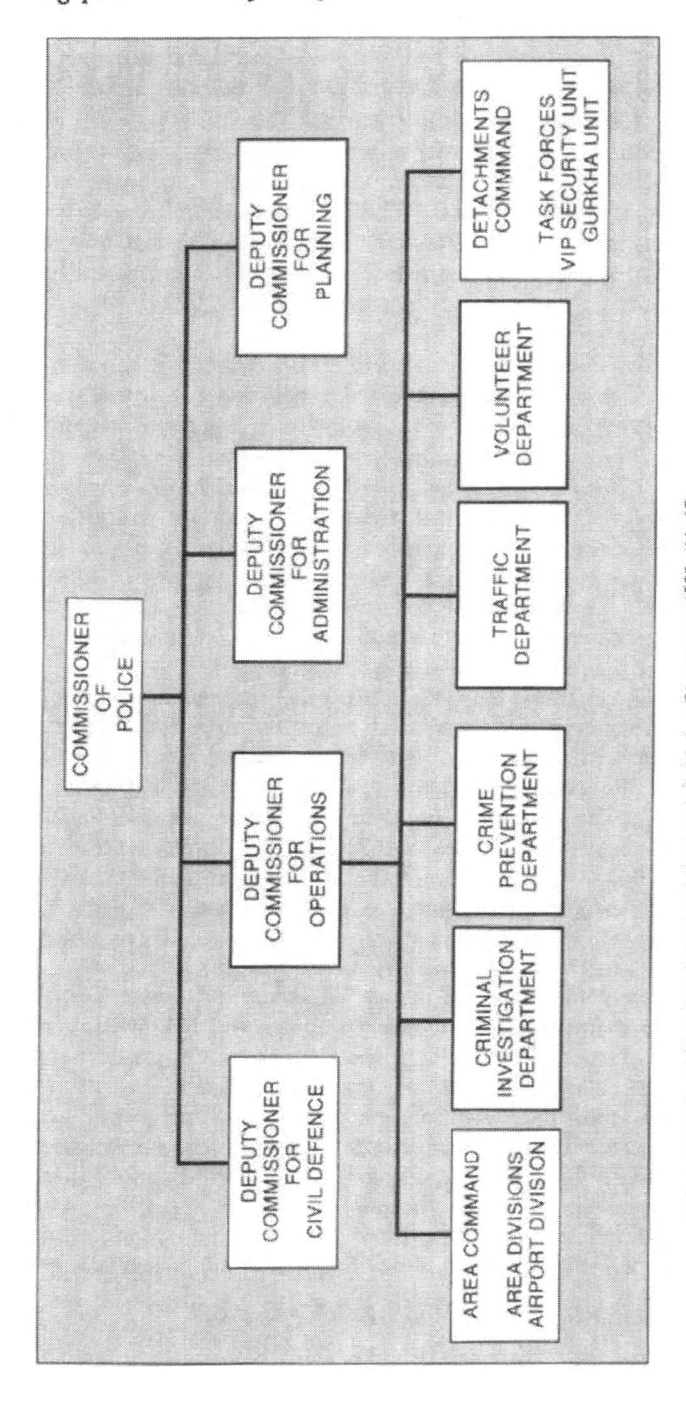

Source: Based on information from John Drysdale, *In the Service of the Nation*, Singapore, 1985, 44–45.

Figure 16. *Organization of the Police Force, 1989*

National Security

3,000 national service conscripts, and 2,000 volunteers. The commissioner of police was responsible for law enforcement in all civil jurisdictions of the country. He was assisted by deputy commissioners for administration, civil defense, operations, and planning (see fig. 16). Two auxiliary police organizations employed an additional 2,300 persons trained to provide security for the Port of Singapore and private businesses. The Port of Singapore police, with 300 personnel in 1989, was delegated responsibility for maintaining law and order on the docks, checking cargo manifests, and inspecting vessels that were suspected of having contraband. The other auxiliary police force was the Commercial and Industrial Security Corporation, which was operated as a public service under the control of the minister for home affairs. The corporation was established in 1972 to relieve regular police from routine security and escort duties for private businesses. The 2,000 security personnel employed by the corporation were delegated the same powers and immunities as police officers in the course of their duties. The Commercial and Industrial Security Corporation was the only civilian security organization whose personnel were authorized to carry firearms.

The deputy commissioner for operations of the police force was responsible for overseeing two commands and four departments. The main island was divided into ten police divisions, which, along with the airport police division, came under the Area Command. The one other command, known as the Detachments Command, comprised police units responsible for counterterrorism, crowd management, protection of government officials, and the marine police. Two police task forces, with probably fewer than 200 specially trained officers, had replaced the police reserve units of the 1960s. Counterterrorist operations most likely would be conducted by elite units belonging to one of the task forces in coordination with army commandos and other units taken from the police and armed forces. A 700-member Gurkha unit was responsible for prison security and for supporting the police task force in the event that a civil disturbance got out of control. The British-trained Gurkhas, recruited in Nepal, had been employed by the police since 1949. The four departments under the control of the deputy commissioner for operations had jurisdiction over crime prevention, criminal investigation, traffic control, and the special constabulary, which included an estimated 2,000 volunteer constables who were trained to assist the regular police in patrolling residential neighborhoods.

The three other deputy commissioners were responsible for administration, planning, and civil defense. The deputy commissioner for administration managed recruitment, training, and logistics and was responsible for the National Police Cadet Corps, a student organization that in the late 1980s had more than 20,000 members and units in 129 secondary schools located throughout Singapore. The deputy commissioner for planning was responsible for research and force development and proposed plans for the purchase of state-of-the-art equipment and the introduction of new law enforcement tactics to improve the efficiency of the police force. The deputy commissioner for civil defense was in charge of civil defense planning and civil defense organizations (see Civil Defense, this ch.).

Police personnel primarily were recruited from among high school graduates who were interested in law enforcement as a career. The professional force was augmented, as necessary, with national service conscripts and volunteers. In 1989 women comprised 15 percent of the force and were employed in all occupational fields. The high number of students interested in belonging to the National Police Cadet Corps provided the police with a large pool of potential recruits. Police recruits were required to be high school graduates without a criminal record and to be in excellent physical condition. Officers selected for promotion to senior grades had to be approved by the Public Service Commission. There were ten senior-grade levels: inspector, four grades of superintendents, and five grades of commissioners.

Basic and advanced training for recruits and national service conscripts was provided at the Police Academy. Selected officers were awarded scholarships to attend local universities and to take courses in other countries. The six-month basic course for recruits emphasized legal procedures, police station and field operations, use of weapons, dealing with the public, and physical fitness. National service conscripts were given a three-month basic course, but with less emphasis on legal procedures. Most divisions of the areas and detachments commands selected from within to fill vacant billets for corporals, sergeants, and higher level positions. Officers were encouraged to enroll in career development courses that were devoted to such subjects as crisis management, community relations, crime investigation, and interrogation techniques. Exceptional junior officers received merit scholarships to the National University of Singapore to study management and other disciplines needed by the force. Senior officers were required to travel overseas for training to broaden their understanding of law enforcement practices in other countries. Some of the foreign schools attended were the Police Staff College in Britain, the Federal Bureau of Investigation Academy in the United States, and the Police Academy in Japan.

Judicial System

Prosecution of criminal cases was the responsibility of the Office of the Attorney General. The attorney general was appointed by the president on the advice of the prime minister. Public prosecutors were attorneys appointed by the Public Service Commission to advise police on the law in criminal matters and to present the government's case against the defendant. Criminal cases in which the maximum sentence did not exceed three years were referred to magistrates' courts, while more serious offenses were assigned to the district courts. There also was one Juvenile Court, which handled cases that involved children under the age of sixteen. Criminal cases appealed to the Supreme Court went through a three-stage process. Judges known as judicial commissioners eliminated cases that did not meet legal criteria for appeal. The High Court of the Supreme Court heard all cases appealed from a district court in which the convicted criminal received the death sentence and also selected cases approved by the judicial commissioners. The High Court also had unlimited original jurisdiction for cases deemed important to the state. The Court of Criminal Appeal was the final arbiter in criminal cases where the interpretation of law was subject to question.

Prisons and Rehabilitation Centers

In 1989 there were six types of correctional institutions: two maximum security prisons for males; three medium security prisons for males; one prison for females; four day-release camps; one reformative training center for persons between the ages of sixteen and twenty-one; and seven drug treatment centers. Queenstown Remand Prison, a short-term, maximum-security facility, served two basic functions: receiving and classifying newly convicted male offenders and holding persons awaiting trial or sentence. Changi Prison, a maximum security prison for males, was used for hardened criminals considered to be unlikely candidates for rehabilitation. Political prisoners detained under the Internal Security Act usually were also placed in the Moon Crescent Center within the Changi complex. Females convicted of crimes are thought to have been sent to separate maximum and medium security complexes.

All adult prisoners spent the last six months of their sentence in day-release centers. These prisoners were allowed to spend days at work and to visit their families without supervision. The purpose of the reformative training center for young adults was to provide rehabilitation. Sentences to this facility usually were for not

Singapore: A Country Study

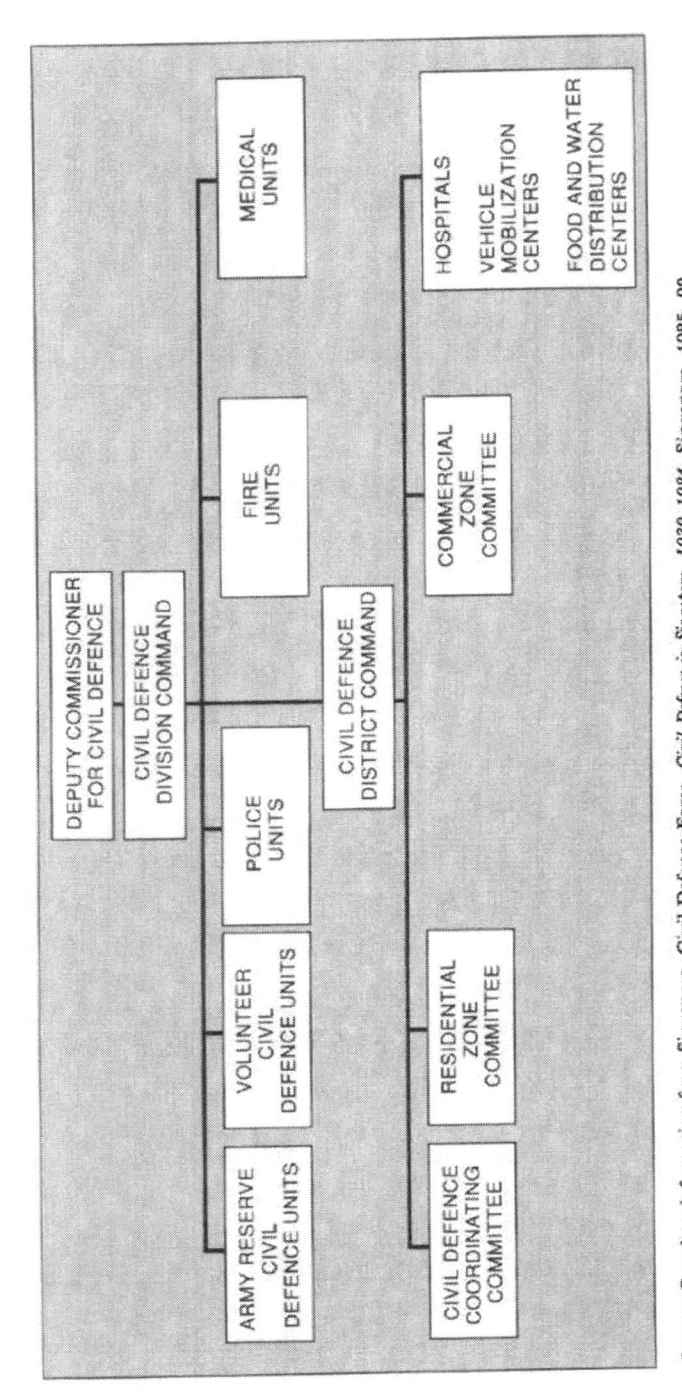

Source: Based on information from Singapore, Civil Defence Force, *Civil Defence in Singapore, 1939-1984*, Singapore, 1985, 98.

Figure 17. *Organization of the Civil Defence Force, 1989*

National Security

less than eighteen months and not more than three years. Juveniles fifteen years old and under convicted of crimes were sent either to reform homes for girls or to reform schools for boys. Whereas persons convicted of importing and selling drugs were prosecuted as criminals and served time in prison, drug abusers usually did not go to jail. Singapore's Central Narcotics Bureau operated six rehabilitation centers and one anti-inhalant abuse center. Individuals who tested positive for drugs were required to spend up to six months in a rehabilitation center and possible additional time in halfway houses operated by the Central Narcotics Bureau.

In 1989 two privately operated programs attempted to assist prisoners and drug abusers find jobs and stay out of the correctional system. The Singapore Corporation of Rehabilitative Enterprises operated job training programs in the prisons and managed day-release programs for the prisons. The Singapore Anti-Narcotics Association provided counseling for drug abusers after their release from rehabilitation centers. Although it did not have job training or placement programs, the association worked closely with the Singapore Corporation of Rehabilitative Enterprises to find employment for drug abusers and monitored their progress after placement.

Civil Defense

In 1964, as a response to Confrontation, the government established the Vigilante Corps to assist police by patrolling communities and reporting suspicious activities. The Corps gradually evolved into the nation's first civil defense force. Initially comprised entirely of volunteers, members were given some weapons training and instruction in general police procedures. The Police National Service Command was established in 1967 to train and organize conscripts assigned to perform police duties in either the Special Constabulary or the Vigilante Corps. At that time, the Corps had approximately 12,500 volunteers. In the 1970s, most new members of the Vigilante Corps were conscripts who assisted police in their home communities at nighttime, on weekends, and during emergencies.

In 1981 the Vigilante Corps was disbanded, and its members were assigned to units of the newly established Civil Defence Force (see fig. 17). The force's division headquarters were set up in each of the police divisions under the Area Command. Numerous local civil defense units were organized and were assigned responsibility for such specialized duties as blood collection, food and water distribution, and providing shelter to the homeless. In 1989 about 40,000 national service reservists and 18,000 civilian volunteers served in the Civil Defence Force.

The deputy commissioner of police for civil defense was the government official responsible for all military and civilian civil defense units. In 1989 he controlled ten division-level organizations, which were subdivided into districts and zones. Each division headquarters was assigned a small staff of regular army officers who were responsible for coordinating civilian and military cooperation within the district during an emergency and for training national servicemen for civil defense assignments. Between 1981 and 1989, more than 7,000 conscripts were trained in various construction skills and assigned to construction brigades subordinate to the civil defense division headquarters. In emergencies, construction brigades would be deployed to damaged and destroyed buildings to clear debris and to construct temporary shelters for residents. Reservists also were assigned to rescue battalions, shelter battalions, and medical units subordinate to each division headquarters.

In 1989 civil defense organizations below the division level were in various stages of development. Each of Singapore's fifty-five electoral districts had a Civil Defence Coordinating Committee. The government enlisted members of Parliament and other community leaders to serve on these committees in order to promote civil defense programs. Local civil defense units were established in residential neighborhoods and at some businesses. Nine underground Mass Rapid Transit (MRT) stations also served as blast-proof shelters for up to 100,000 people. The government frequently organized civil defense exercises in selected jurisdictions, and in 1989 the installation of a sophisticated electronic blackout and civil defense warning system was under study.

* * *

Three books provide in-depth coverage of the evolution of the armed, police, and civil defense forces since 1965. *The Singapore Armed Forces,* published by the Ministry of Defence, covers all aspects of military life and includes useful information on the types of military equipment used by the army, navy, and air force. *In the Service of the Nation* by John Drysdale is a good reference on police organization and training. *Civil Defence in Singapore,* published by the Civil Defence Force, presents an overview of civil defense organizations past and present and explains how military and civil defense units would function during wartime or a national emergency. Two books on the development of armed forces and defense spending in Asian countries include discussions on Singapore. *The Armed Forces in Contemporary Asian Societies,* edited by Edward A. Olsen and Stephen Jurika, Jr., includes a chapter by Patrick M.

Mayerchak on the evolution of the armed forces and strategic planning, and Chih Kin Wah's *Defence Spending in Southeast Asia* discusses how changing perceptions of potential adversaries and domestic economic considerations affect the amount of money the government budgets for defense. A number of articles on Singapore's armed forces have been published in recent years in military journals, and Singapore also publishes its own defense magazine. *Asian Defence Journal* probably provides the best overall reporting on current developments in the armed forces and Singapore's military relations with other countries. *Pacific Defence Reporter* and *Far Eastern Economic Review* are also good sources for current information on military subjects. *Pioneer*, a monthly news magazine on the armed forces, published by the Ministry of Defence, has useful articles on military organization, weapons, logistics, mobilization policies, civil defense, and other subjects. Human rights and internal security issues are covered yearly in reports to the United States Congress by the Department of State titled *Country Reports on Human Rights Practices* and in *Amnesty International Report*, which is also published annually. Statistics on crime can be found in *International Crime Statistics*, which includes coverage of Singapore. Occasional articles on crime and the criminal justice system in Singapore can be found in *Far Eastern Economic Review* and *Asiaweek*. (For further information and complete citations, see Bibliography.)

Appendix

Table

1 Metric Conversion Coefficients and Factors
2 Population Growth, Selected Years, 1824-1988
3 Population by Ethnic Group and Language, 1980
4 Singapore Chinese Speech Groups and Their Alternate Names
5 School Enrollment, Selected Years, 1972-88
6 Employed Persons Aged Fifteen Years and Over by Sector, 1984-88
7 Gross Domestic Product by Sector, Selected Years, 1978-88
8 Balance of Payments, 1984-88
9 Exports by Commodity, 1984-88
10 Imports by Commodity, 1984-88
11 Trade with Selected Countries, 1984-88
12 External Trade, 1984-88
13 Defense Personnel and Expenditures, Selected Years, 1970-88
14 Major Equipment of the Singapore Armed Forces, 1988

Appendix

Table 1. Metric Conversion Coefficients and Factors

When you know	Multiply by	To find
Millimeters	0.04	inches
Centimeters	0.39	inches
Meters	3.3	feet
Kilometers	0.62	miles
Hectares (10,000 m^2)	2.47	acres
Square kilometers	0.39	square miles
Cubic meters	35.3	cubic feet
Liters	0.26	gallons
Kilograms	2.2	pounds
Metric tons	0.98	long tons
	1.1	short tons
	2,204	pounds
Degrees Celsius (Centigrade)	9 divide by 5 and add 32	degrees Fahrenheit

Table 2. Population Growth, Selected Years, 1824–1988

Year	Chinese	Malays	Indians	Others	Total * Population
	(as percentage of total population)				
1824	31	60	7	2	10,683
1840	50	37	10	3	35,389
1860	61	20	16	3	81,734
1891	67	20	9	4	181,602
1911	72	14	9	5	303,321
1931	75	12	10	4	557,745
1947	78	12	8	2	938,144
1957	75	14	7	2	1,445,929
1970	76	15	7	2	2,074,507
1980	77	15	6	2	2,413,945
1987	76	15	7	2	2,612,800
1988	76	15	6	2	2,670,000

* Figures may not add to total because of rounding.

Source: Based on information from Cheng Lim-Keak, *Social Change and the Chinese in Singapore*, Singapore, 1985, 7; *Singapore Facts and Pictures, 1988*. Singapore, 1988, 3; and *Singapore Bulletin* [Singapore], April 1989, 15.

Table 3. Population by Ethnic Group and Language, 1980

Ethnic Group and Language	Number	Percentage of Ethnic Group	Percentage of Total Population
Chinese			
Hokkien	799,202	43	33.0
Teochiu	409,269	22	17.0
Cantonese	305,956	16	13.0
Hainanese	137,438	8	6.0
Hakka	131,975	7	6.0
Other Chinese	72,397	4	3.0
Total	1,856,237	100	78.0
Malays			
Malays	312,889	89	13.0
Javanese	21,230	6	0.9
Boyanese	14,292	4	0.6
Other Malays	3,097	1	0.1
Total	351,508	100	14.6
Indians			
Tamil	98,772	64	4.0
Malayali	12,451	8	0.5
Punjabi	12,025	8	0.5
Gujarati	1,619	1	0.1
Other Indians	29,767	19	1.0
Total	154,634	100	6.1
Miscellaneous			
European	23,169	45	1.0
Eurasian	10,172	20	0.4
Japanese	7,590	15	0.3
Arab	2,491	5	0.1
Others	8,164	16	0.3
Total	51,586	100	2.1
TOTAL*	2,413,965		

* Figures may not add to total because of rounding.

Source: Based on information from Eddie C.Y. Kuo and Seen-kong Chiew, *Ethnicity and Fertility in Singapore,* Singapore, 1984, 9.

Appendix

Table 4. Singapore Chinese Speech Groups and Their Alternate Names

Singapore Group	Alternate Names
Hokkien	Fujian, Fukien, Amoy, Xiamen, Hsia-men
Teochiu	Chaozhou, Chao-chou, Swatow, Shantou, Teochew, Chaochou
Cantonese	Guangzhou, Kuang-chou
Hainanese	Hailam, Qiongzhou, Ch'iung-chou
Hakka	Kejia, K'e-chia
Hokchiu	Fuzhou, Foochow
Hokchia	Fuqing, Fu-ch'ing
Henghua	Xinghua, Hsing-hua
Sam Kiang	Sanjiang, San-chiang, Shanghai

Source: Based on information from Cheng Lim-Keak, *Social Change and the Chinese in Singapore*, Singapore, 1985, 15–23.

Table 5. School Enrollment, Selected Years, 1972–88

School	1972	1980	1985	1988
Primary schools	354,748	299,252	278,060	259,270
Secondary schools	161,371	173,693	190,328	201,755
Technical and vocational institutes	5,841	12,542	18,894	26,911
Universities and colleges	15,206	22,511	39,693	46,904
TOTAL	537,166	507,998	526,975	534,840

Source: Based on information from Singapore, Ministry of Communications and Information, *Singapore Facts and Pictures, 1989*, Singapore, 1989, 73.

Table 6. Employed Persons Aged Fifteen Years and Over by Sector, 1984-88

Occupational Group	1984 Number	1984 Percentage	1985 Number	1985 Percentage	1986 Number	1986 Percentage	1987 Number	1987 Percentage	1988 Number	1988 Percentage
Manufacturing	322,200	27.4	293,800	25.5	290,100	25.2	318,900	26.7	352,600	28.5
Construction	99,800	8.5	102,800	8.9	99,500	8.7	91,500	7.7	83,300	6.7
Commerce	264,600	22.5	271,100	23.5	265,700	23.1	279,400	23.4	283,600	22.9
Transport, storage, and communications	122,400	10.4	117,000	10.1	114,100	9.9	120,900	10.1	120,200	9.7
Finance, insurance, real estate, and business services	100,900	8.6	100,700	8.7	99,900	8.7	105,700	8.9	111,400	9.0
Community, social, and personal services	242,200	20.6	248,300	21.5	259,200	22.6	256,700	21.5	271,600	21.9
Others [1]	22,700	1.9	20,600	1.8	20,500	1.8	19,800	1.7	15,800	1.3
TOTAL [2]	1,174,800	100.0	1,154,300	100.0	1,149,000	100.0	1,192,900	100.0	1,238,500	100.0

[1] Includes agriculture, fishing, mining, quarrying, and utilities.
[2] Figures may not add to total because of rounding.

Source: Based on information from Singapore, Ministry of Communications and Information, *Singapore, 1989*, Singapore, 1989, 292.

Appendix

Table 7. Gross Domestic Product (GDP) by Sector, Selected Years, 1978-88
(in millions of Singapore dollars) *

Industry	1978	1980	1982	1984	1986	1988
Agriculture and fishing	237.7	322.0	349.1	339.7	244.5	203.4
Quarrying	37.5	82.2	128.1	132.2	75.6	51.2
Manufacturing	4,575.9	7,312.7	8,153.5	9,863.4	10,185.5	14,509.7
Utilities	351.5	555.0	600.9	773.0	1,056.9	1,135.2
Construction	1,118.8	1,613.2	3,146.1	4,943.7	3,149.1	2,755.9
Commerce	4,283.3	5,435.1	6,387.5	6,885.5	6,516.3	8,826.8
Transport and communications	2,554.7	3,522.2	4,435.8	5,222.3	5,297.0	6,625.0
Financial and business services	3,165.6	4,906.1	7,697.6	9,879.6	10,573.9	13,111.4
Other services	1,867.2	2,326.3	3,399.7	4,321.8	4,594.1	5,221.0
Less imported bank service charge	−737.6	−1,410.9	−2,109.0	2,827.4	−3,869.5	−4,990.0
Import duties	340.2	426.8	481.5	514.1	393.6	596.3
TOTAL	17,794.8	25,090.7	32,670.8	40,047.9	38,217.0	48,045.9

* For value of the Singapore dollar—see Glossary.

Source: Based on information from Singapore, Ministry of Trade and Industry, *Economic Survey of Singapore*, Singapore, Second Quarter 1989, 24.

Table 8. Balance of Payments, 1984-88
(in billions of United States dollars)

	1984	1985	1986	1987	1988
Exports	22.7	21.5	21.3	27.3	39.0
Imports	26.7	24.4	23.4	29.8	41.8
Trade balance	−4.0	−2.9	−2.1	−2.5	−2.8
Services	3.9	3.2	3.0	3.7	4.5
Transfers	−0.2	−0.3	−0.4	−0.6	−0.7
Current account balance *	−0.4	−0.0	0.5	0.5	1.1

* Figures may not add to total because of rounding.

Source: Based on information from WEFA Group, *World Economic Historical Data*, Bala Cynwyd, Pennsylvania, April 1989, 266.

279

Table 9. Exports by Commodity, 1984-88
(in millions of Singapore dollars) *

Commodity	1984	1985	1986	1987	1988
Food, beverages, and tobacco	3,105	2,434	2,958	3,104	3,838
Crude materials	3,410	2,700	2,459	3,003	4,046
Mineral fuels and bunkers	16,179	16,452	12,361	12,198	12,353
Animal and vegetable oils	1,541	1,535	880	796	885
Chemicals and chemical products	2,464	2,717	2,840	3,762	5,199
Manufactured goods	7,033	6,976	7,675	10,079	7,579
Machinery and transport equipment	16,865	16,567	18,900	26,274	37,939
Miscellaneous	743	798	912	1,050	1,151
TOTAL	51,340	50,179	48,985	60,266	72,990

* For value of the Singapore dollar—see Glossary.

Source: Based on information from Singapore, Ministry of Trade and Industry, *Economic Survey of Singapore*, Singapore, Second Quarter 1989, 32.

Table 10. Imports by Commodity, 1984-88
(in millions of Singapore dollars) *

Commodity	1984	1985	1986	1987	1988
Food, beverages, and tobacco	4,618	4,036	4,407	4,547	5,397
Crude materials	2,510	1,988	1,905	2,267	2,999
Mineral fuels	16,961	17,031	10,994	12,526	12,422
Animal and vegetable oils	1,436	1,380	720	792	941
Chemicals and chemical products	3,096	2,890	3,246	4,082	5,809
Manufactured goods	12,242	11,276	12,501	15,591	20,993
Machinery and transport equipment	19,420	18,317	20,781	27,534	38,299
Miscellaneous	850	898	991	1,078	1,367
TOTAL	61,133	57,816	55,545	68,417	88,227

* For value of the Singapore dollar—see Glossary.

Source: Based on information from Singapore, Ministry of Trade and Industry, *Economic Survey of Singapore*, Singapore, Second Quarter 1989, 31.

Appendix

Table 11. Trade with Selected Countries, 1984-88
(in millions of Singapore dollars) *

Country	1984	1985	1986	1987	1988
China					
Imports	2,881	4,972	3,110	2,926	3,386
Exports	519	730	1,244	1,547	2,369
Hong Kong					
Imports	1,281	1,082	1,310	1,802	2,432
Exports	3,176	3,197	3,183	3,815	4,944
Japan					
Imports	11,218	9,870	11,052	14,029	19,364
Exports	4,807	4,722	4,204	5,449	6,828
Malaysia					
Imports	9,180	8,301	7,403	9,477	12,929
Exports	8,324	7,787	7,245	8,560	10,721
Taiwan					
Imports	1,998	1,922	2,244	3,144	3,997
Exports	830	855	1,097	1,637	2,235
United States					
Imports	8,923	8,775	8,314	10,057	13,718
Exports	10,292	10,619	11,436	14,674	18,826
European Community					
Imports	6,140	6,546	6,468	8,238	10,613
Exports	4,980	5,312	5,455	7,353	10,253
Total World					
Imports	61,134	57,818	55,545	68,415	88,227
Exports	51,340	50,179	48,986	60,266	79,051

* For value of the Singapore dollar—see Glossary.

Source: Based on information from Singapore, Department of Statistics, *Monthly Digest of Statistics,* Singapore, July 1989, 36, 37.

Singapore: A Country Study

Table 12. External Trade, 1984-88
(in millions of Singapore dollars) *

	1984	1985	1986	1987	1988
Exports	51,340	50,179	48,985	60,266	79,051
Domestic exports	33,051	32,576	32,062	39,071	49,555
Re-exports	18,289	17,603	16,923	21,195	29,496
Imports	61,134	57,818	55,545	68,415	88,227
TOTAL TRADE	112,474	107,997	104,530	128,681	167,278

* For value of the Singapore dollar—see Glossary.

Source: Based on information from Singapore, Ministry of Trade and Industry, *Economic Survey of Singapore*, Singapore, Second Quarter 1989, 30.

Table 13. Defense Personnel and Expenditures, Selected Years, 1970-88

Year	1970	1975	1980	1985	1988
Personnel					
Army	14,000	25,000	35,000	45,000	45,000
Air force	300	3,000	4,000	6,000	6,000
Navy	500	2,000	3,000	4,500	4,500
Reserves	6,000	12,000	50,000	132,000	182,000
Total personnel	20,800	42,000	92,000	187,500	237,500
Expenditures					
Defense spending (in millions of United States dollars)	106.4	269	574	1,046	1,003
Defense as percentage of gross national product *	7.4	5.0	6.7	6.0	6.0

* Gross national product—see Glossary.

Source: Based on information from *The Military Balance* (annuals 1970-71 through 1988-89), London, 1971-89.

Appendix

Table 14. Major Equipment of the Singapore Armed Forces, 1988

Type and Description	Origin	In Inventory
Aircraft		
A-4S/S1 (ground-attack fighter)	United States	63+
TA-4S/S1 (ground-attack fighter)	-do-	13+
F-74 (ground-attack fighter)	Britain	29
T-75 (ground-attack fighter)	Unknown	4
F-16 (ground-attack fighter)	United States	On order
F-5E (interceptor)	-do-	35
F-5F (interceptor)	-do-	9
E-2C (early warning)	-do-	4
C-130 (transport)	-do-	10
Skyvan 3m (transport)	Britain	6
S-211 (training)	Italy	30
SF-260(training)	-do-	26
Helicopters		
UH-1B	United States	24
UH-1H	-do-	16
AS-332B	France	3
AS-332M	-do-	19
AS-350	-do-	6
AB-205	Italy/United States	4
Air-to-air missiles		
AIM-9J Sidewinder	United States	Unknown
Surface-to-air missiles		
Bloodhound 2	Britain	28
Rapier	-do-	Unknown
HAWK	United States	6
Naval vessels		
Corvette (MCV)	West Germany and Singapore	6
Fast-attack craft (with Gabriel and Harpoon surface-to-surface missiles)	West Germany	6
Patrol craft	Britain and Singapore	6
Landing craft, tank (LCT)	United States	6
Minesweeper (MSC)	-do-	2
Tanks and armored personnel carriers		
AMX-13 (light tank)	France	350
V-150/200 (armored personnel carrier)	United States	250
M-113 (armored personnel carrier)	-do-	750
V-100 (armored personnel carrier)	-do-	30
Towed Artillery		
M-71 (155mm)	Israel	38
M-114A1 (155mm)	Singapore	16
M-68 (155mm)	Israel	Unknown
FH-88 (155mm)	Singapore	Unknown

Table 14.—Continued

Type and Description	Origin	In Inventory
Rocket Launchers		
89mm	Unknown	Unknown
Recoilless, guns		
106mm	Unknown	90
84mm	Sweden	Unknown
Antiaircraft artillery		
20mm	Unknown	30
35mm	Switzerland	34
40mm	Swedish	16
Surface-to-air missiles		
RBS-70	Sweden	Unknown
Mortars		
120mm	Unknown	50
160mm	Unknown	12

Source: Based on information from the International Institute for Strategic Studies, *The Military Balance* (annuals 1970–71 through 1988–89), London, 1971–89.

Bibliography

Chapter 1

Boyce, Peter. *Malaysia and Singapore in International Diplomacy.* Sydney: Sydney University Press, 1968.

Brailey, Nigel J. *Thailand and the Fall of Singapore.* Boulder, Colorado: Westview Press, 1986.

Callahan, Raymond. "The Illusion of Security: Singapore 1919-42," *Journal of Contemporary History* [London], 9, No. 2, April 1974, 69-92.

Clutterbuck, Richard L. *Conflict and Violence in Singapore and Malaysia, 1945-1983.* Singapore: Graham Brash, 1984.

———. *Riot and Revolution in Singapore and Malaya, 1945-1963.* London: Faber and Faber, 1973.

Colless, Brian E. "The Ancient History of Singapore," *Journal of Southeast Asian History* [Singapore], 10, No. 1, March 1969, 1-11.

Crawfurd, John. *Journal of an Embassy from the Governor-General of India to the Courts of Siam and Cochin China,* II. London: H. Colburn, 1828.

Dartford, Gerald Percy. *A Short History of Malaya.* London: Longmans, Green, 1957.

Drysdale, John. *Singapore: Struggle for Success.* Singapore: Times Books International, 1984.

Esterline, John H., and Mae H. Esterline. *"How the Dominoes Fell": Southeast Asia in Perspective.* Lanham, Maryland: Hamilton Press, 1986.

George, F.J. *The Singapore Saga.* Singapore: Fernandez Joseph George, 1985.

Hall, D.G.E. *A History of South-East Asia.* New York: St. Martin's Press, 1968.

Jack-Hinton, Colin. *A Sketch Map History of Malaya, Sarawak, Sabah and Singapore.* London: Hulton Educational, 1966.

Kennedy, J. *A History of Malaya, A.D. 1400-1959.* London: Macmillan, 1962.

Lowe, Peter. *Great Britain and the Origins of the Pacific War.* Oxford: Clarendon Press, 1977.

Mackie, J.A.C. *Konfrontasi: The Indonesia-Malaysia Dispute, 1963-66.* Kuala Lumpur: Oxford University Press, 1974.

Makepiece, Walter, Gilbert E. Brooke, and Roland St.J. Braddell (eds.). *One Hundred Years of Singapore.* (2 vols.) London: John Murray, 1921.

Marshall, David. "Singapore's Struggle for Nationhood, 1945–1959," *Journal of Southeast Asian Studies* [Singapore], 1, No. 2, September 1970, 99–104.

Moore, Donald. *The First 150 Years of Singapore.* Singapore: Donald Moore Press, 1969.

Ooi Jin-bee, and Chiang Hai Ding (eds.). *Modern Singapore.* Singapore: Singapore University Press, 1969.

Pluvier, Jan. *South-East Asia from Colonialism to Independence.* Kuala Lumpur: Oxford University Press, 1974.

Rose, Saul. *Britain and South-East Asia.* London: Chatto and Windus, 1962.

Ryan, N.J. *A History of Malaysia and Singapore.* Kuala Lumpur: Oxford University Press, 1976.

_____. *The Making of Modern Malaysia and Singapore.* Kuala Lumpur: Oxford University Press, 1969.

Sheppard, Tan Sri Datuk Mubin (ed.). *150th Anniversary of the Founding of Singapore.* Singapore: Journal of the Malaysian Branch of the Royal Asiatic Society, 1973.

Short, Anthony. *The Communist Insurrection in Malaya, 1948–60.* New York: Crane Russak, 1975.

Singapore. Ministry of Communications and Information. *Singapore, 1988.* Singapore: 1988.

_____. Ministry of Communications and Information. *Singapore Facts and Pictures, 1988.* Singapore, 1988.

_____. Ministry of Culture. Information Division. *Singapore: An Illustrated History, 1941–1984.* Singapore: 1984.

Song, Ong Siang. *One Hundred Years' History of the Chinese in Singapore.* Singapore: Oxford University Press, 1984.

Tan, Ding Eing. *A Portrait of Malaysia and Singapore.* Singapore: Oxford University Press, 1975.

Tarling, N. *Piracy and Politics in the Malay World.* Melbourne: F.W. Cheshire, 1963.

Tregonning, K.G. *A History of Modern Malaysia and Singapore.* Singapore: Eastern Universities Press, 1972.

Trocki, Carl A. *Prince of Pirates: The Temenggongs and the Development of Johor and Singapore, 1784–1885.* Singapore: Singapore University Press, 1979.

Turnbull, Constance M. *A History of Singapore: 1819–1975.* Kuala Lumpur: Oxford University Press, 1977.

_____. *A Short History of Malaysia, Singapore, and Brunei.* Stanmore, N.S.W.: Cassell Australia, 1979.

_____. *The Straits Settlements, 1826–67.* London: University of London, 1972.

Bibliography

Wurtzburg, C.E. *Raffles of the Eastern Isles.* London: Hodder and Stoughton, 1954.
Yen Ching Hwang. *The Overseas Chinese and the 1911 Revolution with Special Reference to Malaya and Singapore.* Kuala Lumpur: Oxford University Press, 1976.

Chapter 2

Balakrishnan, N. "Singapore 2: Pledge of Allegiance," *Far Eastern Economic Review* [Hong Kong], 143, No. 6, February 9, 1989, 32-37.

――――. "Singapore 3: Speak Singaporean," *Far Eastern Economic Review* [Hong Kong], 143, No. 6, February 9, 1989, 40-42.

Barton, Clifton A. "Trust and Credit: Some Observations Regarding Business Strategies of Overseas Chinese Traders in South Vietnam." Pages 46-64 in L.A. Peter Gosling and Linda Y.C. Lim (eds.), *The Chinese in Southeast Asia, 1: Ethnicity and Economic Activity.* Singapore: Maruzen Asia, 1983.

Benjamin, Geoffrey. "The Cultural Logic of Singapore's 'Multiracialism.'" Pages 115-33 in Riaz Hassan (ed.), *Singapore: Society in Transition.* Kuala Lumpur: Oxford University Press, 1976.

Buang, Zakaria. "A Matter of Survival," *Mirror* [Singapore], 25, No. 7, April 1, 1989, 1.

Chen, Peter S.J., and Tai Ching Ling. *Social Ecology of Singapore.* Singapore: Federal Publications, 1977.

Cheng, Lim-Keak. *Social Change and the Chinese in Singapore: A Socio-Economic Geography with Special Reference to Bang Structure.* Singapore: Singapore University Press, 1985.

Chew, Shirley. "The Language of Survival." Pages 149-54 in Riaz Hassan (ed.), *Singapore: Society in Transition.* Kuala Lumpur: Oxford University Press, 1976.

Chew Sock Foon. *Ethnicity and Nationality in Singapore.* (Monographs in International Studies, Southeast Asia Series, 28.) Athens, Ohio: Center for Southeast Asian Studies, Ohio University Center for International Studies, 1987.

Chia, Lin Sien (ed.). *Environmental Management in Southeast Asia.* Singapore: Faculty of Science, National University of Singapore, 1987.

Clammer, John R. "Singapore's Buddhists Chant a Modern Mantra," *Far Eastern Economic Review* [Hong Kong], 142, No. 52, December 29, 1988, 26-28.

――――. *Straits Chinese Society.* Singapore: Singapore University Press, 1980.

de Terra, Diane. "The Effects of Language Planning on a Penang Hokkien Kampong." Pages 126-46 in L.A. Peter Gosling and Linda Y.C. Lim (eds.), *The Chinese in Southeast Asia, 2: Identity, Culture, and Politics*. Singapore: Maruzen Asia, 1983.

Deyo, Frederic C. *Dependent Development and Industrial Order*. New York: Praeger, 1981.

Djamour, Judith. *Malay Kinship and Marriage in Singapore*. London: University of London, Athlone Press, 1959.

Freedman, Maurice. *Chinese Family and Marriage in Singapore*. (Colonial Office, Colonial Research Studies, 20.) London: Her Majesty's Stationery Office, 1957. Reprint. New York: Johnson Reprint, 1970.

Hassan, Riaz (ed.). *Singapore: Society in Transition*. Kuala Lumpur: Oxford University Press, 1976.

Jenkins, David, and V.G. Kulkarni. "Joining the Mainstream." *Far Eastern Economic Review* [Hong Kong], 124, No. 26, June 28, 1984, 26-32.

Jeyaretnam, Philip. *First Loves*. Singapore: Times Books International, 1987.

_____. *Raffles Place Ragtime*. Singapore: Times Books International, 1988.

Kuo, Eddie C.Y. "Measuring Communicativity in Multilingual Societies: The Cases of Singapore and West Malaysia." Pages 287-302 in Evangelos A. Afendras (ed.), *Patterns of Bilingualism*. Singapore: Singapore University Press, 1980.

Kuo, Eddie C.Y., and Riaz Hassan. "Ethnic Intermarriage in a Multiethnic Society." Pages 168-88 in Eddie C.Y. Kuo and Aline K. Wong (eds.), *The Contemporary Family in Singapore*. Singapore: Singapore University Press, 1979.

Kuo, Eddie C.Y., and Seen-kong Chiew. *Ethnicity and Fertility in Singapore*. (Research Notes and Discussion Paper, No. 48.) Singapore: Institute of Southeast Asian Studies, 1984.

Kuo, Eddie C.Y., and Aline K. Wong (eds.). *The Contemporary Family in Singapore*. Singapore: Singapore University Press, 1979.

Lee, Sharon Mengchee. "Intermarriage and Ethnic Relations in Singapore," *Journal of Marriage and the Family*, 50, No. 1, February 1988, 255-65.

Leong Choon Cheong. *Youth in the Army*. Singapore: Federal Publications, 1978.

Li, Tania. *Malays in Singapore: Culture, Economy, and Ideology*. Singapore: Oxford University Press, 1989.

Lim, Linda Y.C. "Chinese Business, Multinationals and the State: Manufacturing for Export in Malaysia and Singapore." Pages 245-74 in L.A. Peter Gosling and Linda Y.C. Lim (eds.), *The*

Chinese in Southeast Asia, 1: Ethnicity and Economic Activity. Singapore: Maruzen Asia, 1983.

Mani, A. "Caste and Marriage among the Singapore Indians." Pages 189-210 in Eddie C.Y. Kuo and Aline K. Wong (eds.), *The Contemporary Family in Singapore.* Singapore: Singapore University Press, 1979.

Ow Chin Hock. "Singapore: Past, Present, and Future." Pages 366-86 in You Poh Seng and Lim Chong-Yah (eds.), *Singapore: Twenty-Five Years of Development.* Singapore: Nan Yang Xing Zhou Lianhe Zaobao, 1984.

Pan, Lynn. "Singapore 1: Playing the Identity Card," *Far Eastern Economic Review* [Hong Kong], 143, No. 6, February 9, 1989, 30-32.

Phillips, David, and Anthony G.O. Yeh. *New Towns in East and South-East Asia: Planning and Development.* Hong Kong: Oxford University Press, 1987.

Salaff, Janet W. *State and Family in Singapore: Restructuring a Developing Society.* Ithaca: Cornell University Press, 1988.

Saw, Swee-Hock. "Singapore." Pages 118-54 in Hermann Schubnell (ed.), *Population Policies in Asian Countries: Contemporary Targets, Measures, and Effects.* (Centre of Asian Studies Occasional Papers and Monographs, 0378-2689; 57.) Hong Kong: Centre of Asian Studies, University of Hong Kong and the Drager Foundation, Federal Republic of Germany, 1984.

Siddique, Sharon. "The Administration of Islam in Singapore." Pages 315-31 in Taufik Abdullah and Sharon Siddique (eds.), *Islam and Society in Southeast Asia.* Singapore: Institute of Southeast Asian Studies, 1986.

Siddique, Sharon, and Nirmala Puru Shotam. *Singapore's Little India: Past, Present, and Future.* Singapore: Institute of Southeast Asian Studies, 1982.

Singapore. Ministry of Communications and Information. Information Division. "Land Reclamation: Our Resources Stretched," *Mirror* [Singapore], February 1, 1986, 1-4, 6-7, 16.

———. Ministry of Communications and Information. Information Division. *Singapore, 1989.* Singapore: 1989.

———. Ministry of Communications and Information. Information Division. *Singapore Bulletin,* April 1989.

———. Ministry of Communications and Information. Information Division. *Singapore Facts and Pictures, 1988.* Singapore: 1988.

———. Ministry of Communications and Information. Information Division. *Singapore Facts and Pictures, 1989.* Singapore: 1989.

Skinner, G. William. *Leadership and Power in the Chinese Community of Thailand.* Ithaca: Cornell University Press, 1958.

_____. "Mobility Strategies in Late Imperial China." Pages 83–126 in Carol A. Smith (ed.), *Regional Analysis*, 1. New York: Academic Press, 1976.

_____. "Overseas Chinese Leadership: Paradigm for a Paradox." Pages 191–207 in Gehan Wijeyewardene (ed.), *Leadership and Authority: A Symposium*. Singapore: University of Malaya Press, 1968.

Sng, Bobby E.K., and Yoh Poh Seng. *Religious Trends in Singapore, with Special Reference to Christianity*. Singapore: Graduates' Christian Fellowship, 1982.

Stough, John. "Chinese and Malay Factory Workers: Desire for Harmony and Experience of Discord." Pages 231–65 in L.A. Peter Gosling and Linda Y.C. Lim (eds.), *The Chinese in Southeast Asia, 2: Identity, Culture, and Politics*. Singapore: Maruzen Asia, 1983.

Tan, Chee Beng. *The Baba of Melaka: Culture and Identity of a Chinese Peranakan Community in Malaysia*. Petaling Jaya, Selangor, Malaysia: Pelanduk, 1988.

Tan, Ern-Ser. *Employees and Social Mobility: The Mobility Game in Singapore*. (Ph.D. Dissertation.) Ithaca: Cornell University, 1988.

Tan, Kok Seng. *Son of Singapore*. Singapore: University Education Press, 1972.

Tham Seong Chee. *Religion and Modernization: A Study of Changing Rituals among Singapore's Chinese, Malays, and Indians*. Singapore: Graham Brash, 1985.

T'sou, B.K. "Critical Sociolinguistic Realignment in Multilingual Societies." Pages 261–86 in Evangelos A. Afendras (ed.), *Patterns of Bilingualism*. Singapore: Singapore University Press, 1980.

United Nations. Department of International Economic and Social Affairs. Statistical Office. *Demographic Yearbook, 1986*. New York: 1988.

United States. Central Intelligence Agency. *The World Factbook, 1989* (CPAS WF89-001.) Washington: May 1989.

Walter, Michael A.H.B., and Riaz Hassan. *An Island Community in Singapore: A Characterization of a Marginal Society*. (University of Singapore, Department of Sociology, Sociology Working Papers, No. 61.) Singapore: Chopmen Enterprises, 1977.

Wan Hussain Zoohri. "Socio-Economic Problems of the Malays in Singapore," *Sojourn* [Singapore], 2, No. 2, August 1987, 178–208.

Wang, L.H. "Residential New Town Development in Singapore: Background, Planning, and Design." Pages 23–40 in David Phillips and Anthony G.O. Yeh (eds.), *New Towns in East and*

South-East Asia: Planning and Development. Hong Kong: Oxford University Press, 1987.

Wee, Vivienne. " 'Buddhism' in Singapore." Pages 155-88 in Riaz Hassan (ed.), *Singapore: Society in Transition.* Kuala Lumpur: Oxford University Press, 1976.

Wong, Aline K., and Eddie C.Y. Kuo. *Divorce in Singapore.* Singapore: Graham Brash, 1983.

Wong, Aline K., and Yiu-chung Ko. *Women's Work and Family Life: The Case of Electronics Workers in Singapore.* (Working Papers, No. 64.) East Lansing, Michigan: Office of Women in International Development, Michigan State University, 1984.

World Bank. International Economics Department. Socio-Economic Data Division. *World Development Indicators, 1989.* Washington: 1989.

Chapter 3

Altback, Philip G. "Economic Progress Brings Copyright to Asia," *Far Eastern Economic Review* [Hong Kong], 139, No. 9, March 3, 1988, 62-63.

Au-yang, Karen. "Moving Ahead," *Mirror* [Singapore], 24, No. 12, June 15, 1988, 1-4.

Balakrishnan, N. "Springing a Leak," *Far Eastern Economic Review* [Hong Kong], 143, No. 7, February 16, 1989, 44-45.

Buang, Zakaria. "Moving into the Fast Lane," *Mirror* [Singapore], 24, No. 20, October 15, 1988, 1-3.

Chanda, Nayan. "Concessional Bending," *Far Eastern Economic Review* [Hong Kong], 139, No. 6, February 11, 1988, 68-69.

Chiang, Yin Pheng. "Productivity: Why Bother about It," *Mirror* [Singapore], 25, No. 12, June 15, 1988, 1-3.

Chin, Elizabeth. "The CPF: Enhancing Our Social Security," *Mirror* [Singapore], 25, No. 11, June 1, 1989, 5-7.

"Country Watch: Singapore," *Asian Finance* [Hong Kong], 15, No. 9, September 15, 1989, 82-85.

Crawford, Morris H. *Information Technology and Industrialization Policy in the Third World: A Case Study of Singapore, Malaysia, and Indonesia.* Cambridge, Massachusetts: Program on Information Resources Policy, Center for Information Policy Research, Harvard University, August 1984.

―――. "Singapore's Offshore Information Services Industry." (Paper presented at Seminar on Information Services Marketing, Bermuda.) May 19, 1989.

Goh Keng Swee. "A Socialist Economy that Works." Pages 77-85 in C.V. Devan Nair (ed.), *Socialism that Works . . . The Singapore Way*. Singapore: Federal Publications, 1976.

Holloway, Nigel. "Saving Is no Virtue," *Far Eastern Economic Review* [Hong Kong], 136, No. 14, April 2, 1987, 52-53.

Krause, Lawrence B., Koh Ai Tee, and Lee (Tsao) Yuan. *The Singapore Economy Reconsidered*. Singapore: Institute of Southeast Asian Studies, 1987.

Krausse, Gerald H. "The Urban Coast in Singapore: Uses and Management," *Asian Journal of Public Administration* [Hong Kong], 5, No. 1, June 1983, 33-67.

Lee Soo Ann. "The Economic System." Pages 3-29 in Riaz Hassan (ed.), *Singapore: Society in Transition*. Kuala Lumpur: Oxford University Press, 1976.

Lee (Tsao) Yuan. "The Government in the Labor Market." Pages 174-216 in Lawrence B. Krause, Koh Ai Tee, and Lee (Tsao) Yuan (eds.), *The Singapore Economy Reconsidered*. Singapore: Institute of Southeast Asian Studies, 1987.

Lim Chong-Yah (ed.). *Policy Options for the Singapore Economy*. Singapore: McGraw-Hill, 1988.

Lim, Linda Y.C. "Singapore's Success: The Myth of the Free Market Economy," *Asian Survey*, 23, No. 6, June 1983, 752-64.

Liu Thai Ker. "Vision for the City," *Mirror* [Singapore], 25, No. 11, June 1, 1989, 8-9.

Marchand, Christopher. "Singapore Girl Jilted," *Far Eastern Economic Review* [Hong Kong], 144, No. 23, June 8, 1989, 124-25.

Moskowitz, Michael. "SIA's Success Story," *Mirror* [Singapore], 24, No. 21, November 1, 1988, 14-15.

Mulcahy, John. "Setting a New Flight Path," *Far Eastern Economic Review* [Hong Kong], 136, No. 25, June 18, 1987, 67-68.

People's Action Party. Central Executive Committee. *People's Action Party, 1954-1984*. Singapore: 1984.

Raman, Virram. "Bigger Things to Come for Small Companies," *Mirror* [Singapore], 25, No. 12, June 15, 1988, 8-9.

Salem, Ellen. "Back to School," *Far Eastern Economic Review* [Hong Kong], 141, No. 34, August 25, 1988, 59.

_____. "Flexible Response," *Far Eastern Economic Review* [Hong Kong], 141, No. 36, September 8, 1988, 141.

_____. "No Give, No Take," *Far Eastern Economic Review* [Hong Kong], 139, No. 11, March 17, 1988, 78-79.

_____. "Twinned Hinterlands," *Far Eastern Economic Review* [Hong Kong], 141, No. 33, August 18, 1988, 76-77.

Bibliography

Sean, Chiang Nee. "The Social Strains of Singapore's Economic Growth," *Far Eastern Economic Review* [Hong Kong], 136, No. 21, May 27, 1987, 24-5.

Singapore. Department of Statistics. *Monthly Digest of Statistics.* Singapore: July 1989.

_____. Department of Statistics. *Yearbook of Statistics, Singapore, 1987.* Singapore: 1988.

_____. Ministry of Culture. Information Division. *Singapore, 1984.* Singapore: 1984.

_____. Ministry of Trade and Industry. Economic Committee. *The Singapore Economy: New Directions.* Singapore: February 1986.

_____. Ministry of Trade and Industry. *Economic Survey of Singapore, 1988.* Singapore: 1989.

_____. Ministry of Trade and Industry. *Economic Survey of Singapore, 1989, Second Quarter.* Singapore: 1989.

Singapore MRT Limited. *MRT Guide Book.* Singapore: 1987.

Sullivan, Margaret W. *"Can Survive La": Cottage Industries in High-Rise Singapore.* Singapore: Graham Brash, 1985.

Tan, Diana. "Shipyards Shaping Up," *Mirror* [Singapore], 24, No. 15, August 1, 1988, 6-7.

United States. Congress. 100th, 2d Session. House of Representatives. Committee on Foreign Affairs. Senate. Committee on Foreign Relations. *Country Reports on Human Rights Practices for 1987.* Washington: GPO, February 1987.

You Poh Seng, and Lim Chong-Yah. *Singapore: Twenty-five Years of Development.* Singapore: Nan Yang Xing Zhou Lianhe Zaobao, 1984.

WEFA Group. *World Economic Historical Data.* Bala Cynwyd, Pennsylvania: April 1989.

Wong, Aline K., and Stephen H.K. Yeh (eds.). *Housing a Nation: 25 Years of Public Housing in Singapore.* Singapore: Housing and Development Board, 1985.

Chapter 4

Ahmad Ibrahim (ed.). *Constitutions of the Countries of the World,* 14. Dobbs Ferry, New York: Oceana, May 1981.

Amnesty International. *Amnesty International Briefing: Singapore.* London: Amnesty International, January 1978.

_____. *Amnesty International Report, 1987.* London: 1988.

"Asia Major: A Delicate Balancing Act," *Asiaweek* [Hong Kong], 15, No. 12, March 24, 1989, 21-22.

Balakrishnan, N. "Back to Steady Growth," *Far Eastern Economic Review* [Hong Kong], 144, No. 17, April 27, 1989, 74.
_____. "The Family Way," *Far Eastern Economic Review* [Hong Kong], 143, No. 11, March 16, 1989, 80.
_____. "Marching to the Top," *Far Eastern Economic Review* [Hong Kong], 144, No. 16, April 20, 1989, 33-34.
_____. "Pledge of Allegiance," *Far Eastern Economic Review* [Hong Kong], 143, No. 6, February 9, 1989, 32, 34, 37.
_____. "Politics of Housing," *Far Eastern Economic Review* [Hong Kong], 143, No. 10, March 9, 1989, 24.
_____. "Singapore's Sleeping Booty," *Far Eastern Economic Review* [Hong Kong], 144, No. 21, May 25, 1989, 68.
_____. "Speak Singaporean," *Far Eastern Economic Review* [Hong Kong], 143, No. 6, February 9, 1989, 40-41.
_____. "Two Ports in a Storm," *Far Eastern Economic Review* [Hong Kong], 144, No. 26, June 29, 1989, 58.
Bellows, Thomas J. "Singapore in 1988: The Transition Moves Forward," *Asian Survey*, 29, No. 2, February 1989, 145-53.
Bernstein, Jonas. "A Unique State of Governance Anchored in Sea of Instability," *Insight*, September 26, 1988, 26-27.
Buszynski, Leszek. "Singapore: A Foreign Policy of Survival," *Asian Thought and Society*, 10, No. 29, July 1985, 128-36.
Chan, Heng Chee. *The Dynamics of One Party Dominance: The PAP at the Grass Roots.* Singapore: Singapore University Press, 1976.
Chen, Peter S.J. *Singapore: Development Policies and Trends.* Singapore: Oxford University Press, 1983.
Duthie, Stephen. ". . . But Succession Less Clear in Singapore," *Wall Street Journal*, December 31, 1986, 12.
_____. "Singapore's PAP: Always on Guard, a Review of Dennis Bloodworth's *The Tiger and the Trojan Horse*," *Asian Wall Street Journal* [Hong Kong], July 28, 1986, 6.
Economist Intelligence Unit. *Country Report: Singapore*, Nos. 1-2, London: 1987.
George, Thayil Jacob Sony. *Lee Kuan Yew's Singapore.* London: Andre Deutsch, 1973.
Holloway, Nigel. "Private Roaders," *Far Eastern Economic Review* [Hong Kong], 136, No. 14, April 2, 1987, 50-53.
_____. "Rising on New Foundations," *Far Eastern Economic Review* [Hong Kong], 134, No. 43, October 23, 1986, 152-58.
Kulkarni, V.G. "Amid Speculation the Younger Lee Takes a High-Profile Line," *Far Eastern Economic Review* [Hong Kong], 129, No. 27, July 11, 1985, 38-39.

Bibliography

Kulkarni, V.G., and Rodney Tasker. "Don't Talk Down to Us," *Far Eastern Economic Review* [Hong Kong], 129, No. 27, July 11, 1985, 34–37.

Lee Boon Hick. "Constraints on Singapore's Foreign Policy," *Asian Survey*, 22, No. 6, June 1982, 524–35.

Lee Hsien Loong. "U.S.-Singapore Relations." Speech delivered to the Asia Society, Washington, D.C., May 16, 1989.

"Lee Kuan Yew Still in Charge," *Wall Street Journal*, December 31, 1986, 12.

"Lee Kuan Yew Views Ties with PRC, Taiwan," Singapore Domestic Service [Singapore], March 9, 1989. Foreign Broadcast Information Service, *Daily Report: East Asia*. (FBIS-EAS-98-046.) March 10, 1989, 48–49.

"Lee Warned Not to Crush Dissenters," *Bangkok Post* [Bangkok], August 9, 1988, 8.

Lim, Linda Y.C. "Singapore's Success: The Myth of the Free Market Economy," *Asian Survey*, 23, No. 6, June 1983, 752–64.

Low, Linda. "Public Enterprises in Singapore." Pages 253–87 in Yoh Poh Seng and Lim Chong-Yah (eds.), *Singapore: Twenty-five Years of Development*. Singapore: Nan Yang Xing Zhou Lianhe Zaobao, 1984.

"Party Politics for One and All," *Economist* [London], 301, No. 7473, November 22, 1986, 10, 15.

Quah, Jon S.T. "The Public Bureaucracy in Singapore." Pages 288–314 in Yoh Poh Seng and Lim Chong-Yah (eds.), *Singapore: Twenty-five Years of Development*. Singapore: Nan Yang Xing Zhou Lianhe Zaobao, 1984.

Quah, Jon S.T., Chan Heng Chee, and Seah Chee Meow, (eds.). *Government and Politics of Singapore*. Singapore: Oxford University Press, 1985.

Rigg, Jonathan. "Singapore and the Recession of 1985," *Asian Survey*, 28, No. 3, March 1988, 340–52.

Ropke, Jochen. "The 'Second Industrial Revolution' in Singapore: Industrial Policy in a Newly Industrializing Country," *Asian* [Hamburg], No. 13, October 1984, 46–57.

"Shut Out in Singapore," *Asian Wall Street Journal* [Hong Kong], April 12, 1989, 6.

"Singapore Govt. Proposes More Powerful President," *Bangkok Post* [Bangkok], July 30, 1988, 2.

Singapore. Ministry of Communications and Information. Information Division. *Singapore, 1989*. Singapore: 1989.

"Singapore." Pages 212–18 in *Asia Yearbook, 1989*. Hong Kong: Far Eastern Economic Review, 1989.

"Singapore." Pages 2345-60 in *Europa Year Book, 1988: A World Survey*. London: Europa, 1988.

"Singapore Soundings," *Far Eastern Economic Review* [Hong Kong], 143, No. 10, March 9, 1989, 8.

"Singapore to Move Slowly on Relations with China," *Far Eastern Economic Review* [Hong Kong], 143, No. 11, March 16, 1989, 14.

United States. Central Intelligence Agency. Directorate of Intelligence. *World Factbook, 1988*. (CPAS WF-88-001.) Washington: May 1988.

_____. Department of State. Bureau of Public Affairs. Office of Public Communication. *Background Notes: Singapore*. (Department of State Publication, No. 8240.) Washington: GPO, February 1987.

Vasil, Raj K. *Governing Singapore*. Singapore: Eastern Universities Press, 1984.

Wain, Barry. "Singapore Link with Malaysia Grows Stronger," *Asian Wall Street Journal* [Hong Kong], September 12, 1983, 1.

Young, P. Lewis. "Malaysia and Singapore Defense Forces," *Journal of Defense and Diplomacy*, 6, No. 2, February 1988, 27-29.

Chapter 5

Amnesty International. *Amnesty International Report, 1988*. London: 1988.

"An Exclusive Interview with Singapore's Defence Chief," *Asian Defence Journal* [Kuala Lumpur], 19, No. 3, March 1989, 44-48.

"Are You There?" *Asiaweek* [Hong Kong], 12, No. 13, March 30, 1986, 12-14.

"Armed Forces Training Institute," *Pioneer* [Singapore], No. 122, December 1987, 8-9.

Asia Yearbook, 1988. Hong Kong: Far Eastern Economic Review, 1988.

Aznam, Suhaini. "Room to Maneuver: Singapore-Malaysian Exercises Signal Improved Ties," *Far Eastern Economic Review* [Hong Kong], 143, No. 8, February 23, 1989, 27.

"Back to Basics," *Pioneer* [Singapore], No. 98, December 1985, 14-15.

Balachandrer, S.B. "Flying High," *Mirror* [Singapore], 22, No. 7, April 1, 1986, 1-4.

Balakrishnan, N. "Eyes on the Job: Dissident under Watch in New York," *Far Eastern Economic Review* [Hong Kong], 143, No. 4, January 26, 1989, 12.

_____. "Singapore: Fatal Flaws, Legal Lacuna," *Far Eastern Economic Review* [Hong Kong], 142, No. 50, December 15, 1988, 14-16.

Bilveer, S. "Defence Production in Singapore," *Asian Defence Journal* [Kuala Lumpur], 19, No. 1, January 1989, 10.

Bowring, Phillip, and Patrick Smith. "The Citizen Soldier," *Far Eastern Economic Review* [Hong Kong], 119, No. 2, January 13, 1983, 26-32.

"Bruneians Sail In," *Pioneer* [Singapore], No. 97, November 1985, 23.

"Budget Cut Will Not Weaken Defence," *Pioneer* [Singapore], No. 102, April 1986, 12-13.

Cheong Wye Mun. "Ex Chariot II: Civil Resources Mobilisation," *Pioneer* [Singapore], No. 88, February, 1985, 6-7.

Cheong Wye Mun, and Bernard Chan. "Training at Home: SAF Women's BMT, 3 Special Weeks," *Pioneer* [Singapore], No. 99, January 1986, 17-19.

Cloughly, Brian. "Singapore Fortifies Defence Stance," *Jane's Defence Weekly* [London], 10, No. 8, August 27, 1988, 368.

"Defence and Economics in ASEAN Nations," *Military Technology* [Bonn], 9, No. 12, Supplement, December 1985, 95-103.

Drysdale, John. *In the Service of the Nation*. Singapore: Federal Publications, 1985.

"Elements of the Support Company," *Pioneer* [Singapore], No. 115, May 1987, 36-37.

Far Eastern Economic Review Yearbook, 1971. Hong Kong: Far Eastern Economic Review, 1971.

Fernandez, Warren. "Arty's 98 Years," *Pioneer* [Singapore], No. 102, April 1986, 30.

_____. "Weapons: The Rapier Guards Our Skies," *Pioneer* [Singapore], No. 97, November 1985, 4.

Foss, Christopher, F. (ed.). *Jane's Armor and Artillery, 1987-88*. London: Jane's, 1987.

"From the Desk to the Field: Women Teach Combat Skills," *Pioneer* [Singapore], No. 119, September 1987, 9-11.

"Government Releases Three ISA Detainees," Singapore Domestic Service [Singapore], March 11, 1989. Foreign Broadcast Information Service, *Daily Report: East Asia*. (FBIS-EAS-89-047.) March 13, 1989, 52.

Heussler, Robert. *British Rule in Malaya*. Westport, Connecticut: Greenwood Press, 1981.

Hogg, Ian V. (ed.). *Jane's Infantry Weapons, 1985-86*. London: Jane's, 1985.

Howarth, H.M.F. "Singapore's Armed Forces and Defense Industry," *International Defense Review* [Geneva], 16, No. 11, November 1983, 1565-72.

"Internal Security Measures," *Keesing's Contemporary Archives* [London], 29, December 1983, 32569.

International Criminal Police Organization. *International Crime Statistics, 1983-1984.* Paris: 1985.

Jack-Hinton, Colin. *A Sketch Map History of Malaya, Sarawak, Sabah, and Singapore.* London: Hulton Educational, 1966.

"Joint Air Weapons Range Planned with Indonesia," AFP [Hong Kong], September 16, 1988. Foreign Broadcast Information Service, *Daily Report: East Asia.* (FBIS-EAS-88-184.) September 22, 1988, 33-34.

Kennedy, Paul M. *The Rise and Fall of British Naval Mastery.* New York: Charles Scribner and Sons, 1976.

Khalid, A. "Procurement Trends in ASEAN," *Military Technology* [Bonn], 10, No. 1, January 1986, 29-51.

Kim, Gordon-Bates, and George K. Mathews. "Joint Maneuvers in Uncle Sam's Wake," *South* [London], No. 101, March 1989, 33-34.

Kulkarni, V.G. "Coming Out of the Closet," *Far Eastern Economic Review* [Hong Kong], 120, No. 26, June 30, 1983, 13-16.

"Lee Kuan Yew on Bases, Regional Progress," *The Manila Chronicle* [Manila], January 22, 1989, 14. Foreign Broadcast Information Service, *Daily Report: East Asia.* (FBIS-EAS-89-015.) January 25, 1989, 39-42.

Lintner, Bertil. "Passing in the Dark: Singapore Is Accused of Supplying Military Regime with Arms," *Far Eastern Economic Review* [Hong Kong], 142, No. 44, November 3, 1988, 17.

The Military Balance (annuals 1970-1971 through 1988-1989). London: International Institute for Strategic Studies, 1971 to 1989.

"Mobilization System Works," *Pioneer* [Singapore], No. 103, May 1986, 14-15.

Moore, John (ed.). *Jane's Fighting Ships, 1982-83.* London: Jane's, 1983.

"More about the Super Puma," *Pioneer* [Singapore], No. 99, January 1986, 10-13.

Morgan, Joseph R., and Abu Baker Jaafar. "Strait Talk," *United States Naval Institute Proceedings,* 111, No. 3, March 1985, 120-27.

"New Indonesia-Singapore Air Weapons Range Opened," *Indonesia Times* [Jakarta], March 22, 1989, 1, 8.

Olsen, Edward A., and Stephen Jurika Jr., (eds.). *The Armed Forces in Contemporary Asian Societies* (Special Studies in Military Affairs Series.) Boulder, Colorado: Westview Press, 1986.

Paribatra, M.R. Sukhumbhand. "ASEAN and the Kampuchean Conflict: A Study of the Regional Organization's Response to External Security Challenges." Pages 146-65 in Robert A. Scalapino and Masataka Kosaka (eds.), *Peace Politics and Economics in Asia*. Washington: Pergamon-Brassey's International Defense, 1988.

Pochhacker, Christian. "Defence Profile. Singapore," *Defence Update* [London], No. 94, March 1989, 44-49.

Pocock, Chris. "The Republic of Singapore Air Force," *Armed Forces* [London], 4, No. 3, March 1985, 103-6.

Pretty, Ronald T. (ed.). *Jane's Weapon Systems, 1986-87*. London: Jane's, 1986.

Ramanujan, Chandra Sekar. "Training Abroad: Ex Malapura 4/87," *Pioneer* [Singapore], No. 116, June 1987, 2-3.

"Republic of Singapore Air Force," *Asian Aviation* [Singapore], 9, No. 2, February 1989, 36-38.

Richardson, Michael. "More Eyes in the Sky," *Far Eastern Economic Review* [Hong Kong], 118, No. 49, December 3, 1982, 16-17.

_____. "Setting Their Sights on Space," *Pacific Defence Reporter* [Prahran, Australia], 14, No. 4, October 1987, 14.

_____. "Southeast Asia: Year of Uncertainty," *Pacific Defence Reporter* [Prahran, Australia], 15, Nos. 6-7, December 1988-January 1989, 41-45.

Ross, Russell R. "Singapore's Defense Industries." *Journal of Defense and Diplomacy*, 3, No. 1, January 1985, 24-27.

Ryan, N.J. *The Making of Modern Malaysia and Singapore*. Singapore: Oxford University Press, 1969.

Salem, Ellen. "Singapore Budgets for Slower Growth," *Far Eastern Economic Review* [Hong Kong], 139, No. 11, March 17, 1988, 78-79.

Sassheen, R.S. "Exercise Lima Bersatu," *Asian Defence Journal* [Kuala Lumpur], 18, No. 10, October 1988, 13-19.

_____. "The Singapore Armed Forces—Geared For Total Defense," *Asian Defence Journal* [Kuala Lumpur], 19, No. 4, April 1989, 4-15.

Saw, David. "Singapore. A State Prepared to Defend Itself," *Military Technology* [Bonn], 13, No. 3, March 1989, 64-70.

Sim, Terence. "Computer Power for Manpower," *Pioneer* [Singapore], No. 107, September 1986, 16.

Sim, Vernon. "Warning: Keep Out!" *Pioneer* [Singapore], No. 85, November 1984, 18-19.

Singapore. Civil Defence Force. *Civil Defence in Singapore, 1939-1984*. Singapore: 1985.

Singapore: A Country Study

_____. Law Revision Commission. *The Statutes of the Republic of Singapore.* Singapore: 1970.

_____. Ministry of Communications and Information. Information Division. *Singapore, 1988.* Singapore: 1988.

_____. Ministry of Defence. *The Singapore Armed Forces.* Singapore: 1985.

_____. Ministry of Home Affairs. Police Department. *Annual Report, 1971.* Singapore: 1972.

"Singapore: The Long Arm of the Law," *Asiaweek* [Hong Kong], 15, No. 14, April 7, 1989, 24.

"Singapore, Malaysia and Indonesia: General Defence Cooperation," *Asian Defence Journal* [Kuala Lumpur], 19, No. 5, May 1989, 69-71.

"Singapore: The Reserves Provide the Teeth," *Pacific Defence Reporter* [Prahran, Australia], 10, No. 4, October 1983, 18-21.

"Singapore Acquires Missile Corvette," *Singapore Bulletin* [Singapore], 17, No. 2, February 1989, 14.

"Singapore Corvette," *Navy International* [London], 94, No. 2, February 1989, 85.

Singh, Bilveer. "Singapore's Management of Its Security Problems." *Asia-Pacific Community* [Tokyo], No. 29, Summer 1985, 77-96.

Siong, Ng Poey. "A Lesson in Total Preparedness," *Mirror* [Singapore], 25, No. 4, February 15, 1989, 8-9.

SIPRI Yearbook. Oxford: Oxford University Press, for Stockholm International Peace Research Institute, 1988.

Smith, Patrick. "The Ricochet Round-Up," *Far Eastern Economic Review* [Hong Kong], 115, No. 3, January 15, 1982, 13.

Soon, Lau Teik. "National Threat Perceptions of Singapore." Pages 113-24 in Charles E. Morrison (ed.), *Threats to Security in East Asia-Pacific.* Lexington, Massachusetts: D.C. Heath, 1983.

Speed, F.W. "The Military Potential of ASEAN," *The Army Quarterly and Defence Journal* [London], 115, No. 3, October 1985, 412-17.

"Stepping Up the Defence Drill," *Asiaweek* [Hong Kong], 12, No. 39, September 28, 1986, 28.

Ta, Dong. "The Soviet Military Threat and the Future of ASEAN," *Military Technology* [Bonn], 10, No. 1, January 1986, 52-58.

"Taiwan Minister Denies Rumored Exercise With Singapore," CNA [Taipei], CNA, April 4, 1989. Foreign Broadcast Information Service, *Daily Report: China.* (FBIS-CHI-89-064.) April 5, 1989, 69.

Tan, Adrian. "Reservist Officers Train for Higher Appointment," *Pioneer* [Singapore], No. 101, March 1986, 8.

Tan, Adrian, and Yong Po Wer. "Armour School Has New Training Aid," *Pioneer* [Singapore], No. 116, June 1987, 4-5.

Tan, Reginald. "Training Abroad Ex Elang Indopura IV," *Pioneer* [Singapore], No. 107, September 1986, 11-15.

Tan, Reginald, and Warren Fernandez. "Reservists Are Ready," *Pioneer* [Singapore], No. 98, December 1985, 2-3.

Tan Siew Kia. "Strengthening Our Air Defense: 149 Sq Takes to the Skies," *Pioneer* [Singapore], No. 96, October 1985, 23.

United States. Arms Control and Disarmament Agency. *World Military Expenditures and Arms Transfers, 1988*. Washington: GPO, 1989.

_____. Congress. 100th, 2d Session. House of Representatives. Committee on Foreign Affairs. Senate. Committee on Foreign Relations. *Country Reports on Human Rights Practices for 1987*. Washington: GPO, February 1987.

Wah, Chin Kin (ed.), *Defence Spending in Southeast Asia*. Singapore: National University Press of Singapore, 1987.

_____. *The Defence of Malaysia and Singapore*. Cambridge: Cambridge University Press, 1983.

"World's Most Densely Defended Area," *Asian Defence Journal* [Kuala Lumpur], 18, No. 8, August 1988, 75-76.

Yong Po Wer. "Weapons: The Big Guns," *Pioneer* [Singapore], No. 105, July 1986, 14-15.

Glossary

Asian Development Bank (ADB)—Established in 1967, the bank assists in economic development and promotes growth and cooperation in developing member countries. The bank is owned by its forty-seven member governments, which include both developed and developing countries in Asia and developed countries in the West.

Association of Southeast Asian Nations (ASEAN)—Founded in 1967 for the purpose of promoting regional stability, economic development, and cultural exchange. ASEAN's membership includes Brunei, Indonesia, Malaysia, the Philippines, Singapore, and Thailand.

Baba Chinese—Descendants of marriages between Chinese men and Malay women, many of whom moved to Singapore from Malacca in the early nineteenth century. Although mixed parentage gradually disappeared through marriage with Chinese immigrants, the Babas usually spoke Malay or English as their first language and identified more closely with Singapore and Malaya than with China. After establishment of Straits Settlements (*q.v.*) in 1826, their descendants also came to be known as Straits Chinese (*q.v.*).

Barisan Sosialis—The Socialist Front, a left-wing political party that was the primary challenger to the People's Action Party (*q.v.*) in the 1960s and early 1970s.

Commonwealth of Nations—Often referred to as the British Commonwealth, the Commonwealth is formally an association of forty-nine sovereign, independent states that acknowledge the British monarch as symbolic head of the association. Commonwealth membership is expressed in cooperation, consultation, mutual assistance, and periodic conferences of national leaders.

Communist International (Comintern)—Founded in Moscow in 1919 to coordinate the world communist movement, the Comintern was officially disbanded in 1943.

Communist Party of Malaya (CPM)—Known as the Malayan Communist Party (MCP) until the 1960s. Founded in Singapore in 1930 with a predominantly Chinese membership, the party carried out armed resistance to the Japanese during World War II. From 1948 to 1960, its military arm, the Malayan Peoples Liberation Army, practiced guerrilla warfare in the rural areas of peninsular Malaya with the support of underground organizations in Malaya and Singapore. In the late 1980s, an estimated 500 guerrillas and the party leadership maintained themselves in the jungles of the Malaysian-Thai frontier.

Confrontation (Konfrontasi)—Indonesia's 1963–66 effort to disrupt the new state of Malaysia, which Indonesian leaders regarded as a front for a continued British colonial presence in Southeast Asia.

Emergency—The 1948–60 communist insurgency in peninsular Malaya and Singapore; most active between 1948 and 1951.

European Economic Community (EEC)—Originally established by the 1957 Treaty of Rome and sometimes referred to as the Common Market, an association of twelve West European nations with common economic institutions and policies toward trade with non-Community nations. One of three communities; besides the EEC, there are the European Coal and Steel Community and the European Atomic Energy Community, collectively known as the European Community.

fiscal year (FY)—April 1 to March 31.

Five-Powers Defence Agreement—A 1971 agreement (not a treaty) in which Australia, Britain, and New Zealand promised military support for Malaysia and Singapore if they were attacked by a foreign power.

Generalized System of Preferences (GSP)—A policy promoted by the United Nations Conference on Trade and Development under which developed countries grant tariff exemptions to imports from developing countries. The United States GSP program was authorized by the International Trade and Tariff Act of 1974 and was extended by the International Trade and Tariff Act of 1984. Singapore "graduated" from the United States GSP program as of January 1, 1989, as it was no longer considered a developing country.

gross domestic product (GDP)—The value of domestic goods and services produced by an economy in a given period, usually a year. Only output of goods for final consumption and investment is included, as the value added by primary or intermediate processing is assumed to be represented in the final prices.

gross national product (GNP)—Gross domestic product (q.v.) plus income from overseas investments and wages minus earnings of foreign investors and foreign workers in the domestic economy.

Group of 77—Founded in 1964 as a forum for developing countries to negotiate with developed countries for economic aid, by the 1980s its membership had expanded from the original 77 nations to include the 127 members of the Nonaligned Movement (q.v.).

Her Majesty's Privy Council—As the final court of appeal for certain Commonwealth (q.v) countries, the Judicial Committee of

Glossary

> Her Majesty's Privy Council includes privy counsellors who hold or have held high judicial offices in Britain and present or former chief justices of Commonwealth countries.

International Monetary Fund (IMF)—Established along with the World Bank in 1945, the IMF is a specialized agency affiliated with the United Nations and is responsible for stabilizing international exchange loans to its members when they experience balance of payments difficulties.

International Telecommunications Satellite Organization (Intelsat)—Established by two international agreements effective in February 1973, Intelsat promotes the development of the global telecommunications satellite system. In the late 1980s, there were 109 signatory member nations and 30 nonsignatory user nations.

Jawi-Peranakan—Malay term for the descendants of marriages between Indian Muslim men and Malay women.

Malayan Communist Party (MCP)—*See* Communist Party of Malaya.

Nanyang—Chinese term meaning southern ocean and used to refer to Southeast Asia.

newly industrializing economies (NIEs)—A category of economies of nations or other political entities that experienced rapid industrial expansion and concomitant growth in their per capita GNP in the 1980s.

Nonaligned Movement (NAM)—Formed at a conference in Belgrade, Yugoslavia, in 1961, the NAM promotes the sovereignty and territorial integrity of nonaligned nations. By the late 1980s, there were 127 member nations.

Organisation for Economic Co-operation and Development (OECD)—Organized in Paris in 1961, the OECD represents developed nations. Its twenty-four-nation membership, originally confined to Western Europe, includes the United States, Japan, Canada, Australia, and New Zealand.

People's Action Party (PAP)—Singapore's dominant political party, which has controlled the government by winning every general election since 1959.

sharia—Muslim law, based on the Quran and precedents established by early Muslim jurists.

Singapore dollar (S$)—Singapore's monetary unit, which in late 1989 had an exchange rate of US$1 to S$1.94.

Straits Chinese—Chinese born in the Straits Settlements (*q.v.*) in the nineteenth and early twentieth centuries and more oriented to Southeast Asia than to China. They often spoke Malay or English as their first language.

Straits Settlements—Trading ports along the Strait of Malacca that were under direct British rule during the colonial period in contrast to the Malay States, which retained their native rulers. Governed from 1826 as part of British India, the Straits Settlements became a crown colony in 1867. Although the major settlements were Singapore, Penang, and Malacca, the Straits Settlements also included Dindings, south of Penang, and Labuan Island, off the northern coast of Borneo.

Total Defence—Singaporean national defense strategy calling for a small but well-equipped military force backed by trained reserves and an extensive civil defense organization.

World Bank—The informal name used to designate a group of three affiliated international institutions: the International Bank for Reconstruction and Development (IBRD), the International Development Association (IDA), and the International Finance Corporation (IFC). The IBRD, established in 1945, provides loans to developing countries for productive projects. The IDA, a legally separate loan fund administered by the staff of the IBRD, was established in 1960 to furnish credits to the poorest countries on much easier terms than those of conventional IBRD loans. The IFC, founded in 1956, supplements the activities of the IBRD through loans and assistance intended to encourage the growth of productive private enterprises in developing countries. The three institutions share a common president and senior officers and are owned by the governments of the countries that subscribe their capital. To participate in the World Bank group, member states must first belong to the International Monetary Fund (*q.v.*).

Index

Abdul Rahman, Tengku, 49, 53-54, 55, 56, 57
Abdu'r Rahman, Temenggong, 13; settlement in Singapore of, 8-9, 15; treaties signed by, with Raffles, 10-12, 16
abortion, 73-74
acquired immunodeficiency syndrome (AIDS). *See* AIDS
Aden, 260
adoption, 101
Afghanistan, 30; Soviet invasion of, 209; Soviet withdrawal from, 251
agriculture, 171-74; agro-technology parks, 172; farms, 172; fish farming, 174; flower farming, 172; main crops, 171, 172; pig farming, 172
AIDS: policy, 112; National Advisory Committee, 112; Task Force, 112
Air Defence Command, 227, 228, 234
Air Engineering Training Institute, 245
air force, 234-35, 249; air defense, 234-35; basic training, 243; combat support training, 245; control units, 234; evolution of, 228; expansion of, 229; ground attack, 235; helicopters, 235; interceptors, 234; pilot training, 244; structure of, 234
Air Traffic Control School, 245
alcoholic beverages, 13, 42
A level exams, 114
Aliens Ordinance of 1933, 32
Amalgamated Union of Public Employees, 97
Ambassador Hotel, 55
Amnesty International, 206, 260
Amoy University, 33
Anglo-Dutch Treaty of London, 16
anticorruption campaign, 58
Anti-Pollution Unit (*see also* environmental protection; Pollution Control Department), 69
Approved Investments Scheme, 134
Arab residents, xxi, 3, 13, 23
Arab traders, 3
Arabic-language education, 107
arak, 13
armed forces (*see also* air force; army; national service; navy; reserves), 185; advanced training, 243-44; basic training, 243; combat support training, 245; conscription, 220, 240, 250, 257; disaster relief, 238; history of, 221; Israeli system as model for, 228; joint international training, xxvii, 213, 241, 250-51; Malays in, 83, 240; mobilization of, 237; NCO training, 244; officer training, 244, 245, 250; pilot training, 244; role of, in society, 239-40; salaries, 199-200, 239; tour of duty in, 239; training in Singapore, 241, 250; training in Taiwan, 213, 241; training in United States, 239; training in Western Europe, 239; uniforms and insignia of, 240; women in, 241
Armed Forces Act (1972), 221, 231
Armed Forces Council, 221, 231
Armed Forces Training Institute, 228, 244, 246; Officer Cadet School, 244
Armenian residents of Singapore, 13, 23
army, 231, 233-34; advanced training, 243-44; Advanced Training School, 244; armor, 233; Armor School, 243; artillery, 233; Artillery School, 243; Basic Combat Training Center, 246; basic training, 243; capability, 249; combat support, 233-34; Command and General Staff College, 244; evolution of, 228; expansion of, 229; General Staff, 236; infantry, 231-33, 243; NCO training, 244; number of personnel, 229, 230; officer training, 244; School of Infantry Section Leaders, 244; School of Infantry Weapons, 243; structure of, 231
Asia Society, 212
Asia, Southeast, xxvi; demand for foreign investment in, 163; Japanese military operations in, 224; as participant in Greater East Asia Co-Prosperity Sphere, 40; Soviet role in, 213
Asian Development Bank, 165, 207, 209
Asian dollar market, 163
Asian values, 68, 90
Association of Southeast Asian Nations (ASEAN) (*see also* under names of

307

members), xxvii, 61-62; cooperation with, 209-10; members of, 209, 219; members' reaction to Singapore, 210; military relations with members of, 248; opposition of, to Vietnamese occupation of Cambodia, 62, 210, 219-20, 250, 251-52; relations with, 207, 209-10; telecommunications with, 159; trade with, 154, 156-57
associations, 98; Chinese, 94-96; Indian, 94; Malay, 94; networks of, 94
attorney general, 182, 185, 262, 267; office of, 267
Attorney General's Chambers, 185
Auditor General's Office, 186
Australia: emigration to, 73; flowers exported to, 172; food imported from, 172; foreign workers from, 72; military support by, 252; recognition of independent Singapore by, 57; security of Singapore guaranteed by, 211, 221; training for Singaporean military officers in, 245, 250
Australian troops, 37, 38
Automotive Engineering, 247
Aw Boon Haw, 32
Ayer Rajah Expressway, 167
Ayutthaya Empire, 3, 6

Baba Chinese: attraction of homeland for, 33; cuisine of, 82; culture of, 81-82; defined, 13; education of, 32, 81; education concerns of, 32; as go-betweens, 22; inter-war population increase, 32, 43; language of, 81-82, 89; loyalty to British, 27; origins of, 13, 81; population size, 81; political participation restricted to, 46, 256
Bangkok, 13
Bangladesh: foreign workers from, 144, 167; immigrants from, 73, 79
Bank of America, 163
Bank of China, 56
banking, 162-63; foreign, 28; offshore, 163
Bannerman, James, 10, 12
Barisan Sosialis, 206, 207; opposition to Malaysia, 54, 55; origins of, 54
Basic Education for Skills Training, 146
Batam, xxvii
Batavia, 9, 13
Baturaja, 251

Bazaar Malay, 85, 90, 91
Bawean Island, 83
Bencoolen, 12, 13; convicts brought to, 23; exchanged with Dutch for Malacca, 16; occupied by British, 9-10, 12
Bengal, 17
Bengkulu. *See* Bencoolen
Bible Society of Singapore, 110
Bible study, 93, 109
Bintan Island, 7
birth control. *See* Family planning program
Black, Robert, 50
Black Thursday, 50
Bonham, George, 20
Borneo. *See* Sabah, Sarawak
Britain: as caretaker of Dutch territories, 9-10, 222; defense of Singapore by, 37; East Indian trade of, 9; in Five-Powers Defence Agreement, xxviii, 252; importance of influence in Malaya to Singapore as trading center, 4; military advice of, 250; military bases in Singapore of, 221; military training in, for Singaporean officers, 245, 250; recognition of independent Singapore by, 57; security of Singapore guaranteed by, 211, 224; trade harassment by Dutch, 10; trade with, 154, 157; withdrawal from Singapore of, 124, 238, 257
British armed forces, 258; decline of influence of, 227; in emergency, 227; employment of Malay Singaporeans by, 86; in Singapore, 222-24; withdrawal of, 124, 221, 227, 238; in World War II, 223-24
British Borneo, 5
British Colonial Office, 17, 41, 43, 50, 223
British East India Company, 3, 9, 10, 17, 20, 151, 222; law and order maintained by, 252; Singapore taken over by, 16; trading post established at Singapore by, 12, 16, 123
British Military Administration, 41, 42-43, 44
British War Office, 223
Brunei, 54; decision not to join Malaysia, 55; joint military training with, 241, 250-51; as member of ASEAN, 209; telecommunications hookup of, with Singapore, 159
Buddha, 104

308

Index

Buddhism, 103; percent of population practicing, xxiii, 108; popularity of, 109-10; as secondary school course, 93; schools of, 104
Buddhist Society, 109
Bugis, xxi; conflict of, with Malays, 7-8; control of Riau Archipelago and Sumatra by, 7; control of Johore Sultan by, 7-9, 10; as residents of Singapore, 12; traders, 3, 13, 19, 20, 23
Bukit Gombak, 227, 234
Bukit Larangan, 6
Bukit Timah, 38, 68, 159
Bukit Timah Expressway, 167
Burma, 79
Burma-Siam railroad, 41
Bush, George, 212

Cabinet: meetings of, 180; ministers chosen for, 179
Calcutta, 9, 16, 20, 24; reaction to Raffles' takeover of Singapore, 12
Cambodia: Singapore's economic ties with, 209; Vietnam's invasion of, 62, 210, 211, 219-20, 250, 251-52; Vietnam's promise to withdraw from, 251
Cambridge University, 48, 114
Canada: emigration to, 73
Canton. *See* Guangzhou
Cantonese Chinese dialect, 21, 92, 104; distribution of speakers of, 80; occupations of speakers of, 95
Carimon Islands, 10
Castlereagh, Lord, 12
Celebes, 7
censorship, 36
Central Expressway, 167
Central Narcotics Bureau, 269
Central Provident Fund, xxiii, 97, 98, 99, 127, 188; administration of, 134-35; benefits of, 190; effect of, 135; employee contributions to, 143, 159, 160, 190; employer contributions to, 59, 127; funds in, 134; funds used for construction of mosques, 107; interest rate on, 134; mandatory contributions to, 133; Medisave Scheme, xxiii, 111, 139; Mendaki contribution to, 86-87; retirement plans, changes to, 142; savings used to pay for apartments, 76, 131; size of, 135; topping-up scheme, 139; types of accounts in, 134; used as capital to build housing, xxvi, 189
Ceylon (*see also* Sri Lanka), 29
Changi, 38, 41
Chartered Industries, 246-47
Chia Thye Poh, 206
Chiam See Tong, 63, 205
Chicago Mercantile Exchange, 164
Child care, 101-2
Chin Peng, 43, 45, 256
China (*see also* Taiwan), 3, 4, 5, 43, 212-13; British trade with, 9; civil war in, 22; diplomatic relations with Indonesia, 213; diplomatic relations with Singapore, xxix, 212, 219; economic ties with, 208; food imported from, 172; immigrants from, 71, 79; Japanese war against, 35, 40; as participant in Greater East Asia Co-Prosperity Sphere, 40; potential for diplomatic relations with Indonesia, 212, 219; trade with India, 13; trade with Singapore, 157, 212; traders from, 19
China, Republic of (*see also* Taiwan), 34
Chinatown, 15, 58
Chinese Advisory Board, 26
Chinese associations (*see also* secret societies), 94-96; functions and activities of, 94-95; leaders of, 95; structure of, 94
Chinese, Baba. *See* Baba Chinese
Chinese businesses, 100, 157
Chinese Communist Party: Chinese Singaporeans' support for, 4, 46, 256; collaboration of, with Guomindang, 34
Chinese consulate, 27
Chinese culture, retention of, 22-23
Chinese dialects (*see also* Cantonese; Hainanese; Hakka; Hokkien; Mandarin; Teochiu), xxii
Chinese dialect groups: employment patterns of, 26
Chinese High School, 47
Chinese immigrants, 24
Chinese-language education, 33, 52; of Baba Chinese, 32; for Chinese women, 30; decline in support for, 43; under Japanese occupation, 40; quality of primary education, 29; reform of, 30
Chinese-language schools, 30, 46, 257
Chinese Malaysians, 210
Chinese Middle School Students Union, 257
Chinese middlemen, 19
Chinese, Nanyang. *See* Nanyang Chinese

309

Chinese nationalism, 34
Chinese New Year, 103, 106
Chinese popular religion, 103-104, 108; festivals of, 103
Chinese Protectorate, 26
Chinese Singaporeans (*see also* Baba Chinese; Nanyang Chinese) xxi, xxii, 78-82, 252; attraction of homeland for, 4, 27; anti-Japanese boycott by, 34; associations of, 94-96; communist influence among, 253, 256; composition of, 26; criticism of colonial policy, 46; culture of, 93; defense of Singapore by, against Japanese invasion, 38, 40; dialect groups, 79-81; employment of, 26, 95-96, 97; ethnicity and, 67, 96; growth in population of, 26; as imported labor in Johore Sultanate, 7; languages spoken by, 80-82, 86, 91; maltreatment of, by Japanese during occupation, 40; in multiracial communities, 76; origins of, 21; population of, 79; precolonial Singaporean settlements of, 3, 6; recruitment of, for army, 200, 240; recruitment of, for police force, 254; status for, 82
cholera, 24
Christian Fellowship, 109
Christianity, xxiii, 103; popularity of, 109, 110
Chulalongkorn (King) (Rama V), 28
Chung Kuo Council, 37
Churchill, Winston, 37-38
citizenship, process for, 72
Citizenship Ordinance, 51-52
Citizens' Consultative Committees, 191-92
Civil Aviation Authority of Singapore, 171
Civil Defence Act (1986), 220
Civil Defence Coordinating Committee, 270
Civil Defence Force, 220, 269; duties of, 249; reservists in, 230
civil defense, 269-70
civil service, 185; hierarchy in, 187, 196; lack of corruption in, 187, 199; recruitment, 187-88; salaries, 187
Clementi-Smith, Cecil, 26
Cochinchina, 19, 20
Coleman, George Drumgold, 20
College of Physical Education, 114
Commercial and Industrial Security Corporation, 265

Commercial Square, 19
Commonwealth of Nations, 44, 187; admission of Singapore to, 57; defense of Singapore by, 37, 38, 224, 225
communist movement, 253, 260
Communist International (Comintern): Far Eastern Bureau of, 34
Communist Party of Malaya (CPM), 206 256, 259; breakup of, 253; as cause of Emergency, 227
communist threat, 256-58
community associations, 106
Community Center Management Committees, 191
Community Health Service, 111
computer industry, 149
Confrontation, 56, 124, 207, 209, 211, 221, 249; defined, 54, 258; effect of, 55, 154; end of, 58, 259; entrepôt trade curtailed by, xxv, 124; example of, 56; and Malaysia, 258; response to, 269
Confucian values: in civil service, 187; as deterrent to military service, 240; and relations with other Asian countries, 121, 144
Confucianism, 92, 93, 204
constituency, group, 177, 184; single-member, 177, 184, 205
Constitution, 180, 181, 221, 262
Constitutional Commission on Minority Rights, 58
convict labor, 23-24
copyright, law, 150; piracy, 149-50
Corrupt Practices Investigation Bureau, 180, 186, 187
Court of Appeal, 181
Court of Criminal Appeal, 267
Crawfurd, John, 16
crime: classes of, 262-63; death penalty, 262; drug-related, 220, 261, 262, 269; incidence of, 261; juvenile, 263; rates of solving, 263; report computer network, 262; trends in, 262-263; trials, 262
criminal justice system, 253
cultural preservation, 203, 204
currency, 160-61; exchange controls on abolished, 161; exchange market in, 163

Dalforce. *See* Singapore Chinese Anti-Japanese Volunteer Battalion

310

Index

Dalhousie, Lord, 17
Dalley, John, 37
Daoism, xxiii, 109
Deepavali, 105, 106
Defence and Internal Security Council, 50
defense, in colonial Singapore, 30-32, 35
defense industries, 228-29, 246-48; export production of, 248; foreign-owned, 246; government-owned, 246-48
defense spending, 238-39; parliamentary committee to review, 239; percent of national budget, 238; in recession of 1985, 238-39; on salaries, 239
Democratic Party, 49
Devan Nair, C.V., 47, 51, 52
Development Bank of Singapore, 129, 162; services of, 162
Dhanabalan, Suppiah, 207
divorce: causes of, 103; in Chinese community, 103; in Indian community, 103; in Malay community, 101; Muslim, 102; rates, 102
drug use: among Malays, 84; of opium, 13, 24, 29, 42
Dunman, Thomas, 253
Dutch East Indies, 24, 27

East Asiatic Squadron (Germany), 31
East Coast Parkway, 167
East Indies, 10
Europe, Eastern, 161; economic ties with, 209
Europe, Western, 172, 239
economic boards, 128-33; Economic Development Board, 129; National Productivity Board, 130; Small Enterprise Bureau, 129; Trade Development Board, 130-31
Economic Committee, 199; Report of, 137, 138, 160, 161
Economic Development Board, 128, 129, 147, 148
economic diplomacy, 208-9
economic growth, xxix, 97, 121; in 1970s, 125; of real GDP, 125; reasons for, 125
economy: between world wars, 32; development of, after independence, 53; domestic market as sector of, 121; internationalization of, 151; problems with, after independence, 58; sectors of, 121-22
education (*see also* Arabic-language education; Chinese-language education; English-language education; Malay-language education; Mandarin-language education; Tamil-language education), 53, 112-16; British-style, 114, 115; career prospects, 115-16; enrollment, 114-15; goal of, 112-13; higher, 114; junior colleges, 114; operation, 114; reforms in, 113; secondary schools, 114; and Singaporean identity, 116; and social mobility, 113; and social stratification, 96-97, 98, 99; spending, 113; tracking system, 113; tuition, 113; vocational, 114, 116
Education Code (1902), 29
Education Ordinance (1957), 52
elections, 45-46, 61-63, 184, 193, 197; election of 1955, 49-50; election of 1959, 52; election of 1988, 204
Elections Department, 180
Electricity, 136
Emergency of 1948-60, 43, 46, 48, 205, 258; British military presence under, 227; described, 45, 257
Employment Act (1968), 147; 1988 amendment, 144
employment patterns of Singaporeans, 140, 171
English common law, 15
English language, xxii, 67, 88, 92, 182; Chinese speakers of, 79, 80, 81, 82, 96, 104, 109; as key to upward mobility, 96, 98; newspapers in, 214; radio and television broadcasting in, 215; skill levels, 146
English-language education, 29-30, 43, 114, 116; of Baba Chinese, 32, 81; under Japanese occupation, 40
Enlistment Act (1970), 220
enterprise, domestic, 148
entrepôt, 165, 207; colonial Singapore as, xxiv, 15, 24, 123-24, 151; defined, 122; Singapore as petroleum-servicing, 126
entrepôt economy, 53, 147
entrepôt trade, xxiv, 3, 5, 7, 121, 151-52, 154; curtailed by World War II, 40-41; curtailed by Indonesia's Confrontation, xxv, 124; description of, 17, 19; facilities for, 133; as reason for early success, 17
environmental protection: air pollution controls, 69-70; intentions of, 70; oil

311

spill controls, 70; water pollution controls, 70
ethnic distribution (*see also* Chinese Singaporeans; ethnicity; Indian Singaporeans; Malay Singaporeans; multiracial policy; Tamil Singaporeans), 92-96; Chinese identification with, 96; decrease in importance of, 93; multiracialism policy and, 93; and occupation, correlation between, 96; and religion, 106-8
European Economic Community (EEC), 154, 157
European investors, 59
European settlers, 3, 12, 13, 254
European traders, 3
exchange rate, 161
executive authority (government) (*see also* President of Singapore), 181-82
Executive Council, 22, 24, 32, 45
Export Expansion Incentives Act (1967), 147
exports, 151; domestic, 151; of flowers, 172; growth of, 152; insurance plan for, 161; petroleum, 152; reexports, 151, 152

family: Chinese, 101; and class, 101-2; functioning of, 101; Indian, 100-101; kin networks in, 102; Malay, 101; structure of, 100; Tamil, 101
Family Planning and Population Board, 73, 188
family planning program, 60; abortion, 73-74; voluntary sterilization, 73
Farquhar, William, 10, 12, 13; legalization of gambling, opium, and liquor by, 13; replaced, 16
fashion industry, 149
Federal Bureau of Investigation Academy, 266
Federated Malay States, 37, 223
Feedback Unit, 192
fertility: decline in, 74; of female university graduates, 74-75
Fifth Light Infantry Regiment, 222-23; mutiny of, 31, 254
financial services, 161-63; incentives for development, 162
fish farming, 173
fishing, 172-73
Five-Powers Defence Agreement, xxviii, 211, 221, 248, 252

Flying Training School, 228
Fong Swee Suan, 47, 49, 51, 52
Food Control Department, 111
food: imports of, 152
Foreign Correspondents' Association, 54
foreign policy, 207-14; balance of power in, 209; goals of, 62, 207-9; in late 1980s, 208-9; and national security, 219; neutrality rejected in, 209
foreign reserves, 159-60
France, 224, 250
free market: Singapore as, 121, 122, 123
free trade policy, 121, 122; effect of, 12, 13; established by Raffles, xxiv, 12
Fujian, 21
futures trading, 164

gambier, 7, 13, 21, 23, 24
gambling, dens, 15; legalized by Japanese, 42
gas, 136-37
General Labour Union, 44
Generalized System of Preferences (GSP), 155, 209
Germany, Federal Republic of, 228, 250; trade with, 157
go-betweens, 22
Goh Chok Tong, 179, 212; authority of, 231; as most likely successor to Lee, xxvii, 63; political career of, 200; as prime minister, xxix; as second-generation leader, 62
Goh Keng Swee, 48, 52, 58, 227, 227-28; support for Singapore's integration with Malaysia, 53
Gold Exchange of Singapore, 164
Gorbachev, Mikhail, 214
government control: focus of, 203; to foster Singaporean identity, 203; of media, 214-15; and national security, 219; opposition to, 203, 204; over labor, 141-42; over newspaper circulation, 212
government of Singapore: absence of limits on, 197; activism of, 197-98; anti-proselytizing policy of, xxiii, 110; budgeting and taxation, 127-28; controlling imports, 147; decreases in, 202; economic roles of, 202-3; encouraging trading of international securities, 164; impact of, on private business, 127; perceptions of, 202-3; privatizing, 202;

Index

policies and practices, 200–201; recruitment of university graduates by, 146; regulating distribution of enterprises, 147; regulating exchange markets, 161; regulating savings rate, 190; and society, relations between, 200–205; structure; style of, 177; wage controls, 202; in workers' welfare, 127
Government Hill, 15
Government Securities Market, 164–65
Government of Singapore Investment Corporation, 160
Great Depression, 32, 71, 125
Greater East Asia Co-Prosperity Sphere, 40
gross domestic product (GDP), xxiv, xxv, xxvi; information services' percentage of, 158; manufacturing's percentage of, 147; percentage of devoted to education, 113; ratio of, to trade, 151
Group of 77, 207
Guangdong, 21, 108
Guangzhou, 9, 22
Guomindang: banned by colonial administration, 34; collaboration of, with Chinese Communist Party, 34; precursor of, 27; Singaporean Chinese support for, 4; support of, for Singaporean Chinese, 33; under Japanese occupation of Singapore, 35, 37
Guoyu. *See* Mandarin Chinese dialect

Hainan, 36, 224
Hainanese Chinese dialect, 80
Hakka Chinese dialect, 21, 80; occupations of speakers of, 95
Hari Raya Haji, 106
Hastings, Lord, 10, 222
Hawkers Department, 111
health: AIDS policy, 112; causes of death, 111; epidemics, 111–12; occupational diseases, 112
Heaven, Earth, and Man Society, 22
Henghua, 80, 95
High Court (*see also* Supreme Court), 181, 267
Hindu religion, xxiii, 108, 109; Brahman priests, 87; customs, 88, 102; holidays, 105; studies, 93; temples, xxii, 103, 105
Hindu Advisory Board, 94, 106
Hindu Endowments Board, 106
Hindu New Year, 105
Hitachi Zosen, 166
Hokchia, 80
Hokchiu, 80
Hokkaidō, 48
Hokkien Chinese dialect, 21, 92, 104; in Baba Malay, 81; as market language, 90, 91; occupations of speakers of, 95; percentage of Singaporean speakers of, 80
Home Protection Insurance Scheme, 134
Hong Kong, 17, 29, 31, 82, 142, 222, 223; Chinese Singaporeans from, 72, 79; as financial center, xxvi, 162; foreign investment from, 59; foreign workers from, 73, 144; as newly industrializing economy, 121, 154; Singapore investment in, xxix; Singapore trade with, 157
Honors Degree Liberal Arts and Social Science program, 116
Hoo Ah Kay, 22–23, 27
Housing and Development Board, 133, 134, 188–90, 192; accomplishments, 53, 131; community programs sponsored by, 78; establishment of, 53, 131; powers of, 76, 189; rehousing under, 76, 189–90
Housing and Development Board apartments, xxiv, 97; assignment of, 75; forced savings used for, 190; government encouragement to buy, 131; as improvement in standard of living, 76; management of, 192; purchase prices for, 189; rents for, 189; residents of, 98
housing estates, 58; as communities, 78; defined, 131; ethnic clustering in, 78; Town Councils in, 192
housing policies, 75–78; social effects of, 76
Human Organ Transplant Law, 112
Hundred Days' Reform Movement (1898), 27
Hussein (Tengku Long), 8, 12, 13; acknowledged to be sultan of Johore, 12; agreement to help suppress piracy, 16; treaty establishing settlement boundaries signed by, 12; treaty establishing trading post at Singapore signed by, 12

Ibrahim, 20
Illanun pirates, 20
immigrants: categories of, 71–72; origins of, 71–72

313

immigration: effect of, on population, 73; restrictions on, 32, 71-72
Immigration Department, 72
Immigration Restriction Ordinance (1930), 32
income, per capita: in 1965, 125
income distribution, 97
income level (class): increases in, 99; lower, 97-98; middle, 98; upper, 98-99
India, 3, 5, 9, 10, 29, 37, 87, 222, 223; foreign workers from, 144; goods traded by, xxiv, 5; immigrants from, 24, 71; population, 79; trade with China, 13
Indian Ocean, 5
Indian Singaporeans (*see also* Tamil), xxi, 3, 12, 34, 67, 76, 87-88, 94, 252, 253; associations of, 94; background of, 23; caste distinctions, 88, 102; composition of, 27-28; ethnic composition of, 79, 87; in government, 177, 200; intermarriage with Malays by, 24, 88; issues, 87; jobs held by, 13, 28, 88; languages spoken by, 87-88, 91; population of, 23, 43; as race, 89; recruitment of, for police force, 254; religion of, 87; sex ratio, 87; untouchables, 87
Indian traders, 3
Indian troops, 38-40
Indochina, 36, 224; economic ties with, 208-9; investments in, 211; relations with, 211
Indonesia, 5, 54, 82, 154, 236; Confrontation policy of, xxv, 124, 207, 209, 211, 221; food imported from, 172; foreign workers from, 144; military exercises with, 250, 251; potential diplomatic relations of, with China, 212, 219; relations with Singapore, xxvii, 62, 211, 227; tensions between Singapore and, 56, 61, 227; trade with, 154
Indonesia Raya, 54
Indonesian immigrants, 24
Industrial Arbitration Court, 142
industrial development, 151
industrial estates, 59, 133
industrial relations, 140-42
Industrial Relations Act (1960), 141
Industrial Training Board, 188
industrialization, 125, 146-49; emphasis on high-technology, 146-47, 148-49, 149; export-oriented, 147; in 1960, 147; in 1988, 147

inflation, 125
information technology, 149-50
Institute of Education, 114
Integrated Air Defence System, 252
Integrated Manpower Information System, 240-41
integration, as goal of Singapore government, 58
Intelsat Business Service, 159
Inter-Governmental Committee, 211
Internal Security Act (1960), xxviii; purpose of, 205-6; uses of, 212, 220, 258, 259, 260
Internal Security Council, 52, 55
Internal security plan, 255
International Criminal Police Organization (Interpol), 261
International Finance Corporation, 165
International Maritime Organization, 165
International Monetary Fund (IMF), 165
International Telecommunications Satellite Organization (Intelsat), 208
Inter-Religious Organization, 106
investment: foreign, xxv, 59, 125, 147, 159; government support for, 161; Singapore as magnet for, 59-60
Ishak, Yusof bin, 57, 59
Islam, xxiii, 74, 102, 109; study of, 93
Islamic revival movement, xxiii, 28, 108, 110, 210
Israel, 250; military advisers from, 61, 228

Jackson, Phillip, 18
Jaffna, 87
Japan (*see also* Japanese invasion of Singapore; Japanese occupation of Singapore): attack on Malaya by, 4; bombing of Singapore by, 36; boycott against, 34; capture of Singapore by, 36-37; demonstrations against, 35; flowers exported to, 172; invasion of Malaya by, 225; invasion of Manchuria by, 34; investments by, xxv; level of spending on education by, 113; market orientation of, 156; military training of Singaporean officers in, 250; as progenitor of Greater East Asia Co-Prosperity Sphere, 40; rearmament, 212; sentiment against, in Singapore, 34; Singapore's trade deficit with, 155;

Southern Army of, 224; surrender by, to Mountbatten, 41; trade with Singapore, 58-59, 151, 154, 155-56; Twenty-One Demands of, 33; workers from, 72
Japanese community in Singapore, 155
Japanese invasion of Singapore, 224-26, 248; British preparation for, 223, 254; goals of, 224; Japanese strategy for, 37; preparatory attacks, 224; strength of Japanese force, 37
Japanese investors, 59
Japanese Malaya Campaign (*see also* Japanese invasion of Singapore; Japanese occupation of Singapore), 36-41
Japanese occupation of Singapore, 38-41, 256, 258; control of schools under, 40; damage to infrastructure by, 42, 227; recovery from, xxv, 42-43
Japanese Red Army: terrorist attack by, 260-61
Java, 3, 9, 79; goods traded by, 5-6; Malays as immigrants from, 82; occupied by British, 10; people of, 73; traders from, 3
Java Sea, 83
Jawi-Peranakan, 24, 28
Jeyaretnam, J.B., 63, 205, 206
Jewish residents, 23, 109
Jiangsu, 81
Jiangxi, 81
Johor, xxv, 144, 156, 258; economic ties with, 156; foreign labor from, 144
Johore, 21, 31, 51, 224
Johore Baharu, 37, 69
Johore Causeway, 29
Johore Strait, 37, 169, 225, 226
Johore Sultanate, 3; Bugis control of, 7-9, 10; as entrepôt, 15; establishment of, 7
Judicial Committee of Her Majesty's Privy Council, 181, 184-85
Judiciary, 184-185; Court of Appeal, 184; Court of Criminal Appeal, 184; Judicial Committee of Her Majesty's Privy Council, 181, 184-85; Supreme Court, 184-85
Jurong, 41
Jurong Camp, 244
Jurong Industrial Estate, 53, 77, 166
Jurong Marine Base, 133
Jurong Port and Market Complex, 166, 167, 172
Jurong Town Corporation, 59, 132-33

Justice Party, 206
Juvenile Court, 267

Kalimantan Army Command, 258, 259
Kallang, 38, 136
Kallang Gasworks, 136
Kallang River, 70
kampongs, 58, 76, 84
Kampuchea, Coalition Government of Democratic (*see also* Cambodia), 62
Kapitans, 15
Kedah, 224
Kelantan, 224
Keppel Wharves, 166, 167
Kew Letters, 9, 10
Khatib Camp, 243
Khota Baharu, 36, 225
King Edward Medical College, 30, 42
King George V Graving Dock (*see also* Sembawang Shipyard), 35, 60
Konfrontasi. *See* Confrontation
Korea (*see also* South Korea), 35, 60
Kota Tinggi, 258
Krause, Lawrence B., 140
Kuala Lumpur, 5, 37, 52, 53, 54, 55, 56
Kuomintang. *See* Guomindang
Kuwait, 261

labor law, 59, 141-42
labor unions, 140-42, 202, 256; collective agreements for, 143; membership in, 142; organization of, suppressed by colonial government, 34; role and structure defined, 142; role and structure modified, 142; strikes, 255
Labour Court, 142
Labour Front, 4, 48, 52
Labour Front government, 50
Lai Teck, 45
land development and management, 131-32
land reclamation, xxi
land use policy, 77-78
Lands Acquisition Act (1966), 189
language (*see also* under names of individual languages): high and low variations, 90-91; planning, 58, 90-92; understood by Singaporeans, 91
Laos, economic ties with, 209
law enforcement, 253

315

Lee Hsien Loong, xxvii, 180, 197; political career of, 63, 199-200; as potential successor to Lee Kuan Yew, 63; and Speak Mandarin campaign, 92; speech by, on U.S.-Singapore relations, 212
Lee Kuan Yew, xxi, xxvi-xxvii, xxviii, xxix, 92, 192-3, 227, 230, 251; antiproselytizing policy of, 110; as delegate to Merdeka talks, 50; early political career of, 48-51; education of, 48; executive presidency proposed by, 160, 180; family planning schemes under, 74-75; formation of People's Action Party, 4; independence of Singapore under, 5, 57-62; industrialization promoted by, 54; and international relations, xxvii, 210, 211, 213, 219; labor relations controlled by, 141-42; leadership style of, 196; merger into Malaysia supported by, 53-54, 56-57; national unity promoted by, 53-54; as People's Action Party secretary general, 194; People's Action Party victory under, 52, 256, 257-58; referendum on merger question announced, 54; succession to, 62, 63, 198-99, 249; suppression of political opposition by, 60-61, 205
Lee Siew Choh, 205, 207
legal service, 185
Legal Service Commission, 186
Legislative Assembly (*see also* Parliament): description of, 47-48; first elections for, 4-5, 52; and Merdeka talks, 51; merger with Malaysia, vote on, 54; People's Action Party control of, 193; preparations for self-government by, 52; Singapore Independence Bill passed by, 180
Legislative Council, 22; Chinese members of, 26; under colonial rule, 33, 45-46; description of, 24
legislature (*see also* Parliament of Singapore), 182
Leong Mun Kwai, 207
Li Teng-hui, 213
Lim Chin Siong: appointed to government post, 52; communist activities of, 47, 51; seat in legislature, 50; as secretary general of Barisan Sosialis, 54-55
Lim Kim San, 53
Lim, Linda Y.C., 139-40
Lim Yew Hock: as chief minister, 50-53; 255; formation of Labour Front by, 48; at Merdeka talks, 52
liquor, tax on, 15
living standards, 205
Lürssen Werft, 228, 235-36

Macao, 72; foreign workers from, 144
Macassar, 23
machinery industry, 148
Madras, India, 167
Mahathir, Mohammad, xxvii, 62, 210
Majapahit Empire, 3, 6
Malacca, 3, 13, 21, 23; as part of Malayan Union, 41; medieval role of, 7; occupied by British, 10, 222; occupied by Japanese, 37; as part of Straits Settlements, 3, 17, 24; Portuguese capture of, 7; traders, 12, 19
Malacca, Strait of, xxi, 3, 28, 68; as border between British and Dutch control, 16; Dutch control of, 10, 12; Japanese control of, 225; oil spills in, 70; security of, 211
Malacca Sultanate, 3, 7; as entrepôt, 15; establishment of, 7; Singapura controlled by, 7
Malay Archipelago, xxiv, 3, 19; as entrepôt, 5; as rendezvous point for traders, 5; as supply point for traders, 5
Malay immigrants, 24
Malay language: Bazaar Malay, 85-86, 90, 91; as "mother tongue," 90; as national language of Singapore, 53; newspapers in, 214; radio and television broadcasting in, 215; spoken by Chinese Singaporeans, 79, 80, 81, 91; spoken in legislature, 182; spoken by Indian Singaporeans, 88, 91
Malay-language education, 29, 43, 52, 114; under Japanese occupation, 40; Mendaki tutoring, 86; number of students in, 32; special considerations regarding, 85-86
Malay Peninsula, xxiv, 3, 7, 9, 19, 20, 23, 68, 71; British occupation of, 20; British defense of, 223, 224; controlled by Malacca Sultanate, 7; opposition to separating Singapore from, 41, 44; overland connecting roads, 169; as source of rubber and tin, xxiv, 24, 124; unstable conditions in, 24
Malay press, 56

316

Index

Malay Singaporeans, xxi, 3, 67, 76, 89, 177, 200, 252, 253, 254; associations of, 94; background of, 23; birth patterns of, 84; education of, 86; ethnic composition of, 79; government view of, 75; intermarriage with Indians by, 24, 88; jobs held by, 28, 83, 84, 86; language used by, 85-86; marriage patterns of, 84, 102; military service by, 74, 240; origins of, 82-83; population of, 79, 82; precolonial Singaporean settlements of, 6; religion, 84, 102, 106, 108; social position of, 74

Malay traders, 3

Malay troops, 38-40

Malaya, 36, 43, 54, 54, 222, 257; Chinese consulates established in, 27; Japan's attack on, 4, 225; Malay immigrants from, 82; Singapore's merger with, 53, 124

Malaya, Federation of, 45; formation of, 44; Merdeka talks regarding, 51; merger of Singapore with, 52; proposed, 54

Malaya, University of, 43

Malayan Chinese, 37

Malayan Chinese Association (MCA), 49, 52, 56

Malayan Communist Party (MCP), 4, 34, 35, 45, 46; labor activities of, 44; popularity of, 43

Malayan Democratic Union, 44, 45

Malayan National Liberation Front, 259

Malayan People's Anti-Japanese Army, 40, 43, 45, 256

Malayan Union, 41, 44

Malayans, 55, 56

Malaysia, Federation of, 82, 93, 236, 260; conflicts of, with Singapore, 57, 221; and Confrontation, 258; first year of, 56; food imported from, 172; formation of, 5, 124, 180; as member of ASEAN, 209, 219; military exercises with, 251; opposition to formation of, 54, 258; percentage of Singaporeans from, 72; police force, 259; political tensions in, 56; proposed, 54; relations with Singapore, xxvii, 62, 210-11, 221, 252; separation of Singapore from, xxv, 57, 61, 67, 88, 124, 125, 180, 210, 227, 250; Singapore as part of, 55-57, 221, 227; as source of foreign workers, 71, 144, 167; stock exchange of, 162; trade with, 154; water imported from, 69, 136

Malaysia-Singapore Airlines. *See* Singapore Airlines

Malaysian Agreement (1963), 55

Malaysian National Alliance Party, 56

Malaysian Solidarity Convention, 56

malnutrition, 24

Manchukuo, 40

Manchuria, 35

Mandarin Campaign Secretariat, 91

Mandarin Chinese dialect (Guoyu), 82, 88, 109, 182; as "mother tongue," 90; newspapers in, 214; radio and television broadcasting in, 215; Speak Mandarin Campaign, 91-92

Mandarin-language education, 33, 43, 52, 114; discouraged by British, 33-34

Manila, 13

manufacturing industry, 28; export-oriented, 121

markets, international, 121; services for, 121-22; Singapore's dependence on, 121; Singapore's vulnerability to, 121, 122

Marshall, David, 4, 48, 50

marriage (*see also* divorce), 100-103; Chinese, 101; interethnic, 102; Malay, 101; Tamil, 101

Maternal and Child Health Service, 111

media, 214-15; government restrictions on, 214; newspapers, 214-15; radio, 215; television, 215

medical services, 110-11; facilities, 111; fees, 111

Medisave Scheme, xxiii, 111, 134, 139

Members of Parliament Constituent Advisory Groups, 93

Mendaki, 86; Central Provident Fund contribution, 86-87

Mercantile activity, 19-20

merchant houses, 19-20

merchant marine, 166

Merdeka talks, 5; first round of, 50; second round of, 51; third round of, 52

Middle East, 37

middlemen, 22; system of, 19

military. *See* armed forces

Military Maneuvers Act (1963), 241

military relations, 250-52; exercises, 250-51, 252; joint international training, 213, 239, 241, 245, 248, 250-51; matériel, 250

Mindanao, 20

Min-def mafia, 199

317

Minimum Sum Scheme, 134
ministries (*see also* cabinet; individual ministries): ministers chosen for, 179; ministerial portfolios, 179-80
Ministry of Communications and Information, 91
Ministry of Community Development, 108, 191
Ministry of Culture, 191
Ministry of Defence, 238, 241; business interests of, 191, 228-29; civilian as minister, 221; conscription regulations of, 240; National Cadet Corps administered by, 236; organization of, 231; political power of former members of, 199; reserve units monitored by, 249
Ministry of Education, 114, 115, 186, 236
Ministry of Environment (*see also* Pollution Control Department), 69, 70, 111
Ministry of Finance, 186, 190, 200; Public Service Division, 186
Ministry of Foreign Affairs, 211
Ministry of Health, 111, 140, 186
Ministry of Home Affairs, 186, 211
Ministry of Interior and Defence, 228
Ministry of National Development, 172,
Ministry of Social Affairs, 191
Misuse of Drugs Act (1973), 263
Mohammad, Mahathir, xxvii, 62, 210
Moluccas, xxiv, 6
Monetary Authority of Singapore, 161, 162, 163
monsoons, 19
mortality rate, 29
mother tongue, xxii, 90
motor vehicles, 167-69
Mountbatten, Louis, 41, 43
multiracialism policy, 210; description of, 93; and ethnic clustering, 78; in housing estates, 76, 190
Mushroom Unit of the Primary Production Department, 172
Muslim, Chulia, 103; law, 15, 107; mosques, 107
Muslim Law Act (1966), 102, 106-7
Muslim Ordinance (1957), 107-8
Muslim Religions Council, 106, 108, 188

Nagarakertagama, 6
Nakhodka, 214
Nanyang, 33, defined, 6
Nanyang Chinese, 13, 27, 34

Nanyang Chinese National Salvation Movement, 34, 35
Nanyang Chinese Relief General Association, 35
Nanyang Communist Party, 34
Nanyang Technological Institute
Nanyang University, 46
National Association of Securities Dealers (NASDAQ), 164
National Cadet Corps, 236
National Computer Board, 149
National Day, 106
national holidays, 105-6
National Police Cadet Corps, 266
National Productivity Board, 130, 138
national security: communist threat to, 219; defensive outlook, 248-49; and foreign policy, 219; people's reaction to, 249; perceptions, 219; Total Defence concept, 249-50
national service, 219, 250; conscription for, 220, 228, 250
National Service Ordinance, 47, 257; demonstration against, 47, 48
National Trades Union Congress (NTUC), 135, 141, 193
National University of Singapore, 109, 114; employment of graduates of, 116; enrollment, 115; military scholarships to, 239; police scholarships to, 266; tuition, 113
National Wages Council, 142, 147-48, 193, 202; description of, 143
Nationality Law of Republic of China, 34
navy, Singapore, 235-36, 249; advanced training, 245; basic training, 243; capabilities of, 236; combat support training, 245; evolution of, 228; expansion of, 229; Maritime Command, 227, 228; Midshipman School, 245; mission of, 236; officer training, 245; structure of, 235
Negri Sembilan, 223
Neighborhood Police Force System, 262
Neptune Orient Line, 60
Netherlands, 3, 222, 224; capture of Malacca by, 9; as colonial rulers of Malay Archipelago, 9; East Indian trade of, 9; monopoly by, on China-India-East Indies trade, 3; restrictive trade policies of, 10; taxation of trading ships by, 10; trade with, 157; treaty of, with sultan of Johore, 9

Index

New Guinea, 40
New York, 60
New Zealand: emigration of Singaporeans to, 73; in Five-Powers Defence Agreement, xxviii, 211, 221, 252; invested in by Singapore, xxix; military relations with, 252; recognition of independent Singapore by, 57, 250
Newly industrializing economy (NIE), 154; Asian, 121; Hong Kong as, 121, 154; Singapore as, 67; South Korea as, 121, 154, 155; Taiwan as, 121, 154
Newspapers and Printing Presses Act (1974), 214
Ngee Ann Polytechnic, 114
Nonaligned Movement, 207
North Borneo (*see also* Sabah), 54

occupation: of Chinese, 26, 74, 95–96, 97; correlation between ethnicity and, 95, 96; of Indians, 13, 28, 88; of Malays, 28, 83, 84, 86; mobility in, 99; patterns in, 140, 171
Official Secrets Act, 191
oil. *See* Petroleum
O level exams, 114, 116
Ong Teng Cheong, 62, 141
opium, 13, 24, 29, 42
orang laut, 9, 23
Ord, Harry, 253
Ordnance Development and Engineering, 247
Organisation for Economic Co-operation and Development (OECD), 154
Ottoman Empire, 31
Overseas Training Awards, 239, 250

Pahang, 224
Pakistan, 73, 79
Palembang, 6
Pan-Island Expressway, 167
Pan-Malayan Federation of Trade Unions, 44
Paramesvara (King): Johore Sultanate founded by, 7; Malacca founded by, 7; Malaccan Sultanate founded by, 7; takeover of Singapura by, 6
parapolitical institutions: functions of, 191–92; purposes of, 191–92
Parliament: members of, 196–97; functions of, 179; party functions of, 194; terms of, 177

Parliament of Singapore, 57, 177–80, 181, 186, 188, 205; constituency system in, 177; meetings of, 182; passage of laws by, 182; procedure in, 182
Parliament Privilege, Immunities, and Powers Act (1962), 206
Parliamentary Elections Act, 179
Parsis, 23, 109
Pasir Laba Camp, 243, 244, 246
Pasir Panjang, 29, 38
Pasir Panjang Wharves, 166
Patani, 36
Paya Lebar Air Base, xxviii, 244
penal system, 23
Penang, 9, 10, 12, 17, 222, 253; Chinese immigrants from, 13, 21; control of, by British East India Company, 9; Japanese occupation of, 37, 225; Malays from, 13; as part of Malayan Union, 41; as part of Straits Settlements, 3
People's Action Party (PAP), xxvi, 192–95, 205, 256; cadre system, 194; communist alliance with, 257; communist opposition to, 56–57; dominance of, 60, 139, 193; electoral vote for, 204; founding of, 4, 193; hierarchy of, 196; housing and development program of, 76, 188–89; inauguration of, 48, 49; labor policy of, 193, 202; landslide victories of, 5, 55, 59, 62; leadership of, 193, 196, 197; low profile of, 195, 199; platform of, 49, 52; purge of, 51; relations of, with labor, 141; relations of, with National Trades Union Congress, 141; structure of, 194
People's Action Party (PAP), Central Executive Committee: communist attempt to take over, 51, 257; second-generation leaders in, 63; structure of, 194
People's Action Party (PAP) government: close relationship of, with National Trades Union Congress, 141; Confucianism promoted by, 204; first-generation leaders in, 199; future economic goals of, 137–38; goals of, 197; leadership in, 196, 197; leadership style, 204–5; and organized labor, 141–42; paternalistic approach of, 60–61; plans to inspire national unity, 52–53; power structure of, 196; privatization policy of, 138–40; role of, in macroeconomic management, 122–23,

319

127-35; second-generation leaders in, 141, 198-200; successes of, 206; transformation to industrialized society, 53
People's Association Community Centers, 93, 191
People's Defence Force, 230, 236-37; function of, 236-37; origins of, 236
People's Liberation Organization, 260
pepper, 7, 21, 122
Perak, 224
Percival, Arthur E., 37, 38, 224, 226
petroleum, 150-51; exports of, 152; price collapse in 1970s, 125; price erosion in 1980s, 150; refineries, 68; refining, xxv, 60, 121, 150; Singapore as entrepôt for, 126, 150
Philippines, xxviii, 238; foreign workers from, 71, 144; as member of ASEAN, 209; opposition of, to Malaysia, 54; pirates from, 20
Pickering, William, 26
piracy, 16, 17, 19, 20; of intellectual property, 149-50
plantation agriculture, 21
Police Academy (Japan), 266
Police Academy (Singapore), 266
police force, 84, 185, 254, 263-67; Area Command, 265; auxiliary, 265; British reorganization of, 254-55; counterterrorist operations, 265; deputy commissioners, 265-66; Detachments Command, 265; education, 266; Gurkha unit, 265; Internal Security Department, 259; number of personnel, 265; recruitment for, 266; roundup of communists by, 258; training, 266; women in, 266
Police Reserve Unit, 255
Police Staff College (Britain), 266
political corruption, 199
political culture, structure of, 197
political opposition, 193-94, 205-7; government reaction to, 185; government suppression of, 205-7; parties, 206-7
political participation, 46
political power: distribution of, 195-96; nature of, 195-96
political succession, 198-99
politics, government opposition to, 198, 199
Pollution Control Department, 69
population (*see also* family planning program): abortion, 73-74; birth rate, 70,
73, 197, 203-4; causes of death, 70; control policies, 73-75, 128, 204; death rate, 70; density, 131; distribution, 75-78, 79, 190; ethnic categories, 79; fertility rate, 71; government disincentives, 74; growth of, 71; infant mortality rate, 70; native-born, 71; natural increase, 71, 73; sterilization, voluntary, 73, 74
Port Dickson, 223
port facilities, 29
Port of Singapore, 60, 165, 265
Port of Singapore Authority, 70, 133, 165, 188
Port of Singapore Police, 265
Portugual, 3; destruction of Singapore by (1613), 3, 7
Post Office Savings Bank, 127, 133
poverty, 29, 97
Presidency of the Straits Settlements. *See* Straits Settlements
President of Singapore: duties of, 181; election of, 180; power of, 180; role of, 180; term of, 181
Presidential Council for Minority Rights, 182
Prime Minister, Office of the, 180, 191
Prince of Wales, 36, 224, 225; sinking of, 36
printing and publishing industry, 150
prisons and rehabilitation centers, 267-69; day-release centers, 267, 269; reformative training center, 267-69; types of, 267
Private Sector Investment Committee, 138
privatization, 138-40; divestment plan, 138-39; recommendation against, 139-40; and role of state, 139
processing industry, 28
productivity, 143, 148, 149
Productivity 2000, 138
Progressive Party, 45-46, 49
prostitution: Chinese women forced into, 26; legalized by Japanese, 42
Public Affairs Department, 111
public enterprises, 186, 187, 190-91, 196; Government Printing Office, 190-91; Neptune Orient Line, 191; Singapore International Airlines (SIA), 191; Singapore National Printers, 191; Temasek Holdings, 190
public health, 110-11; facilities, 111; fees, 111

Index

public service, 186-88; boards and councils, 187; civil service, 186-87; prestige of employment in, 187
Public Service Commission, 181, 266, 267; description of, 185-86; scholarships awarded by, 187-88
public transportation, 169
Public Utilities Board: electricity, 136; established, 136; gas, 135-37; water supply system, 136
Public Works Department, 167
publishing industry. *See* printing and publishing industry
Pulau Brani, 28, 228, 245
Pulau Bukum, 28, 260
Pulau Seraya Power Station, 136
Pulau Tekong, 244
Punjabi language, 91
Punjabi Muslims, mutiny of, 31, 254

Queen's Scholarships, 30
Qing dynasty, 22; fundraising in Singapore by, 27
Qing Ming, 103
Quayle, Dan, 212

Raffles College, 42
Raffles Institution, 29, 48
Raffles Place, 14, 19
Raffles, Sir Thomas Stamford, xxi, xxiv, 3, 13, 222; abolishment of slavery by, 15; administration regulations promulgated by, 15; career of, in British East India Company, 10; criminal justice under, 15; dream of, for education for settlers, 16; establishment by, of trading post at Singapore, 3, 12; gambling abolished by, 15; occupation of Singapore by, 10-12; plan for town drawn by, 12, 13-15; settlement of, with Hussein and *temenggong*, 15-16; taxes imposed on liquor and opium by, 15; treaties signed with Hussein and the *temenggong*, 12
Rajaratnam, Sinnathamby, 48, 52, 58, 207
Rama V (King Chulalongkorn), 28
Ramadan, 106
recession of 1985, 126-27, 145, 148; defense spending in, 238-39; effect of, on business loans, 148; government response to, 127; growth rate in, 162; recovery from, 164; savings, capital during, 159
reclamation schemes, 133
Registry of Citizens, 72
Registry of Societies, 94
religion, 103-10; Buddhism, 103; changes in, 108-10; Chinese popular religion, 103-4; Christianity, 103; distribution, 108-9; and ethnicity, 106-8; Hinduism, 103; Islam, 103; Jainism, 103; Judaism, 103; Sikhism, 103; Zoroastrianism, 23, 103
religious education: government monitoring of, 110
religious festivals, 105-6
Rendel, George, 47, 48
Repulse, 36, 224, 225; sinking of, 36
reserves, armed forces, 250, 270; length of duty in, 220; number of personnel, 229, 230; training, 246
resettlement policy: aims of, 131-32
Residents' Committees, 93, 191, 192; Group Secretariat, 192
retirement age, 142
Riau Islands, 8, 12; Chinese immigrants from, 13, 21; entrepôt trade in, 7; Malay immigrants from, 13, 23, 79; occupied by Dutch, 9, 10; plantations in, 7
riots, 254, 255
road-building program, 167
Rotterdam, xxv, 60
rubber, xxiv, 24, 35, 62, 122
Russia, 30
Russian navy, 30

Sabah, as part of Malaysia, 5, 54, 55, 56, 124, 258
Saigon, 224
Sale of Sites Programme, 132
Sarawak, as part of Malaysia, 5, 54, 55, 56, 124, 258
savings, forced, 133-35; effect of, 160; rate of contribution, 133-34
savings rate, 121, 122-23, 159
School Health Service, 111
scorched-earth policy, 38
Seah Eu Chin, 22-23
secret societies, 21-22, 24, 256-57; banned, 22, 26; as criminal groups, 22, 253; membership, 22; origin of, 21-22

321

Securities Industry Council, 165
Sejara Melayu, 6
Selarang barracks, 38
Seletar, 224
Seletar Air Base, 245
Seletar Airport, 171
Sembawang, 224, 245
Sembawang Shipyard, 60
Sembawang Wharves, 166, 167
Sentosa Island, 157, 159, 228
Seow, Francis, 205
Seow Khee Leng, 205
sex ratio, 24, 71, 87
Shah, Zinul Abiddin Mohammed, 260
sharia, 94, 108
Sheng-Li Holding Company, 229
ship repair, 166, 167
Shōnan, 4, 38-41
Siabu Air Weapons Range, 251
Siam (*see also* Thailand), 7, 19, 28
Sikhs, 93, 109
Sikh Advisory Board, 106
Singapore, 93; alteration of landscape of, 68-69; climate of, 69; location of, 68, 69; threat to, 210; topography of, 68
Singapore Aerospace Corporation, 247
Singapore Aircraft Industries, 235
Singapore Armed Forces. *See* Armed forces
Singapore Association of Trade Unions (SATU), 141, 193
Singapore Broadcasting Corporation, 215
Singapore Bus Workers' Union, 47
Singapore Chamber of Commerce, 22
Singapore Changi Airport, 169-70
Singapore Chinese Anti-Japanese Volunteer Battalion, 37, 38, 40
Singapore Chinese Chamber of Commerce, 26, 34, 49, 94
Singapore Chinese General Association for the Relief of Refugees, 34
Singapore Chinese Middle School Students' Union, 50, 51
Singapore Chinese Party, 206
Singapore City Committee, 43
Singapore Civil Service. *See* civil service
Singapore, colonial: administration of, 33; under Bengal, 17; Chinese consulates established in, 27; under Dalhousie, 17; defense of, against Japanese invasion, 37-38; education in, 29-30, 113; ethnic friction in, 13; ethnic residential districts established in, 15; overnight success of, 13; settlers attracted to, 13; shipping transportation, 29; surrender of, to Japanese, 38, 226; town plan of, 13-15
Singapore Corporation for Rehabilitative Enterprises, 269
Singapore Democratic Party, 63, 205
Singapore Factory and Shop Workers' Union, 47
Singapore Family Planning Association, 73
Singapore Foreign Exchange Market, 163
Singapore Harbour Board, 29
Singapore Improvement Trust, 131
Singapore Independence Bill, 180
Singapore, independent, 52, 57; organization of, 57; reaction of, to independence, 57
Singapore Institution, 16
Singapore Islamic Party, 206
Singapore International Airlines (SIA), 138, 171; earnings, 171
Singapore Labour Party, 45, 48
Singapore Legal Service. *See* legal service
Singapore Police Force. *See* police force
Singapore, postwar: as crown colony, 44, 223; food shortages in, 42; new constitution, 44-45; population in, 43; reconstruction of, 43
Singapore People's Alliance, 52
Singapore Polytechnic Institute, 114, 239
Singapore, Port of. *See* Port of Singapore
Singapore, precolonial, 3; Bugis-Malay factionalism in, 7-8; as entrepôt, 5, 17-19; etymology of, 3, 6; history of, 3, 5-9; means of livelihood in, 9; as part of Straits Settlements, 3; as rendezvous point for traders, 5; as supply point for traders, 5; trading post established by Raffles on, 12; written descriptions of, 6, 10
Singapore River, 3, 70
Singapore Science Park, 133
Singapore Shipbuilding and Engineering, 248
Singapore Strait, 211, 222
Singapore Teachers' Union, 47
Singapore Technology Corporation, 246-47
Singapore Tourist Promotion Board, 104, 106, 157
Singapore Town Committee, 257
Singapore Trade Union Congress, 141

Index

Singapore Tramway Company, 136
Singapore University, 30, 114
Singapore Volunteer Artillery, 31, 32
Singapore Volunteer Corps, 48, 236
Singaporean identity, xxii, 5, 58, 67, 88-90; bilingualism and, 89; creation of, 89; as Eastern and Western, 89, 90, 197; education and, 116; ethnic identity in, 89; government efforts to foster, 203, 204; institutions for promoting, 191-92; and international culture, 90
Singapura, 3, 6-7; destruction of, by Portuguese, 3, 7
Singlish, 89, 91
Singora, 36, 225
Sino-Japanese War, 34
slavery, abolished by Raffles, 15
smallpox, 23, 24
Small Enterprise Bureau, emphasis of, 129; established, 129
Small Industry Finance Scheme, 129
Social Development Unit, 75
social mobility: effect of education on, 99-100; potential for, 99-100
social stratification, 96
society and government: relations between, 200-205
Soeharto, xxvii, 62, 211, 258-59
sojourning, 21
Sōka Gakkai, 110
Songkhla. *See* Singora
South China Sea, 225
South Korea (Republic of Korea): foreign workers from, 144; as newly industrializing economy, 121, 154, 155
Southeast Asia, 40, 187
Soviet Union: aggression in Asia, 220; diplomatic relations with, 213-14; economic ties with, 208-9, 213-14; invasion of Afghanistan, 209; relations of, with Vietnam, 213-14, 219; withdrawal from Afghanistan, 251
Soviet-Vietnamese Treaty of Friendship and Cooperation (1978), 214
Speak Mandarin Campaign, 91-92; goals of, 92
Sri Lanka (*see also* Ceylon), 71, 73, 79, 87; foreign workers from, 144
Sri Mariamman Temple, 103, 105
Sri Tri Buana, 6
Srivijaya Empire, 3, 6; as entrepôt, 15; Singapore as port in, 6
state-owned enterprises: MND Holdings, 135; Sheng-Li Holding Company, 135; Singapore Broadcasting Corporation, 135; Temasek Holdings (Private) Limited, 135
statutory boards (*see also* under name of board), 186, 187, 188-90; activities of, 188-90; defined, 188; employees of, 188; management of, 188, 196
Statutory Bodies and Government Companies Act (1984), 191
sterilization, voluntary, 73; rewards for, 74
Stock Exchange of Singapore, 162, 163-64
stock market crash of 1987, 164
Stockholm International Peace Research Institute, 248
Straits Chinese. *See* Baba Chinese
Straits Chinese British Association, 27
Straits Settlements, 3, 17, 20, 29, 222, 252-53; civil service in, 17; components of, 3; as crown colony, 3-4, 17, 24; under British Colonial Office, 17; in World War II, 35
Straits Settlements Volunteer Corps, 36, 223, 254
Subramanya, 105
Suez Canal, 4, 28
Sukarno, 54, 211
Sumatra, 3, 6, 7, 40, 251; Dutch occupation of, 20; Malay Singaporeans as immigrants from, 13, 23, 71, 79, 82
Sulawesi, 79
Supreme Court, 184-85, 254, 262, 267; appointment of judges to, 185; subordinate courts in, 184
Surabaya, 73
Sun Yat-sen, 27, 33; support for, 27
Sungai Gedong Camp, 243

Taiwan (Republic of China): Singaporean immigrants from, 72, 79; foreign workers from, 144; investment in Singapore by, 59; military training in, 213; as newly industrializing economy, 121, 154; relations with, 212-13; Singapore's trade with, 156
Tamil language, 87, 91, 182; education, 29, 32, 43, 52, 114; newspapers in, 214; radio and television broadcasting in, 92, 215
Tamil Nadu, 87

323

Tamil Singaporeans, 87-88
Tampines Aquarium Fish Farming Estate, 174
Tan, Augustine, 160
Tan Cheng Lock, 32, 33, 49
Tan Kah Kee, 32, 33, 34, 37, 46
Tan Lark Sye, 46
Tan, Tony, 62
Tanjong Pagar Dock Board, 29
Tanjong Pagar Terminal, 166
tax farmers, 29
tax farming, 13, 22; defined, 13
Technical Training School, 245
telecommunications, 28-29, 158-59; industry, role of, 149
Telecommunications Authority of Singapore (Telecoms), 149, 158; financial autonomy of, 158; growth of, 158; international telephone links, 159; services offered, 158-59
Temasek, 3, 6-7
Temasek River, 7
temenggong, defined, 8
Temenggong of Johore, 23; Ibrahim as, 20
Tengah, 224
Tengah Airfield, 35, 38
Tengah Air Base, 228, 234
Teochiu Chinese dialect, 21, 91, 92; occupations of speakers of, 95; profile of speakers of, 80
Teochiu community, 22
Terengganu, 224
textile industry, 148-49
Thailand, 36, 40, 251, 260; food imported from, 172; foreign workers from, 71, 144, 167; in Japanese Malaya campaign, 224, 225; as member of ASEAN, 209, 219; military training of, with Singapore, 248; Singapore's trade with, 156; traders from, 3
Thaipusam, 105
Third World, 198
Thomas, Francis, 48
Thomas, Shenton, 37, 38
Three Rivers People, 80-81
tigers, 21; hunting of, 21
tin, xxiv, 62; mines, 23, 24; production, 35
Toh Chin Chye, 48, 52
Tokyo, xxvi, 162
Tongmeng Hui, 27
Topping-up Extension, 134, 139

Total Defence concept, 209, 219; defined, 249; as deterrent to war, 219; strengths of, 249; weaknesses in, 249-50
tourism, 157-58; number of arrivals, 158; origins of, 158; planned increase in, 157-58
Tourism Task Force, 157
Town Councils, 192
Trade Development Board, 130-31
trade, international, 19, 121, 151-52, 152-57; amount of, 152; with Asian communist countries, 152; balance in, 151; deficit, 151, 152, 157; patterns in, 154; ratio of, to GDP, 151; summary of partners in, 152-53; with United States, 154-55, 212
Trade Union Act, 142
trading season, 19
traffic control system, 167
training, worker, 145-46; goals of, 145; job retraining, 60
transportation, air, 169-70; Headquarters, 234; land, 167-68; sea, 165-67
Triad Society (Heaven, Earth, and Man Society), 22
Twenty-One Demands (Japan), 33

Unicorn International, 248
United Malays National Organization (UMNO), 44, 49, 52, 56
United Nations, 55, 57, 208
United People's Front, 206;
United States, xxv, xxviii, 151, 209, 213, 224, 252; emigration of Singaporeans to, 73; flowers exported to, 172; level of spending on education in, 113; market orientation of, 156; navy, 229; recognition of independent Singapore by, 57; relations with, 211-12; removal of Singapore's GSP status by, 155; Singapore's exports to, 154-55; trade ratio, 155; trade with, 58-59, 154-55; training for Singaporean military officers in, 239, 245, 250, 251
Unsinkable, 224
Urban Renewal Authority, 132, 133

Vector Control and Research Department, 111
Vesak Day, 104, 106
Victoria Memorial Hall, 48

Index

Vietnam, 209; aggression in Asia, 220, 251; economic ties with, 209; fall of South, 219
Vietnamese invasion of Cambodia, 211; ASEAN reaction to, xxviii, 62, 210, 219-20, 250, 251-52; and Singapore-Soviet relations, 214; Singapore's reaction to, 207-8, 249; Total Defence as response to, 209
Vigilante Corps, 269
Vladivostok, 214
Volunteer Rifle Corps, 223, 254
Vosper Thornycroft, 228, 236
voting, compulsory, 52, 177; universal suffrage, 177

wage policies, 143-44; description of, 143; guidelines, 143; increases, effect of, 143; reform of, proposals for, 144; restraint policy, 143
wages and benefits, 97
Wang Dayuan, 6
water: importation of, 69, 136; supply system, 136
Wavell, Archibald, 37, 38, 226
West Indies, 224
Western values, 68, 110
wildlife, 21
women: in armed forces, 241; in civil service, 187; education for Chinese, 30; forced prostitution of Chinese, 26; in police force, 266; in work force, 140
Women's Charter, 102
Wong Kan Seng, 209, 210, 211
work force, 143; education levels in, 146; employment patterns in, 140; men in, 140; as nation's natural resource, 140; percentage of, in financial services, 162; retraining in, 160; shipyard, 167; women in, 140
work permits, 144
workers, blue-collar, 143
workers, foreign, 144-45; dependency on, 145; living standards of, 97; proportion of, 144, 145; skilled, 144; source of, 144; unskilled, 144
workers, native: living standards of, 97; provisions for welfare of, 142
Workers' Party, 205, 206, 260
Workers' Protection Corps, 257
Workers, white-collar, 143
World Bank, 188, 209; as source of capital for government, 189; loans from, 165
World Health Organization (WHO), 112
World War I, 4, 31, 223, 253
World War II, xxiii, 253; economic problems following, 124
Wu Tian Wang, 43, 44
Wuchang Uprising, 27

Xiamen, 32
Xiamen University. See Amoy University

Yamashita Tomoyuki, as commander of Japanese Malaya campaign, 36; strategy of, 225; surrender of Percival accepted by, 38, 226; troops commanded by, 37
Yemen, People's Democratic Republic of, 260
Yeo Ning Hong, 179

Zhejiang, 81
Zoroastrianism, 23, 103

Published Country Studies

(Area Handbook Series)

550–65	Afghanistan	550–87	Greece
550–98	Albania	550–78	Guatemala
550–44	Algeria	550–174	Guinea
550–59	Angola	550–82	Guyana and Belize
550–73	Argentina	550–151	Honduras
550–169	Australia	550–165	Hungary
550–176	Austria	550–21	India
550–175	Bangladesh	550–154	Indian Ocean
550–170	Belgium	550–39	Indonesia
550–66	Bolivia	550–68	Iran
550–20	Brazil	550–31	Iraq
550–168	Bulgaria	550–25	Israel
550–61	Burma	550–182	Italy
550–50	Cambodia	550–30	Japan
550–166	Cameroon	550–34	Jordan
550–159	Chad	550–56	Kenya
550–77	Chile	550–81	Korea, North
550–60	China	550–41	Korea, South
550–26	Colombia	550–58	Laos
550–33	Commonwealth Caribbean, Islands of the	550–24	Lebanon
550–91	Congo	550–38	Liberia
550–90	Costa Rica	550–85	Libya
550–69	Côte d'Ivoire (Ivory Coast)	550–172	Malawi
550–152	Cuba	550–45	Malaysia
550–22	Cyprus	550–161	Mauritania
550–158	Czechoslovakia	550–79	Mexico
550–36	Dominican Republic and Haiti	550–76	Mongolia
550–52	Ecuador	550–49	Morocco
550–43	Egypt	550–64	Mozambique
550–150	El Salvador	550–35	Nepal and Bhutan
550–28	Ethiopia	550–88	Nicaragua
550–167	Finland	550–157	Nigeria
550–155	Germany, East	550–94	Oceania
550–173	Germany, Fed. Rep. of	550–48	Pakistan
550–153	Ghana	550–46	Panama

550-156	Paraguay		550-53	Thailand
550-185	Persian Gulf States		550-89	Tunisia
550-42	Peru		550-80	Turkey
550-72	Philippines		550-74	Uganda
550-162	Poland		550-97	Uruguay
550-181	Portugal		550-71	Venezuela
550-160	Romania		550-32	Vietnam
550-37	Rwanda and Burundi		550-183	Yemens, The
550-51	Saudi Arabia		550-99	Yugoslavia
550-70	Senegal		550-67	Zaire
550-180	Sierra Leone		550-75	Zambia
550-184	Singapore		550-171	Zimbabwe
550-86	Somalia			
550-93	South Africa			
550-95	Soviet Union			
550-179	Spain			
550-96	Sri Lanka			
550-27	Sudan			
550-47	Syria			
550-62	Tanzania			

Made in the USA
Lexington, KY
16 August 2013